NOBODY'S SON

BY

FRANK D. KEELING

Cover Photograph:
"Auntie Nance" and Frank, age 10.
Restored by Wallace W. Briggs, Aldergrove, BC, Canada.

Canadian Cataloguing in Publication Data

Keeling, Frank D. (Frank Dennis), 1919-
Nobody's son

ISBN 1-55212-499-1

1. Keeling, Frank D. (Frank Dennis), 1919- 2. Adult child sexual abuse victims--Biography. 3. Public health personnel--British Columbia--Biography. 4. National health insurance--Saskatchewan--History. 5. British Canadians--Biography.* 6. World War, 1939-1945--Personal narratives, British. I. Title.
FC3828.1.K43A3 2000 920.71'0971 C00-911167-0
F1088.K43A3 2000

TRAFFORD

This book was published *on-demand* in cooperation with Trafford Publishing.
On-demand publishing is a unique process and service of making a book available for retail sale to the public taking advantage of on-demand manufacturing and Internet marketing. **On-demand publishing** includes promotions, retail sales, manufacturing, order fulfilment, accounting and collecting royalties on behalf of the author.

Suite 6E, 2333 Government St., Victoria, B.C. V8T 4P4, CANADA
Phone 250-383-6864 Toll-free 1-888-232-4444 (Canada & US)
Fax 250-383-6804 E-mail sales@trafford.com
Web site www.trafford.com TRAFFORD PUBLISHING IS A DIVISION OF TRAFFORD HOLDINGS LTD.
Trafford Catalogue #00-0164 www.trafford.com/robots/00-0164.html

10 9 8

IN LOVING MEMORY
OF MY WIFE, JOY.

"ASK NOT WHERE THE PATH LEADS
GO WHERE THERE IS NO PATH
AND LEAVE A TRAIL"

Anonymous West Coast Indian Chief.

ACKNOWLEDGEMENTS

I am grateful to my daughter Jennifer and husband Ron for providing and setting up the computer hardware that got me started. Thanks also to Michelle my other daughter who lives near Spokane, Washington. Having read an early manuscript she was reduced to tears and begged me to continue when I was about to give up.

To Professor Jim London, University of Victoria, I express my appreciation. He steered me in the right direction and restored my self-confidence.

My thanks to Sue Archer of Langton's Registry Office in Hornchurch, England and to Steve Brock of the Office for National Statistics in Southport England, they were most helpful. I am also grateful to Graham Chorley, the Deputy Town Clerk for the Town of Epping, England. He produced crucial information when all else had failed.

Thanks also to Colleen Mills of Thistle Creek Communications in Victoria, she was my first editor and suggested the title.

To Margaret Devenny at Trafford Publishing my sincere thanks. She guided me through the final process with patience and courtesy for which I am truly grateful.

Above all, my deepest appreciation goes to my wife and partner of fifty-three years. In the final two years of her life, time together was precious but she gave willingly of it so that this project might succeed.

Frank D. Keeling.
Victoria. BC. Canada.

Author's Note

"Nobody's Son" is based on a true story. The names of some characters have been changed in order to protect their privacy.

Personal encounters during World War Two are mentioned only briefly. A few anecdotes and enough detail to set the scene and add continuity to the story. To do otherwise would require a book unto itself.

Some of the dialogue is fictional. But much of what was said, especially in the early years, was so painful and so disturbing that every word, every nuance was forever etched on my mind.

Also, I made a conscious decision to use plain and simple language so that young and old alike may read and understand. And at times I may have done so at the expense of style or grammar. But to write any other way doesn't sound right to me, it isn't the way I talk. After all, what is written is but a conversation with you the reader.

Frank D. Keeling.
Victoria. BC.
June 16, 2000.

One

Once Upon A Time

Everybody came to dinner on Sundays, it had become the custom in our house. My mother would cook the traditional English mid-day meal of roast beef and Yorkshire pudding with new potatoes and peas fresh from the garden.

My sisters would lay table, the big one in the front room. The tablecloth of fine Irish linen was crisp and white, the cutlery clean and shiny and laid strictly according to protocol. A well-polished glass stood beside selected place settings for those adults who enjoyed a glass of fine old English ale with their meal. In the centre of the table there was a vase of freshly cut flowers, sometimes sweet peas and the aroma lingers to this day.

My earliest recollection is of one such very special gathering. It was the last time everybody was present and became a much-talked about event. Thus, it was kept alive in my memory for all time.

It was Sunday, August 26, 1923, and even Selena, my oldest sister was there. Lena, as we called her was rarely home on weekends because she worked in domestic service in Woodford, a long way away in those days. She was twenty-one, two years younger than my oldest brother Frank. I was Jack, the baby of the family also known in the community as Jacky Patchit because of a patch on the seat of my pants. I'd be four come November. In between were Alfred Charles (Charlie) George, Minnie, Evelyn, Jessie and my favourite brother Vic, he was six.

After dinner we assembled in the back garden for a family picture, everybody wearing his or her Sunday best. Even Paddy, my father wore a suit; they called him Paddy because he was born in Paddington, now a borough of London, England. But at the time of his birth in 1865, it was way out in the country in the County of Middlesex.

The girls were wearing their best frocks too. Evelyn had a new one that mum bought just the previous day. She got it from a peddler who sold all kinds of clothing from a barrow in the yard of the Lion, that's Paddy's favourite pub just up the street.

It was a hot sunny day. My three big brothers, also wearing suits and ties looked most uncomfortable. George kept sticking his finger inside his collar and pulling on it; Charlie had his hands in his trouser pockets and continually pushed down as if his braces were too tight. We didn't call them suspenders.

Vic and I wore our Sunday best, except we just had short pants, a clean shirt, knee high socks and boots all nicely polished. Paddy made Vic and me earn our "pocket money" by cleaning all the boots and shoes on Saturdays, and living in the country they were often caked with mud.

In the garden Mr. and Mrs. Walford our neighbours next door but one joined us. He was to take the picture and she would help by putting everyone in the right place and making sure their clothes were in order.

Miss Dennis a middle-aged spinster lived next door, she wasn't home. She was a nice lady, treated me extra special.

"Hello Jack" she would say, "And how are you today?" Talked a bit posh, mum said she had to because she worked in the Post Office. That's up town.

A trellis covered with beautiful English rambling roses separated the gardens, an ideal backdrop for the picture. But the camera would be facing directly into the sun so we had to move to the back wall of the scullery.

Vic was on Paddy's lap and wouldn't sit still, we weren't used to such goings on. Mrs. Walford grabbed me but I refused to co-operate. The more she tried to make me to sit on mum's lap like a good little boy the more I kicked and screamed. By now everybody was feeling the heat and some were threatening to leave. So, while Mrs. Walford held me well away from the action still kicking and screaming, her husband was told to go ahead. Thus I was excluded from the only picture ever taken of the whole family.

The film was developed and the picture wasn't very good. A small brownish coloured snapshot with a streak of light across the bottom and badly out of focus. Charlie put it in a box where it remained until his death almost seventy years later. Vic, as Executor of the estate sent it to me. I had it restored, enlarged to eight by ten and framed. It now hangs in a place of honour in our living room.

My father, Frank Thomas Bunton was the first born son of John Bunton a Park Constable and his wife, the former Sarah Ann Cockram from nearby Marylebone. He was a carpenter and joiner by trade and for many years worked for Noble's the local builder. He always wore a bowler hat which distinguished him from the other workers. We were poor; like all in the building trade, Paddy fell victim to both season and depression. But at least he had a trade and there were periods of relative prosperity.

He married the former Elizabeth Ann Surridge from the quaint little hamlet of Matching Green. The ceremony on March 27, 1898 took place in All Saints Church. He was eleven years her senior.

We lived close by in Ongar, a small town in the County of Essex. Agriculture and a flourishing dairy industry dictated its fortunes, but I first remember it as one main street running through town and a few houses on a couple of side streets.

It was nestled in the heart of the country with its patchwork of tiny fields of lush green pasture and fine cereal crops. Each bordered by a hedgerow, a mixture of crab apple, hazel, holly and hawthorn, as well as beech, blackberry, privet and more. In the spring they would be ablaze with honeysuckle, may blossom and wild rose, the symbol of everything beautiful about the English countryside.

Wild flowers grew at their base, primrose, cowslip and here and there a splash of wild violets, and they were sanctuary to hundreds of birds. Each year Vic and I would gather the rarest of eggs to add to our collection, kept in a shallow box with sawdust in the bottom to protect the fragile shells.

There were all kinds of wonderful trees for little boys to climb and a river called Cripsey Brook flowed by the bottom of our garden, the source of much fun and adventure for the children. It joins the larger River Roding about a mile downstream from our house.

Our back garden was a long one with what, in golfing circles, would be called a dogleg to the left about half way down. It was there our outside toilet stood, we called it the Privy. Just as the outhouse was once the pride of the Canadian prairies, so also were those of rural England. They ranged from a simple wooden box to the most elaborate with stained glass windows and ornate carvings or hunting trophies mounted above the door.

Ours was plain by comparison but a solid little structure built of red brick and fluted red tiles on the roof. Dark green ivy meandered aimlessly up the west side and onto the roof creating a kind of rustic elegance. And it was a triplex, ours was to the north, Miss Dennis' the centre and the Walford's to the south side.

There was an apple tree opposite the Privy and a little further down Paddy had built a small tool shed. The ground between the apple tree and the shed was covered with prickly bushes; gooseberry, raspberry and black currant and I hated it. To push my way through so as to see what was going on in the stable next door left me with a mass of scratches. And I could never resist defying mum's warning not to pick the gooseberries till they were ripe and I got the bellyache.

"Serves you right," she would say, "for disobeying me."

She wasn't very fond of it either but it produced an abundant crop of berries to make delicious pies. That piece of ground would again become the focus of attention in the years to come.

The stable housed a pair of handsome horses belonging to a local haulage Company. By my reckoning I was four and a half when first introduced. In my memory I see myself outside the stall with those gentle beasts towering over me. Looking in awe at their massive shoulders, long necks and wistful eyes; their huge muscular haunches and big shaggy feet. Then, with heads bowed, their large round nostrils barely touching the water as they drank from a pail placed before them by a master anxious for his own supper.

After a while a goat that made its presence known by constantly bleating joined them.

"Jaaaaaack!" It would seemingly wail.

"Listen Jack," my brother Frank would say, "That goat's calling you."

To an innocent little country boy it really did sound as if the animal was calling me.

I would run to the gate and shout at the top of my lungs. "If you don't tell me what you want you won't get it." Then listen, half expecting the goat to make some kind of request. Before long I realized they were teasing me.

We had a dog called Gyp, short for Gypsy, so named because he loved to roam the countryside with Vic and me. A happy little dog but getting old and going blind. Eventually he had to be put down, it was a long time before I got over his loss and we never had another dog.

It seems hard to believe but all nine children were raised in a four-room cottage yet I can never remember any sense of overcrowding. When times were really tough Minnie would go and stay a while with Granny Surridge. There was no so-called safety net then. These were the days when family, neighbours and community came together to alleviate poverty and hardship and we never went hungry.

As children Vic and I were very close. He was always patient and protective of his little brother. He taught me much about rural life, about imagination and creativity. We roamed the local countryside together; paddled in small streams catching tadpoles with a jam jar and the occasional small fish with our bare hands.

If I wasn't with him I invariably got into trouble. Like the time when I wandered off with two older boys to Brentwood seven miles away, telling no one. I was only four but wanted to see Jesus on the cross. Half the population of Ongar was out searching for us and it was midnight before we were found.

The talents of my oldest brother Frank deserve further mention. Radio was one of his hobbies beginning in the days of the old crystal set. Keeping abreast of new technology, he built and rebuilt wireless sets for years. I recall the family sitting around the fire on a winter's night sharing a pair of earphones listening to those early primitive broadcasts.

He was also an accomplished artist in both oils and water colours. I watched him create many beautiful landscapes and to this day his works are still in demand. We have a much-cherished water-colour of the village of Little Torrington in Devonshire where Frank and wife Edie spent many of their vacations.

He was an excellent musician too, playing several stringed instruments but the violin was his forte. Charlie played the banjo and with two friends, Len Root on piano and Joe Childs on drums, they formed a dance band known as "The Dominoes." It was in great demand in towns and villages for miles around. Frank was working for Carter the butcher at the time but his paintings and the dance band brought in some much-needed extra cash.

All the other siblings played at least one instrument. Minnie played the piano having had some lessons. Her tutor got fresh with her or she would have continued. Jessie was learning the piano too and Vic the guitar while George played the mandolin. I wasn't old enough to play anything but I would sing along with them at our family gatherings. Jessie taught me my very first song, "Little Brown Jug." It became one of Paddy's favourites and he would often insist I sing it for him.

Christmas in our house was the happiest of times with everyone contributing. The younger children made all the decorations, paper chains, paper lanterns and the like. Sprigs of holly from nearby hedgerows were spread around and a piece of mistletoe always hung in the doorway between the kitchen and front room.

I remember too, the excitement of Vic and me hanging our stockings on Christmas Eve; then, too excited to sleep, straining our ears to hear Father Christmas come down the chimney. Awake long before dawn, we were eager to see what was in our stockings. Usually a variety of little items, a tangerine, a few nuts, a piece of coal for good luck I was told. In addition, there were small toys, things that cost little but gave no end of pleasure.

As the day progressed the older children would arrive bearing gifts. Nothing elaborate, mainly necessities. Socks, shirts and ties for the boys; dresses, skirts and sometimes scented soap or inexpensive perfume for the girls.

By early afternoon Christmas dinner would be served. We never had turkey but we kept a few chickens and a couple of them were always guests at our table.

Mum's homemade Christmas pudding followed the main course. The smallest silver coin of the realm at the time was known as a three-penny piece. Mum would include a number of them in the pudding mixture. Imagine the excitement when it was served, everybody eagerly looking to see if his or her portion contained a coin. As well, there were mince pies, sausage rolls, nuts and candies. Mum made delicious coconut ice too. Common fare in to-day's world of plenty but in those days, just before the onset of the dirty thirties, we were extremely fortunate. Many families were so poor they could only afford to exchange glances.

It was also a tradition on Christmas day for Paddy to select a special log for the fire. One year he chose Jacky Patchit's log, so called because I had hammered nails into it for as long as I can remember. The next morning mum removed ten pounds of nails from the hearth.

In the evening it was time for carol singing. With Minnie on the piano, Frank his fiddle, Charlie on the banjo and George the mandolin. We would all join in, singing with great gusto. What wonderful times they were.

We always seemed to have a white Christmas. On Boxing Day all the families went tobogganing. The toboggans were hand made from scrap material and we took them to a hill on Bennett's farm. Our river ran along the bottom of the hill and there was a barbed wire fence and a hedge to keep cattle out of the water. One year the Bunton toboggan crashed through the barbed wire fence, through the hedge, sailed over the river bank stopping just short of the water's edge. Miraculously, there were no serious injuries, just a few cuts and bruises.

Come spring, my greatest joy was to pick a bunch of primroses for my mum. Later, the surrounding woods were awash with bluebells and we would gather them for family and friends. There's nothing more pleasing on a warm summer day than to stroll through the woods enjoying the delicate, tantalizing fragrance of bluebells.

Then came summer and a whole new world. Haymaking, with the little children building hay castles. Piling the hay in a circle and having a picnic lunch, sandwiches and home made lemonade.

Next came harvest time, wheat, oats, barley and corn. Following the horsedrawn binder as it cut its swath closer to the centre of the field, hundreds of rabbits would try to escape. We chased them armed with nothing more than a stick with a knob on the end. Great fun, and rare the day we didn't take home a dinner or two for the whole family.

These were, without doubt, the happiest years of my childhood. I had a mother whom I adored and a devoted father. I was the youngest of nine siblings and a little spoilt perhaps. I had Vic whom I idolised and a faithful dog. In those early years we were inseparable and I began to learn about nature and the simple things in life, kindness, compassion, love and trust.

As I look back, it's like reading one of those, "Once upon a time" fairy tales in a child's favourite bedtime story book . . . without the happy ending.

Come the fall, I would celebrate my fifth birthday, time to start school. But because of a sharp rise in the birth rate following World War One, I had to wait till the January term. In the mean time, Jessie and Vic started teaching me my numbers and my ABC's and how to write my name.

I was born on November 5, an infamous day in English history. In 1605 a Mr. Guy Fawkes smuggled large quantities of gunpowder into the basement of the House of Lords in London. He was part of a conspiracy to blow up this noble, upper house of the British Parliament. He was caught in the act and, along with his co-conspirators, put to death.

To this day it is the custom in England to mark the anniversary by building huge bonfires and burning Guy Fawkes in effigy. We also set off fireworks and the little children got to hold sparklers, great fun and it was my birthday too. Being a large family there were lots of presents. Nothing big or expensive but always something I had wanted for a long time, 1924 was no exception.

Fall and winter came, we celebrated Christmas as usual and then it was off to school, at first with Vic who showed me the ropes. I got out before him so I would slowly make my way home alone. I recall lingering a while at the window of Mott's store gazing at the wonderful array of toys.

My first term ended and I don't recall being a particularly bright student or being very fond of school. But thanks to the pre-school tuition from Jessie and Vic I was as good as my classmates.

That summer holiday was especially exciting and ended all too soon. I'd been back at school about a month when, returning home one day, I found Jessie in the kitchen with mum and I was sure they'd both been crying.

"What's wrong?" I asked.

"Oh, mind your own business," Jessie said curtly.

She had never spoken to me like that before. What had I done to deserve that? I wondered. The next day it all became clear.

It was the day that life, as I had known it, came to an abrupt end. The day that everything I'd learned to love and trust was lost. And I was only five!

Two

Without Compassion

When you're five you don't bother much about dates but I knew it was Monday and a school day. I now know it was 5 October 1925. I arose from my bed prepared for another day at school but when I sat down for breakfast something was obviously wrong. Jessie and Vic were there as usual but Jessie was wearing her best Sunday clothes, that was most unusual.

"Why have you got your best frock on?" I asked.

Mum answered my question saying, "You're not going to school today Jack, we're going for a ride on a big bus."

"Oh boy! Is Vic coming too?"

"No, Jessie is though." With that she went upstairs.

This was exciting, I'd never been on a bus before. I'd often seen the bus drive off and wondered where it went and what it was like there. We had a railway line that ran from London to Ongar, the terminus for the London, North Eastern Railway (LNER). I used to peek through a knothole in the fence and watch the fireman uncouple the old steam locomotive which was then moved to the other end of the train for the return journey.

A bus line had recently started in competition. Cheaper than the train it took passengers right into the villages and towns it served and soon became the preferred mode of travel.

While eating my breakfast a multitude of questions came to mind and usually I could rely on Jessie for answers, but not this time.

"Where're we going?" I asked.

"You'll see," said Jessie.

"Why are we going?" I was getting impatient.

"Oh! Wait and see, don't ask so many questions."

This wasn't my Jessie something was wrong, I just knew it. I'll try again, I thought.

"What's mum doing?"

"Changing her dress."

"Oh! Are we going to see somebody?"

"Yes." I waited.

"Who?"

"Jack" she said, obviously frustrated, "don't ask so many questions."

Vic left for school with little more than a hasty, "'bye Jack." He glanced furtively at me as if jealous that I was going on a bus ride and he wasn't.

"'Bye," I said, feeling a bit smug, "see y'after school."

Mum came down stairs wearing her best Sunday dress and carrying a small brown paper parcel tied with string.

"What's in the parcel mum?" I asked.

"Oh just some things we're taking."

What things? Where're we going? Why are we going? When will we be back? And a host of other questions came to mind but were never asked. Jessie, sensing mum's discomfort made what, under the circumstances, seemed a wonderful suggestion.

"Jack, don't you think Teddy would like to go with us?"

That old bear was a hand me down from Vic, Jessie and maybe others. He was threadbare in places, his ears and limbs floppy and he was a bit grubby, but I had hugged him to sleep every night for as long as I could remember. He was very precious to me.

I rushed over to her and gave her a big hug. For some reason she wasn't her usual responsive self, but then, things were different today weren't they. Oh well, I had more exciting things to think about.

I bounded up the stairs, grabbed Teddy and told him we were going on a bus ride. I didn't know where but I just knew it would be an exciting adventure. When I got back down stairs mum was blowing her nose and her eyes were all watery. Here we go again, what on earth's wrong? I wondered.

"Can I go down the garden, mum?" I asked.

"Yes but don't get yourself dirty and don't go near the river. We're having an early dinner and if you get yourself in a mess you won't come with us."

I took her threat very seriously and walked carefully down the garden. It looked rather desolate, the last of the potato crop had been dug and the tops lay rotting on the ground. The plum tree stood bare and leafless, just a few plums lying on the ground and the birds had pecked at them. Only the brussel sprouts looked green and healthy.

I reached the river's edge and sat on a log under the big willow tree. I had climbed that old tree many times, I called it my lookout. My brother Frank had driven large square spikes all the way up the trunk and had fixed our wireless aerial to the top. I didn't climb that high, bit scary for a little boy like me.

So there I sat wondering what makes grown-ups cry. The only thing I could think of was that somebody had died. I remembered seeing a funeral once and all the grown ups were crying. There I was, standing on the sidewalk looking at the hearse, drawn by four black horses frothing at the mouth. Through its glass sides I saw the solid oak coffin with brass handles gleaming in the sunlight. Several horse drawn cabs carrying the mourners followed, everyone wearing black with the ladies heavily veiled. I remember the stark contrast of little white hankies as the bereaved dabbed their eyes. And all those wreaths, hundreds of them.

Back in doors, mum was in the scullery preparing dinner and Jessie was in the front room. I joined her and whispered, "Are we going to a funeral?"

"Of course not," she said in a loud voice, "Don't talk silly Jack."

Mum came in and wanted to know what we were talking about. Jessie told her and mum looked really sad.

"No Jack, we're not going to a funeral, we're just going to see some Aunts and Uncles whom you've never met."

So there it was, why didn't they tell me that in the first place and if that's the case why is everybody so upset? I gave up, grown ups could be so peculiar at times. It would soon be time to catch the bus, that would be great fun and all that mattered for the time being.

A little country boy, a month shy of his sixth birthday hasn't much sense of time. But some time that morning we ate our early dinner. I remember being too excited to eat, impatient to get going.

Finally it was time to leave, all warmly dressed in our best winter clothes. Mum had that little brown paper parcel tucked under her arm and to this day I clearly recall the scene.

The Blacksmith's was directly opposite our house, next door to Wingar's cycle store. As we turned at the end of the drive, Eph Ransome the smithy was standing outside the shop with arms folded. Despite a chill in the air, he was in shirt sleeves and wearing his leather apron. He was a stocky little man, very muscular and thinning on top. He knew the Bunton family almost as well as we knew ourselves.

During hard times both Charlie and George had worked for him. He was a good man, always willing to help if he could. Several times in the last year, I too had gone into the shop and pumped the bellows, watching wide eyed as he shaped a piece of metal or shod a horse. He gave us a casual wave and we moved on.

Up the High Street, past Mrs. Maynard's sweet shop then the Lion, Paddy's favourite pub. Then Lavender's butcher shop, Snellings the Ironmongers and Meads Bakery. A little further on, the first of two more butchers both named Carter but not related.

Each shop had its own peculiar smell. The blacksmith's of burning hoofs and the pubs of stale beer. The Ironmonger's of turpentine and the butcher's of sawdust spread on the floor. The Baker's, that delightful smell of newly baked bread and the Post Office of ink and sealing wax. Isn't it strange how we remember these little things.

Big brother Frank worked in George Carter's butcher shop; the dapper little proprietor was standing in the doorway. He always wore a Boater, a hard straw hat with a black band. He was also wearing his bow tie and the traditional butcher's apron, navy blue with white stripes and tied with a piece of butchers twine. As we approached he passed the time of day with mum.

"Mornin' Missis Bunton, lovely day." He stared for a moment, curious that we were all dressed in our Sunday best.

"Morning, Mister Carter," and as if to satisfy his curiosity, "We're off to Epping for the day."

"That'll be nice," he replied.

And it was on past another pub, The Bell. Then Surridges' the cycle shop with shiny, new bikes standing just inside the door. Next was Pat Carter the second butcher, then the King's Head another pub; finally, the Post Office where we would catch the bus. It hadn't yet arrived and I could hardly contain my excitement. I recall my frustration when it stopped on the other side of the street and unloaded. Then drove empty all the way down High Street, past our house, over the bridge, round the old Fire Engine shed and back.

At last we clambered aboard and I made straight for the big seat at the back. Mum made no attempt to stop me knowing what a thrill it was. Jessie tagged along but was strangely quiet. I couldn't understand that, how could anyone not be excited on such an adventure?

Finally the nearly full bus was off. It was a new one, very comfortable and the big back seat was soft and springy. I remember looking out the back window watching trees and telephone poles recede into the background as we proceeded at, what seemed to me, an incredible speed. Looking toward the front of the bus, I was fascinated by the way the driver, then each row of passengers, would lean first to one side then to the other as the bus proceeded along the winding road. I saw the all-too-familiar sights of the autumn countryside, cows grazing, a bit of "muck spreading" here and there and some early ploughing.

The main bus stops were North Weald and Blake Hall but occasionally it would stop in what seemed the middle of nowhere, a narrow side road or lane. A passenger or two would get on or off, being met or dropped off by someone with a pony and trap.

It was less than ten miles and all too soon my first bus ride was coming to an end. I remember as the bus made it's way slowly through the busy main street of Epping, seeing more and bigger shops than I could ever have imagined. It was a market town much larger than Ongar. One shop in particular caught my attention, a toy store; its two large windows packed with toys, huge compared to Mott's. I would pay another visit to that store before sundown.

Our stop was opposite St. John's Church, a huge building the likes of which I had never seen before. Almost a hundred years old, this massive sandstone structure had a huge clock hanging on the front of the tower. It rang out the Westminster chimes every quarter hour. Jessie suddenly came to life and informed me the bells we used to hear at home sometimes, when the wind was in the right direction, were located in this very same tower. As we proceeded down St. John's Road to the home of the new Aunts and Uncles, I skipped gleefully along singing a song Jessie had taught me within the last few months. "Oranges and Lemons, Hear The Bells of Saint Clemens." Mum and Jessie were strangely quiet. I too would have little to sing about as the day wore on.

Mum knew the house, number 40, she'd been there before. It was bigger than ours but small by today's North American standards. The first thing that struck me, everything was so clean and neat. That's not to say our home wasn't clean, it certainly was. Mum was a wonderful housekeeper and a proud one too, but our home had that lived in look.

A kindly looking gentleman greeted us at the front door. Old to me but, in fact, had barely reached his fiftieth birthday. He had a large bushy moustache just like Paddy's so that's a good sign, I thought. He was introduced as Uncle George Mason and took us down a hallway into a room at the back of the house.

I felt uncomfortable from the moment we were inside the door. Everyone was so prim and proper and everywhere you looked it was so orderly, not a thing out of place. It even smelled of carbolic soap and furniture polish. They had an old-fashioned coal and wood stove and the steel had been burnished so that you could almost see your face in it. It was the typical Victorian home, frigid and impersonal; obviously no children lived here. From the window I caught a glimpse of a well-kept garden.

Meeting the others left me somewhat bewildered. There was this little old lady dressed in a long black dress with a high necked fancy collar, the likes of which I had never seen before. It looked as if it was too small and draped right down to her ankles. She wore those old fashioned boots that you fastened with a hook. She sat bolt upright, a little lace handkerchief tucked up her sleeve which she constantly removed, patted her nose then replaced. Her gray hair was arranged in a bun high on the top of her head. She looked rather like old Queen Victoria, but to me she was a little scary.

In time, I learned that all her garments were handmade by a dressmaker, Annie Bunyan, a spinster who lived alone on Chapel Road, that's at the bottom of St. John's Road. I would get to know her well as the years went by and found she was also the old girl's confidant. She knew all the family secrets which later proved very valuable. As a young woman she had to look after ailing parents so her social life, especially a very deep fondness for George Mason, suffered accordingly. He subsequently married, to Annie's bitter disappointment, the lady to whom I was about to be introduced.

"This is your Auntie Mason," mum said.

I later learned her maiden name was Draper and she was named Emma after a favourite Aunt. As time past, this led to complications so she was called Lizzie and hated it. She would allow none but those closest to her to use it. And so it was from that day forward, Auntie Mason and Uncle George.

There were two younger people in the room, a man and a woman. She was tall and slim but I was immediately struck by how stern she looked. She reminded me of the headmistress at school who scared me to death.

"This is your Auntie Nance," mum said, and after a pause, "and this is Uncle Fred."

"Oh! 'ello" I said. I was shy, and besides, I wasn't used to all this formality and I didn't like it very much. Neither said a word, she just glared at me as if she'd never seen a little boy before and he just sat there.

To this day it is hard for me to deal with what followed, it has remained an imperishable memory all my life. In a faltering voice mum said, "Now Jack, Auntie Nance and Uncle Fred don't have any children and they would like you to go and live with them."

Until then, I had only a limited awareness of fear, pain or loneliness and even less comprehension. But I remember an overwhelming sense of terror, of feeling my heart pound within its tiny frame, convinced I was about to die. Questions flashed through my mind. Why was mum doing this? Why would she want to give me away? What had I done wrong?

In the past I could always rely on Jessie but again, not this time. She couldn't bear to look at me and, for reasons beyond my childish understanding, stood motionless and strangely quiet. I looked in turn at the others. The new Aunt cold and stone faced, her husband looking down at his shoes as if uncomfortable with the proceedings; Auntie Mason staring straight ahead and Uncle George hovering above me, a smug look of satisfaction on his face.

It would not happen, I told myself. I would just say no, mum would agree and stop talking like this and we would all go home and live happily ever after. But it was not to be. Mum continued and there was this horrible pounding in my ears, making her voice sound muffled as if she were speaking from another room.

"They live in a big city by the sea called Brighton. You could paddle in the ocean there, not a little old river like we've got. And you could build sandcastles; you'll have no end of fun. Wouldn't you like that?"

I began to regain my composure and I could be a stubborn little bugger; I turned to face her.

"No, I would not like that, and I'm not going to live with anybody else. I belong to you and Paddy and the others and I love you and I don't want to be with anybody else; why are you doing this to me? Don't you love me anymore?"

The realisation, at such a tender age, that I was being abandoned was unbearable. The only mother I had ever known was handing me over to strangers. The same mother who had helped me take those first faltering steps and taught me my first words. My tiny world was crumbling before my very eyes and it was all so sudden. No warning, no time to adjust to new surroundings or strange people, nothing to help me understand what was happening or why.

There followed a host of bribes. Everything they could collectively think of was offered if I would just be a good little boy and go with my new Auntie and Uncle. I stood my ground and refused.

Finally, Uncle George said, "Come along young man, you and I are going for a walk."

To me, he seemed aloof but kindly and even though I hardly knew him, I agreed. I was so confused by now that I welcomed the relief.

We walked hand in hand and I noticed he had dirt under his fingernails so at least he was human. Later I learned he was a heavy-duty mechanic who repaired railway engines for the London, North Eastern Railway.

We turned left on to High Street, crossed to the other side and stopped in front of that very same toy store I had seen from the bus. I couldn't believe my eyes; they sold nothing but toys. Literally everything a boy of any age could possibly wish for. Rocking horses with real horse's hair tails. Bicycles, tricycles, toy cars and engines you could sit in and pedal. There were small games, big games, every toy imaginable, and some way beyond my imagination. And here I was in the middle of it all.

"So, what do you think," said uncle George. "Have you ever seen anything like this before?" There was an awkward silence, then, "You can have anything in this store if you'll just go and live with Auntie Nance and Uncle Fred."

Ah! So that's it, I looked him in the eye, stamped my foot and said "NO," then stalked out of the store.

I had a hard job fighting back the tears but nobody was going to take me away from my mum. I just knew she didn't really mean what she had said. It was, I told myself, all a big mistake. We walked back to the house in silence.

Entering the same room, everyone was still there. Tea and biscuits were being served, I was asked if I would like some and stubbornly refused. Then this new Auntie Nance said in a very stern voice, "Well, is he coming or not?"

Uncle George explained that he had taken me to the toy store, offered me anything if I would go but I had refused.

"What he needs is a jolly good hiding," Auntie Nance replied in an even more hostile voice.

Uncle George said there was no need for that kind of talk and suggested I might like to go in the garden and look around. Again, I welcomed the chance to get away. Seems I was wrong about mum, she really does want to get rid of me.

I walked the length of the garden and found a secluded spot behind a large bush where I could hide from everything and everybody. All kinds of thoughts went through my mind as I sat there in absolute despair. I felt hurt, frightened and alone and I could hold back the tears no longer.

After a while, my sobbing ceased and I thought perhaps I should jump the fence and walk the ten miles back to Ongar? I would beg Paddy to let me stay. Then I remembered that long walk to Brentwood and how scared I was. The early morning sun had given way to a dull, gray October sky and it would soon be dark. I remembered too, that just before we reached town, the bus went through Epping Forest. The trees were so dense it was dark and scary. No, I couldn't bring myself to do that.

A trio of involuntary sniffles shook my body, the kind that come long after the tears have ceased but before the hurt has completely gone. Try as I may, I could think of no way out of this dreadful predicament. I felt unwanted and unloved but, more than anything, I was scared.

Strangely enough, what bothered me most was the reference to a "jolly good hiding." I couldn't for the life of me understand why she thought I deserved one. I'd had the odd spanking in my life and I remembered how much it hurt both my backside and my pride. So what was I to do? I decided I'd better agree to go. The thought scared me to death but what else could I do? Obviously mum didn't want me anymore, nor did Jessie; and presumably none of the others cared. What's wrong with me? I wondered again. Why are they giving me away? . . . Why?

I shuffled reluctantly back into the house, they were all there. Uncle George did the talking. He told me, if I went to live with Auntie and Uncle I'd be allowed to spend every summer and Christmas holiday with mum and the family. That sounded pretty good, especially since I'd decided to go anyway. He rambled on, offering a few more goodies then told me I should think about it and they all left the room.

I gazed out the window, wasn't much to think about was there, I'd already decided to go. There was an array of autumn flowers at the front of the garden, a mixture of brownish red, bright yellow and bronze. Never before had I seen such large blooms, and I was thinking how beautiful they were when old Auntie Mason came back into the room.

"You've got some nice flowers in your garden haven't you," I said.

"Yes they are beautiful, they're called Chry-san-the-mums" she said, emphasizing each syllable. There was a pause, then, almost as an afterthought she said, "If I were to give you some would you go with Auntie and Uncle?"

Looking back, it's hard to understand her rationale. After all I'd been offered did she really believe I would go for a bunch of flowers?

She was more than surprised when I said, "Yes."

For a moment she stood motionless, then ran out the door gleefully shouting, "Frank has agreed to go, Frank has agreed to go and he only wants a bunch of my "chrysants."

Silly old woman, she really did think I was going for a bunch of flowers. And she couldn't even get my name right.

Three

The Brown Paper Parcel

I heard rapid footsteps as one by one they all filed solemnly back into the room. All that is, except old Auntie Mason. As if afraid I might change my mind, she had hurriedly thrown a large black shawl around her shoulders and was in the garden gathering the floral bribe.

There was an uneasy silence; no one wanted to speak it seemed for fear of saying the wrong thing. I glanced at Jessie, eyes filled with tears she quickly turned away; couldn't bear to look at me. Then, one last questioning look at mum, she was about to say something and in my childish innocence I hoped for a miracle.

"We really must be going," she said, "it's getting late and we have to get back for Paddy's supper."

Obviously relieved the ordeal was over, she was anxious to get away from a difficult and heartrending situation.

So, the die was cast, now I had to say good-bye to her and Jessie, knowing only that I would see them at Christmas. And to a five-year-old that seemed an awful long way away. I saw mum give the parcel to Auntie Nance and realized for the first time, it contained my things. How cruel! All my worldly goods in a little brown paper parcel tied with string.

Our parting was hasty and sorrowful. One minute I was clinging to the only mother I had ever known and whom I loved so dearly, then to my favourite sister. The next moment they were gone, the front door closing with a resounding clang that echoed down the empty hallway. The finality of it all was too much and again the tears flowed.

It was then that I began to realize the full impact of what had occurred. I felt a strange emptiness and there was no one to whom I could turn for comfort or counsel. I was in a strange town, a strange house with four people I had known but a few hours. The dreaded feeling of loneliness, abandonment and betrayal swept over me yet again. Above all I was terribly frightened, more so than ever before or since. Even in the darkest days of World War Two I knew no such fear. The only comforting thing was Teddy. I was clutching him close to me, he was all I had left now.

No sooner had mum and Jessie left than Auntie Nance really took over. She showed no sign of affection or pleasure or that I was in any way a welcome addition to her family. There and then I became aware that I was a burden not a joy to my newfound guardians. Why then had they taken me from my home and those I loved? Fourteen years would pass before I learned the answer.

Now everyone was rushing to catch the train. Working for the railway, Uncle George knew the departure times.

"If you hurry," he said, "you could catch the six o'clock." With that he left the room and we were alone.

"Do you want to go to the lavatory before we leave Frank?" Auntie Nance said.

"Why does everybody keep calling me Frank, my name's Jack, don't you know that?"

Well, I thought she would explode. She grabbed me by the shoulders and shook me so hard I thought my eyeballs would fall out of my head.

"Your name's FRANK . . . FRANK DENNIS KEELING, d'you understand?"

She made no attempt to hide her anger and I'm sure if Uncle George hadn't been around she would have hit me, something she would soon do at the least provocation.

Now I'm completely confused. Not only have I lost my family, I've lost my name. Got a new one, I know I'll never remember it. Frank's no problem, my big brother's name is Frank; Miss Dennis lives next door so I'm familiar with that. But this er, Keeling thing? Very strange, very troubling. Why do I have to have a new name? I like Jack Bunton.

"I 'spose you mean the privy, that's what we call it at home," I replied.

"Well, you're not at home now and it's lavatory. So get yourself out there and do what you have to do and be quick about it or you'll be in trouble. And don't forget to pull the chain."

As I passed her, she gave me a whack across the backside with her hand. It didn't hurt though, my trousers were thick. Uncle George had returned and saw what she did; as I walked through the kitchen to this place called the lavatory, I heard him say, "Now then Nance, that's no way to treat a child."

It was an outside toilet like ours at home except it was joined to the house. There was no window, the only light coming through V shaped cut outs at the top of the door. I could only just reach the door latch and there was a high step. It was now late afternoon so that when I closed the door it was dark and smelled of carbolic.

Now, I hadn't had much practice. Until recently, Vic had to lend a hand with this particular operation. It was an old fashioned toilet, the bowl completely boxed in with a wooden seat. But the bowl was quite a long way in, so is it any wonder an inexperienced little five-year-old would miss the mark? Ah! well, it couldn't be helped.

Now, what was it she said about a chain? I'd better hurry up or I'm gonna be in trouble again, these darn buttons on my fly are hard to do up. I'll just leave'em.

I ran back in doors, she took one look at me and got mad again.

"Look at you" she said, grabbing me by the britches, "you haven't done your buttons up, what's the matter with you, don't you know it's rude to walk around like that?"

"The buttons are jolly hard to do up and I'm only five yer know," I said, holding up the outstretched fingers and thumb of one hand. Jessie taught me that. At this point everything seemed just too much for me and I broke down again and cried bitterly.

For the first time old Auntie Mason showed a little compassion. She came to me, gently but firmly pushing Auntie Nance aside and put her arms around me.

"There, there now, it's been a hard day for you, hasn't it. Don't cry. Look I've got your "chrysants" ready for you aren't they beautiful?

Flowers were the last thing in the world I wanted; all I really wanted was my mum. Oh how I missed her and Jessie and home already.

"I wanna go home," I sobbed.

But I might as well have asked for the moon. I took the flowers, it was such a large bunch I couldn't grasp it in my little hand. Seeing this, Auntie Mason deftly made a loop in the string and hung it on my thumb.

"There," she said, "that's better isn't it?"

I daren't tell her it was almost breaking my thumb. I knew the old girl was trying to be nice so I managed to stop crying long enough to say, "Thank you."

She bent down and in low voice, as if it were some big secret, "When you say please or thank you, or yes or no, you should say yes Auntie or no Auntie, not just yes, or no; and for heavens sake don't say what? Say pardon. We're quite grown up now aren't we and we must talk nicely mustn't we? Auntie Nance would like that."

I didn't know what to make of it. The old gal had hardly spoken since I arrived, but she had obviously been studying my command of the English language and it didn't meet with her approval.

While this was going on, Auntie Nance had gone to the lavatory. Back in the house she said, "Did you pull the chain when you went to the lavatory as I told you?"

My heart sank I knew she had said something about a chain but I didn't see one. It was so dark in there, and anyway, I didn't have to pull the one at home. I was scared stiff and without thinking I said, "Yes." And after a pause, "Auntie."

She was beside herself but thank goodness Uncle George was there.

"Come along Nance" he said, "if you don't hurry, you'll miss your train."

She was putting on her coat; "This little tyke is a liar he did not pull the chain and what's more he wetted all over the seat. I can see we're going to have problems."

Uncle Fred, who had also said little, piped up, "Oh Nance, never mind, let's go, I've had enough of this for one day. We're going to miss that train if we don't get going."

And there the matter ended for the time being.

I was hustled out the door after a quick good-bye to old Auntie Mason. I had Teddy tucked under one arm, that damn bunch of flowers hanging on the thumb of the same hand and the other hand in the tight grip of Uncle George.

We were late and they walked so fast my feet hardly touched the ground. Up St. John's Road, past that great big church, across the High Street, down Station Road, a steep hill, and me still being half dragged along. Uncle George didn't seem to realize my short legs were no match for his. Finally, the station; he bought the tickets because as a railway employee he got a discount. The train was already in the station blowing off steam and making a heck of a noise. We had to cross to the other side. Up the stairs we went, across the two sets of tracks, down the other side and into an empty compartment. Whistles blew a quick wave to Uncle George and we were off.

I'd never been on a train before, what a day! First on a big bus now a train. Normally I would consider myself the luckiest boy in the world and would be beside myself with excitement. But all I could think of was that I was going further away from mum and Jessie and Vic and dear old Paddy. I loved them all sooo! much and missed them. I wanted to go back to them right now, not Christmas, right now. Why couldn't I? What have I done to deserve all this?

Auntie Nance insisted she had to have a window seat and face the way the train was going, so she and Uncle Fred sat on one side of the compartment me on the other. I had a window seat too but I wasn't interested. Couldn't see much and anyway, the train was going backwards to me and it was getting dark so it was just a blur of lights. The train stopped every few minutes; I couldn't read much then, but I later learned there was Theydon Bois, Debden, Loughton, Buckhurst Hill, Woodford that's where Lena lives, Snaresbrook, Leytonstone, Leyton, Stratford and Bethnal Green where it didn't stop; just carried on slowly into London.

I mentioned the little railway station in Ongar didn't I. It was just a small waiting room and a tiny hatch where you bought your ticket, with another room for luggage and parcels. We were at the other end of the line now and it was awesome, it was called Liverpool Street. I got off the train and had to strain my neck to look up at the roof.

I was quickly told, "Don't stand there garping and stay close to us or you'll get lost."

I couldn't get over the size of this place; the roof was all glass, just a few openings here and there to let out the smoke and steam from the locomotives. It must have been a hundred feet up and there were twelve platforms Uncle Fred said. The noise was awful and the walls were black from a hundred years of smoke, soot and steam. For a little country boy who had never been outside Ongar, save for that ill-fated jaunt to Brentwood, it was terrifying.

We quickly reached the barrier and Uncle Fred showed our tickets to a uniformed ticket collector. There were thousands of people rushing hither and thither like ants in an anthill. Most carrying heavy suitcases, others just milling around. I'd never seen so many people in all my life, not even at the football match where I watched Charlie and George play for Ongar Town.

It was scary but there was worse to come. We walked through a long tunnel to a row of glass booths where uncle Fred bought more tickets. Through a turnstile, I'd never seen one of them before, and then there was this moving staircase! How can I walk down stairs with Teddy under my arm and clutching a bunch of "chrysants" if the stairs won't keep still? It was an awful long way to the bottom too, but Uncle Fred grabbed my arm and dragged me on. Then he decided to show off, much to the annoyance of Auntie. He walked down the stairs while they were moving. She didn't like being left behind and told him to "Stop being such a fool." I noticed even he had to do as he was told.

We reached the bottom and somehow I half jumped and was half dragged off the monster. There were two tracks, one to the right one to the left. There was an argument about which was ours, Uncle Fred insisted it was the left.

"In any case" he ended, "it doesn't matter, this is the Inner Circle." I had no idea what they were talking about.

I didn't realize it but I was seeing, for the first time, the most extensive and most efficient subway system in the world known as, what else? "The Underground."

Soon, with a mighty roar a little train came rushing out of the tunnel, screeched to a halt, the doors opened by themselves and I was pushed in. I heard a man shout something like "minethdoooors," his voice finishing a full octave higher at the end of his admonition. The doors closed and we lurched forward. There was only one seat available which Auntie Nance took. Uncle Fred stood in front of her holding a strap hanging from the roof. There was a big fat lady beside him also clinging for dear life to a strap. I had to hold onto a rail and as the train gathered speed it swayed from side to side and the fat lady squashed me against the rail.

No sooner did we get up speed there was another blur of lights, the train screeched to a halt and the routine repeated. I lost count of the number of stops, but in later years, learned them by heart: There was Aldgate, Tower Hill, Monument, Cannon Street, Mansion House, Blackfriars, Temple, Embankment, St. James's Park and finally, our destination, Victoria.

It was another huge terminus, this time the Southern Railway, similar to Liverpool Street but a lot cleaner. There was about the same number of platforms, as many steam engines and just as many people rushing around. By the way, we had another moving staircase to cope with but this time it was going up; a lot easier for me anyway.

The Brighton train was a long one. We trudged past coach after coach looking for seats. Two of the coaches were yellow in colour.

"Pullmans" said Uncle Fred. Didn't mean a thing to me.

The journey to Brighton, the big city seaside resort would take about an hour and fifteen minutes with only two stops. I had now been on the go for thirteen hours but it seemed more like thirteen weeks to me, so much had been crowded into this day. I got up expecting a routine day at school and what had transpired was almost impossible to believe. In my innocence, I fantasized that it was all a dream, that I would wake up and mum would be there telling me to hurry up and get ready for school.

It was hot and I began to feel faint, I'd had little to eat all day. I looked at my new guardians; both asleep, no help from there. Now I wanted to pee, what on earth can I do? There's no corridor in this coach and I can't do it out the window can I.

The train had made its first stop and the next one was a long way off. It was ever so hard to hold it. I fidgeted and squirmed around and somehow managed to avoid an accident. The train entered a long tunnel and another one passed us going in the opposite direction, it made the most horrendous noise, I was terrified!

When the train finally slowed for the next stop, Haywards Heath, I leaned across to Uncle Fred too scared to say anything to Auntie, and whispered, "I have to go wee wee real bad."

She piped up, "What's the matter with him?"

Uncle Fred told her in a loud voice, just to embarrass me I'm sure, that I wanted to go to the lavatory. Auntie made it clear there wouldn't be time at the next stop, I would have to wait and woe betide me if I did anything I shouldn't do.

We finally arrived at Brighton, waited for everyone else to leave then got off. Uncle Fred led me, still clutching Teddy and the flowers toward the public toilet, but he had other ideas.

"Would you like to see the big steam engine that pulled us all the way from London?"

I replied with a half-hearted "Yes." I was busting and would much rather have gone to the toilet.

We approached and the Engineer was leaning out of the cab watching people leave. It was monstrous; with its huge wheels, a mass of pipes, smoke coming out of the chimney and the heat was awesome! Then the Engineer turned a brass lever sharply to the right. With a tremendous roar, steam gushed out completely engulfing us. It was another terrifying experience, I was sure I was going to die. It was a despicable thing for a grown man to do to a little child but they all thought it was a huge joke.

Uncle Fred was determined to avoid any problems in the toilet. He decided to undo my fly and help me, but I was still shaking with fear and in such a hurry to relieve myself that I let it all go too soon.

"No, no," cried Fred, "not yet, not yet."

But it was too late. Most of it went anywhere but where it should have and I walked home in great discomfort.

One would have thought after such a long day, they would at least use public transit but I learned then how cheap they could be. We walked all the way to their home. It seemed like miles to me and took about thirty minutes.

I was so tired after such a long and eventful day, I was neither thrilled nor excited at my first glimpse of a big city. There were huge buildings reaching right up to the stars and big wide streets. One in particular, London Road, was very wide. There were trams (street cars) rattling along all lit up, crowded with people; an endless stream of them going in both directions. There were lots of horse-drawn cabs and I'd never seen so many motor cars either. We had a couple at home owned by rich people, but here there were hundreds, some of them the very latest models.

The street lamps intrigued me though. There were so many of them, some on short poles but many were on the high poles holding up the trolley wires. And they were all electric; we never had anything like that in Ongar. We had a lamp on our street once, fixed to an iron bracket on old Mr. Bailey's house next door. But it was a gas lamp and sometimes the gasman forgot or was too drunk to turn it on. Mr. Bailey didn't like it one bit, it kept him awake at night. So one day some men came with a ladder and took the lamp down but for over sixty years the bracket remained.

We finally made it to their home at 26 Queens Park Rise. It consisted of two rooms on the second floor of a large house. The kitchen, dining room and living room were combined plus a large bedroom.

"The lavatory is down stairs," Auntie said, "but there is a chamber under our bed for night use."

I was too exhausted to say anything and felt sick. The emotional strain was taking its toll.

"Do you want a drink of water?" Auntie asked.

"No," I said.

She glared at me, "No thank you, where's your manners?"

Then I was shown to my bed and I was in for another shock. It consisted of an old army topcoat on the floor and another dark blue topcoat to cover me. I had a cushion for a pillow and no sheets or blankets. Both coats had heavy brass buttons so the bottom one was very uncomfortable to lie on.

Auntie explained that tomorrow night things would be better. Next I had to undress, I was scared she would notice the dampness in my trousers and underpants but somehow she didn't. I had no pajamas so slept in my shirt but I was so tired I didn't care.

Uncle Fred came into the room, "What'll I do with these flowers?" he asked.

"Oh, throw them in the dustbin."

I had carted those flowers all the way from old Auntie Mason's place only to see them trashed, and there was to be yet another heartbreak.

I was holding Teddy close to me. Auntie looked at him, snatched him out of my arms, walked to the kitchen and shoved him in the garbage along with the flowers. My bed was opposite the door so I saw everything, then she returned.

"You don't need that dirty looking thing," she said in her usual stern manner. "You're a big boy now, go to sleep it's school tomorrow."

The door closed and I was alone in the darkness. I was despondent and desperately afraid. The picture of Teddy, one leg sticking out of the garbage pail amidst a bunch of withered chrysanthemums would haunt me for years. My little world had come to an end. I had lost everything, my home, my Mum, Jessie, Vic, Paddy and the others, and now dear old Teddy. I'd even lost my name for God's sake! Utterly exhausted, I drifted into a stressful sleep.

Four

Reluctantly To School

I awoke with a start, something was wrong. It was pitch dark, my heart was pounding and I was scared stiff. I opened my mouth to call Vic but nothing came out. I felt a button pressing on my bum and it all came flooding back.

Mum had said Auntie Nance and uncle Fred had no children and wanted me to go and live with them. How come if they wanted me so bad they didn't have a bed for me? And why had she thrown poor Teddy in the garbage? That was mean.

Somehow my makeshift pillow had moved up against the glass door, rain was beating on it and the wind was howling, that's what woke me. Then I needed to pee but my mind wandered. Why did mum want to get rid of me? I loved her so much and thought she loved me. I used to sit on her lap and she would give me a big hug. That made me feel good. She got mad at me if I was naughty but I'd been a good boy for a long time. Better find that po.

Paddy sat me on his lap and I would sing "Little Brown Jug" for him, he liked that. I'm sure he loves me, and I know Jessie does 'cause she told me so. And Vic, well him and me are always having fun. I wonder what I did wrong?

I gotta find that po or I'll pee myself! What did she call it, a changer? Nah! That's not right. I crawled across the floor to Uncle Fred's side and reached under the bed, no po; must be on her side. It was double size but seemed a mile to her side. I crawled as quietly as I could, felt under her side, still no po. What the heck! I know she said there was one.

A shiver went through my body. Now where in the world could that darned po be? At home we always put it just under the bed so it was easy to find. Maybe it's further under? I got right down on my stomach, squirmed under the bed my hand outstretched and sure enough there it was. It was bigger than ours at home. Oh! well, I'm busting, better hurry up.

I had to ease myself back while at the same time pulling the po with me. I pulled it a bit too sharp because it slip, slopped and some went on the floor. Hope it dries by morning or I'll be in trouble again. I relieved myself and returned the po to it's original spot with the utmost care, then crawled back to my makeshift bed. I tried to get back to sleep but kept thinking of home and family, wondering if they missed me as much as I missed them.

I felt really cold but must have dozed because I was suddenly awakened by an alarm clock. Unlike ours at home, it made a terrible racket. Sounded like the bell on the counter of Mrs. Maynard's sweet shop. If she wasn't there when you went in, you just rang the bell and she would come hurrying to serve you. Sometimes, if you only wanted a hap'orth (halfpenny worth) of sweets she wouldn't be very pleased, but she was a nice lady. Come to think of it, everybody at home was nice.

Uncle Fred got out of bed grunting and groaning, I pretended to be asleep. He went into the kitchen and lit the gas lamp, I could see the light under the door. I heard him washing himself under the tap just like Charlie and George did in the scullery at home. They would puff and snort and shudder 'cause the water was cold. Then the rattle of teacups and a while later he came in the room carrying a cup of tea for Auntie. She got mad because he woke her up.

"I'd much rather sleep, I'm so tired after yesterday."

"Sorry," he replied, "but you always want a cup when I'm on early shift, you get upset if I'm late and don't bring one. You're pretty hard to please sometimes."

To my surprise, he was dressed in a dark blue uniform like a policeman's. Don't tell me my Uncle's a "Bobbie." No couldn't be, he had a peaked cap, they wore big helmets. Wonder what he is? I'll have to ask Auntie. Then I realized the coat he was wearing looked exactly the same as the one covering me.

It was still dark and I wondered what time it was. Couldn't tell time properly; I knew some, like when the little hand is on the seven, and the big one on the twelve it's time to go to bed, Jessie taught me that.

I dozed off again and had a horrible dream; I was back home and that damn goat kept calling me and mum was mad.

"Jack, if you don't get rid of that goat, I'm gonna send you away."

I was crying 'cause I didn't know what to do with the goat. Then I woke up, tears running down my face and Auntie shaking me, telling me to get up and be quick about it.

In the months that followed I had similar nightmares, sometimes reaching frightening proportions. Always dominated by a monster hovering over me intent on taking me away.

I got up and Auntie had opened the curtains. I looked out the window, what a surprise! Across the street there was this huge school. It had a big playground and from the light of a street lamp I could see lines painted on it. Some were straight, some in big rings and there was a lavatory just like ours at home only much bigger. I stood there staring, couldn't get over how big it was. Our three-room school at home was all at ground level, this one had four floors.

Yep, one, two, three, four, never seen so many windows in all me life!

Next thing you know, Auntie's standing there holding my trousers and underpants, I knew it meant trouble, she had that look about her. Just shows you how her 'n me got off on the wrong foot right from the start.

"You dirty little tyke, you wet yourself last night didn't you? First you wet all over the lavatory seat at Auntie Mason's, now this; and I see you've made a mess on the floor, what's wrong with you? Haven't you been taught anything?"

She ranted on at all my shortcomings. How little I'd been taught and how I had been "Simply dragged up like some little gutter snipe," whatever that was. I got mad, she was talking about mum, Paddy and home and I didn't like that.

"You're an old witch," I said, "And I hate you. My mum's better than you. I wanna go home, they all love me and you don't. Why did you take me away from my mum?"

She slapped my face so hard I felt my neck crack, I saw stars and it hurt so much I screamed. The more I screamed the more angry she got. She was concerned about what the landlady would say, and if I didn't stop she would get the stick to me! I was terrified. I'd seen grown ups mad before but nothing like this, and what was that about a stick?

She made breakfast; greasy bacon and fried bread, a slice of bread and marmalade and a cup of weak tea. I was so upset and my face still burned I didn't feel like eating. She saw my reluctance to eat but simply didn't understand why. She went to a cupboard and brought out a stick with a silver knob on the end. It was Uncle Fred's old army cane. She held it right under my chin.

"If you don't behave yourself or you tell anyone my business, you'll feel this stick across your backside." I couldn't understand it.

I dressed in clean clothes taken from the little brown paper parcel. I recognized my brown short trousers, a beige shirt and gray knee socks. I also had a gray pullover that dear old mum had knitted. The sight of it brought a lump to my throat and I began to think back.

I recalled mum sitting by the fire manipulating the knitting needles; occasionally glancing at a pattern that looked very much the worse for wear. She would mumble something about plain and purl and I would become more impatient knowing it was for me. Jessie sometimes held the skein of wool on her outstretched arms while mum rolled it into a ball. It looked so easy and I pestered her to let me do it. When she finally gave in I found it too tiring for my little arms, I thought they would break long before the ball was completed. The wool on my arms got into a tangle and I felt sure mum would be mad, but no.

"Some skeins are like that, you just have to be patient Jack," she said, in the most matter of fact way.

I never volunteered again and when asked to do it, always found an excuse.

I sat twiddling my thumbs, my mind wandering from thoughts of home to the ordeal of going to a new school. My biggest concern was my new name. Why, I wondered, did I have to have a new name? I'd been Jack for as long as I could remember, I could even write J A C K. At our school back home I always wrote my name on the top of my drawings and some were still hanging on the wall.

I don't think I can even spell Frank, I said to myself. I know what it looks like, 'cause I remember seeing it on my brother's birthday card. As for Keeling well, I had a job to remember it let alone spell it. What would I do if the headmistress asked my name and I couldn't remember? She would think I was daft or something.

Auntie came into the room.

"Is Uncle Fred a Bobbie?" I asked.

"Of course not, don't be silly," she said, "He's a Conductor on the trams. Now get your coat on its time for school."

I had no idea what she meant by Conductor or trams. In time, I learned that a tram was a streetcar and in those days, each car had both driver and conductor. The latter responsible for collecting fares. Also, instead of displaying a sign, NOT IN SERVICE when a vehicle returns to the barn, the sign would read DEPOT ONLY. Learning to read, I had difficulty with the word Depot. It caused a stir when I asked my Aunt where Dee-pot was. I was chastised and ridiculed for my ignorance and then grudgingly, the silent "t" was explained.

"It's time to leave," Auntie said in her usual stern voice, she was still angry.

And so, on this the first day of my new life, I was dragged reluctantly to school.

Through the now crowded playground we went, children laughing and screaming, running in all directions and thoroughly enjoying themselves. A few stopped and stared as I was being pulled along. Up the steps, through huge double doors and up the widest staircase I'd ever seen. Then down a hall with its highly polished lino into a small office.

"Ah! Good morning, you're Mrs. . . . er!"

"Ince," said Auntie.

"Oh! Yes, I remember now, we met last week didn't we. Just take a seat won't you, I'll let the headmaster know you're here. Won't be a moment."

Blimey! A headmaster, I don't like the sound of that, I thought. I wish I could run away and hide somewhere.

Auntie sat on one chair loosening her coat and taking a big envelope from her handbag, I sat on the other. Actually I sat on my hands with my feet dangling, then I started to swing them back and forth to take my mind off things.

"Stop fidgeting and sit still" Auntie said in a hoarse whisper, "Undo your coat it's hot in here."

The door to an inner office opened and she was invited to step inside. I heard the muffled sounds of a conversation between her and a high pitched but manly voice. After a while the lady came out and said I should go in. The headmaster was a funny little man, almost completely bald. He had a big nose and his mouth was all pinched up, looked as if he'd just eaten a sour plum.

He said, "Your Aunt has told me all about you and I'm going to start you in Miss Bud's class. Now, if you behave yourself and work hard there's no reason why you shouldn't do well at St. Luke's."

With that we were ushered out.

Auntie left saying, "Now you come straight home at dinner time."

Where else would I go? I thought, I only have to cross the road. I wish I could go back home to mum.

The lady told me to sit down and after a while a big girl came in and was told to, "Kindly take Frank to Miss Bud's room and give her these papers."

The girl seemed a bit bossy.

"What's your other name?" she demanded.

We were walking down the hall but she was going so fast that I had to run to keep up with her.

"Oh! . . . Jack" I said, wondering how she knew I had another name.

"No silly, I mean your surname."

Surname? I'd never heard of it, so I said, "Oh don't ask me!"

She looked at me as if I was stupid or something; she took me to a cloakroom and told me to hang my coat on a peg and not to forget the number. I had no idea what she meant.

Into the classroom we went, the children were seated at funny looking desks, not like my school at home. There, we had nice little chairs and tables just the right size for little'uns. All the children stared at me as we walked to Miss Bud's desk. I wanted to crawl into a hole.

Then the girl said in a loud voice, "This is Frank, he doesn't know his surname and I was told to give you these."

And as she walked away she nearly knocked me off the platform. All the children laughed . . . I felt terrible but Miss Bud was very nice about it.

"Come children, that is not the way we greet new students," she said in a stern voice. "Carry on with your work," and she dismissed the monitor with a curt, "Thank you, that'll be all."

Her desk was on a platform just big enough for her desk and chair. On both sides of the desk the platform was only wide enough for one person to walk, and there were two steps at each end. I'd never seen anything like this before but realized at once that from her elevated position she could see everything! I could.

She glanced at the top sheet of paper and from her desk took out "The Register." All the names were down one side and lots of columns in which there were black ticks and the occasional red cross. There was a space between most of the names and about half way down, she wrote my name and put a tick beside it. Then walked to the other end of the platform and printed something in the top left hand corner of the blackboard which stretched the entire length of the wall.

"Attention children" she said in a much nicer tone. "Our new student's name is Frank Keeling, I shall leave it on the board as usual so that you become familiar with it."

She turned slightly in my direction and continued.

"Frank is the second new student to join us isn't he, and he comes from the small Town of Ongar in the County of Essex. That's on the other side of London, just about here," she said, pointing to a spot on a map of England pinned to the blackboard.

All the children oohd! and ahd! I began to feel quite important I must say.

A boy and a girl sat side by side at each of four desks in a row, and there were four rows. Miss Bud told me to sit at one with an empty seat, exactly as I would have chosen.

"Frank, I would like you to sit next to Molly Stevens. She will help you get settled and show you around wont you Molly?"

Molly agreed and was obviously pleased.

The desk was right in front of Miss Bud's, I could almost reach out and touch it. It felt good to be close to her. And I'd never seen such a pretty girl as Molly Stevens. She had long, blonde, wavy hair the same colour as mine. And the bluest eyes I'd ever seen, and so clean and neat. She wore a white blouse and a black pleated skirt and she smelled nice too. One of her front teeth was missing so she had a bit of a lisp but that's nothing. Maybe this new school wasn't so bad after all.

Miss Bud gave me a sheet of lined paper, the lines were in sets of three with the bottom two closer together. Similar lines were drawn on the blackboard and Miss Bud had written some letters on it. Boy! Could she ever write nice?

"Write your name in the top right hand corner," she directed. "And just see how many letters you can copy from the board. Take your time there's no hurry."

What a nice lady she is, I thought, and I'm just gonna do my best. I'll show her how good I can do my letters. I took up the pencil and slowly, with the utmost care, printed J, A, C, K, and put a nice big full stop at the end. I could feel my tongue curling in the corner of my mouth, a habit I'd developed that helped me concentrate.

I carefully copied the letters from the board, making sure the big letters reached right up to the top line. The little ones I had to keep inside the two bottom lines and the ones with a long neck like ells and effs had to go halfway between the middle and top lines. That's how Jessie showed me and she could write real nice, honest she could.

After a while the bell rang, a monitor collected our papers and Miss Bud gave us our next assignment; to draw a picture of something of interest that we may have seen during our summer holiday. That was easy for me, I just drew a picture of the bottom of our garden at home, with the big willow tree and the bushes and the river flowing by. I even drew a water rat going into his hole in the bank. Then the bell rang again and it was time to go out to play.

I was about to leave my desk when Miss Bud said, "Just a minute Frank, I would like a word with you."

As the last child left the room, she walked to the door and gently but deliberately closed it. Returning at floor level she sat casually on the platform. I wondered what was up. I was nervous and didn't know what to do with my hands. I liked Miss Bud though and besides, I knew I hadn't done anything wrong. She swiveled to one side and said, "Don't be upset Frank, come and sit here," patting the floor of the platform beside her.

I sat beside her feeling honoured at the attention. She had the paper with my letters on it. Looking at it, then at me she said, "You did very well with your letters Frank, but why did you put JACK at the top?"

"Oh!" I said, feeling myself go all hot, "I forgot, that was my name before and it's hard for me to remember my new one sometimes."

"Really, when did you get this new name?"

"Yesterday Miss. I got up to go to school and mum said you don't have to go to school today Jack, we're going on a bus ride and we went to Auntie Mason's, and mum said Auntie Nance and uncle Fred don't have any children, and we've got lots so she wants you to go and live with her. I didn't want to, but my Auntie said I'd get a jolly good hiding if I didn't, so I thought I better go. I got a bunch of flowers but they died and she "throwed" them in the dust bin and she "throwed" my Teddy in there too! I loved that Teddy, I always took him to bed with me." And I started to cry.

Poor Miss Bud, for one brief moment she appeared taken back by this sudden and protracted outburst, but she quickly regained her composure.

"Now, now, Frank don't cry, let's talk about this a little more, would you like that?"

I didn't have a hankie so I wiped my eyes with the sleeve of my sweater, swallowed hard and timidly replied,

"Yes Miss."

So, for what seemed a very long time, we sat there and step by step I tearfully described all the terrible things that had happened to me since the previous morning.

When I'd finished she said, "Do you like your Auntie?"

"No, I don't," I replied, "I hate her, she's an old witch. She hit me across the face this morning and it really hurt. Then she got a stick with a silver knob on the end and she said, `If you don't behave yourself, or if you tell anybody my biz'ness, you'll get this across your backside and hard too,' honest she did Miss."

Miss Bud looked real sorry and I thought she was going to cry too, so I said, "It don't matter Miss, I'll be all right. I'm going to see my mum at Christmas and I'm gonna tell her everything. I know she'll let me stay 'cause she loves me, so does Jessie, I'll be all right Miss."

"Well," she said it's probably just as hard for your Auntie. She hasn't had children before; sometimes even for grownups it can be difficult, so cheer up. Look, the others are coming back, you've missed your first play time what a pity. Do you need to go to the lavatory before class?"

"No thank you," I said, and sat at my desk feeling suddenly very, very tired.

At home we always had our dinner at midday. It was the same at Auntie's. She cooked a nice dinner for me, steak and kidney pudding. For the first time I felt hungry and ate it all, then we had prunes and custard. I fell asleep at the table and Auntie was mad but for some reason let me off and I went back to school.

I enjoyed the afternoon because we played games and Miss Bud was real fun. She joined in, laughing and playing around, I wish she were my Auntie.

I was in for another surprise. Passing through the gate after school I saw this man wearing a barrow boys cap and carrying a big thing on his back. It was tied with rope and he was gripping the rope over his shoulder. It was so heavy he was bent double struggling up the hill. Then I realized it was my Uncle Fred out of uniform with a bed on his shoulder.

"Is that bed for me?" I cried, hardly believing my eyes.

"Yes it is boy, just a mattress but it's a start."

I ran up the steps, opened the door and he struggled up stairs to the bedroom dropping the mattress in my corner. Auntie produced a sheet and folded in half lengthwise; I had my first bed. Two weeks later she made me a real pillow. I remember there were feathers all over the place but it was nice and soft. I also had to make do with the Army coat as a cover for some time but that wasn't so bad.

Could it be Miss Bud was right and it really was hard for Auntie? I wondered. Perhaps she wasn't so bad after all; perhaps things would be better now. Perhaps! Then I remembered what dear old mum used to say.

"Perhaps this, perhaps that, perhaps the other. Wait and see Jack."

Five

Spare The Rod

It was hard growing up in those early days, everybody had a mum and dad except me. It was family I missed more than anything but school was difficult too. In Brighton the education system was more sophisticated, a student who was five before Christmas could start in September. So all the children in my class had completed a full year whereas I had only started in January.

Mrs. Winkworth taught Grade One, we called her "Winky." She was a very large lady with legs like tree trunks that overflowed into seemingly undersized shoes, and an unsightly wart on the left side of her chin. She had a shrill voice that echoed round the high walled classroom like the screech of a nervous sea gull. Nothing like our Miss Bud and hardly what one would expect for a first grade teacher. I had no desire to be relegated to her class so there was lots of incentive to work hard.

Miss Bud couldn't intervene in my home life but without showing favouritism, she gave me lots of individual help and encouragement. She also gave me additional homework and discussed any difficulties I was having.

I struggled through that year, only just achieved a passing mark and made it to Grade III. And, praise the Lord! Miss Bud moved up with us, so except for two lengthy and unforeseen absences, I had my favourite teacher for two years.

At home things changed little. The severity of the punishment and verbal abuse was appalling. The Army cane was replaced with a smaller, thinner one, in the shape of a walking stick. It was stuck behind a picture on the wall with only its ugly little handle showing. The sight of my Aunt's hand reaching for it haunts me to this day. Her philosophy was, "Spare the rod, spoil the child." And she made no secret of it.

Hardly a day passed without a whipping. My buttocks, legs and sometimes my hands had welts on them for days. I was constantly nagged and criticized for the way I spoke. Colloquialisms and pronunciation common to the little town of Ongar were totally unacceptable to Auntie.

Dress, personal hygiene, etiquette, courtesy and manners, especially at the meal table, were often the cause of the most severe reprimand. "Sit up straight, elbows off the table, close your mouth when you eat, don't talk with your mouth full, eat your salt, please Auntie, thank you Auntie, yes auntie, no Auntie, and so it was day after day.

That is not to say such admonitions are entirely invalid. A child should be cted and taught the niceties of every day living. In my case, however, it was tter of extremes. At age six or seven, I was expected to grasp everything the first time and if I repeated a mistake the punishment was harsh and unforgiving. There was nothing tender or loving about the manner in which I was disciplined and never any let up. The harsh treatment was administered no matter the time or place, even though it made everybody's life a misery, including her own. In some perverse sort of way she seemed to derive pleasure from it. It was almost as if she couldn't bear to be happy herself or to see anyone else happy.

She was aloof, cold and unapproachable, like an old Victorian governess. "Children should be seen and not heard," was a common expression. If I did something wrong or that didn't meet with her approval it would never be forgotten. For months, even years, she would resurrect things. And I was always being compared to somebody else.

"Why can't you be like so and so," she would say, and the child with whom I was being compared was usually much older.

I could never make my own decisions, always what Auntie decided. For years she firmly believed I couldn't think for myself. She was always suspicious, "What's that little tyke up to now?" she would say. Never could bring herself to trust me entirely.

I was never allowed to keep any money. If I were given or earned some, it had to be put in a "Money Box" (piggy bank). A halfpenny would be doled out when she felt like it and I would run to the store and buy whatever I could. But more often than not, my piggy bank was a source of revenue when she or Uncle Fred was hard up.

When I was about thirteen, relatives who became aware of this encouraged me to secretly maintain a Post Office Savings Account and would occasionally contribute. I hid the passbook in my toy box. One day she raked through the toy box found the book and there was hell to pay. I was forced to withdraw the money and close the account. She bought me a raincoat, which I certainly needed the remainder she spent on herself.

In 1932 I spent my summer holiday in Ongar as usual and mum decided to buy Vic and me a pocket watch. Well, this was really something, few children were so lucky. The previous September Minnie had married Arthur Bird, whose father was the Innkeeper at the Red Cow and he gave me a silver chain. I was so thrilled and so proud of that watch and chain I was forever taking it out of my pocket to look at the time, but really just to show it off.

When I returned home I proudly showed it to my Aunt and Uncle. He, as a tram conductor, should have had a watch but could never seem to afford one. Without so much as a "May I?" or "By your leave," it was decided his need was greater than mine. Two days later he brought the watch home smashed beyond repair, he had hit it on the side of the tram. There was never a word of apology and the broken watch lay in my toy box for years.

Her actions were not those of a concerned and loving parent. In those early days she was obsessed, there is just no other way to describe her. It was as if she had taken this little urchin and was bound and determined to turn him into a "Little Lord Fauntleroy."

Thirteen years later, as a grown man and off to war, I had a long conversation with Annie Bunyan, old Auntie Mason's dressmaker and confidante; keeper of the family secrets. I mention it now because I think it explains the person my Aunt had become, and more importantly why. Most of the information I have been able to verify but I have no reason to doubt Annie's integrity. She was a deeply religious person, not prone to gossip and a kindly soul.

Auntie Nance's mother, the former Louisa Draper, was married in 1892 at the tender age of sixteen, and over the next five years gave birth to four children. Nance, the youngest, was born on March 3, one month before her mother's twenty-first birthday, April 5, 1897. There were two brothers, Arthur and George, and a sister Edie.

Following Nance's birth, Louisa's prolific childbearing ceased and over the next ten years her health and behaviour deteriorated to the point where, in August 1907, the Draper family decided that she was no longer a fit mother and took the children under their care.

Louisa, having been robbed of her adolescence, made up for it after reaching the age of majority. She frequented the local bars and there were times when she was incapable of fulfilling her role as either housewife or mother. Few details are known of her conduct or whereabouts following the children's departure, only that she was absent for long periods. She died at home, 47 Shaftsbury Road in Romford, on December 6, 1922, age forty-six. Cause of death, peritonitis following perforation of a gastric ulcer.

Nance was placed in the care of her mother's sister, Emma Mason and her husband George in Epping. After several years of marriage they were childless. Nance's sister Edie stayed in Romford. At fourteen I believe she went into domestic service. I was never able to trace, Arthur or George, but must confess I made little effort to do so.

The Mason home was nicely furnished in a timely style and they wanted for little. They were strict but Nance adapted well. Old Auntie Mason was raised in the traditional genteel Victorian manner and Nance was to be raised the same. She was well dressed, well mannered, well read, well everything! It was a kind of Cinderella story. She was an excellent student and graduated from Secondary School four months after her sixteenth birthday and just one year before the commencement of World War One.

She wasn't pressured to find work but instead, stayed home, helped Auntie Mason and learned well the art of good housekeeping. After a year she became restless and got a job in domestic service with a well to do local family, but unlike most servants she continued to live at home.

World War One, 1914-1918, had a profound effect on Epping and the area was inundated with soldiers. Searchlight and Anti-Aircraft units moved into the strategically located region a few miles outside the Greater London area.

Uncle George, like his wife, was a religious man but brought up in the

Wesleyan faith and refused to change. He regularly attended services at the local Chapel and was involved in many of its activities. This caused problems because Auntie Mason was Church of England. She declined her husband's invitation to join his religion and refused to attend her church unescorted. "It wouldn't look right," she insisted.

Uncle George was a "Sidesman" for his Chapel. He gave out hymnbooks and prayer books to people and ushered them to their seats. He would leave home earlier and return later than the ordinary parishioner and Nance took advantage of this. She walked with him as far as St. John's Anglican Church but instead of entering the Church, she would walk around the grounds and out again. By then he would have turned on to Chapel Row where his Church was located; she would go and have fun.

On one such occasion she met and fell in love with a Sergeant in a Royal Artillery Anti-Aircraft unit encamped in fields nearby. He was older than she and a man of the world. Tall, dark and handsome, a real charmer! They would meet at the bottom of Bower Hill. He was wonderful and she was so much in love that it was only a matter of time before the inevitable happened, she lost her virginity. She gave little thought to the consequences because he had assured her that if anything happened he would marry her.

By now, Nance had Saturday afternoons and Sundays off, so when her Sergeant was off duty, they spent the weekend together. The Masons' were told she was staying with friends and thus she was taught all there was to know about sex.

After one such episode in April 1915, her lover was posted overseas. He promised to write but never did. She missed her next two periods, a doctor confirmed her pregnancy and said her due date was early January 1916.

Auntie Mason was beside herself, an unwed mother was an outcast in those days. "How could this wretched child do such a wicked thing after all we've done for her?" She stormed. "To bring such disgrace upon our good name is unforgivable!"

But fate was to take a hand. She turned to her father who welcomed her and she kept house for him while awaiting the birth. Everybody was told she had gone to Romford to look after her father who was ill. She was just two months pregnant when she left, a fact not difficult to conceal. Her employer was exceptionally good about the whole affair, allowing her to resign, "To tend a sick father," and gave her an excellent reference.

It was a difficult time for Nance though, back in her hometown with little money, no friends and reluctant to be seen in public. She spent most of that summer in-doors or in the garden, with sister Edie visiting occasionally.

Early in December 1915, she went into premature labour. A midwife attended and, after many difficult hours, she gave birth to a male child; it was stillborn. Those close to her are quoted as saying she showed none of the usual emotional symptoms following such an ordeal.

After six months she was back in Epping. "Father had sufficiently recovered to look after himself," the curious were told, and the story was accepted. After all, what else could have happened in such a short time?

Following her departure back in June, Uncle George had made inquiries of the military regarding a certain Sergeant. He was informed that after only two weeks in France he had been killed in action, leaving a young widow and two small children!

Upon her return Nance visited Uncle George at work. He gently told her about the fate of her former lover. She was stunned and declared her intention to trace his family to express her condolences. He was forced to tell her of the young wife and children. At first she couldn't believe it but was finally convinced. It took her a long time to get over it.

She then visited her old employer and a member of the staff knew of a family looking for domestic help. She applied for the position and was accepted. This was December 1915 and she continued working in domestic service, with a couple of minor interruptions, for ten years. During that period at least one position included assisting a governess in raising and educating small children. These were children of the very rich, trained in all the niceties of upper class English society, with impeccable manners and behavior and a command of the English language without equal.

Nance enjoyed this environment. She was fascinated by the way in which these children developed into such charming and captivating little individuals. To this day I am convinced her philosophy was, if she was going to raise a child it would be done in such a way as to emulate the children of that superior class. So my fate was sealed.

We must now return to my school days.

I've already mentioned the difficulties of a different education system, my relationship with fellow students was equally difficult.

"Why did you move here? What does your dad do? What's your mum like?"

How was I to answer these embarrassing questions? When I told them I lived with my Auntie and Uncle they wanted to know why? If I told them the truth, as I knew it, they would sneer at me.

"My mum would never give me away, your mum must be horrible," they would say. I learned early how cruel children can be.

A red haired boy, Rufus, living on our street, asked me one day, "How come you live with your Auntie and Uncle, ain't yer got a dad?" Irritably and without thinking I replied "No I haven't got a Dad."

"Well," he said, "my dad told me that anybody what don't have a dad is a bastard so you must be a bastard, I ain't gonna play with you."

He seemed to like using swear words . . . Thought it was big. Anyway, he danced around taunting me as he sang, "Keeling is a bastard, Keeling is a bastard" and before you knew it the others joined in. I was so humiliated I wanted to run home and cry but I'd get no sympathy there, so I ran and hid in bushes nearby and sobbed my heart out.

Then I began to invent stories. "My parents were killed in a big train crash,"

I would say.

"Where, when, what happened?" They would ask. "Oh what a tangled web we weave when first we practice to deceive."

I told this story to one inquisitive playmate that in turn told his mother. The next time she saw Auntie she expressed her sorrow at what happened to poor Frank and admired her for raising "Such a nice little boy." She was politely told there was no truth whatsoever to the story, and "Frank will most certainly be dealt with appropriately." I got the biggest thrashing of my life; I never told stories after that.

When my much loved teddy bear was so unceremoniously disposed of, I was left without a single toy, and that's the way it stayed until I went to Ongar for Christmas. I amused myself indoors by cutting out the Rupert cartoon in the daily newspaper and pasting it in a large, discarded drawing book. Outside, I would play for hours with snails, "Hodney Dodds" we called them; our front garden was plagued with them. I would try to race them one against the other up the garden wall.

Eventually, I made one little friend. His father owned a small Print Shop near our house. One day he invited me to visit the workshop. All the wonderful machinery involved fascinated me. Somehow, I got printers ink on my white shirt; back at home, I got the stick across my backside and was forbidden to play with the boy.

Then another heartbreak; my blonde, curly hair that everybody admired so much was a little longer than usual. Auntie decided it should be cut. When Uncle Fred next needed a haircut, I accompanied him.

I had never been to a barber's before, mum or one of the girls had always trimmed my hair. It was a Saturday morning and the barber's shop was crowded with working men. I sat nervously waiting my turn, listening to a conversation dominated by politics, unemployment and the terrible state of the economy. This was 1925, one year before the general strike. I didn't understand a word and I was restless and growing more nervous all the time.

Finally, after his haircut, Uncle Fred motioned me to get in the chair. The barber added a stool to raise me to a comfortable height and began to hack away. I hated it and had difficulty holding back the tears. Chop, chop, chop, more and more of my curls fell to the floor.

"Now," the barber asked Fred, "is this short enough?"

"A little bit shorter at the back, if you don't mind."

The clippers went further up the back and in order to give it balance, more came off the top.

Even Auntie was horrified at what later became known as the "Crew cut," short all over with just a little tuft of hair at the front.

"Oh Fred," she said, "What on earth have you done! You have no sense at all. My God! He looks like some urchin from the Work House." That didn't make me feel any better.

For weeks after that, everybody wanted to know what happened to those lovely curls. The children at school had a field day teasing about my haircut until poor Miss Bud, who I thought was going to cry when she saw me, told the class she would not take kindly to any teasing.

The following Sunday I met Uncle Fred's family. His elderly mother, Grandma Ince had been a widow for many years. Her husband Samuel was killed in a horrible accident on Brighton Station. He was an Inspector and seeing someone trying to board a moving train without a ticket tried to board the train but slipped between the first two coaches and was run over by the remaining six.

Grandma was left with six small children. The oldest boy, Harry, was killed in action in France in 1917. I met Walter the oldest surviving boy and his wife Mabel, she had a son James by a previous marriage. Then Beatrice the oldest daughter and her husband Harry. Florence, who I would meet much sooner than expected, lived in Wales. Arthur, the youngest, lived in Coventry and it was sometime before I met him.

The entire family were deeply religious, especially his mother. She was almost completely blind and anybody who visited her was asked to read a scripture or an excerpt from the prayer book; this later became a regular task of mine. They had obviously been told all about me because they asked no questions. It seemed they knew all about "Frank" and, apart from the "Hello, young man, how are you, pleased to meet you," nothing more was said. I sat there being seen and not heard.

Now it was November and on the fifth I would celebrate my first birthday in my new surroundings. What would it be like, I wondered? It sort of crept up on me; nobody said anything about it before hand. Back home it was always, "Be a good boy Jack, it's your birthday on such and such a day," usually a week or more before hand.

That Thursday I was about to sit down to breakfast when Auntie Nance came into the room with two parcels, a letter and a shiny postcard with a picture of a beautiful rose. I had never received anything by mail before and suddenly felt quite important.

"It's your birthday today, many happy returns. Eat your breakfast then you can look at your presents."

"Can't I open my presents first?" I asked.

"Do as you're damn well told or you won't open them at all," she barked.

Just because it's my birthday should I expect it to be any different? Well I thought it might.

I ate my breakfast while several times she rebuked me for "gobbling" my food too fast. It didn't seem to dawn on her that I could be a little excited. I was sure one of the parcels was from mum.

I wiped my hands and took off my bib. Yes she made me wear a bib like a little baby. I was almost ten before she allowed me to eat without it. I recall how embarrassed I was when we had company, especially if children were included or if we were on holiday. No other child, to my knowledge, had to wear a bib at that age. I was laughed at and teased by cousins and friends for years over that darned thing. And I was tall for my age too, which made me look even more ridiculous.

I opened the biggest parcel first, the one with string around it, each knot sealed with red sealing wax and stamps in the corner. I knew the postman must have brought that one from mum. There was a nice thick pullover, just like the one she knitted me before, only this one was brown, just right for the on-coming winter. I knew my dear old mum had knitted it and the memories came flooding back.

The other parcel was a pair of slippers from Auntie Nance and Uncle Fred; we called them carpet slippers, very utilitarian. The card was from Jessie and Vic, something I treasured for a long time, repeatedly taking it out of my toy box, gazing at it and dreaming of home.

The letter from auntie Mason and uncle George caused a bit of a hassle. It contained a Postal Order (money order) for two shillings and sixpence, a small fortune for a six-year old. I got that same gift every birthday for the next fourteen years, nothing more, nothing less. Auntie Nance explained what a Postal Order was and that she would cash it. I asked if we could buy fireworks to let off later and I thought she would explode, pardon the pun.

"If you think for one moment I would spend money on such rubbish, you have another think coming. Money to be burned?" To her it was preposterous, unthinkable.

I went to school with my tail between my legs, so to speak. I never did find out what the money was used for.

At school Miss Bud informed the class, as she always did, "We have a birthday, Frank is six today."

And the class chanted, "Happy birthday Frank."

Later, my fireworks display consisted of three sparklers. It had been a typical English November day, the sort of day when you couldn't see where the ground ended and the sky began. The evening was no better, cold, damp and foggy. I wasn't allowed to light my sparklers in doors, Auntie was nervous.

Uncle Fred and I took them into the back garden. He lit the match and I just held them till they petered out, miserable little things they were. Not like the big long ones we had at home that we swung round and round, they looked much better that way. And the older boys would be setting off their Rockets, Wizz Bangs, Ferris Wheels, and Roman candles. The bonfires would be blazing away by this time. It was all so much fun, so much excitement. But this was like a "Damp squib." It was all over in five minutes flat. And I was put to bed at six o'clock . . . as usual!

Six

If Only

I lay in my bed amid the sights, sounds and smells of Guy Fawkes Night. It was a month since mum had handed me over to these strange people. I couldn't believe that so much had happened in such a short time. What had become of that happy little country boy from Ongar? Whatever happened to Jack?

If only I could have stayed with mum. If only I had refused that bunch of "chrysants". If only I had jumped that garden fence in Epping and walked back to Ongar. I could've done it, I know I could. These were thoughts that constantly dominated my mind.

Following my birthday I fell into a routine. I began to better understand my Aunt and acted accordingly. Christmas was coming and we practiced carols at school and made paper chains to decorate the classroom. Also, Christmas meant going home! I could hardly contain my excitement. I did my best to please Auntie Nance for fear she wouldn't let me go.

We had one major upset when she decided I must say prayers every night. Learning the Lord's prayer was difficult enough but Auntie was so impatient. I eventually recited it to her satisfaction, with emphasis here, a pause there, proper breathing, not too fast, "Don't gabble" she would say. Then, just as things were going well she decided I must learn another prayer. My knuckles were rapped a few times but again, I eventually performed to her satisfaction.

School plays were dutifully performed before an appreciative audience of parents and staff although my Aunt and Uncle were never present. Carols were sung with great gusto, albeit a little off key and finally, the great day arrived.

I bade farewell to my fellow students and many were jealous because I was going on a long train ride, through London too!

"Wow! You lucky dog," was the common reaction.

Foolishly, I told many of them I wouldn't be coming back, that I was going to stay with my mum. Miss Bud asked me to stay a moment after class.

"I'm sure I wont be coming back Miss" I babbled. "I just know when I tell my mum about things she will let me stay, I know she loves me. So I'd better say good-bye, thank you Miss for being so nice, if it hadn't been for you I don't know what I would have done. I like you very much, you're my favourite teacher." And the tears started to flow.

Miss Bud, after blowing her nose, put her arm around my shoulder.

"There, there, don't cry Frank, you're a big boy now and I'm relying on you to be brave. You might not come back, but you mustn't be too upset if you can't stay with your mum. Sometimes, we have to do things we don't like doing. That's what makes us good people and strong. Besides Frank, I would be very disappointed if you didn't come back and I know the other children would miss you."

Boy! Wasn't she nice? Made you feel real important. I wiped my eyes on the sleeve of my pullover.

"Well, all right Miss" I said, "It's good to know you like me, but I really do want to stay with my mum."

She said, "We'll see what happens," and I left the school with mixed feelings, knowing I would miss her too.

When I got home Auntie Nance said, "You've been crying, what have you been up to?"

Well I couldn't tell her what Miss Bud and me had been talking about could I. So I said, "I haven't been crying."

"Don't lie to me, you've got smudges all over your face and your eyes are red, tell the truth, what have you been up to?" She roared.

I told her some boy hit me.

"Why did some boy hit you? You must have done something to cause him to hit you."

On and on she went, and the more she did so the more confused I got. I was sent to bed without any supper for lying but I didn't care, I was just glad to get out of it all.

The next morning dressed in my best clothes I was given one whole shilling as spending money. A shilling in those days seemed a lot but would buy very little. I was also briefed on behaving myself while away, minding my manners and talking nicely. "Not like those hooligans in Ongar."

I was warned that if I came back with any of the old habits I would never be allowed to go again and, "Don't tell the Buntons any of my business, what goes on in this house is my business no one else's, do you understand?"

"Yes . . . Auntie," I dutifully answered. But to myself I thought, I'm going to tell mum everything about you, everything!

Then it was up to Brighton station, the train to London, the Underground to Liverpool Street and finally, by train to Ongar. To my surprise, when we reached Epping, Uncle George was on the platform in his working clothes to see me; he worked half days on Saturdays.

There wasn't much time to talk because the train stopped only a few minutes but he said, "Hello Frank, it's good to see you looking so well, merry Christmas." He shook my hand and left another shilling in it.

A lady in the compartment offered to keep an eye on me and I was told to sit still and someone would meet me at Ongar. There were only two stops, Blake Hall and North Weald, so I reached my destination in no time and there on the platform waiting for me was my mum.

I leaned out the window as the train rounded a curve and slowly entered the station. I recognized her at once, she wore the same coat as when I last saw her in Epping. Golly, that seemed a long time ago. But I was here, there was mum, I could hardly believe it. I grabbed my bag and was off the train almost before it stopped. I ran to her, threw my arms around her and kissed her.

Mum was her same dear old self, she said how smart I looked and how much I had grown.

"I like your school cap Jack, it suits you."

I thought, wait till you see what's underneath it. Then I remembered I should have raised my cap when greeting mum, Auntie Nance had drummed that into me ever since I had lived with her. "Always raise your cap when greeting a lady," she would say. But at that moment I didn't care I just grabbed mum's hand, picked up my bag and said, "Can we go home mum?"

As we walked up the hill to the High Street I was full of questions.

"Where's Vic and Jessie, what are they doing, why didn't they come to meet me as well?"

"Well they wanted to but they've been busy running errands, earning some extra money for Christmas. Now they're doing their Christmas shopping; Friday is Christmas Day you know, so there's not much time. We might run into them as we go through town." We didn't though.

Home! What a wonderful thought, what a wonderful home this was. We walked down the yard as we called it, actually it was the driveway leading to the stables. Gyp heard us coming and as we reached the gate, he was wagging his tail, making a little whimpering noise and jumping around in circles. I made a fuss of him, saying to mum, "Oh, how I miss dear old Gyp, we don't have a dog, we only have two rooms, it's terrible there mum, I don't want to go back."

"Come now Jack," said mum, "You've only just got here let's not talk about going back."

We went through the scullery to the kitchen and there was the most delicious smell as I opened the door for mum. We never locked our doors in those days. She had a big stew simmering on the hob. Without thinking I removed my cap as I entered, another thing Auntie had taught me. For the first time in a long time I felt really hungry.

"Mmm...." I was about to say how nice it smelt and please could I have some but mum had turned around and she saw my hair. It had grown a little but still not a curl to be seen. I thought mum was going to faint, she grabbed the edge of the table, I saw her swallow hard and her other hand went tentatively up to her mouth.

"My God! Jack, what on earth happened to your hair!"

I saw the tears well up in those loving eyes.

"Who did that to you . . . how could anyone be so cruel? You had the most beautiful hair."

She let out a deep sob and then knelt down and hugged me and we both cried.

I had risen very early that morning, it was hardly light when the eight o'clock pulled out of Brighton Station. It had seemed an awful long time since then but it was still only a little past twelve.

Mum got up, "Don't cry Jack," she said very softly "sit yourself down; I know you're hungry, do you still like stew?"

Suddenly I didn't feel quite so hungry but I knew I must eat.

"Of course I still like stew" I said, "And you make the best. Auntie Nance is a pretty good cook, she makes some nice things but not as nice as yours and she never makes coconut ice like you do."

"Well, I'll make you some Monday perhaps, now eat your dinner."

She cupped my face in her hands and kissed my forehead.

I was determined to tell her all the terrible things that had happened since I left and how cruel Auntie Nance was. I just couldn't wait to tell all, but before I had finished my stew, old Mrs. Walford came through the gate her arms full of parcels. She dumped them on top of the water butt; Paddy had made a lid for it because the damn cat kept jumping up there. She whirled into the scullery.

"Heard young Jack arrived, let me look at him, where is he?" She poked her head into the kitchen; I was in Paddy's chair, in the corner beside the chimney with my spoon poised for a last mouthful.

Mrs. Walford had always treated us Bunton children as her own, helping the whole family through our early years. Her eyes went straight to my hair too, with the same reaction as mum.

"Goodness gracious, Jack, whatever became of those lovely curls of yours, oh! What a crying shame . . . whose grand idea was that then?"

"My Auntie's," I said, "And she's horrible, she hits me with a stick and smacks my face real hard and I hate her and I'm never going back there."

And I had a hard job fighting back the tears but I didn't want Mrs. Walford to see me cry.

"Well I never did Mrs. Bunton, what a dreadful shame!"

Mum agreed but, "There's nothing we can do about it now," she said. "Let's forget about it. It's Christmas." But I knew she was sad.

Mrs. Walford left saying she was dying for a cuppa tea. I was about to continue my tirade against Auntie when Vic and Jessie came through the gate, I was out of my chair like a shot. Both dropped their parcels on the copper, Vic was the first to give me a big hug.

"Hello Jack, how long you been here then?" He looked a bit surprised.

I turned toward Jessie, she just threw up her hands and shrieked.

"I can't believe it, Jack, what happened, who did this to you. Muuum! It looks awful, what are we going to do?"

This was the way it would be for days, as everyone wanted to know what had happened to my curls.

One by one each member of the family came home or dropped by to say hello to Jack. It couldn't be anything but Jack. Two Franks just didn't sound right. Evelyn came home looking more grown up than ever, I don't quite know what it was but she looked different. She would be fourteen in January and closely resembled mum. She already had a job to go to mum said, at the Star Grocery Store.

It was Saturday afternoon and the Ongar Town soccer team was playing North Weald, so Charlie and George wouldn't be coming by till later. Minnie came, shocked by my hair but said little. She knew how much it hurt and she always seemed to say the right thing to make you feel good.

Frank dropped by carrying his butcher's basket with some meat for mum. For as long as I can remember he did this almost daily, and long after Paddy passed away he would drop something off.

For tea we had bread and home made raspberry jam and some nice cake she had made especially for me, bless her. Those who had not had dinner helped themselves to stew and mum lit a fire in the front room. By now it was just about the time Auntie would say, "Come along Frank, it's time for bed, it's six o'clock. Early to bed, early to rise, makes a man healthy, wealthy and wise." God, she got on my nerves.

The family gathered in the front room, the lid of the piano was raised and we all started to sing. Charlie came in with George in the middle of "The First Noel" with only a nod and a smile in my direction he took up his banjo and joined in. Later, Frank came by all dressed up. It was Saturday night and he was going to see Edie in Toot Hill. Most Saturday nights, Frank and Charlie would be playing in the dance band but not this week.

Then I heard Paddy come in. Paddy loved his pint and after he had consumed a few, sometimes more than mum liked, he would walk jauntily through the back door singing some little ditty. Never ever saw him drunk . . . never, just jolly. After eating his supper he would sit in his favourite chair in the corner by the chimney. He'd have a little doze then join us in song. He wasn't much of a one for carols though, preferring more boisterous songs like Little Brown Jug or, Knick-Knack Paddy Wack, Give a Dog a Bone those were his favourites.

That Christmas seemed extra special, everybody was so nice. It seemed they all missed me and were determined to make up for it. We hung up our stockings as usual on Christmas Eve and had great fun in the morning emptying them on the bed, comparing the contents and stuffing ourselves with the chocolate and other goodies that were right down in the toe.

I got a Fort from Father Christmas (Santa Claus) made of thick cardboard and collapsible so you could set it up and then fold it and put it back in the box. Then, to my utmost joy, I got a box of lead toy soldiers. "From: Mum, Paddy and the Family", it said on the box, in big letters so that even I could read it. There was a row of six soldiers carrying rifles at the top of the box and beneath those, four soldiers on horseback. I got years of pleasure out of that gift, adding to the collection whenever possible.

It had started to snow Christmas Eve and by morning there was a white blanket as far as the eye could see. The all too familiar trees had a layer of snow on each branch. As they swayed gently in the breeze a little bit of snow floated majestically to the ground.

Then a little robin landed on our windowsill where mum had put some crumbs. I stood not daring to move for fear I would frighten him away. He would pick up a crumb, raise his beak up in the air to swallow, pause as if to thank God for his little meal and then he was gone. I saw him several times that holiday but he never came back to the windowsill. Some big old Black Birds ate what was left.

We didn't go for a sleigh ride that year. Not enough snow the boys said. I was disappointed but there were lots of other things to do. Vic got a meccano set complete with screwdriver and wrench. We built a crane with a pulley on it and had great fun loading and unloading an old truck, a gift from another time. There were the two horses in the stable next door to visit, as magnificent as ever, I spent hours with them. The goat had gone, I think the horses complained.

I had to return to Epping on Sunday, January 3 1926, on the nine fifteen train but on the Saturday afternoon I found myself alone with mum. Here was my opportunity to tell her all the terrible things about auntie Nance.

"She hit me with a stick with a knob on the end, honest she did mum."

I told her about the big welts I had on my legs and bum, I told her she was always boxing my ears, as she called it.

"She smacked me on the side of my face once and it nearly knocked me out" I declared, with all the drama I could muster. "Put to bed without any supper," and on and on I went.

At last mum said, "Oh! Jack, she can't be that bad, surely you're exaggerating."

"No I'm not mum, honest I'm not, you must believe me mum," I pleaded.

I was getting desperate. I couldn't bear the thought of leaving everyone again, and returning to Auntie Nance horrified me. Surely mum knew I would never lie to her. I had to convince her somehow.

"Mum" I said after a little while, "Why did you give me away to auntie Nance? I loved it here and I love you and Vic and Jessie and all. And why did I have to have a new name? I liked Jack and I hate Frank. Why mum? . . . Why? . . . Don't you love me anymore? . . . Don't I belong to you mum? . . . Please tell me, I'm so unhappy!" And I could hold the tears back no longer.

Mum sat beside me looking very serious and she took a deep breath.

"Jack, we didn't give you away. You see, you didn't belong to us in the first place. I know it's hard for you but one day when you get bigger you'll understand."

"What do you mean I didn't belong to you." I swallowed hard. "Aren't you my mum then?"

Mum very gently and very quietly said, "No Jack I'm not your mum."

For the second time in less than two months I was hearing words that cut like a knife. My beloved mum was telling me that, in fact, she was not my mother. Again, my chest was pounding and my body seemed to wilt under the crushing weight of this latest revelation. That feeling of emptiness and despair came over me again.

There was a deathly silence for what seemed an eternity, broken only by the loud tick of the old fashioned clock on the mantelpiece. Then, the real meaning of what had been said slowly seeped into my mind.

"Well, if you're not my mum who is then? And where did I come from?"

"Jack, one of these days Auntie Nance will explain everything, that's a promise. All I can tell you now is that we got you from a lady in Biggleswade when you were a tiny baby. She could only keep you a little while so we took you. But there came a time when I had too many children and Auntie Nance didn't have any, and her and Uncle Fred decided they would like to have you."

My mind was a jumble but after a while I said, "Well where did that lady get me from and why was my name Jack then and now it's Frank?"

Mum forced a little smile. "You know we already had a Frank and it was Paddy who named you Jack . . . And the lady got you from the hospital when you were just six weeks old."

The hospital? What on earth would I tell kids now?

"Well I still hate her and I still don't want to go back there. She's cruel mum, honest she is, can't I stay here with you mum? . . . Can't I?"

Mum put her arm around me and gave me a hug.

"No Jack, you can't. We made a promise that Auntie Nance should have you and I know that if you're a good boy things will get better, you'll see. I know she likes you, and Jack, of course I love you, we all do. We will always love you and you can always come here for your holidays."

My mind in turmoil I slept little that night.

The next day mum and Vic took me to the station. The good-byes were hard; a shrill blast of the guard's whistle, one last hug and it was over. I leaned out the window waving frantically until they were lost from view.

Alone in the empty compartment I had time to think. So, mum was not my mum, Vic and Jessie and all the others were not my brothers and sisters. Jessie had said something about a foster parent yesterday; I didn't quite understand that. After my talk with mum, her and me went for a walk down the garden. It was cold so we stood inside the wooden shed where Paddy kept his gardening tools. Being next to the stable we could hear the horses snorting and stomping their feet. Every now and then one of them would give out a little whinny.

Jessie tried to help me understand it all. She said a "tempry" foster mother had taken me from the hospital because my real mother couldn't look after me. She said I was only six weeks old when that happened. She also made me promise faithfully that I wouldn't tell anybody what she had told me.

So, I thought, there's this foster mother, that's one, and I grabbed my little finger; then there's mum, that's two, and I grabbed my second finger; then there's Auntie Nance that's three; the first three fingers of my right hand were now firmly gripped in my left. I'd had three mothers and I was only six, some children would think I was lucky but somehow I didn't feel at all lucky. Ah! But wait a minute, I've forgotten something. There's my real mother, the one that couldn't look after me, that makes four! But I still didn't feel any better.

I wonder what she's like? I wonder what her name is? I wonder why she couldn't look after me? Perhaps she also had so many children she didn't know what to do. I'll ask Auntie when I get home. Oh! No, I can't do that, I promised Jessie I wouldn't tell anybody what she told me didn't I. Ah well, I'll ask Jessie next time I see her, she'll tell me I know she will. Again I had that dreadful feeling of not belonging, of being abandoned and of being very much alone, that nobody loved me, nobody cared.

I was still sobbing when the train pulled into Epping station. The door opened and Uncle George got in. I didn't realize it but this had all been pre-arranged. He tried to comfort me by telling me he worked on these big engines that pulled the train. That if I would like to stay with him and Auntie Mason next year, just for a few days, he would take me down to the sheds and I could play on the engines. I wasn't really interested but I said thank you.

He took me by bus to London Bridge station and put me on the Brighton train. Again, a lady in the compartment was asked if she would kindly keep an eye on me, I was going all the way, she was told.

At Brighton station there was Auntie Nance standing at the barrier, forbidding as ever.

"So, you got here then, I hope you behaved yourself; how was Uncle George, he didn't look too good to me. Anyway come on, we're late, got to get home for dinner and your nose is running, haven't you got a handkerchief?"

Here we go again!

Seven

A Modicum Of Privacy

Miss Bud greeted my return in her usual kindly manner and I settled down to a routine of difficult but enjoyable schoolwork. My classmates seemed friendlier and at last I was accepted. At home I did my utmost to please Auntie, if I succeeded she never showed it. Compliments were rare but reprimands and the use of the cane were not.

On April 1, we moved to 23 DeMontfort Road. It was half a block from Elm Grove and on Uncle Fred's tram route, making life easier for him. It too, consisted of two rooms, one in the basement and a very large bedroom on the third floor. We shared a large kitchen with the owners of the house, an elderly retired couple and their daughter Flossie.

Although the living/dining room was below ground level, it was bright and we faced a pretty and well-kept garden. A large concrete retaining wall with steps leading to our front door, the only things spoiling an otherwise pleasant view. Our huge bedroom had a large bay window and another, smaller window in the corner. Finally I got my very own complete bed bought from the "Workhouse," an institution for the poor and destitute. They had a sale of surplus furniture including iron beds.

This one had folding legs and a folding head rail, but it also had springs so at last I could sleep in relative comfort. It was placed under the corner window so that if I sat up in bed I could watch the comings and goings of the neighbours and other outside activities.

The street lamps had long been converted from gas to electricity so the old Lamp Lighter played a regular part in the street scene. As dusk approached he arrived on his old fashioned bicycle and without stopping, reach up with his long pole and switch on the lights. Around dawn he repeated the performance extinguishing them.

The middle class house was quite distinguished looking, completely covered with ivy. Not the evergreen type, but the kind that, like the trees, greeted the advent of spring with a burst of new leaf. Then as the season progressed the leaves would grow quite large and by autumn would be a glorious blaze of crimson, russet and gold.

With the first high wind of the approaching winter our street would be awash with the fallen leaves, arousing the wrath of the homeowners. Every year there would be threats to "tear the whole damn lot down." But it would be another twenty-five years before they did. The leaves would be swept into the gutter and I would gleefully wade through them, creating a swishing sound as I kicked my feet forward in goose step style.

The ivy was also home for hundreds of the little Common House Sparrow. For the next four years I would lie in my bed and watch with great anticipation the annual ritual of mating, nest building and the raising of young.

Auntie improvised a modicum of privacy in our shared sleeping quarters, at least so she thought. Her solid, dark oak bedroom suite, a wedding gift from the Masons, included an old-fashioned wooden wardrobe. It was a stately looking piece with a full-length mirror and a big drawer at the bottom. At the top it had a large, heavy, removable molding, kept in place by its weight alone.

When I was put to bed she would remove the cover from her bed and secure one corner under the heavy molding. The other corner she would tie to the brass knob of the bedpost at the bottom of her bed. All this so that she could undress and perform other bedroom activities without being seen. There was just one problem and it always amazed me that, for a woman of her intelligence, she didn't realize it.

She always insisted that a candle or later on, a little battery operated lamp, be left on during their bedroom activities. I was a normal, healthy, curious young lad and the cover was of such thin material that I could see everything that transpired. Not just in silhouette either, the real thing! I could hear too and, occasionally, the word experiment arose. I had no idea of its meaning, but there came a time when Auntie introduced a little variation for their mutual enjoyment. So at a very tender age I learned what it is that mothers and fathers do in bed besides sleep.

Maybe I should have told her, but I was too scared because I was supposed to be asleep, even when they lay in bed for hours in the mornings. And I was never allowed to leave my bed without permission.

As I grew older, I would often become aroused by what I saw and heard and eventually surrendered to what came naturally. But my soccer coach insisted such activities were a drain on one's stamina and mentally harmful. So again I let nature take its course and experienced the occasional erotic dream.

Perhaps, in fairness to Uncle Fred, a word about his background might be in order. He told me this many years later when, as a grown man I joined him for a beer.

He was the second youngest in a family of six. His father was killed in 1902 when he was six, and thirteen-year-old Harry became the man of the house. For the next twelve years he ruled the younger children with an iron hand.

Their mother, always religious, became fanatical. Sex was only for procreation, anything else was sinful and the guilty would be forever condemned to hell. Pre-marital sex was an even greater sin and to masturbate was to invite insanity. Harry, once gave Fred a beating when he was thirteen because he was "touching himself." Harry was killed in action in France in 1917, at the age of twenty-eight having never courted a woman. He had devoted his entire life to his widowed mother and his siblings.

At the outbreak of the Great War in 1914, Fred enlisted as a regular soldier in the Royal Sussex Regiment. After initial training in Chichester, not far from Brighton, he was sent to India where he spent the next six-and-a-half years, he was stationed in Rawalpindi in northern India for most of that time. There were few white women in the area and those that were there showed no interest in a lowly Private in the British Army. And Fred, unlike some of the troops, had no interest in the local native or half-caste women.

He was twenty-six when he returned to England in 1921. By this time all his surviving brothers and sisters were married. He lived with his mother and, being under her roof, lived by her rules. He told me he felt obligated to support her because he had been away so long and in his absence, the other children had helped her. He was also lucky enough to get a steady job with the city as a streetcar conductor. The pay was reasonable for a person of his limited education and skills and regular work was at a premium.

He met Nance the following year, but long courtship was the order of the day and he was in no hurry to marry. Grandma Ince didn't want him rushing into anything either. The bride to be had to meet her rigid standards - a God fearing girl who lived strictly by the tenets of the Ten Commandments. All this would have far-reaching and profound effects on many lives, especially mine.

They eventually married in February 1925, she was a month short of her twenty-eighth birthday and he was thirty. Whatever sexual urges he may or may not have had in his young life had been suppressed until his wedding night and by his own admission he was ill prepared.

"I am small made," he said, "I was inexperienced and had been taught that sex was dirty and lustful unless for the purposes of procreation."

On the morning of their wedding he learned that Nance was not a virgin which did little to enhance his desire. She spent the next seven months patiently coaching this reluctant husband in the art of lovemaking. But he was a poor student. Now, back to my story.

For two years before we moved and I had my own room, I would hear her implore him to indulge in foreplay. To fondle her breasts which for her, was the ultimate pleasure. Or to let her take the dominant position giving her greater satisfaction. But Fred thought this dirty, lustful and refused. Nothing but the traditional missionary position was acceptable to Fred. Nor would he make love more than once a month despite her frustration and her pleading.

Another bone of contention was Fred's gruesome looking hands. His job required him to handle coins all day every day. As a result they were like leather, covered with calluses, cracked and badly stained. She would suggest ways to improve them but he flatly refused.

It almost seemed as if he enjoyed tormenting her. When he did agree to participate, he showed very little emotion; sometimes lying there neither amused nor aroused and the proceedings would come to a premature and tearful end. Occasionally, Nance would cry out when reaching climax. He would chastise her, often using abusive language, fearful that Flossie, the occupant of the adjoining bedroom might hear or that I might be awakened.

Our new house was in a different school district, but I don't think Auntie ever told St. Luke's that we had moved. For four more years I made the thirty-minute walk there and back in all kinds of weather, instead of going two blocks to Elm Grove elementary. I told the curious neighbourhood children St. Luke's was a superior school and besides, I got to keep Miss Bud for another year so I didn't mind.

At this time in England there was a groundswell of discontent among the poor and unemployed. I was too young to fully understand the issues of the day but I did know there were an awful lot of destitute people begging on the street corners. And I also knew many children came to school hungry.

The labour unrest was headline news in the papers every day, with outdoor meetings, huge rallies and much debate on both sides of the issue. At one such meeting, so the story goes, an Honourable Member of Parliament, wishing to placate a raucous crowd, stood on a short stepladder to address the mob.

"I understand your plight," he claimed, "You have my complete sympathy." Such words had not fallen on the ears of the working class for a very long time and the crowd fell silent. The M.P. continued.

"You people deserve better, you are good solid men, I say without hesitation you are the bulwark of the nation."

As he paused for a breath a voice from the crowd was heard to say, "Right you are then gov'ner, let's have less bull and more work."

The issue came to a head on May 3 when a general strike was called and England was plunged into a state of paralysis, everything came to a standstill until May 12.

Unless one has actually lived through a general strike it is impossible to envisage. No electricity, no water, no transportation, communications severely limited, schools closed. Even hospitals were restricted to life-threatening emergencies, and so on.

I remember walking along the streets and it seemed like a ghost town, eerie and a little frightening. At a mass rally at the Brighton Town Hall, the Mayor read the Riot Act. Sir Harry Preston, Chief of Police at the time, prematurely and certainly without just cause, ordered the mounted police to charge the crowd. They obeyed with apparent relish resulting in many broken skulls. The action brought harsh criticism from many quarters and the Chief was condemned by all and sundry. Yet a park was named after him!

Soon it was summer holidays and I would be going home again. I still looked upon Ongar as home and the Bunton family as mum and dad and brothers and sisters. I couldn't bring myself to think otherwise. More important, they showed no signs of wanting to change anything. I was still "Jack" to the family and "Jacky Patchit" to everyone else in Ongar and I preferred it that way. But instead of spending the entire month of August in Ongar I spent one week with old Auntie Mason and uncle George; in that very same house where, less than a year earlier, my life had been so drastically changed

I was a little apprehensive at first but it turned out very enjoyable. Old Auntie Mason was strict but I was used to that. I also got to know Uncle George. Although he had no children he had a natural ability for pleasing young people. Every afternoon I went to the railway sheds and played on the engines in for repair or maintenance.

I clambered over every inch of whatever engines were in. Mostly, they were the small ones but occasionally we would get a larger model. The main repair and maintenance depot was in Stratford, a few miles nearer London; sometimes they were overloaded and would drive or tow a large one down to the Epping facility.

Imagine the thrill and enjoyment for a six-year-old. I would go down in the pit and examine it from underneath and clamber all over the boiler. I would play for hours in the cab pretending to drive the train to London at a breakneck speed. I even climbed down into the firebox of one of them; there was already a man in there repairing a crack in the firewall.

They had a turntable in the yard and Uncle George let me help turn a locomotive round. In later years I would rotate the turntable itself just for fun. When I was ten I had the thrill of a lifetime. Uncle George and his crew were allowed to test drive a repaired engine on a single track for about a mile to the first signal, which was always in the stop position. On this occasion he, carrying a small wooden box, told me to climb aboard. Although tall for my age I had difficulty reaching the first rung of the iron ladder up to the cab. Uncle George placed the box on the floor in front of the controls.

"Right'o Frank," he said, " Up you get, you're the driver."

I was sure he was teasing me but no, he showed me how to release the brake and turn the long steel throttle lever with handles on each end, located in the centre of, and immediately above the firebox. It was operated by giving the top handle a sharp push to the right or by pulling the bottom handle to the left. So designed that the engineer could reach a handle from any position in the cab.

I couldn't believe my ears when, having pushed the lever, just the amount Uncle George had directed, the engine began its familiar Chsssh! Chsssh! And started to move, albeit very slowly. I was then shown how to operate the big brass hand brake and just before reaching the signal, bring the engine to a stop.

Then it had to be placed in reverse, this involved turning a big wheel as far as it would go. We would then repeat the process looking out the back window over the coal tender to make our way back to the shed. I was also shown how the big brake blocks were wound down onto the wheels for extra braking power and how sand was released onto the rails to enhance the grip. I never forgot that day and Uncle George was my hero from then on. Maybe life wasn't so bad after all.

He also had an "allotment" at the bottom of Station Road, a small plot of land leased from the Railway Company on which he would grow vegetables. I would help tend the garden and harvest the crop. The land was atop an embankment with a couple of hundred feet of excellent soil. It stretched from the last property line to the corner.

There was a bridge over the railway line at the junction of Station Road and Kendal Avenue to the left. From the bridge, the railway track veered to the right creating a large triangular shaped empty lot on the corner. There were fields as far as the eye could see on the other side of the track and Uncle George mentioned that during the Great War soldiers were camped in those fields. I pressed him for more information, being interested, as most boys are in soldiers, but for some reason he remained strangely silent.

There were also lots of white daisies or marguerites growing around Uncle George's plot. I recalled when old Auntie Mason had given me the chrysanthemums and thought I might return the favour. I picked a huge bunch and presented them to her with childish glee. She made such a fuss about that little act you would have thought I'd given her the crown jewels, but I must say it made me feel good.

On the Sunday morning I attended Chapel with uncle George then returned home to a magnificent dinner of roast beef and Yorkshire pudding. In the afternoon, I bade farewell to Auntie Mason and took the short train ride to Ongar. Little did I realize that, although I would spend another thirteen weeks under her roof, it was the last time I would see her alive.

To my surprise Uncle George came all the way with me. He traveled free on the railway, of course, but it was a nice thing to do. He saw me into the arms of mum who was there to meet me as usual, then returned to Epping on the same train.

That summer holiday was spent much the same as always. Vic and I were inseparable, involved in all our traditional summer activities. The only difference was Vic seemed even more anxious to please, as did everybody in the family. I felt a bit spoilt which made it even harder to leave and I begged mum to let me stay.

"Don't send me back to her," I would whine.

Mum was always sympathetic but firm; so on Sunday August 29 I caught the nine fifteen to Liverpool Street as usual.

As the train slowly entered Epping station, I lowered the window and hung out looking for Uncle George. This time Auntie Nance was there too, why? I wondered. She yanked me off the train and told me we were going to Romford by bus to visit yet another Auntie and Uncle and a cousin, Desmond. We walked up to the High Street and after a fond farewell to Uncle George, boarded the next bus to Romford.

"Now," she said as the bus rolled along the country road, "We call Desmond your cousin. You're not really related but that doesn't matter. You're to treat him as if you were and mind your manners. Show Auntie Edie what a nice little boy you can be, do you understand?" All I understood was the "mind your manners" bit.

We got off the bus at Romford Station and walked to a house on Hornchurch Road. Another Uncle George greeted us. Boy! This sure is getting complicated, I thought. I was told this was Uncle George Wright, Auntie Edie's husband. He talked very slowly with a distinct cockney accent. He too, turned out to be a good old stick, and very, very henpecked. I guess it ran in the family, no one was more henpecked than Auntie Nance's husband Fred.

I was introduced to Auntie Edie and my Cousin Desmond, he was seventeen months old so of little interest to me. They had a nice garden with flowers, a vegetable patch and a nice lawn to play on. Down the bottom of the garden was a sort of small cellar dug out of the ground, the entrance supported by sandbags. I learned later that this was the beer cellar where Auntie kept her homemade beer. I also noticed that Auntie Edie had a big fat tummy and reference was made to her "having a difficult time." Of course, I had no idea what it all meant but by Christmas I had another Cousin, Jean.

Back to Brighton on the Monday to start school the following Wednesday. Summer holidays were exactly four weeks then, and classes always began on the first unless it fell on a weekend. Auntie Nance was back to her old sullen, moody and irritable self as if completely dissatisfied with life. The cane worked overtime, especially during the evening homework sessions of times table and spelling bees. I would be given a specific period, usually far too short, to learn a times table or to spell several words. Then I would be required to recite them to her. Each error or omission was met with a wrap across the knuckles or buttocks with the cane.

She was irritable and impatient in the extreme with never a word of praise or encouragement. I could never understand why because by that time I liked school and Miss Bud was quite satisfied with my progress, I knew because she wrote that on my report card.

Even at that young age I knew my Aunt's marriage was less than ideal. At night, her whispered pleadings continued but Uncle Fred was still reluctant. His performance didn't improve either; the only time he seemed willing was when he had been drinking. But as Shakespeare wrote in Macbeth, "It (the drinking) provokes the desire but takes away the performance." This is not to say success completely eluded them, but the triumphs were painfully few and far between.

One night he'd had nothing to drink but a crisis had arisen. She and I were leaving the next day and she desperately wanted to make love; he would have nothing to do with it.

That morning, Friday October 22, I was about to leave for school when Auntie handed me an envelope.

"Give this to your teacher," she said.

Naturally I was curious and inquired as to its contents.

"Oh mind your business, you'll find out soon enough, now get off to school and out of my way, I've got a lot to do!"

I walked to my classroom wondering what on earth the note could be about. Miss Bud was taking papers out of her brief case. She paused, then looked up.

"Good morning Frank, what do we have here, a note?"

After she read the note, she put it down on her desk and just sat there for a moment saying nothing. I was about to go and sit at my desk.

"Well then," she said at last, "you're going to Wales, quite an adventure I should think, I've never been to that part of Wales. You'll have to tell me all about it when you get back."

"I didn't know that Miss," I blurted out without thinking. "My Auntie wouldn't tell me. I asked her but she told me to mind my own business."

She frowned saying, "Do you mean to tell me your Aunt told you nothing about this?"

"No Miss, she wouldn't tell me nothing."

"Anything, Frank, anything. If she wouldn't tell you nothing, she'd tell you something. If you're going to Wales for goodness sake remember your grammar. They'll think we can't speak English let alone Gaelic." I was completely befuddled.

Other children were beginning to wander into the room and Miss Bud could sense my embarrassment. She told me quietly that according to the note my Aunt and I were leaving for Wales the following day to look after a sick relative and we would be gone for some considerable time.

"That's all I can tell you, Frank," she said. "But I must say your Aunt ought to have told you herself, and you may politely tell her I said so."

I sat down more bewildered than ever.

Back home, I thought about Miss Bud's suggestion but was too scared to talk to my Aunt like that. I'd get the cane for sure, and that hurt. I could see its ugly little handle protruding from the back of the picture and decided to say nothing.

Eight

The House Of Lords

Florence or Flo as she was called was Uncle Fred's youngest sister, two years older than he. She met Edgar Griffiths while he was on holiday in Brighton and later they married. Now in his mid forties, he had worked for Lord and Lady Palmer for thirty years, the last five as head butler.

The estate is located near the village of Cefn-y-bedd, just outside Wrexham in North Wales. The mansion, known as Cefn Park Hall was built in early Georgian times atop the hill on the east side of Cefn Road.

Two large stone cottages stand side by side in the valley immediately below the mansion, the one to the north was home to the Griffiths family. They had four children: Oliver, then age ten, Douglas, six, Florrie four and Steven ten months.

Edgar had written to Uncle Fred explaining that Flo had a medical condition requiring a long period of convalescence and he wondered if Nance could help.

"I realize," he wrote, "you have adopted (?) a child; he too, would be welcome and could attend school with our children and all expenses would be paid."

Following some discussion it was agreed my Aunt should answer the call.

After a tedious train journey via London and Crewe we reached Wrexham. Greeted by Lady Palmer's chauffeur we were driven to the mansion in her Daimler. The same model used by His Majesty King George V and Queen Mary, quite a thrill for a young lad like me.

A servant with white cap and apron over a black dress stood at the main door. As Auntie approached she curtsied.

"Welcome to Cefn madam, her Ladyship is waiting for you in the library and Thomas will take the young master to the kitchen, cook is expecting him."

I followed Thomas through the main hallway. On it's massive oak-paneled walls there were huge portraits of ancestral Lords and Ladies elegantly dressed in bustles and plunging necklines. The staircase was enormous and suits of armour stood in two corners. Then it was into the kitchen to be greeted by cook.

"So, this is Master Frank is it, you must be starved. Come, let us have your coat now and we will find you something to eat."

I was shown into a small staff dining room off the kitchen and waited on hand and foot. A little ol' country boy from Ongar, here in Wales; in this huge mansion, the House of Lords and Ladies for the better part of two centuries.

On the wall, I noticed two rows of springs with little bells attached and a number behind each bell. Now and then a spring would wave causing the bell to tinkle and one of the staff would hasten to answer the call.

I had two large portions of a delicious scone liberally spread with strawberry jam then a glass of milk. I would never get the latter at home. Auntie always said, "Milk is far too expensive these days to drink like water."

Being waited on I felt quite important. Would the young master like more this, more that? "Would the young master like to use the bathroom?" They didn't seem to realize I was just a little country boy from Ongar.

Returning from the bathroom, one of the bells rang.

"That will be her Ladyship" said cook in her lilting Welsh brogue, "Mrs. Ince will be leaving now. Bronwyn, take the young master to the main hall."

Then to me, "It was indeed a pleasure to meet you young master Frank, I am sure we shall see more of you in the next little while. Now off you go, they will be waiting for you."

Auntie was standing in the hall, with Thomas cap in hand poised to open the door. Then it was into the limousine and off to meet the Griffiths family. As we moved slowly down the drive, I wondered out loud about a small circular iron fence with an opening on each side and a little gate in the centre. On the far side, a footpath crossed the meadow disappearing down the hill.

"It's called a kissing gate," Thomas volunteered. "In the olden days that is where the gentlemen bade farewell to their ladies. The gentleman would open the gate, enter the circle closing the gate behind him. The lady would enter the circle and they would discreetly say their good-byes."

"Ooh! How perfectly romantic, I wish I'd lived in those days," said Auntie.

I thought that was a daft thing to say.

The three older children had obviously been awaiting our arrival. Before we were out of the vehicle they had donned their coats and were greeting us at the side door. Auntie had met them before, of course.

And so it was, "My! Haven't you grown Oliver!" And, "Just look at our Florrie, goodness! You're a big girl. Hello! Douglas, how are you?"

As Thomas took the suitcases, Auntie said, "This is your cousin Frank" and, turning to me, "Frank, this is Florence but we call her Florrie."

"Welcome to Cefn Frank," said little Florrie. Then Oliver chimed in.

"We have been looking forward to meeting you and will do our best to make your stay a happy one, this is my brother Douglas, Steven is upstairs with mother."

What a welcome! Surely it must have been rehearsed, I thought. But I would soon learn my cousins were exceptionally mature, especially Florrie. The head gardener and his wife, who were childless, occupied the cottage next door. The one-room school was in the next valley so Florrie spent most of her time with adults. She was very close to her mother but also spent much time with the staff at the mansion.

Following the introductions Auntie said we should go inside. Thomas was leaving and Auntie thanked him, he saluted saying it was a pleasure to have been of service. Douglas took my coat, Oliver was taking suitcases upstairs and Auntie said she must visit "Mother."

Left alone with Douglas and Florrie, I remember how they immediately made me feel at home. They were so well mannered too, and as for Florrie, she was not yet five but chatted away like someone well beyond her years. I knew at once I would enjoy being with such a delightful family, something I had missed for a long time.

It was just like my home in Ongar, warm and cozy but much bigger than I had imagined. They called it a cottage but it was almost as big as our house in Brighton with what appeared to be four bedrooms. The fourth room turned out to be windowless and used partly for storage but also contained an impressive array of toys.

There was a rocking horse similar to the one in that toy store in Epping. Florrie noticed me staring at it.

"Its tail is real horses hair" she said in her fascinating Welsh accent. "He does not get much work these days because, as you can see, one of his legs is broken; father intends to have it repaired one day soon."

With that Douglas came in the room.

"Father is home and you should come down for supper. It is a quarter to six and we have not started yet and father wishes to talk to us."

We quickly washed our hands and headed for the solid pine table, which easily accommodated six people. The floor was red tile, as was the hallway and the large entrance hall. In the entry recess there stood a huge wooden chest. What could possibly be in there? I wondered.

My cousins made for their usual places; I knew at once where I was to sit because there, beside a place setting was that horrible bib neatly rolled with the ties wound around it. I saw my cousins staring at it; how cruel I thought, for my Aunt to embarrass me in this way. None of the others had such a babyish thing by their plates.

Once seated, Uncle Edgar solemnly addressed the gathering.

"First, I wish to welcome your Auntie Nance and Cousin Frank to Cefn. Grateful it is we are that they would give up the comfort of their own home to help us in our time of need."

What a nice thing to say, I thought.

"Oliver, I hold you responsible for your Cousin's well-being at all times outside this house, especially going to, and coming from school."

"Yes father" said Oliver, and he seemed genuinely pleased at the responsibility.

"And on Monday when you get to school you will introduce Frank to Miss Davis, she is expecting him."

"Yes father" Oliver repeated.

Uncle turned in my direction, "I'm afraid school is a long way from here, Frank, and in the winter it can be quite a difficult journey, but if you would be so kind as to stay close to your Cousins I am sure there will be no trouble."

"Yes I will Uncle, thank you" I said.

"And Douglas, you will show Frank over the estate, including where you may and may not go. I'm sure he will appreciate that."

"Thank you father," Douglas replied, " I shall enjoy doing that."

"And you my little one," he said to Florrie, "You will be Auntie Nance's helper, I know she would like that."

Florrie, obviously overjoyed at such an important task clapped her hands joyfully.

"Oh yes I will father, thank you."

"And you will all obey your Auntie Nance as you would obey me. Let us not have any unnecessary problems, just think of your poor mother lying upstairs. Now let us bow our heads, and Oliver, you will please to say grace."

Grace was said and food passed around. I didn't feel very hungry, it wasn't long since I'd stuffed myself at the Hall. First though, I would have to deal with the bib. I looked at Auntie hoping it might be overlooked but no, she was glaring at me and then down at the wretched thing. I wouldn't mind if it were an apron but it was a bib, no bigger than the ones used by infants and I wanted to crawl away and hide. I unrolled it, placed the strings around my neck and tied the bow at the back with great difficulty. I sensed Douglas watching my every move, I don't think he had ever seen a bib before. Florrie, bless her saw him too.

"It is rude to stare Douglas and please to pass the butter."

The Griffiths children had specific jobs to do around the house and I was soon given some. Nothing of consequence and sometimes one of the others, having completed their own task, would insist on helping me. I was overwhelmed by their kindness. One of Florrie's jobs was to help lay table and the following night there was a serviette beside each place setting. I'm sure that during the day she must have told her mother about it and she suggested using them.

Uncle Edgar was right, it was a long way to school and hard going too. We had to climb the hill to the Mansion, walk through the grounds and down the other side. But from the top of the hill what an incredible sight. There, nestled in the green and glorious beauty of a typical Welsh valley lay the quaint little hamlet where most of the employees of the estate lived.

In its midst, the focal point of the community, stood the little red brick school that was to be my seat of learning for the next ten weeks. Oliver said it was exactly two miles from the cottage to the school. We trudged the four miles each day, later in a foot of snow but always under the watchful eye of big Cousin Oliver.

Sometimes, when we walked through the grounds of the mansion, Lady Palmer would be pottering in the garden. She was very fond of gardening and was especially proud of her rose garden, doing much of the work herself. As we passed, whether she was looking or not, Oliver insisted we doff our caps.

"Just in case she is looking out of the corner of her eye," he said.

There were times when she would be walking toward us, in which case we were to stand on the side of the path facing inwards and as she passed, remove our caps and bow and the girls would curtsy; in unison we would intone, "Good morning M'lady."

"Good morning children," she would reply.

My first day at the new school was fun as everyone went out of their way to put me at ease and make me feel welcome. Oliver proudly presented me to all his friends as his "favourite Cousin."

"He is from Brighton," he would say, "a big seaside resort on the English Channel." Making it sound so important.

The school was very different, one huge classroom serving all the grades. The older children sat at the front at long tables and the younger ones at the back in small groups with one teacher and one assistant. Curiously, we didn't use pencils and paper for our lessons, we were each given a slate. We would write our letters or sums on the slate, the assistant teacher would check our work and we would rub it out and start again. At lunchtime we would sit at our desks and eat sandwiches and surprise, surprise, the warm milk was free.

In fine weather we would go out into a field and play games. On the first day it was windy and cold and while most of the children went out, Oliver and I stayed inside. He had, he said, something important to tell me.

"Mother told us about Auntie Nance getting you from her brother" he said, "and that your parents could not look after you. I want you to know Frank, we all felt so sorry about it, Florrie cried even. It must be terrible not having parents, I don't know what I would do without my dear mother and father."

For a moment I was speechless. My first impulse was to say what a liar my Auntie is. Brother indeed, she got me from mum who got me from a lady in Biggleswade; I could never forget that funny name. And she got me from the hospital, I know, because mum told me so. Not only that, I could not have come from her brother because, when we were at Auntie Edie's in Romford, I heard them talking about their brothers. I remember her saying, "Isn't it strange, we have two brothers and we haven't set eyes on them since the day we all left home." So what was she talking about?

To avoid complications I simply said, "Yes it is hard, but I'm all right. I like staying with you; I wonder how long we'll be here?"

After school Oliver stayed very close to me all the way home.

At supper I was so relieved to see the serviettes but to my astonishment, my Aunt insisted I wear the bib.

"There's nothing wrong with that, it was clean yesterday, you don't need to dirty a serviette." She said in her usual cold, overbearing manner.

I could see in their eyes the others felt sorry for me and we ate in silence.

Suddenly it was my seventh birthday. For days we had gathered anything that would burn and made a huge pile at the bottom of the now empty vegetable garden. We had to put it there because they had chickens and we didn't want to scare them. They had enough to put up with from foxes. Just the other night Uncle Edgar, in his pajamas and overcoat, had to chase one away but not before it had clawed a big hole under the wire and grabbed an old rooster.

From somewhere, a pile of old clothing appeared and we made a Guy Fawkes, it looked more like a scarecrow to me. He was stuffed with straw and as tradition demands, was burnt in effigy on the big night. Uncle Edgar brought home lots of fireworks; all kinds, just like the old days in Ongar. I had lots of nice presents too, small things because we would have to carry them all the way home.

Shortly after my birthday it snowed for three days and nights. At first it was great fun, I'd never seen so much snow. But after a while, walking to school and back in it, I never wanted to see snow again.

Auntie Nance seemed to enjoy the role of nurse and housekeeper and didn't mind the long absence from Uncle Fred. Once a week the tiled floor had to be washed and we all sat up on that big chest to keep out of her way. We would tell stories, recite poetry or sing Christmas carols.

On one occasion, the conversation turned to what we would like to be when we grew up. Oliver wanted to be an engineer and build huge bridges, Douglas a sailor and sail around the world. Florrie said she was going to be a nurse.

Just prior to this, I'd been looking through a pile of old magazines in the playroom. In one of them there were pictures of the celebrations on New Year's Eve 1899, the dawn of the twentieth century. I was impressed by the revelry and thought how thrilling it would be to live through such an historical event.

The others were urging me to respond, I was unprepared and felt embarrassed.

"I want to live to see the year two-thousand," I blurted out.

It was 1926, so that seemed eons away. There was silence for a moment, then they all realized the significance of what I'd said and we all worked out how old we would be; Oliver did Florrie's for her. Uncle Edgar was told about Frank's life long ambition and before long the story spread throughout the estate including to the ear of Lady Palmer. She would comment about it when at last I was formally introduced to her in the Great Hall at Christmas.

Auntie Flo had some difficulty for a while and there was talk of her being re-admitted to hospital. Then things improved but she still had to remain in bed. We would visit her and chat about everyday things. She was always cheerful and very nice to me. She spoke with such love and tenderness to the children. What a contrast to the cold indifference of my Aunt, I thought.

The story Oliver told me was very much on my mind and I felt an urge to tell her it was a big lie but what's the good? Besides, everyone, especially the children were deeply concerned that she would be well enough to make it down-stairs for Christmas. Florrie was beside herself with worry about that, it being such a special time for the Griffiths family.

On Fridays, Uncle Edgar took Auntie Nance up to the Hall for a break and a little socializing with the staff. As she was leaving one night, Florrie remarked how pretty she looked. She was only twenty-nine, so why wouldn't she look attractive? Later, we were sitting around the table doing homework, Florrie was crayoning. Oliver, usually the quiet one, piped up.

"Yes our Auntie Nance is pretty. But I cannot understand why she would go to so much trouble just to go and visit old fat cook and the others."

"Perhaps she has a sweetheart." Douglas quipped.

I knew my aunt was a bit of a flirt and Thomas came to mind. I knew because of an incident on DeMontfort Road. A friend of the family, also a tram conductor, was invited to meals because his wife was away for a few days.

Following an evening meal, my Aunt saw him to the door. On my way to the kitchen I saw them locked in an embrace that was more than friendly. I beat a hasty retreat and never divulged what I had seen but it stuck in my mind.

Monday December 20, we woke at six, it was snowing again and windy so the jaunt to school would be a nightmare. I hated Mondays, but there was more to this particular Monday than snow and school. It was little Steven's birthday, his first. We had wrapped gifts the night before placing them on the chest in the hallway. There was to be a party after school but nobody was in a partying mood. There was still much concern whether Auntie Flo would ever be well enough to come down stairs.

Before we'd finished breakfast Uncle Edgar was out the door with a hasty goodbye, still buttoning his coat he disappeared in the direction of the Hall. Auntie Nance was upstairs, obviously something unusual was afoot.

Oliver told us to finish eating then dear little Florrie broke the silence.

"Father said Christmas Day is less than a week away, I do hope mother will be better soon, it has been such a long time."

Nobody spoke and I felt a big lump in my throat.

Then it was off to school, up that darned hill that seemed to get steeper every day. We climbed in silence, each engrossed in our own thoughts. At school, Oliver told us not to worry.

"Everything will be fine," he said.

Eager to get home we arrived breathless after the long trek through the snow. I think we were all feeling a mixture of excitement and apprehension. The house was quiet as usual, we often returned home to find everybody up stairs. Usually, there would be saucepans bubbling away on the stove, sometimes the smell of newly baked bread.

This time things seemed different, we paused uncertain what to do. There was a crackle followed by a faint hiss, and it came from the rarely used living room. Douglas went down the hallway on tiptoe, I followed close behind with Oliver bringing up the rear. As we drew level with the door there was Florrie's shriek of childish laughter and we saw the cause of the crackling sound.

A huge fire burned in the fireplace and a giant Christmas tree with its trunk buried in a pail stood in one corner its branches outstretched awaiting decoration. Auntie Nance sat in a chair under the window dressed in her Sunday best as if going to one of her weekly visits to the Hall.

Then, what everybody had hoped for. Auntie Flo seated in an armchair beside the fire, the first time in more than three months. She was wearing a pretty dress, hair carefully groomed and her face aglow with the happiest smile. Steven sat wide-eyed on the rug fascinated by the blazing fire. There were whoops of joy and hugs and kisses.

Auntie Flo had recovered enough to gradually return to a normal life; from that day on she would increase her activities and would soon be her old self. This was probably the best birthday present Steven ever had although it is unlikely he remembers much of it.

The following Saturday was Christmas Day, the first time I would spend it anywhere but with the Buntons. I felt a little sad thinking about them but the Griffiths' made up for everything. It was probably one of the best Christmases I had as a child. The other children knew I normally spent it with another family and they went out of their way to make it a joyous occasion.

The big event was the children's Christmas party in the Great Hall at the mansion. Lady Palmer was present and Florrie formally introduced me.

"Merry Christmas, M'lady and may I present my Cousin, he is from Brighton and his name is Frank."

"And a merry Christmas to you Florence," said Lady Palmer. She bent down and shook my hand.

"Ah! Yes, so you're the little boy that wants to live to see the year two thousand aren't you, what an exciting thought; you'll probably make it too. Are you enjoying your visit to Wales?"

I felt awfully shy having never spoken to a real live Lady before and I meekly answered. "Yes thank you M'lady." She moved on to the next child.

We had the biggest feast I'd ever seen. There was an enormous table loaded with everything a child could eat and we all stuffed ourselves. Afterwards we played games and Lady Palmer joined in, she was having great fun.

Lady Palmer herself handed each child a gift from under the Christmas tree. There must have been a hundred children so it took ages to get your present. As we left the hall each child was handed a bag of goodies; chocolates, nuts, oranges and all sorts of chocolate coins wrapped in silver or gold paper. I was sure I had a fortune in my bag.

All this luxury was in sharp contrast to the abject poverty suffered by much of the Welsh population, especially in the coal mining areas in south Wales. I saw none of that, but enough in the surrounding area to make me keenly aware of the plight of the less fortunate and the gross inequities of the British Class system. The experience had a profound effect on me for the rest of my life.

On Friday December 31, we left, having spent eleven weeks under the Griffiths' roof. My Cousins had been kind to me and I had grown fond of them. Auntie Nance had been a lot nicer too, hadn't hit me once all the time we were there.

Thomas drove us to the railway station. As we left, there were hugs and tears and promises to write, but we never did. I never saw Oliver, Douglas or Steven again. In the early part of 1937, there was a tearful reunion with Florrie in Brighton, it lasted all of five minutes.

In 1955, I drove to a suburb of Brighton and visited Auntie Flo who by then had been widowed for many years. She and Uncle Edgar had retired there; she had always expressed a desire to return to her roots. She spoke of the children, saying they were all doing well. I drove her into Brighton to do some shopping and then back to her home where we drank a glass of wine and toasted old times.

Nine

Mrs. Mason's Demise

On Thursday April 28, 1927, my Aunt gave me yet another note to take to school. This one stated that, due to a family emergency I would be absent for an indeterminate period and temporarily enrolled at another school.

The previous day she had received a letter from Uncle George saying Auntie Mason was terminally ill, it was cancer. Miss Bud was most concerned.

"Another untimely upheaval," she said.

On the positive side, going to Epping meant I would be less than ten miles from Ongar and home. Surely I would see lots of the family. In fact, we were there thirteen weeks and during that time I saw mum and Jessie once, and then only for a few moments during recess at my new school. They knew Auntie Mason was dying and had come to bid the old girl a final farewell.

Auntie bought a "Woman's World" magazine at Brighton station and spent most of the journey engrossed in it. I had nothing to do but look out the window or at her. I found myself more and more engaged in the latter as the train clickety! clacked! its way to London. In a juvenile sort of way I was trying to unravel this mysterious personality.

Why was she always so irritable, aloof and unapproachable? And why was she so cruel to me? She never laughed, rarely smiled even. Why did I get the feeling that she hated me, and if she did, why had she taken me away from those I loved in the first place? What had I done wrong? And why me? Why couldn't I be like all the other boys I knew, with a nice mum and dad, a brother and sister maybe and a happy home? These questions and more went through my mind as we reached Victoria, then the clatter of the Underground and on to Epping.

We arrived at Number 40 St. John's Road and everything was just as clean and neat as ever, not a thing out of place. I was tired and hungry; didn't get much sleep last night. There had been the usual bedroom scene.

Annie Bunyan greeted us. She was, she said, "Doing what I can for poor Lizzie but I have so much work on hand, some of it has to be ready by the weekend and here it is Thursday. I really can't spare any more time."

Auntie Nance abruptly told her not to worry; she could leave now if she wished. You could tell there was no love lost between these two.

"I'm here," Auntie Nance continued in her usual cold manner, "To look after Auntie Mason, not for a holiday and I shall stay as long as necessary."

Annie looked a little miffed but meekly replied, "Oh, well . . . All right then,

I'll just pop up and say good-bye to Lizzie, I'll tell her you and Frank are here."

"You needn't bother, I'm going up right away," Nance replied. Annie gave me an odd look and quietly left. We didn't see her again until the day of the funeral three months later.

I gazed out the window looking at nothing in particular. The garden looked pretty but neglected. Being May, there were no blooming chrysanthemums. As I stood there, the events of that fateful day back in October 1925 came to mind and I relived every painful moment.

I recalled my return to Ongar for the Christmas of 1925. That was after the infamous haircut and the question on everybody's mind, whatever happened to Jack?

And mum on bended knee telling me that she wasn't my mother. That had haunted me ever since. Nobody really loves me, I told myself, they can't can they; if they did they wouldn't treat me like they do. Why, I wondered yet again, do all these things happen to me, what's wrong with me?

My Aunt came downstairs looking very stern and a bit pale.

"I want to talk to you," she said.

I could always tell when it wasn't going to be pleasant. I was starving but daren't say anything at this stage.

"Auntie Mason is very ill, she is probably going to die soon, so you are to behave yourself; no running around, you've got to be quiet and you are not to go near her bedroom, do you understand?"

"Yes Auntie . . . could I have something to eat please, I'm really hungry?"

She looked at me as if I had asked for the moon.

"You'll jolly well wait till Uncle George gets home then we'll all eat. What do you think I am, a machine?"

"Can I go out in the garden then?"

"No, go upstairs to the back bedroom, your case is on the bed and don't make a noise; change your clothes and when you come down you can peel the potatoes."

Uncle George arrived home at precisely five twenty as always. He left off work at five, five minutes to wash up, don his street clothes and a brisk fifteen-minute walk home. He had been doing exactly that for twenty-seven years, if he did anything else the world would surely end.

I remember some years later, they had an emergency repair job to do on a big engine and Uncle George had to work about hour overtime. Well, the new Mrs. Mason was fit to be tied, running all over the place worried stiff, what on earth could have happened to George? In those days life was so simple, anything out of the ordinary amounted to a major catastrophe.

He said a quick, "Hello! Frank" and went straight upstairs to see Auntie Mason. This would be the daily routine for the next three months. He hardly went anywhere and the garden and allotment were sadly neglected. To me, he seemed a broken man. There were times when he would descend the stairs, tears streaming from his eyes. I liked him and felt sad.

The next day I was temporarily enrolled at St. John's school in Class Three. The headmaster was quite put out when my Aunt couldn't produce my birth certificate. He always had to "verify a child's age," he said, "it's School policy."

She apologized, saying we had "Left Brighton in a hurry and forgot it, but in any case I don't expect him to be here long."

Another new school, more questions. "Where're you from? How old are yer? Why are you here? What does your dad do? Oh, you don't have a dad, why not? What happened to him?" Can you imagine what it was like for me?

For some inexplicable reason I made life more difficult for myself by deliberately writing JACK BUNTON as my name on the front of one of my exercise books. We were having silent reading while the teacher was marking the books.

"Who's Jack Bunton?" he exploded, in a booming voice that reverberated throughout the classroom like a peal of thunder.

Oh! My God, I'm in trouble now, I thought. I put up my hand and meekly said, "Me Sir."

He looked at me then at papers on his desk, glared back and in the same booming voice, "It says here, your name is Frank Dennis Keeling. Now what's going on, are you trying to be funny?"

I was shaking in my boots and couldn't help wondering why in heaven's name I'd done such a stupid thing. Gotta think fast!

"No Sir, that used to be my name, I just forgot myself. I'm very sorry Sir."

"What do you mean, used to be your name. When was it your name, were you adopted or something? Answer me boy."

Why couldn't he just leave it alone, didn't he know how hard it was for me anyway?

"Well Sir," I said, swallowing hard and with a distinct tremor in my voice, "until two years ago I used to live with the Bunton family in Ongar and I was Jack Bunton, but now I live with my Auntie and my name is Frank Keeling."

He looked at me with disbelief and continued. "Your Auntie eh! And what's her name may I ask?"

"Mrs. Ince," I replied. All the other children laughed.

"Silence," he roared, looked at me yet again and if looks could kill, I'd be as dead as a doornail, he literally threw the book in my direction.

"Your attendance here deprives your village of its idiot," he snapped, his voice full of contempt. "Now put your correct name on that damn book and let's have no more of this nonsense or you'll be in serious trouble, do you understand?"

"Yes, Sir," I said, and there the matter was left. But I was definitely not one of his favourite students.

Life in the Mason household was difficult to say the least. There was little to do and only one boy of my age in the lower part of St. Johns Road, Richard. He went to a Private School in Loughton, a bit of a snob and it took a long time before he would condescend to play with me. We did become good friends but only when it was time for me to leave. Then he said he wished I could stay longer.

I couldn't go to the sheds to play because of school. There were Saturday mornings and I think if things had been normal Uncle George would have allowed me to go but life was very difficult for him. Even at the tender age of seven, I could see in his face that it was taking its toll.

Indoors I always had to be quiet. We all spoke in hushed tones and avoided making noise as much as possible. It was a little weird and unnatural for me. Old Auntie Mason insisted that I not visit her because, it was said, she was weak and emaciated. Her moaning grew louder as the pain got worse. There were times when she would scream, and on two or three occasions I heard her pleading. "Oh! Lord ease my suffering I beseech Thee!" They didn't have the pain control therapy we have today.

There was one particularly harrowing experience for me. I was on my way to my room and her bedroom door was ajar. As I reached the landing I heard the poor old girl cry, in a desperate voice, "Dear Lord, I know I've been a sinner but surely not so bad as to deserve this? I beg your forgiveness and beseech you to ease my terrible pain."

I didn't understand, and I think it would have been better had I not heard it at all.

Sunday July 31, 1927, Auntie Mason passed away. I wish I could say peacefully. She let out one piercing scream that filled the entire house, then it was all over.

She was buried in Epping cemetery on the Wednesday afternoon. It was a beautiful day and I recall peeking through a crack in the curtains in the front room. I watched as, in accordance with tradition, the horse-drawn funeral cortege slowly made its way down St. John's Road. It wheeled around at the bottom and returned, pausing for two minutes outside the house where the deceased had lived these many years. I remember the eerie silence, nothing but the snort of a restless horse and the sound of its hoof clawing on the pavement as if eager to get on with it.

The following Sunday, Uncle George asked if I would like to join him on a visit to Auntie Mason's grave. I liked the old man and readily agreed. He held my hand all the way to the cemetery and I was reminded of the first time we had walked hand in hand.

The grave was to the left, on the main pathway leading from the gate to the little chapel in the centre of the cemetery. Its pile of freshly dug earth was still covered with wreaths. As we reached the graveside Uncle George let go of my hand and somehow I knew he wanted to be alone. He got down on one knee; I saw his body shake and heard a half-smothered sob. His crying made me cry and when he turned and saw my tears it was just too much for him. He came to me and again on one knee, hugged me and we wept together.

But, as is so often said, life must go on. Gradually Uncle George overcame his grief and Annie Bunyan did all she could to encourage him. Thirteen months later, her efforts were rewarded and her life-long dream became a reality when she and George Mason, much to the chagrin of Auntie Nance, were married. She was forty-nine and George fifty-three.

"Poor Lizzie isn't even cold in her grave," Auntie Nance was often heard to say.

All was soon forgiven, however, and two years later I resumed my annual holidays with Uncle George and the new Mrs. Annie Mason. She was far too old to have children but since George was obviously very fond of me, it was easy for her to accept a young boy into her life and we became quite close. Her attitude toward Auntie Nance, however, never changed; she just didn't like her. Uncle George died first, in October 1950. Annie immediately changed her will so that when she died in November 1952, the entire estate was left to a housekeeper.

There was a time when I was the sole beneficiary. I know this to be true because in 1938, Jessie wrote and told me she had that very day visited the Masons and was asked to witness the signing of the new will in the presence of a lawyer. Jessie had married Frank Walker and was living in Coopersale, a small village on the outskirts of Epping.

I hadn't done as well in the end-of-term exams as I would have in Brighton, or was it the teacher? In all fairness I think not. I was ninth in a class of thirty-two. Auntie Nance was livid, I could have done better she declared. And she was not amused when I told her that some of my schoolwork was harder than Chinese algebra. I had been "Lazy and inattentive," she said. The upheaval and the stress I had been under for the previous three months completely eluded her. What else should I expect?

On the Monday, she returned to Brighton and Fred, I spent the rest of the school holiday with the Bunton family in Ongar. But what had transpired in Epping had had a profound effect on me. I couldn't get the thought of old Auntie Mason's death out of my mind.

Ten

An Extra Marital Affair

It was 1929 and I'd been living with my Aunt for almost four years. Occasionally, we went to the beach in the summer with her friend, Dolly and son, Jack. It wasn't long though before that ceased. But I was a country boy at heart, not very fond of the beach so it didn't bother me.

Soon I went nowhere with my Aunt and Uncle; they just couldn't be bothered with me it seemed. I was left to play in the street or put to bed. Dolly visited one day and my Aunt wasn't home, she asked why I never went with them. I told her they just didn't want to take me. She was obviously dismayed and asked if it bothered me. I told her at first it did that I felt lonely and unwanted but I had gotten used to it. She shook her head in disbelief and left saying she felt, "Soo! Sorry," for me.

Some weeks later, after being excluded from an outing and feeling neglected I expressed my displeasure. Then foolishly mentioned that even Auntie Dolly thought it was terrible that I never went anywhere with them. My Aunt flew into a rage and I was beaten with the cane for being insolent. She then went after Dolly, ranting and raving.

"You should jolly well mind your own business and not talk about me behind my back, especially to a child."

Poor Dolly, she was hurt and embarrassed; I regretted mentioning it. They didn't see one another for months, but eventually it all blew over and they remained friends until the day Auntie Nance died.

I recall more beatings that year. One for losing a change purse with a lalfpenny in it on a shopping errand. Another for repeating questions about my parents raised by Uncle Fred's brother Walter and wife Mabel, while on a visit with Grandma Ince. They denied the conversation claiming I was lying. Despite my protests of innocence, Fred whipped off his army belt and beat me until even my Aunt cried "enough!"

I got no answers about my parents either. Whenever I asked, my Aunt would snap, "The Buntons are your family and that's all you need to know."

I would ask myself, if that's the case what's all this nonsense about me being her brother's child? What a liar she is, but I was too scared to say anything.

The one beating I probably deserved was for keeping a pocketknife that I found in the school playground when I should have handed it in. Questioned by the Head Master I foolishly denied having found it, insisting instead that I had bought it. I had a new teacher by then, Mr. Eady, his son sat next to me at the same desk.

After school Miss Bud who lived nearby, paid a visit to Auntie. After a brief conversation, my Aunt summoned me and in front of Miss Bud called me "A miserable, lying little thief." The knife was returned to its rightful owner, Mr. Eady's son who sat next to me at the same desk.

Also in 1929, instead of going to Epping for the first week of my August holiday, we spent five days with the Wright family in Romford.

Uncle George Wright was a nice old man, very good with children. He had an old car with the "Dicky" seat at the back and took us for long rides in the country. Four-year-old Desmond and I would sit in the "Dicky," great fun.

He was also a bit of a magician and would amuse us children for hours with his tricks. He was a good storyteller too. He told us of the Keeling ancestry; about them originally being seafaring folk and boat-builders on the southeast coast of England. How, at the beginning of the Industrial Revolution they had split into three groups. One remained in the area, another moved to the outskirts of London, to which, he said I was directly related. The third group moved to the Birmingham area where industry was flourishing.

He also mentioned a Captain William Keeling, a Ship's Master employed by The East India Tea Company who, in 1609, on one of his many trading voyages to India, discovered a group of islands in the Indian Ocean. They were named after him and are located 2,752 kilometeres Northwest of Perth, Western Australia. They are now known as the Cocos (Keeling) Islands and are governed by Australia. Uncle George insisted I was related to this notorious seaman.

He was also convinced the name, Keeling was derived from their boat building activities. When they laid the keel of a new boat they were "keeling," he insisted. That may be, but my research indicates a "Keeling" can also refer to a small cod. I prefer the former but who knows?

I was fascinated by his story and surprised he knew so much about my ancestry. Being nine years old I didn't appreciate its importance and thought no more about it. Years later I did more research into his claim.

This holiday was memorable for another reason. On August 7, I heard my Aunt say to her sister,

"I'm going to take Frank to see his grandfather, it's the old man's birthday today."

We went to a tobacconist and bought an ounce of pipe tobacco. We had to hurry because the shops closed at one o'clock on Wednesdays. We then walked briskly to 47 Shaftsbury Road, a house that to this day is shrouded in mystery. As we walked she told me we were going to see my grandfather and that I should be on my best behaviour. It took only a few minutes so there was no time for further discussion.

On arrival, she opened the front door and we proceeded down the hallway to a back room. As we did so, she called out.

"Hello there! It's only me, Nance, I've brought your grandson to see you."

Granddad was sixty-one, but to me looked much older.

"Well, hello girl!" he said," It's a long time since I've seen you, and this is that Guy Fawkes boy eh?"

"My! You're a big boy, how old are you now then?"

"I'm nine Sir, I meekly replied, and I've brought you a present. Happy Birthday Grandfather."

I handed him the tobacco, he thanked me then turned to Auntie.

"Well girl what are you doing in Romford?"

"Oh! Just visiting Edie for a day or two."

"Edie eh? She only lives round the corner, never see anything of her."

"Well she's pretty busy you know, she's got the children and George is on shift work so she doesn't get much time to herself."

"Yeah, I 'spose you're right," Granddad said.

Auntie then suggested I go and look at the garden. There wasn't much to see but I always knew when I wasn't wanted. I walked the length of the garden and looked over the wall; the neighbour's was much nicer than Granddad's. It wasn't long before Auntie came and said it was time to go.

"Well, 'bye now boy" Granddad said, "Thanks again for the baccy, you come and see me again some time. And you girl, don't leave it so long next time d'ya hear."

"No I won't, take care of yourself. We'll see ourselves out."

It was all over and I never set eyes on the old man again. He died twenty-seven years later in the same house on January 4, 1955, at the ripe old age of 86. Cause of death - myocardial degeneration and bronchitis. Occupation - General Labourer.

Auntie always insisted he was a successful builder. Her marriage certificate lists his occupation as "Builder," information she would have provided. But reality was never good enough for Auntie Nance and that was another one of her fantasies. On his son, Arthur's birth certificate in 1895, his occupation is listed as "General Labourer," and my research indicates he ended his career as a night watchman.

He worked in the Public Works Department for the city of Romford. After the day shift he would occupy a small hut rather like a prairie out-house without a door, and located beside an excavation. He would tend the red oil lamps warning of a potential hazard and guard the tools neatly stacked beside his shack. Picks, shovels, wheelbarrows, crowbars and the like. This was long before the days of backhoes and front-end loaders. In winter there would be a blazing coke fire in a brazier, shaped from an empty ten-gallon drum with holes in it. It would provide much needed warmth for his aging body.

I also learned there was another woman named Mullett in his life, she had several children but I never did meet them. Now back to my story.

I knew a grandfather had to be somebody's father, so as we walked back to the Wright's house I decided question my Aunt.

"Who are Granddad's children, Auntie?"

"That's Granddad Keeling, your mother's father," she said, somewhat testily.

This was the first time she had ever mentioned my mother and I was curious. I remembered what Jessie had told me and thought I might learn more.

"Well, if he's my mother's father, does she live with him?"

"No she does not," was the irritable reply.

I decided to try again anyway, and as we reached the front gate.

"If she doesn't live with Granddad where does she live?"

"Oh don't ask so many questions, you'll find out one of these days."

We were inside the house by now and I was none the wiser.

Auntie Edie was setting the table and I walked into the dining room.

"So, did you see your Granddad and what did he have to say?"

"Oh, not much, thanked me for the baccy he called it and said I was a big boy for my age."

Auntie Nance came into the room.

"Yes you are a big boy. By the way Nance I really do think Frank is too old for a bib, why don't we throw it out?"

To my surprise she didn't object, at last the end of the bib, I was three months short of my tenth birthday. From that moment, Edie was my favourite Aunt.

At the end of the week I was put on the bus to Ongar where I spent the rest of my holiday. There was the usual emotional plea when it was time to leave but it did no good, mum was very sympathetic but very firm.

On my return to Brighton, I became grandma Ince's little helper. On Saturdays I would go to her house at 43 Crescent Road and perform various household chores.

I walked her to church on Sundays until it became too much for her then I had to take the church to her. First I went to church in the morning, home to dinner, Sunday school in the afternoon and then to grandmas for tea. After that I would do more chores then read the Collect for the day, followed by a chapter from the Bible.

We would end with one of her favourite hymns. In her faltering voice she would join me in a rendition of "Abide with me" or, "The day thou gavest Lord is ended," then it was off to church again for the evening service. Thus, I spent my weekends for eight long years; never received a thank you or a nickel for my efforts.

But, as grandma Ince would so often say, "It is better to give than to receive."

The church was St. Saviour's on Ditchling Road, three blocks away. Just before my tenth birthday I was asked to join the choir. Told I would be handsomely paid for doing something I loved to do anyway, I readily agreed.

The Vicar, a rotund Welshman, loved to sing and placed a high priority on his choir. Its reputation was second only to St. Peter's, the Parish Church of Brighton where many Sunday morning services were broadcast on the BBC.

I saw little of the money I earned but must admit most was spent on clothes, textbooks and school supplies. But with three services on Sundays, a mid-week service, choir practice twice a week for two hours plus weddings and funerals, you would have thought I deserved a little.

Our church offered the Boys Brigade, similar to Boy Scouts. I joined and thoroughly enjoyed it. As an unwanted only child, I welcomed the friendship and the camaraderie. I was interested in First Aid and over the next five years learned basic anatomy and physiology, except that the reproductive systems were discreetly avoided. I wanted to join St. John's Ambulance but was denied the opportunity. All this in addition to a busy school schedule.

Come the July, I would sit the Scholarship Exam, later known as the, "Eleven Plus" exam. This was to determine entry to High School. The education system was vastly different from what we have in Canada today. One had to qualify for entry into high school in much the same way as for University entrance. Those who failed went to a Senior Boys or Senior Girls School, leaving at fourteen with the equivalent of grade nine.

The school year was different too. We had only six weeks holidays, four weeks in August, one at Christmas, and one at Easter. Also, the classes in Secondary School were from nine in the morning to four thirty in the afternoon.

I wasn't a particularly good student after leaving Miss Bud's class but eventually began to apply myself. I was fond of soccer and to participate one had to maintain high marks so there was lots of incentive. In fact, the only time I was ever top of my class in year-end exams was my last year of High School.

Uncle Fred took no interest in my education or my sports activities and my Aunt merely complained about the cost. Thank goodness for the choir money. I was getting used to their indifference but often wondered why they took me in the first place; it certainly wasn't out of love. We were not a family in any sense of the word and they showed no affection for me or for each other.

School ended Thursday July 31, 1930, and the following day we moved to a two-bedroom apartment on the second floor at 94 Ladysmith Road. For the first time I had my own bedroom, no more late night spectacles. We even had a bathtub located in an alcove in my bedroom. Also for the first time since leaving Ongar I had somewhere to play other than the street, our own garden.

That year I spent my first holiday with the new Mrs. Mason. As with Uncle George's first wife, I was a little apprehensive but she turned out to be a good hostess and an even better friend. I could confide in her and she knew my Aunt well. There was little in her life that Annie didn't know about. Also, it was she who established the secret Post Office Savings account.

I went to Church with Uncle George on the Sunday and after dinner he said,

"You and I are going to see someone important and I want you to be on your best behaviour."

We set out and walked up St. John's Road across the High Street and down Station Road. Arriving at a big house we were ushered into a drawing room furnished in typical Victorian style. Uncle George introduced me to the lady of the house, her name was lost to me in the formality of the meeting and I thought no more about it.

Just as uncle had insisted, I acted the perfect little gentleman. Yes madam, no madam, thank you madam. Held my teacup in the proper manner and delicately ate the biscuits. She asked how I was getting along at school and I told her with some degree of pride that I had just passed my scholarship exam.

How did I like living in Brighton she asked, and I told the truth.

"It's all right," I said," but I prefer living in the country."

I avoided the use of double negatives and was careful not to end a sentence with a preposition. But she quickly lost interest in me, spending the remaining time talking to Uncle George. Occasionally, however, she would stare at me, I could feel her eyes studying me intently. And then we left and I couldn't help wondering what all the fuss was about.

Following this holiday I started at my new school, it was a whole new world. Lots of sports including soccer, the training was rigid and taken very seriously. I was tall for my age but under weight so I started a limited weight-lifting programme. We weren't allowed to join the full weight lifting programme until after age fourteen, something to do with puberty. I worked hard at all my sports and two years later represented the school at the annual track and field event in long jump and cross-country running.

But soccer was my priority and I soon made the first team. Auntie refused to buy me the special cleated boots required.

"I'm not going to waste hard earned money on such trash," She screamed.

For a while I had to borrow boots but Uncle George Mason came to the rescue. On one of his brief visits I told him of my plight and without a word he took me to the nearest sports store and bought the best pair of soccer boots money could buy. One size too big, of course, so as to last longer. My career as a player and later as a certified Federation of International Football Association (FIFA) referee was launched.

In the summer of 1931, Vic was fourteen, had left school and was working for Noble's the builder so I was without his company. Mum made it interesting though, she persuaded a traveling Ironmonger (hardware dealer) to let me go with him on his old Model T, Ford truck. We would weigh and package bulk goods early in the morning then travel a different route each day. I turned the crank handle to start the engine after each call. It was fun, I got to see the countryside and earn a few pennies for my trouble.

During that same holiday I learned, for the first time, that Paddy had been involved in a serious accident shortly after I left home in 1925. The truck he was in went out of control on the Chelmsford Road; he was pinned underneath breaking several ribs. He didn't work much after that; always seemed tired, but by this time the construction industry was almost at a standstill. Mum mentioned things had been going downhill even before the accident.

We ended that holiday with another visit to the Wright family in Romford. Auntie Edie had given birth to another baby girl in March. Paula was a beautiful baby, blonde and blue eyes. She blossomed into a very pretty girl, but like her mother, was plagued with a weight problem. It bothered me to see her excluded from so many youthful activities and over the years a fondness developed between us, we were more like brother and sister.

By the fall of 1932, we had lived on Ladysmith Road for over two years and my Aunt continued to insist on bathing me. When I was young I didn't mind but I was almost thirteen. When she washed around my genitals I worried that I might rise to the occasion as it were. I thought she was testing me and I'd had enough.

Following a soccer game, I undressed and ran the bath. Normally, she would come in, sleeves rolled up ready for action. This time I took the key inside locking the door behind me. Right on cue she tried to open the door.

"What are you doing?" she said.

"I'm perfectly capable of bathing myself," I replied.

"Well all right, but make sure you do it properly. I don't want mud on that clean towel. And you don't have to lock the door, what are you afraid of?"

"Nothing," I said defiantly.

This was the first time I had stood up to her and it felt good. I've got rid of that bib, now I'm bathing myself, the only thing left is that darned cane. After my bath she quickly returned the key to its original position.

Two weeks after this incident, on a Friday night, Uncle Fred was on the late shift and I had nothing to do. She seemed a little on edge, fidgety and kept glancing at the clock, I could tell something unusual was afoot. It was about a quarter to eight.

"You've had a lot of late nights this week. You've got a football match tomorrow afternoon and you must go to grandmas in the morning. I think you should get ready for bed."

"Yes Auntie," I said much to her surprise and went to bed.

There was a flurry of activity, back and forth from her bedroom to the kitchen, I assumed she was going out. But after a while she sat in her armchair, most unusual. Then there was the shrill sound of the doorbell. Ah! We have a visitor. She hurried down stairs to the main door to greet our guest and it was a man! They returned and I heard her offer to take his coat and invite him to,

"Sit and relax a moment."

There was a strange man in the house? I was curious and lay for a while listening to a half-whispered conversation. So, Auntie Nance was having an affair. I knew it was wrong but what could I do about it? I crept out of bed and looked through the keyhole. They sat facing each other, both his hands were as far up her dress as they would go.

I froze, one eye closed not daring to breathe for fear of being heard. My heart was pounding, surely the whole world could hear it. I moved slightly, trying to get a better view and my cheek brushed against the doorknob. It made a faint click! Hope she didn't hear it.

I felt uncomfortable, caught up in a strange mixture of youthful curiosity, excitement and disgust. And why did I suddenly feel guilty? I wanted to shout at them to stop what they were doing, even at that age I knew what adultery was. But I was transfixed, unable to move or speak.

"Why don't we go in the bedroom and do this?" I heard her say.

And with that they were lost from sight. As she passed my door she turned the key sharply, my eye was so close it made me wince, I was locked in.

I returned to my bed thinking about what was going on. I didn't know whether to despise or pity her? I recognized the man as the proprietor of a store we patronized. I lay there and based on what I had witnessed before, visualized what was going on in the other bedroom. At first I felt angry but then, knowing there was little love or affection in her life and aware of Uncle Fred's short-comings, I supposed her behaviour was inevitable.

At one point I heard the familiar muffled cry, and knew what it meant. After about an hour they came out of the bedroom and following a brief but inaudible conversation he was escorted to the door. The intrigue was over.

The next morning, just before eight, she gently knocked on my door and quietly said it was time to get up. We now had to face each other and I didn't know how to act. I felt awkward and self-conscious. I could sense that she knew I was aware of what had transpired; perhaps she'd known for years that I knew what went on. Sensing my unease, she quickly broke the silence.

"You've got a birthday coming up soon and I was going to wait until then to buy you some long trousers but I think we should go and get them today, what do you think?"

"I have to go to grandma's this morning and I'm playing football this afternoon."

"Oh, that's all right, I'll go to grandma's, I haven't seen her for ages."

Bribery I thought, but I had wanted long trousers for months, being tall I looked ridiculous in short pants.

It was Fred's day off and he would sleep till noon. We went to a Men's clothing store on Lewes Road near Elm Grove, a long and difficult walk for both of us. On the one hand I wanted to confront her with what happened, on the other, I was too embarrassed. I knew also that she felt uncomfortable in the knowledge that I shared her secret.

She bought me two pairs of gray flannel trousers that needed some alteration and would be ready at four o'clock. Normally I would be expected to pick them up.

"No," she said," I'll do that on my way back from grandma's."

She's certainly going out of her way to placate me, I thought.

Walking home, I thanked her for the trousers saying that I felt foolish in short pants and how much I appreciated what she had done.

"Well if you behave yourself you'll get all you want, you just have to be patient," she said.

There was silence until we turned onto Bear Road.

"I'm very annoyed at what you did last night," she said at last.

So, she did hear me.

"Well, that's too bad," I said defiantly.

More silence, then we turned onto Ladysmith Road, a very steep hill and she was breathing heavily.

"Well . . . I don't think . . . it was very nice . . . you certainly . . . didn't see much."

"Enough to know what was going on," I replied. "I'm not stupid or ignorant you know."

We were at our front door. She looked at me, at first with contempt then a more inquisitive expression.

"Hmm! Is that so?" was all she could muster.

She opened the door and stalked up the stairs.

That same evening she offered yet another bribe. Fred was studying the racing form as usual and I was about to go into my bedroom. She opened the sideboard drawer, took out a popular, weekly Boy's Magazine and handed it to me.

"There, that's for being a good boy. And remember, don't tell anyone my business, not even Uncle Fred."

Fred instantly glanced first at her, then at me . . . and resumed reading his paper. Wimp!

I now shared her secret, which was powerful knowledge. I thought her attitude toward me might change but it didn't. What did change though, was her behaviour around the house. She was notably less modest than before. She would sometimes appear wearing only a slip, which had never happened before.

Other things made me feel uneasy. She would say, "Do me up please," and the zip or buttons often went right down to her backside. In the summer she would stand in front of the glass door and ask if she needed to wear a slip. Sometimes she would pull the back of her skirt way up and ask if the seams of her stockings were straight. Or she'd ask me to put my hand down her dress and scratch her back, then she would purr.

"Oooh! you have such nice soft hands."

Is she testing me? Teasing me? Or trying to goad me into doing something I might regret? I wondered.

My thirteenth birthday came, at last I was a teenager but it didn't make much difference, life went on much the same. I went to Ongar for the Christmas holiday and things were worse. Charlie and George had been unemployed for months and the strain was too much. They got money from somewhere and went out and got drunk. The only time I saw either of them the worse for drink. Poor mum was beside herself. I can see her now, helping them, one at a time, down to the privy. The next day they were full of remorse but their problems were still there.

Minnie and Evelyn had both married the previous year so were no longer at home. Minnie was serving behind the bar at the Red Cow Inn and living in a Council House nearby. Evelyn had married Claud Alderson and was living on High Ongar Road. Jessie was still working at the dressmaker's, but I don't think she earned much money. Frank was still butchering but the dance band no longer existed; there wasn't much to sing or dance about. This was England in the dirty thirties.

Eleven

A Change Of Attitude

Leaving Ongar was always difficult, it was the place where all those wonderful memories of a happier period of my childhood had originated. And even though Mrs. Bunton was not my birth mother, a bonding had developed in those early infant years. She was still my mum and I loved her dearly. Paddy was the only real father I had ever known, I could not have loved him more had he been my natural father. As well, I still looked upon the rest of the family as my brothers and sisters, it was too painful to think otherwise.

Returning to Brighton that year was particularly hard. The family had tried to make it Christmas as usual but the odds were against them. England was in the depths of the worst depression in living memory, money was scarce and employment limited. Many workers, especially those in the coal mining and related industries, had been without work for as much as ten years.

Everybody put on a brave face but somehow the Christmas spirit seemed a little hollow. Paddy was not himself; quiet, didn't join in the singing and rarely left the house. Not even to visit his favourite pub.

The situation was little better in Brighton. Luckily, Fred had a steady job and my earnings from the choir became even more important. The whole of Europe seemed in a state of turmoil. The following year, 1933, would see Hitler come to power and Communism firmly entrenched in Eastern Europe. The future looked grim especially for young people. It would be mid 1936 before things began to improve but by then the clouds of war were already on the horizon. I read the newspapers and at school we discussed the issues of the day as part of our social studies. We were fortunate compared to many parts of the country.

The year 1933 was memorable for another reason. It was a turning point in the relationship with my Aunt. Things came to a head in July.

Having a garden, we wanted to grow as much produce as possible to save money. Earlier in the year, either by accident or design, she became friendly with the mailman. It all started innocently enough with a conversation about gardening. Then, on his days off he brought seedlings; always ensuring that Fred was home. He offered advice on the art of growing things and his visits became routine. Neighbours knew the mailman was a friend of the Ince family. It didn't look out of place, therefore, for him to be invited in for a cup of tea when making his mail deliveries.

Our apartments were built on a slope so that the ground floor was slightly below street level. The master bedrooms, with large bay windows, were at the front of the building. Anyone standing in our second floor bedroom could clearly be seen from the sidewalk if the drapes weren't drawn.

It was end of term exams, I had one test from nine till ten-thirty then free until two, so I went home. Imagine my horror when, as I approached our apartment I saw the mailman in my Aunt's bedroom, naked from the waist up and putting his pants on. She was having another affair!

Disgusted, my first reaction was to storm upstairs and confront them, but what good would that do? There would be a scene and the neighbours would know all our business. The houses on the opposite side of the street were higher than ours. She hadn't bothered to draw the curtains and I was sure neighbours opposite must have seen everything. Then the door opened and without a word he pushed past me. I'll make sure Fred and the Post Office hear about this, I thought.

Once inside there was a terrible scene, during which I picked her up bodily, jostled her out the front door, locking her out. I let her back in only when she agreed to changes in her behaviour toward me. The upshot of it all was, the mailman would no longer be welcome in our home, the cane would be destroyed and her attitude toward me would change. In future I would be treated with the same respect she demanded from me. In exchange I agreed not to tell Fred or cause any problems with the Post Office. In the end, to my utter surprise she put her arms around me, hugged me and cried bitterly on my shoulder. And I felt sorry for her!

Things were much better after that, at last she realized I was growing up. Never again did she attempt to hit me and the only time she laid a hand on me was an occasional and unexpected show of affection. We argued at times but settled our differences through discussion. Our relationship became more congenial and over the next two years life took on a more pleasant atmosphere. During this time, as far as I know, there were no more affairs but she was not a happy woman.

Shortly thereafter a strange thing happened. I'd gone no where with either of them for years but out of the blue, Fred asked if I would like to go for a walk with him. I was surprised but agreed. The tourist season was over so we walked unimpaired, east along the promenade and I sensed he had something on his mind.

He remarked about how suddenly the mailman had stopped visiting. He couldn't understand it; did I have any ideas? I'd agreed not to tell and didn't want to go back on my word. On the other hand, I had a feeling Fred knew and for me to deny any knowledge of the affair would make me not only a liar but also an accomplice. I was torn between two loyalties, what was I to do?

Then he said I could be honest with him; that I should not worry, nothing said would hurt his feelings and it would be in strictest confidence. He would not, he said, disclose the source of his information. I was relieved and convinced he knew even more than I had supposed. Slowly, bit by bit I told him what I knew.

He was unmoved, it was no more than he expected and he was well aware of his shortcomings as a husband and lover. I dared to suggest that perhaps if he spent less time in the pub and studying the racing form, things might be different. He was quite sure it wouldn't make any difference.

"The marriage was doomed from the start," he said.

An astonishing admission, but many years later it all made sense. When we arrived home he betrayed me.

"I think we have something to discuss," he said to my Aunt.

"Well, if you want to listen to his lies, then so be it," she retorted, her irritation obvious.

"All right, if it's lies, there's nothing more to be said."

And for six years nothing more was said.

For a while things were a bit cool. It wasn't long though, before she was her old friendly self, with the occasional warmhearted embrace. The transformation was amazing. At first I was suspicious of this newfound affection and dismissed it as intimidation. It is obvious, I told myself, she is testing me and trying to goad me into doing something I might regret, perhaps in retaliation.

We moved to Park Crescent Terrace in the fall. The South end of the Terrace consisted of typical Georgian style Town Houses with three stories and a basement. These Stately homes of England had been converted into Flats. Our house was at the other end and was one of two semi-detached (Duplex) houses that had been completely remodeled. We didn't live there long though, grandma Ince's health was failing rapidly and the house next door became vacant so we moved there.

While living on the Terrace we were exposed to one of the most gruesome crimes ever committed in England. The Brighton Trunk Murder.

A few doors from us a young lady named, Violet Kaye, lived in the basement suite. There was no outward sign that she worked at the world's oldest profession. But we soon learned she was a high-class call girl, much to the disgust of some of the neighbours. Her live-in male companion murdered her and stuffed the body in a trunk. He then phoned a taxicab and the cab driver helped carry the trunk up the steps to the street and secure it to the luggage rack. He remarked about the extraordinary weight and was told it was full of books. They drove to Brighton railway station and between them carried the trunk into the Left Luggage Office, where it remained for three days.

Eventually, body fluid leaked from the trunk, which led to it being opened by the police thus exposing the body. Tony Mancini was charged with the murder and at the trial the cab driver, Tommy Kay was a key witness. Many years later, that name would resurface under very different circumstances.

We moved into the house next door to grandma Ince in March, 1935. It was further away from school but nearer the college I would soon attend, and it was easier to look after grandma's needs. Unfortunately, she died three months later.

Traditionally, her body was embalmed and placed in an open coffin in the front room. During this period the body couldn't be left alone and so her children took turns, four hours on and eight hours off, day and night, sitting beside grandma. I was expected to take my turn too. It was the first time I had ever seen a dead person. Furthermore, although I didn't know it, I would soon become much more familiar with the four hours on and eight hours off routine.

It had long been agreed that Fred would buy the other children out and take over his mother's house. So again we moved but only next door. If the spirit of our dearly departed grandma haunted the house we shall never know, but it proved an ill-fated house for me.

When we first moved to Crescent Road I met Reg Ellison from the next street. We developed a friendship that lasted until well after World War II. As we strolled along the promenade one day we met two girls, and for a few weeks we were a happy foursome. Then Reg and his girl broke up but I had fallen in love with Mary. She was very attractive and I was the envy of my peers.

This was my first serious teenage affair. I'd been out with girls before but nothing compared to this. It put a strain on my friendship with Reg though, and he would try to persuade me to break my dates with Mary but I declined.

Throughout the summer of 1935 we spent every possible moment together. For the first time I didn't go away on holiday, there was no soccer and so on Saturdays we roamed the countryside. And we got involved in some typical teen-age necking but agreed not to indulge in sex. In England it was a criminal offense to have sexual intercourse with a female under sixteen. We did come awfully close on one occasion though when she allowed me to undo her blouse and fondle her breasts. They were firm and her nipples swelled in response to my touch. Her skin was soft and white and she let my hands roam over her body. She became aroused, and I better understood my Aunt's pleadings. It ended with both of us being totally frustrated.

Now it was early September, I was enrolled at the Brighton Technical College and life was hectic. One might say, I was as busy as the proverbial one-armed paperhanger. School Monday to Friday with lots of homework, choir practice two evenings a week and a mid-week evening service. My Saturdays were devoted to household chores in the morning and soccer in the afternoon. Sundays there were three Church services and Mary was feeling neglected. There were times when I was tempted to give up the choir but that was out of the question, we needed the money. My Aunt was already complaining about the cost of my education.

I'd been to Mary's house and met her parents and we would often spend the evening together when they were out. But her younger sister was always there, so we had to be on our best behaviour. They had a radio and we would listen to the popular shows and the big band music of that era.

The first Saturday in September saw the end of a particularly busy week. I had a soccer game in the afternoon then to Mary's in the evening. At one point while she and her sister were talking I fell asleep. Mary was quite upset and we had our first tiff. I left in a huff, completely unjustified, but I was too pig-headed to admit it.

On the Sunday I went out with Reg. Mary decided to come to our house and my Aunt invited her in, something she had never done before. I was surprised when I got home and was told about Mary's visit, that she was annoyed at my behaviour and it was up to me to make amends. My Aunt also made it clear she didn't like Mary at all, saying that she thought her common.

"She had a skirt on with a split right up to her arse," she said.

It was, of course, the fashion but you couldn't tell Auntie that. She was critical of everything about Mary.

At that time we had a cat, a nice old thing, almost human. When you mentioned it's name, "Puskus," it would meow as if to answer. It was my Aunt's pet and she treated it like a companion, using this unorthodox relationship to add weight to a point of view or to support her in an argument.

Ending her criticism of Mary she said, "We didn't like her at all, did we Puskus," the cat meowed in response.

"See, Puskus agrees with me don't you, Puskus." And again the cat meowed seemingly in agreement. No body really took it seriously but it was amusing.

I was surprised at the intensity of her criticism. She obviously didn't want me to have a girlfriend, but I could not agree with all she had said about Mary. Regretfully, I did accept her point about the consequences of getting too serious at such a young age, and was persuaded to end the romance. Reg was glad though.

I awoke one Tuesday morning and lay pondering the agenda for the day. Then I suddenly realized it was November 5 1935, my sixteenth birthday. I'd been so busy it sort of crept up on me.

Now what could I do to celebrate and with whom? Reg was sick with the flu and David, my College buddy, never went out on school nights. Deep down I knew I was missing Mary. It was over five weeks since I last saw her. Yes, that was my problem, I really did love that girl.

I decided that after supper I'd walk over to Mary's house. I would apologize for my behaviour, say how much I missed her and could we make a fresh start? I was sure it would work. I mean, how could it fail?

I was excited, and like Charles Dickens' Pip, I had great expectations! Mustn't say anything to Auntie though, she doesn't like Mary.

Twelve

The Age Of Consent

I arrived home just before five, had supper then washed and shaved; a dab of after shave lotion and a little Brilliantine on my hair. This was a special occasion and I was determined to look and smell my best for Mary.

As I dressed, the glow from bonfires filled the sky and there was the unmistakable smell of burning. There was also the occasional swish of a rocket as it hurtled skyward, followed by a mild explosion amidst a shower of sparks. Some small child would be getting a big kick out of that. Yes, it was Guy Fawkes Day, which meant birthdays, huge bonfires and firecrackers. But none of that appealed to me anymore.

It was my sixteenth birthday, second only in importance to my twenty-first, when I would legally become an adult. There were very important legal ramifications attached to this one too; yes indeed! I could now go into a tobacconist shop, buy cigarettes and walk down the street smoking my fool head off without breaking the law, only I'd been doing that since I was fourteen. Guess it wouldn't feel quite the same anymore. No rush of adrenaline as you passed a cop, wondering if he was going to stop you and demand proof of age.

Also at sixteen it was legal for two consenting parties to have sex. We had celebrated Mary's sixteenth birthday a couple of months previously, now it was mine. Deep down though I felt uneasy; what was going through my mind was wrong and could lead to all sorts of complications but, what the heck? I knew a couple when we lived on Ladysmith Road who'd been doing it since she was thirteen, nothing happened to them. Didn't use a condom either. "Tried it once," the guy said, "like having a bath with your socks on." Anyway, I felt just a little excited at the thought.

Auntie was sitting in the living room knitting, a fire made the room warm and cozy. Fred was on the late shift and it would be at least one in the morning before he'd be home. Puskas would be her only companion, and I wish she hadn't asked where I was going.

"Oh, I don't know, might just go down town, see what's going on."

There was a pause.

"Well, you could stay home and play with us, couldn't he Puskas?"

The cat meowed its assent and I decided to go along with her little game.

"What on earth would we do?"

Visions of playing Checkers or Snakes and Ladders came to mind and didn't appeal to me one bit.

"Well, we could play mothers and fathers couldn't we Puskas?"

The cat meowed again.

"Mothers and fathers with a cat?," I said, continuing what I thought was a little harmless banter. But I was always a little wary, couldn't be serious surely.

"Are you serious?"

"Of course I'm serious, why wouldn't I be?"

I still had difficulty believing her and to make sure she wasn't having me on. "You're suggesting . . . that you and I . . . play mothers and fathers?"

She came to me, put her arms around me and kissed me full on the lips, at the same time forcing her tongue in my mouth. It was the most passionate kiss of my young life. And all the time she was pressing her body against mine, removing any doubt as to how serious she was.

It is said that, "There is nothing more surprising than reality." To say I was stunned would be an understatement. Here was this woman, my guardian for the past ten years pulling me closer to her. I could feel every curve of her body, she still had her tongue in my mouth and I was shaking like a leaf.

Of course, she wasn't really my Aunt, I told myself. She had often stressed over the years that we were in no way related. For years I had literally hated her guts, it was only in the last two, that she'd been amiable or good-humoured. It dawned on me just how much our relationship had changed since the incident on Ladysmith Road. Those provocative little actions of hers, were they a prelude to what was happening now, now that I had reached the age of consent?

Her tongue was still exploring my mouth. She was pressing her abdomen hard against mine, moving her buttocks from side to side, breathing heavily and I was getting aroused.

"You're shaking," she said, "What's the matter?"

"I'm nervous . . . This is so unexpected . . . I don't know what to do."

"Don't be nervous . . . Relax . . . Just leave everything to me."

She deftly unbuckled my belt and began to pull my shirt out of my pants, at the same time she whispered,

"Undo the hook on my dress."

With both hands I reached to the back of her neck, undid the hook, eased the dress over her shoulders to the floor. She was wearing a satin slip and as I slid the two straps from her shoulders, she pulled both my shirt and under vest over my head and threw them on the floor. Then she undid the top button of my fly and my pants dropped slowly to the floor, her slip followed. And there we were, naked in each other's arms.

From what I'd seen and heard in the bedroom years before, I knew what would please her. I took her breasts in my hands and gently caressed them, plying the nipples between finger and thumb.

"Ooh! That's beautiful," she whispered, "When you do that it drives me crazy."

She had her hands on my buttocks and was pressing me ever closer, I was hard and throbbing, I knew she could feel it and I could feel the moisture from her.

"Let's go to bed," she murmured.

We picked up our clothes and as we climbed the stairs I realized the significance of what was happening. I was going to bed with Fred's wife, the very thing for which I had condemned others.

Under the old common-law, both parties commit adultery if the married participant is a woman. So, I was about to commit adultery. I felt a twinge of guilt but quickly overcame it. Fred didn't care, he'd made that clear years ago. And I wasn't the first one to do this was I. But did that make me less guilty? I wondered.

Now we were on the bed and me still fondling her breasts. I looked at them, they were different, not as firm as Mary's and the nipples weren't pink. But her breasts were large, soft and white and to fondle them was exciting, and I knew it was wrong to compare. Mary was barely sixteen, my Aunt was, well, what age was she? At that point I neither knew nor cared. In fact, she was thirty-eight.

I was shocked by what I saw next.

"What's the big scar?"

Without a moment's hesitation she said,

"Oh that . . . That's my gall bladder operation."

"When did that happen?"

"Oh, years ago, don't ask so many questions."

And with that, as if to stop me talking, she guided one nipple into my mouth and asked me to, "Play with the other one."

We made love, and to me it was the most wonderful thing I had ever experienced. She obviously enjoyed it too, letting out that little cry when she reached a climax. We lay together in silence for a while, then to my amazement she began to tell me about her first love.

He was a Sergeant in the Royal Artillery stationed in Epping during World War One. His camp was located in fields on the other side of the railway track off Kendal Avenue. I knew the area well as Uncle George had pointed it out to me years ago from his allotment. Just last year, he had built a new bungalow on that large triangular-shaped lot at the corner of Station Road and Kendal Avenue.

The Sergeant was the first man to make love to her and she described the sheer ecstasy of that first encounter and the thrill of their subsequent love-making. She told me of the most intimate things he used to do to please and satisfy her including oral sex.

"Do you think that's dirty?"

I was only vaguely familiar with it but said "No," and she gave me a little squeeze.

"That's nice . . . You're a treasure."

She also told of the heartbreak she felt for years after learning of the Sergeant's death.

"We're wasting precious time," she said.

We made love again and it was even more exciting.

She took the dominant position this time and it was obviously more satisfying for her since she had complete control. She would pause as if to savour the moment, then continue with a slow, drawing motion. She was eager to have all of me inside her, the pace quickening as she approached orgasm. Then, reaching a climax she gasped.

"So beautiful darling, don't stop, don't stop now . . . Oh! Oh! Ooooh!"

This was the cry of passion I'd heard so many times.

She lay on top of me for a brief moment kissing me just as she had done at the beginning of this incredible evening. Then rolled over and lay in my arms as contented as a cream fed tomcat in a dairy. After a while we talked about the future and she surprised me.

"You won't ever tell anyone about this, will you."

"Of course not, I'd be scared Fred might find out and I don't want to be named a corespondent in a divorce case. Besides, it's too personal to share with anybody."

She was pleased and we agreed our behaviour when Fred was around would have to be as before. In his presence there could be no outward sign of any change in our relationship. There was one last kiss, then off to my own bed.

It was still quite early. As I lay awake pondering what had happened, I heard the sound of firecrackers exploding followed by shrieks of childish laughter. The sky was still aglow from the multitude of bonfires down at "The Level" a piece of parkland between Lewes and Ditchling Roads, so named because it was the only flat piece of land in an otherwise hilly landscape.

Tonight there had been fireworks in this house but of a different kind. I shall never forget my sixteenth birthday as long as I live, I thought. And I still marveled at the woman under whose roof I had lived for the last ten years. For all that time I had seen her as nothing more than my guardian and most of the time not a very nice one. We've come a long way, I thought.

After so many years she was at last making me feel wanted and worthwhile. For what she had done this night I would be forever grateful. Or at least, so I thought.

What made her change I wondered, from that cold, sullen, unapproachable and sometimes, cruel person I had once known? It was totally beyond my understanding. All I knew was, it had been the most beautiful experience of my young life and I eventually drifted into a deep and contented sleep.

The following days were, indeed, difficult for me. Every time I set eyes on her I thought about those wonderful moments and yearned to relive them. How long would I have to wait? I repeatedly asked myself. I had difficulty concentrating on anything else. At school, church or just walking down the street my mind wandered and sometimes I became aroused. I hated this waiting.

There were subtle changes in my Aunt's behaviour too. She went around the house humming a popular love song, she smiled at me a lot more and was even more pleasant. If Fred noticed any change he showed no sign of it. He would sit for hours pouring over the racing form. He was one of very few people I ever met who actually made money from betting on horses.

He was investigated once by the Criminal Investigation Division (C.I.D) because of a phenomenal wager he had made involving several different horses at different locations, resulting in a very large pay out. The Bookmaker, a large

National Company, refused to pay him until the police had satisfied them there was no fraud involved. Racing and the pub were all he lived for, and I felt sorry for the man.

He was off duty on the Friday following my birthday, Saturday her friend, Dolly visited, Sunday was church all day and Fred began his early shift. He got home about three in the afternoon, slept for a couple of hours and was always there when I got home. He often went to the pub in the evening but was so unpredictable. Sometimes he would be gone an hour sometimes three, and so my Aunt and I would remain at a distance. For me it was hard.

He was off on the Saturday and Sunday following his early shift. On the Monday, thirteen long days and nights after our first encounter we were alone again. With supper over, the dishes stacked away and the table laid for tomorrow's breakfast, little time was wasted. There was a divan under the window in our living/dining room and a blazing fire, just like the first time it was cozy and inviting.

We undressed and lay on the divan kissing and fondling each other. If not for the table I think we would have made love there, but it restricted our movements. Anyway, the heat from the fire made the upstairs bedroom comfortably warm so for the second time we went to bed and I needed no coaching.

She lay on her back and I took one breast into my mouth, gently fondling the other, just the way she liked it. Then we made love and it was even more beautiful than before. Afterward she lay beside me, I knew she was feeling mellow and contented and I wondered if she was in a mood to reminisce again.

"Was that nice?" I asked.

"It was beautiful."

"Am I better than Fred?"

"Oh, poor old Fred, he's not much of a one for love making."

"Am I bigger than him?"

"Yes, but it's not how much you've got, it's how you use what you've got. And I intend to make the best possible use of what you've got my love."

We both giggled.

"There's something that's been bothering me for a long time," I said.

"Oh, what's that?"

"Well, Jessie Bunton once told me that when I was born a lady took me from the hospital because my own mother couldn't look after me. Is that true?"

I felt her stiffen slightly and she was quiet for a moment. I wondered if I had done wrong in asking her such a question, but I wanted to know.

"Yes"

"Did you know my mother?"

This time she was prepared.

"Yes, of course," she said very quietly.

I could feel my heart thumping. I raised myself up on one arm, and looking down at her I said somewhat excitedly,

"You did, why didn't you tell me before, for years I've wondered about her. What was she like, what's her name?"

"Her name was Annie . . . Annie Keeling, she was just a young girl," she said.

I was getting impatient.

"Well what was she like was she pretty, tell me, I want to know."

"Well, I don't know about pretty, she was pleasant looking."

I lay for a while, absorbing this new information about my mother.

"What happened, do you know? I mean about her not being able look after me?"

"Oh, she was just a young girl who fell in love, and they did what you and I have just done and you came along; then he jilted her. You see, you were born prematurely and when he was told, he wouldn't believe it and simply refused to have anything more to do with her."

"Rotten bastard" I said without thinking. Then, "You know, I really would like to meet her, do you know where she lives?"

Silence for quite a while, I was about to ask again.

"You must realize dear, she may not want to be known as your mother now . . . That was a very long time ago . . . You have to think of her feelings you know."

I thought for a moment.

"Yes, you're right," I sighed, "She's probably married and got children now, I'd only spoil things for her I suppose."

I lay quietly for some time still trying to imagine what my mother would be like, I didn't realize I was still fondling my Aunts breast.

"You know, you have lovely soft hands, I love to feel them all over me" she said.

And with that we made love again. Why was it always better the second time, I wondered?.

We talked little after that but I had learned a lot. I felt relieved that at last I knew something about my mother, that she existed and that meant a great deal to me. It was no longer a mystery and for that I was grateful.

I looked down at my Aunt.

"Thanks for telling me about my mother, that's a load off my mind and I'm grateful."

I kissed her one last time, more out of gratitude than anything then retired to my own bed feeling very smug.

She had said I was better than Fred, which did wonders for my ego. She liked my hands and I made a mental note to keep them that way. She said there were other things we could do, how lucky I was. I knew she had enjoyed it too, because she cried out even louder when she came the second time. That was important because I was more concerned for her satisfaction than my own, which surprised me. But, "It is better to give than receive" as grandma Ince used to say.

It was eighteen long and frustrating days before our next rendezvous. Christmas day was less than three weeks away. It began in much the same way, foreplay on the divan then off to bed. That's the way all love making should begin, I concluded. Once in bed I started to perform as usual, but then she dropped a bombshell!

"I don't think you should put it in anymore," she said.

"Why not."

"Well, it's wicked."

I didn't know whether to laugh or cry and it took me a moment to regain my composure.

"Well, yes it's wicked I suppose, but only because we're committing adultery, and who cares about that? Fred doesn't. In any case, it's not the first time is it."

I knew at once that I shouldn't have said that.

"You needn't throw that up," she said testily.

"No" I said. "I certainly shouldn't have, and I'm deeply sorry. It's just that I don't understand what's happening, I thought you enjoyed what we're doing."

"I do, but it's still wicked."

I was even more confused. She had done the same thing with at least two other men, this was our third time and suddenly it was wicked?

"So, if we're not going to do what we've been doing, what are we going to do?" I asked.

I was frustrated, I mean how stupid can you get? Laying there naked, debating moral standards.

"Well, I told you before, there are other ways."

But I had tasted the real thing and nothing else appealed to me. Perhaps I could change her mind.

"Let's think about this for a moment, I said. "What you're proposing is nothing more than glorified masturbation. Is that worth it?"

Before she could reply I went on.

"We'd be running the risk of getting caught doing something we can do for ourselves. Surely, for us to lay here naked and satisfy each other, in whatever manner, is just as wicked. To me, what you're saying just doesn't make sense."

She replied in her old angry, superior way.

"It might be glorified masturbation as you call it but it can be very beautiful, it's better than running the risk of disease with some slut like that Mary."

I wanted to retaliate but she was all worked up now.

"You ask, is it worth it? Am I not worth it? You're saying you only want full-blown sex or nothing at all. That's a Lord All Mighty attitude, I must say. And there's little risk of being caught if we're careful, we haven't been caught yet have we? And you say we can do it for ourselves, that doesn't say much for me does it. I thought you said what I did to you was beautiful . . . Make up your mind boy!"

So, I was a boy again eh?

She carried on.

"I don't care what you say, what I'm suggesting is not as wicked. Anyway, that's the way it's going to be and if you don't like it then to hell with you, you can lump it."

I was amazed at the complete turnaround, there had to be more to it than this. Another man came to mind.

"Look" I said, "I just don't understand. Right out of the blue you take me to your bed, teach me the most beautiful things I have ever known and now you seem as if you just want to use me and push me aside. Is there someone else? If there is, tell me."

She flew into a rage, something I hadn't seen for a long time.

"There is no one else stupid, I'm not using you or pushing you aside. You could have all the satisfaction you want with me but you are not going to fuck me again . . . ever! Now get out of my sight you make me sick!"

I was startled by her use of the four letter word, never before had she uttered more than the occasional damn. I went back to my bed frustrated, a black depression descended over me and I was a little bit scared. There's no telling what she might do when she's in this kind of mood.

For hours I lay awake going over what had been said. I was deeply saddened, not because of the sex but because my unkind and ill-considered words had ruined that short-lived closeness. More than anything I would miss the affection. Why the hell, did I have to go and spoil everything?

Her remarks about Mary cut like a knife, she was not a slut. She was the first person to show me real love, something that had been missing for so long in my life. She used to say I was the nicest boy she'd ever known.

"The others have no class," she would say.

That made me feel good, and I cursed the day I had left her. If only I could turn back the clock to my birthday, put on my shoes and go to her.

The past five weeks had been the best in the ten years I had lived under my Aunt's roof. She had been kind, considerate and treated me like a grown man instead of a naughty, unwanted child. She had, at times, been tender and I don't mean in the sexual sense and I had never before seen her so happy around the house. Perhaps I could change her mind?

Any hopes of reconciliation were quickly dashed the following morning. Instead of the gentle knock on my door and a pleasant, "Time to get up, sleepy head," there was nothing but the thump of an angry fist and her footsteps descending the stairs. I thought of William Congreve's, "Heaven has no rage like love to hatred turned, nor hell a fury like a woman scorned."

She got my breakfast in stony silence, not even a "Good morning." Fred was up stairs sleeping, in the very same bed that just a few hours before we had lain naked together. I wanted so badly to admit I had been indiscreet and ask her forgiveness.

I wouldn't miss the sex as much as the love she'd shown me, I'd enjoyed it so much. And I had to admit what we had done was wicked. Before I could open my mouth she said in a hoarse whisper,

"Fred is upstairs so don't say a word. What happened between us in the last few weeks was wrong, it was wicked. I'm going to forget it ever happened and you should do the same. From this moment on, as far as I'm concerned you are nothing more than a lodger in this house, and the sooner you find somewhere else to live the better. The matter is closed, not another word or you'll regret it."

Over the next eighteen months the suggestion I find somewhere else to live became a familiar refrain. What was I to do? In those days of high unemployment a superior education was absolutely essential. My Aunt repeatedly complained about the cost of everything and obviously, the choir money was never going to satisfy her.

And so it was, on Sunday December 15 1935, I told the Choir Master I was going to leave after the evening service.

"Good heavens, Frank!" he said. "Why on earth would you do that; you know, with Christmas upon us we need you."

"Well Sir, I said, "my voice is beginning to crack, I don't feel confident anymore."

"That's nonsense and you know it, what's the real reason, is it a girl or something."

I didn't want to tell him how close he was to the truth.

"Well Sir, to tell you the truth, my Aunt feels I have to earn more money so I'm going to try and get part time work."

"Oh! . . . I am sorry to hear that Frank, we shall miss you, you've been with us a long time haven't you."

"Six years Sir, and I've enjoyed it very much, I shall miss it too," I said, feeling a lump in my throat.

"I understand" he said, "I'll inform the Vicar and you should collect your pay as usual at the end of the quarter. By the way, what kind of work are you seeking?"

"Oh anything" I said. "Can't be fussy these days."

"Well let's talk about it after the service, maybe I can help," he said.

Following the sermon, it was customary for the choir, led by the two senior boys to walk in procession as we sang the last hymn. Slowly down the centre isle, the pace determined by the number of verses in the hymn, round the west end and down the north isle to the vestry door.

That night the "processional" was, "The Day Thou Gavest Lord Is Ended." As Reverend Hadyn Evans intoned the blessing, I thought how appropriate. My day was ending and tomorrow would be the beginning of a totally new way of life.

Thirteen

A Wise Decision

After the service I talked to the choirmaster. He wished me well, thanked me for my years of service and gave me the name of a business friend. I dropped my Cassock, Surplice, Eaton collar and bow tie in the laundry basket, took a last look around and left.

With only ten days to Christmas and thousands seeking work, there was little hope of finding part-time employment but I tried. The choirmaster's referral led to a second then a third which finally proved fruitful.

At the time, there was a lot of moonlighting and a flourishing underground economy, this was my only hope. My contact, Vic, was a young plumber working for a large building contractor. He loved motor bikes and had just bought a brand new Norton 350cc., which had to be paid for. He also had a girl friend with expensive tastes so it was a case of, "When needs must the devil drives." There was nothing available, however, until 6 January. He would pick me up at the College at five and I could expect three to four hours work daily.

So, what would I do for Christmas? Too late for Ongar or Romford, I couldn't afford it anyway. Reg was out of work and spending Christmas with relatives. The only thing to do was visit Mary and persuade her to give our relationship another chance. I went to great pains with my grooming.

At her door her sister said,

"No, Mary's not home, she doesn't want to see you anyway!"

"Oh, does she have another boy friend?" I asked, realizing it was inappropriate.

"Mind your own business" she said, slamming the door in my face.

I walked home feeling sorry for myself.

Life at home worsened in the days that followed. My Aunt was moody, irritable and nagged me constantly about moving out. So intense was the bickering that finally, on the eve of the festival of giving and forgiving I made one last attempt at reconciliation.

Fred was working the late shift and Christmas Day would be a Sunday schedule. It would be midnight before he got home so we'd be spending a lot of time alone in the house. I made the first move.

After Fred left I suggested that since it was Christmas, could we not talk things over? It was childish, I said, to continue the way we were. At first she just listened. I apologized again, insisting my motive had nothing to do with sex, simply a desire to live in harmony until completing my education. I told her I had given up both the choir and football and had found part-time work. I would contribute what money I could toward my keep and accept full responsibility for all costs relating to my education.

Her reaction was not entirely unexpected. I was selfish, she raged. Making use of her for another three years only to leave; it was unacceptable.

"Besides," she said, "what we did was wicked," and after a pause, "every morning I have to look at you and I feel guilty."

Then, out of frustration I made another mistake.

"Well, you saw the mailman every day after that encounter and didn't feel any guilt. You passed the shop on Ladysmith Road almost every day and saw him. And there have been other affairs so why all the guilt with me?"

She flew at me fists clenched, arms flailing trying to beat me. I grabbed her by the wrists and forced her back into the chair. I reminded her I didn't ask to live with them in the first place. Why had she taken me away from those I loved? I asked. I also reminded her it was she who started the whole thing. I concluded by saying that this had gone far enough, if she continued in this way I would tell Fred everything and to hell with the consequences. She was sobbing, more out of anger than anything else I suspect.

"You go right ahead, tell Fred, I'll say you came on to me. It'll be your word against mine. And what's more, if you want to turn that log over don't be surprised at what crawls out."

And with that she ran out of the room.

I didn't appreciate the significance of the last remark until many years later. But I knew she was right about it being her word against mine and that worried me.

From that day on we spoke only when necessary. You could cut the air with a knife, even Fred noticed it.

"What's wrong with you two?" he asked one evening.

Nothing's wrong he was told, and that was that. Or was it?

Years later, I learned she was nagging him instead of me. Day after day she would berate him for, as she put it, not taking a proper roll in my upbringing. Constantly telling him I was more than she could handle, that I was insolent and beyond her control. So I found myself fighting Fred rather than her.

Christmas was behind us, 1936 arrived and tension grew everywhere, including in our house. Fred and I were always at loggerheads. My education was a waste of time he said, and insisted I get a proper job. This, despite the fact I was working every evening I could and weekends and giving most of the money to my Aunt. But it was a losing battle.

I still hadn't seen Mary, but toward the end of January I was given a free ticket to Xavier Cugat and his band playing at the Dome theatre. I'd been so busy I hadn't been to a show for months, so I put on some decent clothes and felt human for a change.

Just got seated in the balcony, lights still up when I sensed someone staring at me from behind. I turned, looked up and there was Mary! My heart leaped and

I was about to go to her when I noticed she was with a man. He appeared much older than she, which bothered me. She strained her neck, moving her head from side to side looking to see if anyone was with me, maybe she still cares? I didn't enjoy the show, just couldn't get her off my mind.

Afterwards, without knowing why, I followed them. Keeping my distance, I trailed them along Lewes Road, past the Level and Brighton Technical College. Over Elm Grove, on and on we went, the clicking of my heels on the sidewalk echoing theirs. As they approached the railway viaduct at the junction of Lewes Road and Upper Lewes Road I came to my senses. Turning onto Upper Lewes Road I made my way home, never to see Mary again. But somehow, the sight of her with that older man made it easier to forget. I felt sure she was no longer a virgin. But then, neither was I!

At end of term exams I barely made a passing grade, having sacrificed my studies to make a few pounds. I'll never forget my counselor's opening remark.

"With marks like this, one thing is certain, you're not cheating."

I didn't appreciate his humour but the upshot was, I would switch to night school and get myself a full time job.

My old bike just gave up so I went in hock for a new one. Come September there would be more debt for textbooks. I decided to take a week off anyway and cycled all the way to Ongar. I'm glad I did because I got to see Paddy for the last time; he died August 27, 1937.

By now everyone in the Bunton family was married except Vic and he was working. So holidays in Ongar were not the same. Jessie came from Coopersale to see me and was appalled to find I had no identification on me. She painstakingly wrote my name and address on a piece of linen with a laundry marker and stitched it under the flap of the saddlebag on my bike.

I left Ongar and went to Epping for a quick visit with the Masons and then on to Romford to see auntie Edie, but I had more than just a visit in mind.

She was alone when I arrived so a cup of tea and a chat was in order. Following the usual exchange, I came straight to the point.

"Auntie," I said, "I've learned something of my real mother and I would very much like to find her. Do you by any chance know her or where she lives?"

I held my breath not knowing what to expect.

"Yes Frank, I do know you're mother and I do know where she lives, but I'm not going to tell you because she doesn't want to be identified as your mother. She doesn't want to be found, Frank."

There's one thing about Auntie Edie, she never minces her words.

I cycled back to Brighton with a heavy heart. How could a mother be so unkind? Doesn't she know how much it hurts not to know her or what she looks like? How much I want her, though I've never seen her? How much I yearn to put my arms around her and give her a big hug just like I did with mum Bunton. Perhaps I could help her in some way I thought. I'd give anything in this world to find her. Such were my thoughts as my feet mechanically pedaled up and down, up and down for the eighty miles back to reality.

It was a long, tedious journey through Seven Kings, Ilford and Forest Gate. I had left later than planned and by the time I reached London it was dark. Through the East End I pedaled, over Blackfriars Bridge and south alongside Streatham Common, then it started to rain. I felt miserable, all I could think of was a mother that I knew existed but nothing more. And nobody would tell me a thing, no one! How cruel it all seemed. For the umpteenth time I asked myself, why me, why couldn't I be like other people with a nice mum and dad and a happy home?

On through Croydon, Redhill and eventually to the outskirts of Brighton where it stopped raining. I saw the first signs of dawn, a glow over the South Downs to my left as I struggled those last few miles past Preston Park and home.

I got the full-time job with Vic the plumber, working for the same employer. It was a good company and while there I subscribed to five, one-pound common shares. It felt good being a shareholder. But my earnings were little better than part-time because I was paid by the hour. In the underground economy I shared in the total profit of a given project. It was the same with moonlighting and I was compelled to engage in both, although my commitment to school three nights a week had limited what I could handle.

Christmas 1936 came and went. In the January my friend Reg joined the army. He was, he said, "Fed up with being unemployed and the daily search for meaningful employment."

He was sent to Chichester, the same place Fred had enlisted twenty-two years previously. Four months later he came home on leave having completed initial training. The first evening our conversation was about life in the Army. He thoroughly enjoyed it, he said, and described, among other things how one could continue one's education. He had been attending school throughout his military training.

There were four levels of education, he explained. A third and second class certificate was mandatory. First and Special class, voluntary. They had credited him with Third Class by virtue of his civilian education, he had already passed the Second and intended to continue. And he thoroughly recommended the life.

"Why don't you join up Frank? Think of all the fun we could have."

I said I would think about it, but it didn't really appeal to me.

During his leave we spent much time together and I was impressed by how, dressed in his "Blues," he so easily attracted the girls. He wore this non-issue, expensive outfit rather than civilian clothes. It was navy blue with red hatband, red-striped pants, highly polished buttons and cap badge and he carried a cane with a silver knob on the end. I told him of the first beatings I'd had with a similar cane, he was horrified.

One would think, having experienced the joys of sex, I would be chasing all the girls. Strangely, I had no desire to get involved. Was it guilt or a reaction to that final encounter with my Aunt? To this day I've never fully understood.

While out with Reg one evening we met two girls and struck up a friendship. Daphne, my girl was strikingly pretty but I was ambivalent. We went to a show together and she was good fun. After about a week, during which I had made no advances, she asked me what was wrong. Why had I not "Done anything?"

I told her there was a time and place for everything, and at the moment I was interested in nothing more than her company. We were walking toward her home, she stopped in her tracks.

"You really don't have to see me home you know, I'm perfectly capable of making it on my own."

I said it had been nice knowing her, turned on my heel and left. It would be more than two years before I felt completely at ease in female company.

Tuesday June 1, 1937, I was working in Sussex Square on a renovation job. The previous night I had handed in my last assignment at the College so no more school till September. I wouldn't get my marks until the end of July but I knew I had done a lot better. Two down, two to go, years that is; I wondered if I would ever complete the four-year course.

Vic, the plumber offered me a moonlighting job in Peacehaven several miles further up the Channel coast. It was famous for it's orphanage founded by Gracie Fields the illustrious singer. Tuesdays and Thursdays were my only free nights and the house rule was that on those nights, I had to be home by ten o'clock. When I left home I had no idea I would be offered work in the evening and there was no way of informing anyone. Besides, I didn't see the need.

Normally we would have gone on Vic's motor bike but he had something to do in town. He told me the address, what he wanted me to do and I cycled the few miles to the job. He arrived about seven-thirty and we worked until just after nine-thirty.

I'd been riding deep in thought for about ten minutes when there was that sickening hissing sound . . . A flat tire. The bike was little more than nine months old, just my luck, but there was worse to come. When I checked the tube of glue required to stick a patch on the inner tube, it was solid. It was three years old and had never been used. No good moaning I thought, perhaps I'll get a lift. But I didn't and walked all the way home.

It was past midnight as I turned off Ditchling Road and there, waiting on the corner was Fred.

"Where the hell you been boy, it's gone midnight?" he fumed.

"Look," I said, I've just walked all the way from Peacehaven with a flat tire so let's not make a scene, I've had enough for one day."

I was getting annoyed.

He simmered down somewhat and sympathized because, he said, the same thing had happened to him as a youth. Then he continued.

"You're Auntie is flaming mad, she's been on at me all night, you've been staying out late a lot lately."

I said that wasn't true, I had only been to night school and except for the previous night, always came straight home.

"Last night was the last night at school, I spent an hour with Dave and some of the others but I was home by ten-thirty. She's exaggerating and besides, she's not happy unless she's nagging somebody."

He opened the front door and I wheeled my bike down the darkened hall to the kitchen where I stored it overnight. As I returned a fist hit me hard on the side of my face, my head hit the banister and I saw stars. It took me a moment to realize Fred had hit me, the first time since I was a child. I didn't think he had the guts.

Then he went into the dining room where the table was neatly laid as usual for breakfast. I followed, grabbed the edge of the table and with one swoop tipped it on its side. There was a terrible clatter as crockery, cutlery and everything else went crashing to the floor.

"All right Fred, you wanna fight, now we've got lots of room. Come on you bastard, I'm gonna give you the biggest fucking hiding you've ever had. You thrashed me once for something I didn't do and I've never forgotten that. Now it's my turn."

I caught a glimpse of my Aunt going to the front door, learning later it was to call the police. They never came, but I wouldn't have cared if they had, I was in an ugly mood. I looked back at Fred just in time to see him pick up the bread knife with its serrated edge as if to attack me. I sneered at him, calling him a coward and challenged him to go ahead and try it. I taunted him saying he didn't have the guts, that he was a henpecked wimp. Then I went to bed.

I listened as they picked up the pieces. As she took broken crockery to the garbage, I heard my Aunt say,

"The table's broken."

I didn't believe it, but in the morning I looked and sure enough the edge of the table was split from end to end but I was past caring; I knew exactly what I was going to do. Look out Reg, here I come!

The minimum age to join the Army as an adult was eighteen but a new category of service had been introduced known as the Supplementary Reserve. Under this system there were two options. One could join at seventeen-and-a-half, complete six months training then leave, reporting back once a year for further training. Or one could sign on for a period of Regular Service.

The next morning Fred came into my bedroom and told me to get up and go to work or get out. I told him to get lost, I had more important things to do and not to worry, I would be gone by sundown.

"Oh . . . That's all right then," he said, and left.

I was at the Army Recruiting Office when it opened and told the Sergeant I wanted to join this new Supplementary Reserve.

"Are you in any kind of trouble?" he asked.

When I explained my situation he produced the necessary papers. I asked if he needed a birth certificate as I didn't think I had one, he said it didn't matter.

"You'll have to swear the information is true and your guardian will have to co-sign the application."

I was to return the following morning with the form duly signed, then proceed to the Royal Artillery Barracks on Lewes Road for a medical examination.

Fred would have nothing to do with the form but Auntie signed it without hesitation. Her eagerness to get rid of me was offensive, but who cares? The feeling was reciprocal. The next morning, Thursday, June 3, 1937, I produced the signed form, passed the medical and took the oath.

Then came the first disappointment. I was handed a railway travel warrant to Bury St. Edmunds in the County of Suffolk, I'd never heard of it. I asked why I couldn't join my friend in The Royal Sussex Regiment in Chichester and was told it was a matter of quotas.

I spent much of the day trying to sell five pounds worth of textbooks. Finally, in desperation, I sold them to a secondhand bookstore for five shillings, one per cent of their true value. How on earth, I wondered, would I ever pay off that debt? Ah! well, I'd worry about that later.

I also sold a few tools I had acquired while working. Another plumber gave me two pounds for them, exactly the amount owing on my bike. I rode to the store where I bought the bike, asked for a discount for paying out the debt and was flatly refused. I told the proprietor, had I foreseen his attitude I would have left without paying.

Next morning I left home for the last time without even a goodbye. My Aunt was irritable from the moment she got up and again, she couldn't hide her eagerness to see me gone. She was upstairs when I left so I slammed the front door as hard as I could, just to let her know I didn't give a damn!

It was a glorious day so I walked the mile or so to Brighton Station. At the bottom of Ditchling Road, I glanced across the small park known as the Level. Brighton Technical College stood on the far side. The image of a domineering Aunt flashed before my eyes and I thought of the bitter struggle that I'd had trying to further my education. I recalled a line from Shakespeare, "I have too long borne your blunt upbraiding and your bitter scoffs." I first learned it in high school but more recently heard it during a rendition of Richard the Third by the College drama students.

The next twelve weeks were spent in Bury St. Edmunds completing my initial training. In September I was granted leave before being posted to Plymouth in Devonshire for a further ten weeks of more advanced training.

I spent the first few days visiting Ongar and learned of Paddy's death. I hadn't told the Buntons that I'd joined the Army so had only myself to blame. The visit was one of contrasts. On the one hand the family were still grieving at the loss of Paddy, on the other, celebrating the birth of Minnie's first and only child, Brian. Her first outing following his birth was to attend the funeral. Mum and I visited them at the Red Cow and I got to hold the baby. I recall how nervous I was because he was so tiny.

The entire family was shocked that I had joined the Army. Jessie was beside herself and immediately talked of buying me out. But, "It was something I wanted to do," I lied. "And anyway, there's going to be a war sooner or later." It was then that Jessie suggested I make a small weekly allowance to her and she would start a savings account for me, I agreed.

Like my friend Reg, I went to school for precisely two hours and ten minutes each day but it was disappointing. It didn't live up to his glowing report, being designed mainly for young boys joining the army at fourteen.

A First Class Certificate was the equivalent of senior matriculation, something I had already accomplished. I was credited with the Third Class, passed the Second Class in six weeks and looked forward with confidence to the First Class. This was mandatory for promotion above the rank of Sergeant. Classes for this level, however, were only held during the winter months and the curriculum was spread over two years. I had no difficulty with the first half but, following the Munich crisis in September, 1938, all schooling was abandoned. There were more important things to do.

I decided to remain in the forces following completion of my Reserve Service. I enjoyed the life and excelled at my favourite sport, soccer. I was soon playing for my unit and later Southern Command. But, two things influenced my decision more than the life-style. First, the situation in Europe. Hitler had reached the pinnacle of his fanatical career and the consensus among the military was that war with Germany was inevitable. Munich simply bought us another year. And, contrary to popular belief, we put that period to good use, believe me.

But the more compelling reason; having completed endless questionnaires, a number of grueling tests and lengthy interviews, I was posted to the Intelligence Section. The excellent training served me well, long after my military career ended.

It was an interesting, exciting and challenging branch of the Army. We trained with both the Royal Navy and the Royal Air Force. Many hours were spent flying in old-fashioned aircraft studying defense systems from the air. And I took basic parachute training long before Airborne Forces were ever thought of. But more important, it spared me the hardships of the ordinary footslogging soldier. The training intensified and continued daily for the eighteen months prior to the outbreak of World War Two.

I consigned five shillings a week, almost a third of my pay to, Jessie and she deposited it in a Post Office savings account. Unfortunately, after a couple of years it caused an unpleasant disagreement.

I was bored with army uniform and decided to buy some civilian clothes. I wrote to Jessie asking her to send my bankbook so that I could withdraw the necessary funds. She declined, insisting that I not touch my savings. Angry, I wrote a nasty letter demanding she comply at once and to my everlasting regret, canceled the arrangement.

For the entire month of August 1939, Southern Command conducted the most extensive manoeuvres in military history. It was one of the wettest months in living memory and when it was all over, the troops literally staggered back to barracks in Devonport. Being in the Intelligence Section and by now a Lance Corporal, I rode in military transport.

Normally, we would have donned our civilian "threads" and departed on a well-earned leave, but the clouds of war were directly overhead. The last few days of August and early September were hectic, we were on the move twenty-four hours a day. Thus, when Neville Chamberlain, the Prime Minister, made his famous speech at eleven o'clock on Sunday September 3, 1939, we were already fully mobilized.

The Military had, in its wisdom, decreed that no one under age twenty could be sent to an active combat zone. This was a reaction to the scandal of World War One when boys as young as fourteen were killed in action. The edict was later modified but I was just two months short of my twentieth birthday and fell within its purview.

The following morning we entrained for our various destinations. Most to France, but those like myself not yet of age, were posted to Bury St. Edmunds as Instructors. Thus I missed the horrors of Dunkirk where my regiment was severely mauled.

I shall never forget the tens of thousands lining the streets of Plymouth, cheering wildly as we marched behind the Band and Drums to the Railway Station. What a contrast to the shabby way we were treated prior to this day:

"God and soldier we like adore,
In time of danger not before.
The danger past and all things righted,
God is forgotten, the soldier slighted."
Thomas Jordan. 1612-1686.

We reached Bury St. Edmunds about eight o'clock in the evening there was chaos. Hundreds of Territorials and other Reservists, many of them World War One veterans, had been ordered to report that same day and there were two hundred of us. We had been traveling since early morning with nothing to eat but haversack rations and a mug of tea. We were herded into the gymnasium, handed in our papers and assigned to a newly created company.

The temporary wooden huts that were to be our home for the next few months were still under construction. There were no doors or windows and no furniture. We were issued with palliasses and bolsters, which we filled with straw.

Dog tired and hungry, we were angry at the lack of preparation for our arrival. The NAFFI, (an acronym for Navy, Army and Air Force Institute. The Americans call it their PX.) was closed, we weren't allowed out to buy anything and many of us had no cigarettes. To say that tempers were frayed would be an understatement. But there was a war on, what the hell should we expect?

There was much moaning and groaning before, out of sheer exhaustion we slept only to be rudely awakened, long before dawn by the undulating wail of an air raid siren. It proved to be a false alarm and we all trooped bleary-eyed back to our straw beds. One crude individual mused that perhaps we should,

"Shit on our beds and stomp in it."

When asked why such a disgusting comment he replied,

"Well, we're being treated like horses, we might as well act like them."

Another old sweat dryly commented.

"With a remark like that he should be shot at dawn twice a day for a week."

It was too early in the morning for such frivolous talk.

Over the next three days order was restored and we were given our new assignments. I was posted to R2 Company and my job would be to train a platoon of raw recruits every eight weeks. Because of seniority I was promoted to Corporal which was most welcome. Not only did two stripes look better than one, the money was a lot better. In hindsight, joining the army when I did proved a wise decision.

Instructors were to undergo a two week course to ensure we were all "singing from the same page," but the course was not due to commence until the Monday. In the mean time we were granted forty-eight hours leave.

Glad to get away, I dismissed any thought of going to Brighton. I decided to go to Epping, bid farewell to the Masons' and Jessie in nearby Coopersale. Then go on to Ongar and spend the weekend with mum. Vic was the only one at home now so I knew I'd be welcome. I would visit Auntie Edie and Paula on the way back.

This then, was how my war began but I was in for a surprise. A conflict of a different kind had to be settled first.

Fourteen

Stranger Than Fiction

The train to London included a Restaurant Car so I treated myself to a hearty brunch, rationing hadn't yet been introduced. As the old-fashioned steam locomotive clattered through the English countryside, I reminded myself that Uncle George and Annie, his second wife and the former dressmaker, no longer lived on St. John's Road in Epping.

She had never felt comfortable in old Lizzie Mason's bedchamber, so in 1935 they built a bungalow on that large triangular lot at the corner of Station Road and Kendal Avenue. It was but a two-minute walk from the station and the sheds where Uncle George worked. I had visited them briefly at their new home in the summer of 1936 and hadn't seen them since.

Ironically, it was in a field close by that my Aunt had her affair with the soldier back in 1915. That brought to mind the night we lay naked together when she told me all about it. I felt sure Annie and George must sometimes walk past that very same spot and in my innocence, wondered what they would think if they knew what I knew.

It was two years and three months since I left home; I had never returned and had received only one communication back in 1937. A curt letter telling me they were being hounded by a collection agency for the five pounds I owed for textbooks. I wrote to my old employer, redeemed the five common shares and paid off the debt. So much for my dealings in high finance. I had also received a re-addressed envelope from Brighton Technical College containing my marks for the last semester but by then they were of no consequence.

I arrived on the Mason's doorstep a little after one in the afternoon. Annie was surprised but pleased to see me and remarked how tall I'd grown and how smart I looked in uniform.

"And now Frank, you're off to war" she said, as we made ourselves comfortable in the living room. "Oh God, I fear for you my dear boy. It reminds me so much of the last war."

I told her not to worry, that I had been posted to Bury St. Edmunds as an Instructor at least for the time being, she seemed genuinely relieved.

"Can I get you something to eat?" she asked. I told her I'd eaten on the train. "How about a nice cup of tea?" I agreed.

In no time she returned from the kitchen and she poured.

"It's hard to believe you're almost twenty. God knows what the future holds."

She paused as if struggling for words.

"Has Nance ever told you anything about your family?" she finally asked.

"Not much" I said, surprised at the question. "Whenever I've asked, I've been brushed off. Mrs. Bunton told me a long time ago that she took me from a lady in Biggleswade who got me from a hospital. Jessie told me that my real mother couldn't look after me."

"Really?"

"Yes, and on my sixteenth birthday Auntie Nance told me she knew my mother, that her name was Annie Keeling and she had got herself into trouble. But she said I should bear in mind it happened such a long time ago, she probably didn't want to be known as my mother." Annie's eyebrows arched.

"She really said that eh?"

"Yes she did."

"Well, well, well."

"Then I talked to auntie Edie once," I continued. "I asked her to help me find my mother. She said she knew her and where she lived but she wouldn't tell me because my mother didn't want to be identified."

"Well I never," Annie said.

There was an awkward silence.

"I think its time you learned the truth."

And so began the most incredible story.

"You know I used to be Lizzie Mason's dressmaker, Nance lived with the Masons you knew that too didn't you."

I nodded and she continued, "I was more than her dressmaker, I was a friend. She had no one else to confide in poor woman and she told me everything that went on. She told me things she wouldn't even tell her husband."

Pouring a second cup of tea she continued.

"I mention that Frank, because I want you to know that what I am about to tell you is the truth, exactly as Lizzie told me God rest her soul. And most of it at the time it happened."

For half an hour she talked uninterrupted then the doorbell rang.

"Drat" she said. "I'll go and see who that is, won't be a minute."

So, Annie had described my Aunt's childhood and her being raised by the Mason's. That Lizzie Mason, the former Emma Draper, was her mother's sister. How her mother's problems had led to her untimely death and that her name was Louisa. I didn't know my Aunt was related to the Masons, I thought they were foster parents. Strange, nobody ever mentioned it.

Annie also spoke of my Aunt's employment in domestic service and the affair with a Sergeant. I knew about that, of course. But Auntie Nance hadn't told me about going to Romford and having a stillborn baby or that her lover was married and had two children. Boy! The skeletons are really coming out of the closet now.

Annie came back into the room.

"My neighbour," she said, "anyway, where was I? Oh yes, after Uncle

George told Nance about the death of the soldier and that he had a wife and children, she was beside herself, just couldn't believe it. For a long time she was quiet and moody, hardly went anywhere."

"Must have thought a lot of that Sergeant" I said.

"Yes, you're right there," Annie replied. "Of course, we have to remember he was her first love and I think there is always something special about that. There's an old saying, `There's no love like the first love', more tea?"

"No thanks." I said, dubious about the quotation.

"Well anyway" Annie continued. "She flung herself into her new job and did little else. No social life at all, at least that's what we were told. But you know Frank, Nance was such a liar you could never be sure whether she was telling the truth. Drove poor Lizzie out of her mind at times. She would say to me, `That girl Nance, she'll lie just for the sake of lying."

Yeah! I know all about that, I thought.

"Anyway, the war ended in November 1918 and just after Christmas, Nance met a young man who worked at Cottis' Iron Works. He and his younger brother had been working there during the war. They were in lodgings here in Epping but their home was in Ongar."

"She introduced him to Lizzie and Uncle George. Lizzie wasn't all that impressed. He was only eighteen, four years younger than Nance. Mind you, George was three years younger than Lizzie, but then he was in his mid twenties when they met. Anyway, George thought he was a nice young fellow, handsome too. `Handsome is as handsome does', Lizzie always said."

"Why would she get involved with someone that young?" I asked.

"Well the last war played havoc with her generation, it robbed most places of its young men. Then in the winter of 1918 we had a terrible flu epidemic and a lot more died."

"Yeah!, I remember reading about that."

"By the way Frank, Lizzie had a diary, it was a gift from her mother." She paused, "it was a beautiful little thing. When Lizzie died, Nance begged Uncle George to let her have it, reluctantly he gave in. Have you ever seen it?"

"No I haven't" I said.

"Well I'm sure it would prove much of what I'm telling you because Lizzie kept it religiously, I wonder what happened to it?"

She seemed lost in thought momentarily then continued.

"Anyway, early in February, 1919 there was a big party at the house where Nance worked and all the staff had to be there. The drinks flowed and the occasional glass came back to the kitchen with drink left in it, which she drank. By the time it was all over she was feeling a bit tipsy."

Annie took a deep breath, obviously this wasn't easy.

"Nance claims that after the party her employer stopped her on the way to her room. He grabbed her saying how attractive she was and suggested they go to bed. He'd been drinking, she said, but wasn't drunk. They went to bed and had sex. Now we know this is true because later he admitted to it.

A couple of months later, according to Nance, she and her boy friend from Ongar had sex. It was his first encounter and he made some comment about how experienced she was. Foolishly, she told him she had learned from an affair with her employer. He asked how long ago and she told him."

"Why on earth would she say that?" I said. "Why not tell him the truth about the soldier back in 1915?"

"Well this was four years later, I suppose she didn't want to admit being sexually active that long. It was frowned upon in those days. Anyway, it wasn't long before she found herself pregnant again and could no longer hide it."

"Her heir was apparent" I chimed.

Annie didn't appreciate the joke.

"Nance handed in her notice and told her employer's wife about her condition. She was livid and told Nance to pack her things and leave immediately. But it wasn't quite that simple. She went upstairs and told her husband. He, to his credit, admitted having sex with Nance, which raised the possibility that he might be responsible.

The three of them got together and Nance quoted dates she had seen her periods after the affair. They were relieved, of course, but for some reason the wife wasn't entirely convinced although at the time she said nothing,"

There was another pause.

"I think she was afraid of a scandal. Anyway, her attitude toward Nance changed. She told her she could stay another two weeks then gave her a generous severance. Nance assured them she would tell no one about the sexual encounter despite having already told the lad from Ongar.

The next day she told him about her pregnancy and the dates of her periods, leaving no doubt as to the father. He didn't seem overly concerned, much to Nance's relief. In fact, he didn't believe her.

On the Saturday they went to Woodford and tried every Chemist shop in town looking for something to terminate the pregnancy. One chemist sold them some little pink pills but they didn't work and Nance panicked."

It was now two-thirty, Annie had been talking non-stop for over an hour and there was obviously much more to come. She saw me look at the clock and sensed my impatience.

"You're going to wait and say good-bye to Uncle George aren't you?"

I hadn't the heart to refuse.

"Yes of course. I was going to see Jessie too but I'll do that on my way back. Mustn't stay too long though, I have to get to Ongar."

She looked even more uncomfortable as she continued.

"I must tell you Frank, this isn't easy for me."

She stared at the empty fireplace, a far away look on her face and there was silence for what seemed an eternity.

"I wasn't directly involved at first, I was just someone in whom poor Lizzie could confide. But when I married your Uncle George I became part of it all."

"As I was saying, Nance panicked. She went to Ongar to talk to his mother.

When she arrived there was no one home. The next door neighbour saw her and told her that Mrs. Bunton wouldn't be home for a while, would she care to join her for a cup of tea while she waited?"

This brought me up with a jolt, it was the first time the Bunton name had surfaced and I made the connection.

"You're talking about old Miss Dennis." I said.

I saw Annie's chin quiver, then gently she said,

"Yes Frank, I am. And the child Nance was carrying was you."

There are no words to describe my feelings as the full impact of her words registered in my brain. Frank Bunton my father? That was difficult enough. But then the realization that what Annie was saying meant I had been to bed with my own mother!

I felt myself drifting into a dreamlike state, everything around me became vague and unreal. Annie's voice trailed off in the distance and I was seized with a sense of panic, surely she must be mistaken. I went to speak but my throat was so tight I had to force the words out.

"No," I said, in a hoarse and unfamiliar voice, "that can't be true. On my sixteenth birthday we ugh! . . . " I stopped myself just in time. "I mean . . . uhm! She told me . . . ugh! She knew my mother and her name was . . . ugh!" I was repeating myself, caught in a web of deceit, shock and confusion.

Annie seemed startled that I was so profoundly disturbed by what she had revealed. She could never know, of course, the full import of her words.

She was speaking softly now, and with my head pounding I could barely hear her.

"Frank," she said, her voice showing genuine concern, "don't you see, Nance was talking about herself, she was a Keeling. Her real name was ANNIE ELIZABETH KEELING. But just bare with me, I can explain it all."

Explain? How the hell could anyone explain it. If this were true, I'd had sex with my own mother that was incest . . . a criminal offense!

Another thing, if she'd had her way it would have continued. My own mother! No, surely not, Annie must be mistaken. I excused myself and fled to the bathroom.

My heart was pounding and my breathing heavy as I sat on the toilet seat trying to absorb the ramifications of what I had learned. Images of this woman's naked body flashed before my eyes, how in God's name would I deal with all this? My mind turned to Mrs. Bunton, the good, wholesome and caring person whom, as a child, made me feel secure and loved. And now this other woman who Annie insists is my mother! I'd seen her naked, I had been to bed with her and done things that now seemed revolting.

All my life I had waited for the moment when I would know my real mother; that moment was now and I was filled with horror and shame. From somewhere in the depths of my mind I remembered, as an inquisitive youth, reading the bible; the book of Leviticus, about the dire consequences for he that would lie with his own mother.

A play written by Sophocles in the fifth century BC came to mind. About the mythical King Oedipus who was abandoned at birth by his Royal parents because the Courtiers insisted there was a curse upon him. Then as a grown man, and through a series of bizarre circumstances, he returned to Thebes where he was born and unknowingly married his widowed mother and they had children.

But I had long since abandoned traditional religion and was equally cynical of myths, Greek or otherwise. And so I quickly dismissed it all from my mind.

Gotta pull yourself together, I muttered. For two years I'd been trained to deal with all manner of crises and here I was panicking. I must go back into that room and control myself. Annie had always disliked Nance and was well aware of the hostility I felt toward her, to show undue concern might arouse suspicion. There's my guilty conscience at work already, I thought.

I wasn't sure whether I wanted to hear anymore of Annie's story, yet there were so many unanswered questions. Not the least of which was, how could I have lived under the same roof for twelve years and never learn that my Aunt's maiden name was Keeling, the same as mine? Why was I deceived about my own mother for so long?

And how was it possible that a mother could lure a son into her bed, teach him and encourage him to indulge in the most intimate sexual acts? This was the most disturbing thing. Again the dreadful word incest came to mind.

I flushed the toilet and dashed cold water over my face; Annie always had nice soft towels. What a stupid thing to think about at a time like this.

"Would you like some more tea?" Annie asked when I was again seated on the couch.

"No thanks." And more in jest than anything, "I could use something stronger than tea. You'll never know what a shock this has been."

I was surprised at her reply.

"Well, we have a bottle of George's home made dandelion wine from last year, perhaps you'd like a glass of that?"

She quickly removed a bottle from the hall closet and suggested I draw the cork. I did so and poured.

"My goodness!" she stalled, "I can't remember the last time I drank wine in the afternoon. Ah well, we shall drink to your good health," Then, rather sheepishly, "Besides, we deserve this don't we."

I wasn't in the mood but went along, realizing how hard it must be for her and that she was doing it for my benefit. But for her, how long would I have been kept in ignorance?

"Here's to your very good health Frank, and may God be with you in these troubled times."

I took a mouthful of wine and felt the glow all the way down to my toes. I'd had nothing to eat since eleven thirty; not good to drink on an empty stomach but it sure made me feel better. I watched as Annie sipped and almost at once her normally pale face became flushed.

"Now Frank, bare with me" she said, her tongue gently sweeping her upper lip. "I want to tell you everything. God knows you deserve it. But I must tell it in my own way, it's the only way I can do it."

I was feeling relaxed and a little light-headed now, obviously the wine was having its effect.

"OK Auntie fire away, I'm all ears" I said.

And for some crazy reason I wanted to laugh, mustn't do that, she'll think I'm off my rocker, gotta control myself.

"Now, where was I, oh! yes. Nance went indoors with Miss Dennis, she was a dear old soul as you know, very good to Nance all through her ordeal. In fact Frank, you were named after her, Dennis with two ens, just the way hers was spelt. There's more to your name too, but I'll come back to that."

I wondered what on earth she meant by that.

"Nance learned that Miss Dennis was a close friend of the family, and desperate to share her problem with someone, told her the whole story. Miss Dennis told her not to worry, she was sure Frank Bunton would do the right thing.

When Mrs. Bunton came home, Miss Dennis ran next door. They both returned and Nance repeated her story, spelling out the dates of her last periods and where and when it happened. Mrs.Bunton's reaction was that it was all a bit of a shock and she would have to talk to Frank about it. She asked Nance her age and was told twenty-two. Mrs. Bunton expressed surprise, saying she was old enough to know better, then left. Miss Dennis insisted Nance keep in touch, saying she had no family and would like to help her. Nance was glad of her friendship under the circumstances."

My mind flashed back to the days when I used to visit old Miss Dennis; never a hint of what she knew. Now I know why she was always so nice to me.

"Sunday afternoon came, not a word from Ongar," Annie continued. "Nance, getting more agitated, took the bus, arriving just as Mrs. Bunton was leaving with her youngest."

Vic, I thought, shifting myself on the couch.

"Have some more wine" Annie said.

I poured myself another glass, she declined. She could sense my restlessness and hastily added,

"The upshot of it all was, Frank Bunton refused to accept any responsibility whatsoever and again Nance had to turn to her father."

"That would be Granddad Keeling in Romford, would it?" I asked.

"Yes, did you ever meet him?"

I told her of the visit when I was nine, saying neither indicated in any way that they were father and daughter.

"In retrospect," I said, "It seems like a conspiracy."

"Well Frank, you were the victim of a conspiracy in a way, but I doubt if Granddad Keeling was involved. He was very good about it all. She settled in with him again awaiting your arrival. Of course, she had a little money this time so it wasn't so bad. Also, Miss Dennis often took the bus to Romford and always brought a small gift."

That was surprising, but something else came to mind.

"What about grandma Louisa, where was she in all this?"

"Heaven only knows Frank, nobody seems to know much about her or what went on after the children left. I gather she was missing for long periods of time and drinking heavily by then. I know she was at home when she died in 1922, poor soul. She was only forty-six.

"Anyway, getting back to Nance, her story was that about five o'clock on November 5, Guy Fawkes day, some children put a firecracker through the letterbox. The explosion scared her and she fell then went into labour. Later, when complications arose she was taken to Romford Cottage Hospital where you were delivered by Cesarean just before midnight."

Ah! The scar on her abdomen. Visions of her lying naked on that bed flashed before my eyes again. Jeeze! This is terrible, will I ever get this out of my mind?

"You were born on a Wednesday, Annie continued. Miss Dennis went to Romford on the Saturday, and learning Nance was in the hospital, made her way there. Nance was terribly depressed and spoke of you being adopted. Miss Dennis tried to dissuade her, still convinced Frank was the father.

Returning to Ongar, Miss Dennis told Mrs. Bunton you were likely to be put in a foster home prior to adoption. Mrs. Bunton was very concerned and again talked to Frank, but he was unrelenting. This wasn't his child he insisted and, furthermore, he didn't believe the birth was premature. It coincided exactly with the admitted affair with her employer. Nothing it seemed would convince him otherwise. But for some reason Mrs. Bunton was convinced you were, indeed, her grandson and spoke of taking you in as a foster child. On her next visit Miss Dennis told Nance.

Also, it was popular in those days for the first born son to be given the father's name. The Senior Bunton's name was Frank Thomas and his eldest son was Frank John."

I realized immediately how I got my names but wondered where the Jack came in. Later, I remembered mum telling me that Paddy first called me Jack, synonymous with John (John F. Kennedy, for example). Frank's middle name was John, he was alleged to be my father, it all made sense now.

"She persuaded Nance to name you Frank and suggested the addition of Bunton. That way, if Frank changed his mind and they married, the Keeling could be dropped and you would be known as Frank Bunton. Nance agreed but also insisted on Dennis, in appreciation of all Miss Dennis had done for her. And so Frank, that's how you got your names."

So that's what she meant earlier when she said there was more to my name. And I could see now why I had always been denied access to my Birth Certificate. Had I known of the Bunton name I would have asked questions. It struck me too that none of my records, including those of the army, contained my full name. What a can of worms!

"I'm almost twenty," I said angrily, "and only now learning my full name and who my mother is. Why have I been deceived for so long? How could you people be so cruel to an innocent little child? Can you explain that? Are there any more secrets?"

The effects of the wine were wearing off and she could see I was hurt and angry. The full impact of what had happened was overwhelming. Sex with my own mother! Oedipus tore his eyes out on learning the truth and became a wanderer, what the hell would I do? Incest, incest, incest; the word hammered on my brain tormenting me.

"I don't wanna hear any more" I shouted, covering my face with my hands.

For a moment Annie didn't quite know what to do. Then she came to me, put her arm around my shoulder and begged me not to be so upset.

"I only did this because I thought you deserve to know the truth," she said, "but I'm beginning to wish I'd never started it. Frank my dear boy, have courage and listen to me. You must know the whole truth now or it will torment you for the rest of your days and God knows you've suffered enough."

I pulled myself together.

"Toward the end of December you were discharged from the hospital in the care of a temporary foster mother, I don't remember her name. The staff told Miss Dennis you were a happy, healthy and contented baby. I think you got preferential treatment because Nance showed not the slightest interest in you."

Annie shifted in her seat.

"Of course we have to remember she had become an unwed mother for the second time. In those days once was bad enough . . . but twice!"

She shook her head, made a sucking sound between clenched teeth and tutt-tutted as if the very thought of it pained her.

"Anyway," she went on, "the foster mother took you to Biggleswade, sixty miles away. I presume the Buntons' hadn't made a commitment. Nance registered your birth at the Romford Office and according to Lizzie Mason that was a problem."

I looked up, "What now."

"Nothing much," Annie said. "Just that when they asked for place of birth, instead of saying Romford Cottage Hospital, she said 47 Shaftsbury Road which, of course, was Granddad Keeling's address where she was staying. Have you ever seen your birth certificate Frank?"

"No, of course not, if I had, I would have known about my name and would have questioned it."

"Ah yes, of course."

"I've often looked for it, could never find any documents anywhere. I remember she had a big envelope when I was first registered at St. Luke's school in Brighton, I suppose that was it, but never saw it again. I remember too, there was quite a fuss when she didn't have it when I went to St. John's school here in Epping when Auntie Mason was ill.

And I was asked for it when I registered for employment in Brighton when I was sixteen. I just said I hadn't got one. They said I would have to get one but

I never did."

I thought for a moment then continued.

"When I joined the Army in 1937 I was only joining the Reserve so they didn't seem to bother too much. And anyway, I had to swear the information was true. Also, Auntie, I mean my mo . . ." I could not bring myself to say the word, "anyway, she had to sign the form." I was rambling on, wasting time and Annie sensed my agitation.

"Won't be long now Frank, there's not much more to tell. You were in the foster home about five months then Mrs. Bunton went and fetched you. Nance, knowing you were in good hands made a remarkable recovery. Her old employer gave her a reference and in January 1920 she got a job with a family in Brighton."

"You sure you can't remember the name of that foster mother?" I insisted.

"No I can't Frank, I have no idea. That's always been a bit of a mystery to me. I'm not even sure it was Biggleswade but I think it was. Anyway, much of Nance's work involved helping the governess raise two small children and apparently she enjoyed it. She stayed with those people until shortly before she married Fred. She was fascinated with the way those children were brought up. Of course, the people were rich and the children had the best of everything.

Oh, by the way, before I forget Frank, do you remember the first holiday you spent with us after I married your Uncle George?"

"Yes I do, I quite enjoyed it."

Her reply surprised me, she sounded quite nostalgic.

"I enjoyed it too, it was the first time I'd ever played host to a young boy and I was a little nervous. But you were such fun, you made me feel young again and you were so well mannered and everything. . . Aah!" she sighed. "They were good times Frank," and with a sort of far away look she said, "You know, for all her faults Nance really did bring you up well, she taught you a lot."

I wondered what she would say if she knew all that Nance had taught me.

"I know it was hard for you, but you're a better person than you would otherwise have been. I always wished you could have spent more time with us."

"Well auntie, you really do surprise me."

Returning to her original train of thought she said,

"On that same holiday, do you remember Uncle George taking you to a big house on Station Road, you had tea there, remember?"

"Yes I do, very well. I recall the lady staring at me all the time."

"Well that was the wife of Nance's old employer. Her and her husband still live in that house, just around the corner, you remember the house don't you?"

"Yes I do," I said.

"They're both in their seventies now and retired, he was in the Banking business here in Epping."

"I remember her well" I said, "but I didn't see anything of him."

"No, well . . . . . Anyway, remember I told you she didn't seem completely convinced of what Nance had told her the day she gave her notice; about her pregnancy?"

"Yes."

"Well, she insisted Uncle George take you to see her, she was curious to see whether you resembled their family in any way. After the visit she told Uncle she was quite satisfied you didn't but she remarked what a charming young man you were. `Nance should be really proud of him' she said.

Anyhow, in 1922, Nance's employers went abroad and she moved into a boarding house on Campbell Road, in Brighton. Shortly afterwards she met Fred, a Tram Conductor on the Dyke Road route. She had a friend living on Montpelia Crescent and often traveled on his tram.

Because of his irregular hours, Fred had problems with meals, so Nance got him a room in the boarding House. They courted for over two years, never had sex, of course; Fred was taught `nice' people just didn't do such things.

Nance was introduced to his family as Annie Keeling, her second name was Elizabeth they were told. But she had always been known as `Nance' which she preferred. Apparently she measured up to old Grandma Ince's standards and the wedding was arranged for the first week in February, that would be 1925.

Fred took a week's holiday, and following the wedding they were to return to Epping with Uncle George. After a brief honeymoon they would move into the two rooms on Queen's Park Drive in Brighton where you joined them. Problem was Nance had never mentioned anything about her being the mother of a five year old."

"That was stupid," I said.

"The wedding was to be held at St. Saviour's Church where you sang in the choir and Uncle George was to give her away. On the morning of the wedding he paid Nance a visit and asked if she had told Fred about you. She said, no she hadn't and had no intention of doing so, Uncle George was furious and said, `You will either tell him or there will be no wedding.'

Nance was beside herself, she warned Uncle that to tell Fred would probably mean no wedding and that it would be cruel to tell him at such a late hour. `We're getting married in four hours,' she said, `what's the point of bringing it up now?' Uncle George was adamant. He said `If you don't tell Fred, I will not give you away. But, I will stand at the back of the church and when the Vicar asks if anyone knows any just cause or impediment why these two people should not be joined together in Holy Matrimony, I shall speak out."

Annie did her best to imitate his stern voice, and I could well imagine him doing that too.

"Nance broke down and pleaded with Uncle but to no avail. He told her he had recently seen Mrs. Bunton and how difficult things were for her. Most of the older children had been unemployed for months. Mr. Bunton had little work, wasn't in the best of health and there were five young mouths to feed including Frank."

"Yeah, I remember the boys being out of work for a long time now I come to think of it."

"He told her she must face up to her responsibilities, that she should have told Fred before because sooner or later he was bound to find out. Uncle said he simply could not live with such deception neither would Auntie Mason.

Uncle George went upstairs and told Fred there was something important to discuss. Fred was reluctant because in those days it was considered bad luck for the groom to see the bride before the ceremony. But when Uncle George said if he didn't come down there might not be a ceremony, Fred complied. The three of them sat in that room and Nance had to tell Fred about you. Nothing was ever said about the previous pregnancy.

To say Fred was shocked would be an understatement. According to Uncle George he turned deathly pale, clutched the arm of the chair and looked as if he were about to pass out. His response was that he needed time to think about it. He was terribly worried, he said, about how his family would react, particularly his mother. She was in poor health and he was afraid the news might be too much for her.

With that he left and walked for two hours. He returned just before one o'clock and the three of them got together again. Fred said he had thought things over and was prepared to go through with the wedding and, furthermore, he would be willing to accept the child. He said he was very fond of Nance and didn't want to see things end this way but there was one condition.

Under no circumstances was his family, especially his mother, to be told that Nance had a child. Somehow they would have to come up with a suitable story. He said his family would disown him if they learned the truth. That his mother was deeply religious and despised anyone who had sex before marriage. So if everyone accepted that, the wedding could go ahead."

What a way to start a marriage, I thought. It was doomed from the start.

"Uncle George said he admired Fred's courage but was loath to be a part of any deception. The wedding went ahead, but according to Nance the wedding night was a disaster. Fred wasn't in the mood and she lied to him about the scar on her stomach, saying it was a gall bladder operation."

"Yeah! She told me the same thing," I said without thinking. And I felt myself go all hot but Annie didn't catch on.

"The following day they left for Epping. On the train, Nance wanted to discuss what the story might be, Uncle would have none of it. He told them they should discuss the matter between themselves and tell him later. He would then tell Lizzie.

On the Monday, uncle George went to work and Lizzie had an appointment with me. It was a dreadful, wet, windy day. Fred and Nance sat around the fire in the living room on St. John's Road deciding on their story. All his family knew her name was Keeling and yours would be the same. She had never seen you but uncle George had, and he told Nance how much you resembled her. So it was decided the story would be that you were her brother's child, thus explaining the name and the resemblance. They would say his wife was an unfit mother and that you were in a foster home with the Buntons."

"Ah! yes, I've heard that one before." I said.

"Really! When?"

"Back when I was about seven, we went to Wales to look after Fred's sister, she told her children and one of them told me; I knew it wasn't true though."

"Yes well, they knew sooner or later you'd find out, so in the mean time everyone was asked not to mention her maiden name. Nance would eventually explain everything to you, they were told. They would also made sure Fred's family was given sufficient detail that there would be no need for them to question you."

Annie, with a quick glance at the clock said, "You'll have to excuse me Frank, just for a moment, Uncle George'll be home soon."

She retired to the kitchen and I was alone with my thoughts. My mind in a whirl, it was difficult to concentrate but it was all beginning to fall into place. There was Oliver's story about me being her brother's child. Their panic when Fred's brother Walt and wife Mabel started to ask me awkward questions and the beating I got for telling the truth. And no wonder Uncle George Wright in Romford knew so much about the Keeling ancestry, his wife was a Keeling! That reminded me of the visit to Granddad Keeling on his birthday. He had called her "girl," she had used only the name Nance. She sent me out into the garden while she talked to him. Was he too part of the plot?

I recalled her remark about turning over a log that last Christmas Eve I spent in Brighton. I had threatened to tell Fred everything. Of course, it was clear now what she meant. If I told Fred, or anyone else for that matter, the fact that we had committed incest would come to light. And, of course, it was obvious now why I had never been allowed to see my Birth Certificate.

I realized that all those I had loved and trusted for so long had been deceiving me and I felt angry and hurt. How could they have been so cruel, and all to spare the feelings of Fred's family; I would never forgive them. I had heard it said that, "Truth is stranger than fiction." The truth, as disclosed by Annie was difficult enough, but the fact I had been deceived for so long was even harder to bear.

Almost fifty years after this conversation, I took possession of the diary to which Annie had referred. In it I found an example of her determination to conceal her maiden name. Under March 3, there had originally been an entry: `Annie Elizabeth Keeling 1897' which, of course, was her birthday. The entire entry had been heavily inked over and `Anne Ince' written in pencil below. But when held up to the light, the original entry can clearly be seen. Also, several pages had been removed.

Annie had described how determined Nance was to get possession of that diary when Lizzie Mason died. And how some of the events might have been documented. While nothing can be proven, it is obvious someone wanted sensitive and embarrassing information removed.

Now I could understand why, on that third and last time we were in bed together, she suddenly decided what we had done was wicked. It was guilt, no doubt about it now.

I recalled her telling me after the second time we had sex, she'd had a "Huge flood." She was superstitious by nature and no doubt saw that as an omen. Despite all this, she was still eager for me to go to her bed and engage in other sexual acts. I vividly recalled the oral sex and remembered that, at one point, we even discussed anal sex although that never took place. Somehow, she didn't consider that wicked?

I couldn't help wondering whether she would have done what she did before my sixteenth birthday had I responded differently to some of her provocative behaviour?

I remembered her harsh words the morning after that final night, "From now on you are nothing but a lodger in this house and the sooner you find somewhere else to live the better."

What an evil woman, I thought, and she was my mother! But who was my father? Frank Bunton? The Banker? Who knows? After what I had learned this day anything seemed possible. Perhaps I was nobody's son. Now I'm being silly.

My thoughts were interrupted as Annie returned. She had obviously been to the bathroom, her face looked fresh, her hair combed and she was eager to resume. I had no idea how long she'd been gone. Seeing me deep in thought she waited a moment and then continued.

"Uncle George met with Mrs. Bunton and told her what the story had to be and why. He stressed that if Fred's family learned the truth the marriage would be in jeopardy. She was also told that after about six months they would tell his family that Nance couldn't have children and they would adopt Frank."

"God! This is all sickening" I said.

"Yes," replied Annie, "Lizzie and George were appalled at the extent of the deception and George regretted getting involved. I remember Lizzie saying, `Oh what a tangled web we weave when first we practice to deceive'. But they went along with it, to save the marriage they thought."

"Save the marriage?" I stormed, "it was doomed from the start, it wasn't a marriage, it was just a bloody miserable existence for everybody."

Annie ignored my outburst.

"They went to her sister Edie's on their way home. She was told the same story and pledged her support."

Edie was no longer my favourite Aunt!

"Back in Brighton his family was told. Shortly afterwards, arrangements were made for you to join them. At the time, everyone involved thought they were doing the right thing. For my part . . . I regret allowing myself to be drawn into it but by marrying Uncle George I had little choice. I hope Frank that in telling you I have in some way made amends."

She glanced out the window.

"Oh! Here comes Uncle George."

I looked at the clock, it was ten minutes past five. We'd been talking for almost four hours.

He opened the gate and walked to the back door.

"One last question Auntie," I said hastily, "do you think I'm a Bunton?"
She thought for a moment.
"Well, Nance has always stuck to her story, if it's all true you probably are."
There was a pause.
"But you must remember Frank, your mother was such a consummate liar."

Fifteen

In The Mirror

Annie left to greet Uncle George, he would change from his work clothes while she pottered in the kitchen preparing the evening meal. For a few moments I was alone again with unpleasant thoughts that just wouldn't go away.

Annie had referred only to "Nance" throughout our conversation, it was strange at the end to hear her say, "Your mother" She emphasized the word mother I think, because she was relieved and perhaps a little proud that at last she had let the cat out of the bag. To me, feeling sensitive about it, it sounded like she was rubbing it in.

I repeated the words under my breath, my mother, my mother; didn't sound right, not for the woman I knew. Her naked body flashed before my eyes and I heard once more that familiar cry as she reached orgasm, and again I was filled with shame and disgust. How in God's name would I deal with it all.

Uncle George, his usual boisterous self, jolted me back to reality.

"Well, hello there Frank, how are you. My! it's good to see you, it's been a long time."

I stood to shake his hand.

"You look a little pale, not feeling well?"

Before I could reply, Annie swept back into the room insisting I stay for supper.

"You've eaten nothing," she said, "and besides, Uncle George has only just arrived."

That I might decline never entered Annie's head, but I knew there was no way I could stay in that house. I simply had to get away and the sooner the better.

"I've been telling Frank about his family," she said excitedly. "I told him everything George . . . When he walked in here in his uniform I thought to myself, I cannot let this boy go off to war without knowing the truth. I couldn't live with myself if anything . . . "

Her voice trailed, reluctant to follow that line of thought and she sat down looking subdued. I was appalled at Uncle's brusque reply.

"Oh!. . . Well, you shouldn't talk about such things, Nance is the one to do that. I don't think that was at all proper Annie."

I glanced at Annie, she was surprised by his abrupt manner and looked dejected. I decided to come to her defense and with great difficulty, retained my cool.

"Well Uncle," I said, "My mother would never tell me anything. Nobody has had the courage to tell me the truth until today, and I very much appreciate Auntie's decision, even though it's been a terrible shock. You'll never know the extent to which I've suffered and the harm that's been caused by a lifetime of lies and deception."

Now it was his turn to look surprised, I'm sure he thought I was exaggerating. I wanted to say more but feared Annie might suffer further humiliation. I wanted very much to yell at the top of my lungs that they were all a bunch of cowards. That what they had done to me as a child was cruel.

I wanted so badly to tell him they should have spoken out years ago. Had they done so, actions that would haunt me for the rest of my life would have been prevented. I wanted to scream at him that, because of what they had done, I had fucked my own mother! What would he say to that, I wondered? Instead, I simply rose to my feet, offered him my hand again and said quite firmly,

"Now I really must be going, good-bye Uncle. Thank you Auntie, I shall never forget this day."

And with that I strode to the door the two of them at my heels.

Uncle George's reaction triggered an anger in me that was hard to control. He still didn't realize the harm that had been done and was prepared to continue the deception. For this I would never forgive him. At the door I mumbled an apology for my hasty departure and left. As I closed the garden gate I sensed both were watching me but I was determined not to look back. I walked the few yards to the corner and heard their front door close. Come the end of the day, I would never see either of them again.

People were making their way to the railway station. I should too, but couldn't face a crowd. I had to be alone, to sort out my thoughts and decide, after what I'd learned, how to approach mum and Jessie. So instead of going to the station, I turned left onto the Railway Bridge. From the left side I could look down into the Mason's living room so I crossed the road.

In the centre I stopped and leaned on the wall. I gazed at the gleaming steel rails as they appeared to merge and disappear in the distance in the direction of London. There was much activity on the platform, the train to Ongar was due any minute. But I was so engrossed I saw nothing.

My mind was filled with memories of this woman I now knew to be my mother. I thought of Sir James Barrie who wrote, "God gave us memories that we might have roses in winter," what a beautiful thought. But mine weren't of roses, they were of fear, disgust, hatred; and the guilt was overwhelming. If only I had known, if only, if only; how many times had I used those words in my young life? They would torment me again in the days that followed.

I thought back to when, at the slightest provocation, I would be thrashed with that wretched cane, I was terrified of her then. Was that done to keep me in line, to stop me from asking embarrassing questions or making inappropriate remarks about my past? How well I remembered her threats if I were to, "Tell anyone my business." God! How I hated her.

Then the dramatic change after I physically put her out the door on Ladysmith Road. I was barely fourteen but she began to treat me like a man. She was helpful and now and then I was the recipient of an affectionate hug. Was there more to that than I had thought? At the time, I began to think that perhaps she wasn't so bad after all. Perhaps, just as Annie had observed, she was trying to make me a better person. For that I began to respect her.

Next came my sixteenth birthday. I relived the whole sordid affair and how I thought I was in love with her. How sick it all seemed, I felt nothing but hatred now. I remembered the episode with Sam at the front door of our basement suite on DeMontfort Road and the affairs with the mailman and the shopkeeper. After all that, how could I have allowed myself to be seduced into going to bed with her? I rationalized by telling myself I was only sixteen, naive and vulnerable.

I thought of how bitter she was after that last night together and her eagerness to get rid of me. Because of that, I had given up my education, the most important thing.

Annie said we were both born on a Wednesday. According to legend, "Wednesday's child is full of woe." Normally I would ignore these old granny's tales but it seemed, in our case at least, there might be some truth to it. On the other hand perhaps it was all meant to be. There was a war on, I had more than two years service under my belt and was much better prepared than I otherwise would have been.

I was suddenly engulfed in smoke and forced back to reality. The train had passed under the bridge and, despite its huffing and puffing and the blare of its high-pitched whistle, I had hardly noticed it. I would have an hour-and-a-half to wait, so I just walked. To this day I cannot recall where, I only know I kept walking and thinking!

One of my concerns was how to deal with mum and the rest of the Bunton family. Should I even visit them? Maybe I should just slink away and try to forget? No, I had to talk to mum, I simply had to hear her side of the story. But would she want to discuss it?

I began to think about the role the Bunton family had played in my life. Vic was barely three when I arrived, Jessie five and Evelyn almost eight. Minnie was eleven, George thirteen Charlie sixteen and Lena seventeen; obviously they had nothing to do with what happened. They probably had no idea what was going on and I don't know what they were told. It doesn't matter anyway.

So it was Paddy and mum who made the decisions. The way Annie described things I couldn't apportion blame. I knew that over the years, Jessie had become mum's confidante and wondered how much she knew.

My thoughts switched to Frank Bunton, the man alleged to be my father. He had vehemently denied it; his attitude toward me had always been that of a big brother. He and Edie had been happily married for eight years; could I step in now and raise questions. Annie's last words jumped back at me, ". . . . your mother is a consummate liar." Somehow I couldn't imagine myself challenging him.

Then there was mum, she and old Miss Dennis were so convinced I was a Bunton, why? Despite having eight children, she had taken me in and nurtured me as one of her own. She was a wonderful mother to me, always there to give comfort in times of trouble, always kind, gentle and loving. There must have been some compelling reason. Did she see a birth mark, some physical irregularity peculiar to the Bunton family or to Frank himself? My heart ached at the thought of it all.

Why had mum so readily given me away? I couldn't believe she really wanted to. I cast my mind back to 1925 when it all happened. I recalled, just as Annie had described, the older boys being out of work for months, then Paddy's accident and him grumbling about the shortage of work and men being laid off. And Miss Dennis allowing us to use her back garden in addition to our own so that we could grow more produce, and mum accepting a few pennies from a neighbour for some of it. I remembered too, mum taking in washing and for the first time, began to see her dilemma.

Annie had said Uncle George spoke of the difficulties she was facing; there were five young mouths to feed and I wasn't even her child. My mother, on the other hand, had married a man with a good steady job, she wasn't even working, just looking after Fred. The facts were clearer to me now and I was glad I had taken the time to think about it. I would be very gentle with dear old mum.

I re-crossed the bridge having no idea how long I'd been walking. I took a quick peek at the Mason property and saw Uncle George vigorously digging the garden; looked like a man working off some hostility to me. At the corner I glanced up Station Road where my mother's old employers lived. Should I go and see them? What would I say? What purpose would be served? They were in their seventies Annie had said. Nah! What's the point? And I hurriedly made my way to the station.

Twice in the years to come, however, I would attempt to satisfy my curiosity. In 1942, I visited Jessie and decided to visit these people. Any family resemblance would be more apparent now than at nine, I thought. But the old man had died of heart failure two months earlier on July 1st. He was seventy-eight. The family would still be grieving so I didn't go. Then, in 1955, I visited Evelyn and considered visiting his widow only to find she had died on July 2, 1953 aged eighty-five. Bowel cancer had spread throughout her body and she was senile, so it was not to be.

Arriving in Ongar I left the train and began the familiar walk toward what I had always considered home. Past the nursery where, on my summer holidays, I had often bought mum a few roses; my! how she loved them. It was closed now or I would have bought some; such was my love for her despite all I'd learned. Turning right on High Street I passed a row of old houses then the Police station. Next came the Budworth Hall and the clock in the tower struck eight.

Next to the Hall, down a short alleyway, there was the little school I had attended briefly before being whisked away. That was fifteen years ago, my how time flies! I wondered under what name mum had registered me. Jack Bunton? Jacky Patchit? Not Frank Dennis Bunton Keeling, of that I felt sure. It reminded me of the stupid thing I did at St. John's school in Epping. God! was that teacher ever mad when I wrote the wrong name on my exercise book.? Did it deliberately too! What made me do that? I wondered.

Past the International store on the left where Minnie and Frank's wife Edie used to work then Mott's toy store, more memories. Vic and I with our noses pressed against the window looking fondly at some big toy. Then past the Star grocery store where Evelyn had worked. I went in there with mum when I was four, there was a dog, I stroked him and he bit me on my right forefinger. Mum took me to the chemist for repairs. I still bear the scar.

I approached the Post Office and there, among a group of people, was mum and Jessie waiting for the bus to Epping. Our eyes met as I strode toward them. There was a moment of hesitation; they could be forgiven for not recognizing me. A soldier was a common sight now and we all looked much alike. Suddenly, all the pent up feeling associated with the long absence of loved ones was released. I threw my arms around them both and there were tears of joy. Jessie had spent the day with mum and was returning to Coopersale.

What was I doing in Ongar, they wanted to know, how long had I got? Was I off to war? Both expressed concern for my future, so I told them about my initial posting, they were much relieved.

"I've just come from the Mason's in Epping," I said. "Annie spent the whole afternoon telling me the story of my life. For the first time, I know who my mother is and I must say I'm not impressed; and I know my full name too."

And I laughed hoping to lessen the impact of what I was saying, but my laugh sounded hollow and both looked stunned. Jessie spoke first.

"Look Jack, the bus will be here any moment and there isn't a later one or I would stay; we may not see each other for a long time. All I want to say is that I was a little girl of five when you came into my life, I loved you then and I love you now. No matter what others may have said, you were always part of our family and always will be. Mum can tell you all the details but one thing I do know, what happened was just as hard for us as it was for you. It wasn't our choice, we simply complied with your mother's demands. I beg you Jack not to think ill of us, we don't deserve it."

With that the bus arrived.

Mum and I waved good-bye and watched the bus disappear. Then we slowly made our way home, she telling her version of what happened including one little surprise. Apparently, when she brought me home I was suffering from some kind of urinary infection, which simply would not respond to treatment. Night after night my screams kept the whole family awake. In desperation she took me to the doctor who recommended circumcision. Mum agreed and paid him the princely sum of half a crown (fifty-cents) for his trouble; that was all she could afford, she told him and that was that. Much to the relief of everyone, it worked.

By the time we reached the back door, she had confirmed much of Annie's story. How she first met Nance in Miss Dennis' house in 1919, her saying she was pregnant and that Frank was the father. She spoke of how she had approached Frank and he vehemently denying paternity.

Why then had he spent a Saturday in Woodford trying to end the pregnancy?

she had asked. His answer, he `felt sorry for her', there was much more to the story than Nance had disclosed, he declared.

"When Miss Dennis returned from Romford she said you were a very tiny baby. That supported Nance's claim you were premature. She also said you bore a strong resemblance to Vic. I told Frank but he was unmoved. He just didn't believe any of it."

This was obviously difficult for mum, her eyes filled with tears and I wished I'd never started it.

"Miss Dennis said you were to be placed in a foster home, I couldn't bear the thought of that."

We entered that familiar place I first called home, it was strangely quiet and empty. I looked at Paddy's armchair in the corner by the chimney, it was even stranger not to see him there.

I lied, saying I wasn't hungry but would like a cup of tea. Waiting for the kettle to boil, I told mum I knew this was difficult and I didn't want to cause her pain.

"You know I've always loved you and always will, you're still the only mother to me."

And I gave her a big hug. She wiped away the tears, and I felt awful again.

"There are a couple of things I'd like to ask though, just to put my mind at rest then we can forget it."

The teapot was warmed and three teaspoons of tea added. That's one each and one for the pot. Stir, let it brew for a minute and then into the kitchen to pour. I added sugar to mine and stirred.

"I'd like to know what convinced you I was a Bunton? And why was I given to her, a complete stranger, so suddenly; without any explanation and at such a young age? I'd like to hear your side of the story."

Mum took a sip of her tea.

"Well Jack, before you were even born I met with George and Lizzie Mason. For years afterward, well, until Lizzie died, I would drop in for a cup of tea whenever I was in Epping. Sometimes George would have a job to do down here and he would drop by; always insisted on giving me half-a-crown toward your keep. That's something Nance agreed to do right from the beginning but never did. Anyway, I knew all that was going on. So when they told me she was getting married and her future husband had a good job, I told George how difficult life was for us. I suggested Nance should start contributing as she had originally agreed."

Mum's lower lip trembled, I reached across the table, took her hands in mine and gave them a gentle squeeze.

"Did Annie tell you what happened on the morning of their wedding?"

"Yes she did, mum."

"Well the way George Mason explained it to me, Fred said he wanted to go through with the wedding and wanted her child as well. I don't know whether Nance liked the idea or not, I rather fancy she didn't. But with George Mason there I don't think she was in a position to argue. HE thought it was a great idea. And so the decision was made there and then. We weren't asked at all, we were just told what had been decided and the conditions Fred had insisted upon."

I wanted to ask her if any government agency had been involved and again, what was it that finally persuaded her to accept me. But she was having a hard time, the tears were flowing and I hadn't the heart to pursue the matter.

"We would have loved to keep you Jack," she said between sobs. "We had all grown fond of you, you were one of us, and we didn't want to give you up. But she was your birth mother, there was nothing we could do. When you used to ask me who your mother was, it broke my heart that I couldn't tell you. But we had agreed it should be left to Nance to tell you."

I swallowed hard watching mum fight back the tears.

"I really thought when old Grandma Ince died she would have told you. I can't for the life of me understand why she didn't, but you know her better than I."

"I certainly do," I said, "I hate to say it knowing she's my mother, but she's a wicked woman, you'll never know . . ." I stopped myself, realizing I was saying too much.

"Anyway" I said, "it's all over now; I understand mum, don't worry, let's forget it. Where's Vic?"

She didn't answer because at that moment we saw Frank and his wife, Edie, coming through the gate.

It's hard to describe my emotions as they entered the room. Not knowing I was there, they were surprised but happy to see me.

"You look smart in your uniform Jack, are you here for long?" Edie asked.

Mum answered her question.

I stared at Frank and wondered . . . could this man be my father? It seemed ridiculous, I'd known him all my life. No, he was my big brother, nothing more.

I had stood out of courtesy to Edie. That's how my mother had taught me. "Always stand when a lady enters the room," she insisted. This time by doing so, I could see myself in the mirror over the mantelpiece. Did I look anything like Frank Bunton? I looked first at my reflection, then at Frank then back at myself. No, I could see no resemblance whatsoever. I watched him closely as he spoke.

"Whasamatter Ma? Yer look as if you've been cryin'."

"Oh! Seeing young Jack here, all dressed up in his uniform made me shed a tear. I'm all right now."

I looked and listened closely for some small sign, but no, nothing. He neither looked like me nor spoke like me. In fact, I was struck by the obvious differences. We were as different as chalk is to cheese.

Now Edie was talking to mum. They'd just dropped in on their way home, Frank had been working late. And would she care to go up town with her tomorrow afternoon to help pick out some curtain material.

There was a time when they lived next door. When old Mr. Bailey died they moved in, now they live on Clovely Road, that's up Marden Ash Hill. Charlie and his wife Olive live next door. Must visit them before I leave.

When I was a little boy, the baker delivered a loaf of hot, crunchy French bread to old Mr. Bailey every day. He would cut the end off, butter it and give it to me. I would run out to play with my "hunch" of bread, a special treat.

The small talk went on between the two women for several minutes then there was a lull in the conversation.

"Well, we really must be going," said Edie." 'Bye Jack, take care of yourself, all the best."

"Thanks Edie," I said, and gave her a peck on the cheek. Frank grabbed my hand and shook it firmly.

"So long Jack, hurry up and win this war for us, take care."

And they were gone. I looked at the clock, it was ten to ten, my how time flies. I stood there going over in my mind all that had just happened when mum came down stairs with her hair down. We always knew when she was going to bed. She'd be missing a while then come down stairs, her hair almost down to her waist. She'd walk down to the privy, light the candle again and bid everyone good night. Tonight was the same.

She asked if I would like something to eat before she went up, I declined. I hadn't eaten since morning and felt sickly; smoking on an empty stomach. I had hoped she might stay for a chat, but she just pecked me on the cheek.

"Night Jack, God bless, see you in the morning."

With that she climbed the stairs, a little laboriously I thought. I realized then that my dear old mum was getting old. I mustn't upset her anymore, I thought.

I drank a glass of milk and felt better; then decided I had to visit the privy. I walked the few yards down the garden and paused at the privy door. It was a beautiful September night, still not completely dark, with a big harvest moon making it's way above the horizon. I stood looking at all the old familiar sights. The barn; I thought of those two beautiful horses, long since replaced by a big, smelly truck, what happened to them I wondered? Across from the Privy the old apple tree; a little further down, the tool shed, the same where Jessie had first told me in strictest confidence, a little more about my real mother.

Behind the barn was old Mrs. Mead's garden. She was a dear old soul, wonder if she's still alive? I gazed down the long stretch of garden from the dogleg to the river. The fence posts were there but the wire dividing Miss Dennis' property from ours was still missing, and vegetables had obviously been harvested. I saw the huge willow tree I had climbed a thousand times. For a moment I was caught up in the nostalgia of it all.

Back to reality; I had to pee, and there was much to be resolved. I still had this dreadful feeling of guilt, just could not get it out of my mind. Incest, carnal knowledge, my own mother! I was tormenting myself.

Up in the back bedroom I suddenly felt exhausted, but I slept little till long after sunrise. Then there was mum with a cup of tea, gently shaking me.

"It's past ten," she said. "I thought I'd better wake you . . . got any plans for today?"

I felt dreadful and said my only plan was to visit Charlie. Then asked where

Vic was.

"Oh, didn't I tell you? He left Thursday, doing a job for Noble's in Harlow, some big warehouse fire or something. They're working right through. Should be home Tuesday."

"Well, I have to be back tomorrow night so I'll miss him. Damn! haven't seen Vic for ages."

"Well drink your tea. Frank came by, brought us a couple of nice lamb chops for dinner. Edie's gonna come by about half-past-one."

And she went back downstairs.

God! I felt awful, lay awake all night churning things over. Who was to blame? If only they'd told me sooner. If only I'd known, if only, if only. Here we go again!

I went down stairs, got a bowl of cold water out of the butt and, stripped to the waist, washed myself just as Charlie and George had done years before. Then I shaved in cold water. I was used to that, we rarely had hot water in the Army. I suddenly realized there was a war on and wondered how things were going? My thoughts drifted to my buddies who had gone to France. "There but for the grace of God go I."

Mum cooked a nice meal. Lamb chops with homemade mint sauce, peas and potatoes from the garden. Just like old times. Then rhubarb and custard for "afters". Don't get grub like this in the Army. Since mum was going up town with Edie I said I'd visit Charlie.

"What about supper?"

I was looking forward to some fresh country air and was too full to worry about supper, so I said not to worry I'd probably have a bite at Charlie's.

Reaching the end of the drive I noticed Eph Ransome's blacksmith shop was gone; no longer the ring of hammer on anvil, the roar of the bellows or the snort of a restless horse. It had been taken over by the cycle shop next door; all chrome, clean and shiny, nothing resembling a blacksmith anymore. Wonder what happened to Eph? I'll ask mum.

I crossed the street and turned up the lane known as Bushey Lea, the Stokes family lived on the corner. I thought of Harold on the back of the toboggan, the year they nearly went into the river. I recalled the rest of the family: Harold was the oldest, then there was Helen, Freda, Lenny, 'Rene and `Wiggy', that's Wilfred. Their dad was tall and slim and worked at the Gas Works; their mum a very large, jolly lady and very kind.

I passed the same row of cottages on the left, and could see in the distance and to my right, a tree from which I had fallen as a youngster. Looked the same as the day it happened. A little further on, the lane veered to the right over the bridge. On the river bank there was a huge sloe tree, the very same from which Vic and I picked sloes for Paddy to make wine.

I recalled Vic falling from that tree; his feet just touched the water as he grabbed onto the last branch. Scared the hell out of me, but he just swung his feet up and was back picking sloes as if nothing had happened.

I hopped over the stile next to an old tree I had often climbed as a child; followed the public footpath past that part of the river where we used to paddle known as Spring Ponds, and the deep end where I had once fallen in. I still remembered the hiding I got for that.

I walked deep in thought, wondering where all my troubles would end. It was another beautiful day, how good it would be if only I didn't have so much on my mind. Damn that woman. Will I ever get over this?

It was so peaceful, nothing but the rustle of leaves and the singing of the birds. Away in the distance I could hear a cuckoo, and to my left, the gentle swishing sound of Cripsey Brook as it made it's way over rocks.

I walked to the point where Cripsey Brook joins the River Roding then down stream to a spot where, in days gone by, adults and older children would swim and dive. As I approached the river's edge a rabbit ran across my path, so close that had I been alert, I'm sure I could have grabbed him.

I sat and gazed at the river, it was so deep, so still. The only way you could tell the direction in which it flowed was by watching the odd leaf float slowly by. It looked so deep and so inviting; I found myself wondering what it would be like to drown. For a moment I thought how nice it might be just to let myself sink into its depths, just let myself go. All my problems would be solved, I thought.

But I knew I had neither the courage nor the desire to do such a thing and felt restless. I wanted to do something. I'd no idea what, but I just felt I was wasting time, that I ought to be doing something about my problem. I hurriedly retraced my steps and back at the stile, sat a moment thinking about my visit to Charlie. Annie said he was working with Frank in Epping at the time of my conception. He would be about fifteen then, but that's an age when most brothers confide in one another. Perhaps I could glean something from him.

From the stile I could almost see his house on Clovely Road, Frank lived next door. Frank Bunton, my father? Yes, no, who the hell knows? I angrily kicked a stone as I jumped off the stile.

My visit to Charlie was short and sweet. I had said good morning to his neighbour as I passed, and when she saw me approach his front door she said,

"Is it Mr. Bunton you're wanting to see?"

"Yes ma'am, it is," I said, wondering why she would ask.

"He's in the back yard and Mrs. Bunton's out so he won't hear you if you knock. I'll go through and tell him he has a visitor."

I thanked her and in no time Charlie was facing me at the door. He stood with a blank stare on his face and I realized we hadn't seen one another for three years, and me in my uniform. He too could be forgiven for not recognizing me.

"Jacky Patchit" I said.

"No . . . Never . . . Well bless my soul, I wouldn't 'a known yer Jack, come on in."

I followed him in his stockinged feet to the back door, the sweat from his labours showed through his shirt. Olive had gone up town on her bike and he'd promised to dig the last few potatoes and be ready to leave as soon as she got back. They were to visit relatives. As he replaced his muddy boots I apologized for the intrusion saying, I couldn't stay long anyway.

"Have so many people to visit," I lied.

I followed him down the path stopping level with the row he was digging. It was obvious he wanted to continue but felt uncomfortable about it.

"Wish the Missus was here, she'd make a cuppa tea or somethin'," he said.

"Don't worry" I said and, feeling as awkward as he, I made small talk about the wonderful weather and the war. I couldn't help glancing over to Frank's garden and admiring the beautiful flowers. Then I plucked up courage.

"Was over in Epping yesterday visiting the Mason's."

"Oh ah, how they doin'?"

"Fine," I said. "Old Annie spent the afternoon telling me who my real mother is and that Frank might be my father. Do you believe that? Do I look anything like him?"

Charlie gave a hearty laugh. To him, the very idea was obviously ridiculous. Then he plunged the fork deep into the rich soil.

"Nar! Don't believe a word of it Jack, Never did."

His words had a finality to them, I knew the subject was closed as far as he was concerned. I wished I had kept my big mouth shut. I'd gained nothing by asking.

After more small talk I left. He wished me well and suggested I look out for Olive.

"She"ll be on her way back now more'n likely, she always walks up the hill," he said.

I didn't though, I wouldn't have known her if I saw her. And anyway, I went home the same way that I'd come, down the lane. I should have gone by way of Marden Ash though, if I had, I would have bumped into mum and Edie returning from their shopping trip. Mum had been invited to tea. On second thought, I don't think I would have felt comfortable.

I spent a lonely evening wrestling with my thoughts, first feeling sorry for myself then angry. Angry with the whole darn world for what had happened. I felt cheated, used and abused. No matter how hard I tried, the one thought that persisted in my mind was that I had committed incest; that damn word plagued me. I went to bed early, slept no better than the previous night and was walking in the garden when mum got up.

She mentioned the garden was getting too much for her, that she had to rely on the boys. For months she had asked them, without success, to clear the patch between the apple tree and the shed as her little piece of garden.

"Just to grow a few flowers," she said.

This was where the gooseberry bushes and other prickly plants had grown for years; it had become an overgrown, tangled mass of roots and vines but the soil was good. I recalled mum's oft repeated assertion that this was the ugliest part of the garden and I had never liked it either.

Without another word I whipped off my shirt, donned an old pair of Vic's coveralls and set to work. Mum protested but I insisted. Not only would it be helping her, it also would help me to get rid of some of my anger. I worked like a dog on that piece of ground and by noon it was done just as mum had wanted it.

I washed and changed back into my uniform, by which time mum had prepared another big meal. I said she shouldn't have but her reply was charmingly simple.

"You gotta eat Jack, after all that hard work. Besides, the way to a man's heart is via his stomach."

How could I dismiss this extraordinary woman who I loved more now than as a little boy?

She refused my offer to wipe the dishes and I found myself alone in that tiny room pondering over so many of my earliest memories and what lay ahead. Suddenly, I again had the urge to do something, I glanced at the clock it was five minutes to two. There was a train to London at two fifteen and I knew exactly what I was going to do and made an excuse about leaving so abruptly.

"Don't worry Jack, I understand" mum said, a little disheartened.

I felt bad because I knew she had enjoyed my visit. I stuffed a pound note in the vase on the mantelpiece. Then, into the scullery, a big hug, thanked her for everything and told her not to worry. Everything would be fine I assured her, and I was on my way.

Sixteen

A Word In Private

Having said good-bye to mum I had less than fifteen minutes, and although feeling a little self conscious I half walked, half ran to the railway station. Army Regulations required that respirator and steel helmet or, to use the vernacular, tin hat and gas mask, be carried at all times. The respirator was slung over the right shoulder with the helmet attached to it, with both resting on the left buttock. A haversack containing toiletries, clean shirt, clean socks and various other items hung at my right side.

So there I was, dashing through town with these things bouncing up and down on my arse. I'm sure the locals thought I'd been summoned to number 10 Downing Street by the Big Man himself. But I made it and knew exactly what I was going to do. It was time for action and I was off to Brighton to confront the woman I now knew to be my mother.

Finding an empty compartment I wrestled with how best to approach the subject. She is my biological mother, must remember that. I wondered if I could keep my cool, but knew ranting and raving would serve no useful purpose. I searched for the right words but with little success.

I mean, what do you say to a woman who has sexually abused her own son? The more I thought about it, the more difficult it became. I found myself going back to the period prior to my sixteenth birthday. Did I do anything to encourage her? No, for at least two years I had been careful not to fall for her little games lest I do something wrong.

Then I tried looking at it from her perspective. What would cause a mother to do such a thing? Why would she do it? I knew her marriage was without love, or anything resembling a normal relationship. I knew also that physically, Fred was inadequate. I recalled the many tearful nights when their love making ended in failure. But did any of that justify what she had done? To me it didn't.

Frustrated, I began to focus on my arrival, I didn't want to get there just as they were eating. Ideally, Fred would be on a late shift, if he were there it would be impossible to deal openly with the issue.

Then it dawned on me. The earliest train I could catch to Brighton would be the four o'clock, arriving there at five. I would have to leave by six to be back in Bury St. Edmunds by midnight. What a fool I was, why didn't I think this thing through? All that time spent in Ongar; could've left this morning. But then mum wouldn't have got her garden dug, and I felt a sense of satisfaction having done that for her. As it turned out, it was the last thing I would ever do for her so no regrets.

Damn! Now what do I do? Could go to Romford, see Auntie Edie, I now knew her sister was my mother not my Auntie. I pictured myself confronting her, why hadn't she told me years ago? I thought she was my friend. I even toyed with the idea of confiding in her exactly what had happened. But on second thoughts, better not. One doesn't go around telling people they've had sex with their own mother. God almighty! Why do I have to keep thinking about that?

No, I didn't feel like visiting. All I wanted to do was confront her, damn it. I finally decided to go back to Barracks; it would be the first and only time in my military career I would return from leave earlier than required. And so, instead of taking the Underground to Victoria, I simply walked to Platform Twelve and caught the next train to Bury St. Edmunds via Cambridge.

The train was packed, many returning from a weekend in London. The talk was of the sand bagging of all the monuments in London, particularly that of Queen Victoria opposite Buckingham Palace. About the huge numbers of service personnel and equipment; in particular, the anti aircraft units and Barrage Balloons. There was also talk about the impending evacuation of children from the Greater London Area. Such was the conversation of the day. But I had other things on my mind.

I had to change at Cambridge with a twenty-minute wait so I went to the Restaurant and had a cup of railway tea. In six years of war the quality of their tea would deteriorate to the point where it was unrecognizable. The only good "cuppa" to be had in London was provided by good old "Sally Ann." No matter the time of day, or how serious the situation, the Salvation Army was always there with a mug of hot "char" and a bun.

I entered the guardroom in Gibraltar Barracks at eight-thirty and handed my pass to the Orderly Corporal. He thought I was crazy returning from leave three and-a half-hours early. I went to my room and tried to sleep. Physically I was exhausted; mentally I was in turmoil. Sleep was out of the question, apart from my mental state there was the bedlam caused by men returning from their evening activities or from weekend leave.

For most of that night I lay thinking, overcome by a sense of despair. I tried convincing myself things always look worse at night, especially when you're tired. Somebody once said, "The darkest hour is before the dawn," but it didn't help. I felt empty, depressed and alone in the world. No one to love and loved by no one.

My feelings for the Buntons, especially mum, had been challenged during the last forty-eight hours. I couldn't blame them for what happened as a child, but I deplored the way it was done. The more I thought about it the more cruel and heartless it all seemed. How could they love me as much as they claimed? On the other hand, both mum and Jessie had stressed they had no choice and I wanted so badly to believe them.

Worst of all, I could no longer imagine a mother somewhere out there. That someday I would find her and she would be gentle, kind and loving, and I was sure she would be beautiful. No, now I knew who my mother was and she was none of those things. She was cruel and wicked and I had been to bed with her. I had lain naked with her, doing things normally reserved for man and wife not for mother and son.

The seriousness of it was overwhelming. I had been a willing party to adultery; I was guilty of incest; I'd had sex with my own mother. Under British law that was a criminal offense. Suppose, in a fit of temper she told Fred? What would he do, would he go to the police? Or would he just close his eyes as he had with all her other affairs? If it went to court, would she, as she had once threatened, claim that I had been the aggressor?

Would anyone, least of all a court of law, believe I had no idea that she was my mother? Did it seem plausible that I could live under the same roof for over ten years and not know her maiden name was Keeling, the same as mine? Would anyone believe, or would those responsible admit, that I was the victim of a conspiracy? That I was systematically denied any knowledge whatsoever of my heritage? Such was the agony of my thoughts.

I finally drifted off to sleep only to be rudely awakened by reveille. Somebody should shoot that bloody bugler. I went to the mess, but couldn't face "bangers" and mash. As I watched the food being sloshed onto the plates I was reminded of the military version of an old English proverb, "A rolling sausage gathers no gravy." I left with a mug of tea.

This was the first day of the course on how to be an effective Instructor. My mind wandered to the point where twice during the day I was chastised for being inattentive. My thoughts were a mixture of fear, contempt, horror and loathing. Finally, at the end of the day, the Warrant Officer in charge spoke up.

"I've been watching you all day, Keeling, your mind sure as hell ain't where it should be. Now what the hell's the matter?"

"I'm not feeling well, Sir," I replied. "I've been sick all week-end. I thought I could fight it off," trying to make it sound convincing.

"Well if you're sick, for Christ sake go sick, I don't want you here screwing things up all the time."

"Yes, Sir," I said, "I'll report sick in the morning."

And so I found myself in front of the Medical Officer the next morning. When asked the nature of my ailment I was hesitant, not knowing how to explain it to an officious looking Captain in the Royal Army Medical Corps. But I needn't have worried. He was middle aged, had practiced medicine in civilian life and a man of compassion.

"Take your time Corporal, just tell me what's troubling you. Don't worry, I've heard it all before."

I thanked him for his understanding and told him the whole story. I was fearful of the outcome; after all, incest was a criminal offense. How, I wondered would the Army deal with that? My concern was unfounded. He said, while my problem wasn't one he dealt with on a daily basis, it was not as uncommon as I might think.

"Happens quite often, what's unusual is that you didn't know she was your mother. Now I believe you, some may not. But don't worry about that; it's probably better not to say too much about it. Most important, don't feel guilty. She was a grown woman, the responsibility for what happened lies with her not you."

I felt better already.

"There is no magic pill I can give you, it needs time; with a war on, we haven't got much. It happened almost three years ago but you have to face this woman, deal with the problem, and get it out of your system. If you don't, it'll eat away at you and you'll be useless. I'm going to recommend you be granted compassionate leave. Go and get this thing sorted out, get it off your chest and you'll feel a lot better. And good luck."

I waited while he wrote, thanked him again for his understanding and headed to the Company Office. On the way I read the note:

To: O.C. R2 Company.

I recommend this N.C.O. be granted a minimum of forty-eight hours compassionate leave to deal with a very serious family matter.

I couldn't read his signature.

The Company Sergeant Major, somewhat out of character, was most understanding. He said the Company Commander was out but I should go and get packed.

"By the time you get back, I'll have your pass waiting for you."

So, he was human after all.

True to his word he handed me my pass, it was from after duty Tuesday, 12 September to 2359 hrs., Thursday, 14 September. The war was not yet two weeks old and I was on leave for the second time. What a way to fight a war, I thought, and caught the next train to London.

"Change at Marks Tey" the ticket Collector, said.

I did and the platform was deserted, I was the only person catching the London train. I had twenty minutes to wait, time to dwell on what the Medical Officer had said.

When the train pulled into Brighton Station a few minutes before two in the afternoon, I knew exactly how I was going to handle things. My only concern was that Fred might be home.

I walked briskly down Station Street, across London Road and up Ditchling Road, past St. Saviours Church and turned up Crescent Rise. I chose this circuitous route because it was then downhill on Crescent Road to our house. I didn't want to arrive breathless from coming up the hill. I took my time, mounted the three steps, grasped the door handle and turned. It was locked! That's funny, never known our door to be locked at this time of day. I hammered on the door with the old-fashioned iron knocker, no response. She must be out. Damn! Murphy's Law again.

I stood back, and out of the corner of my eye, saw old Mrs. Stanmer's lace curtain move. She was always looking out her window, proper little busy body.

Next thing you know she was at her front door.

"There's no one home I'm afraid, Frank," she said.

"Oh, where's Mrs. Ince, do you know?"

"Well, I'm afraid Mrs. Ince doesn't live there anymore."

I was flabbergasted!

"What do you mean, she doesn't live here anymore?"

"Well, she's left Fred I'm afraid to say, poor old Fred is all on his own, but I have a key. Fred likes me to have one in case she . . . Well anyway, I'll give you the key. I know he wouldn't mind me doing that."

With that she handed me the key, said how nice it was to see me and was gone.

It was obvious my mother wasn't around because the place was in a mess, that's something she would never tolerate. Otherwise, the room was just as it had always been, including that wretched divan. I could swear the bloody thing was mocking me. Maybe Katherine Walker was onto something in 1864, when she wrote, "I believe in the total depravity of inanimate things."

The old fashioned stove stood silent, black and cold, a far cry from the cozy warmth of that long ago November night. The split down the length of the table showed though the cloth, and the memories came flooding back. Almost four years ago, here in this very room the whole sordid affair had begun.

I forced myself back to reality, what should I do now? Wonder where she lives? Wonder if Fred knows or cares? Such were my thoughts. First I'll have to locate him; he could be on a late shift. Damn my hide, I thought, everything in my favour is against me. Just an old army joke, but this was no time for joking.

I was dry; I'll make a cup of tea, I thought. I was just going to the kitchen when I heard a key in the lock. I stood motionless staring at the front door, wondering who would enter. Would it be my mother, deciding after all that there really was no place like home? Or would it be Fred? It was just Fred. I called out to him, for some reason feeling like a burglar.

"I'm here Fred, It's only me, Mrs. Stanmer gave me the key."

I had never addressed him by his first name before; it had always been Uncle. It sounded strange.

"Oh, 'ello there boy, what you doin' 'ere, 'aint seen yer for years" he blinked.

I had to think fast.

"Well, I've got a forty-eight hour pass," I said, "so I thought I'd come home, and maybe bury the hatchet, seeing's there's a war on . . . You know what I mean."

"Well, your Auntie ain' 'ere any more, 'spose old Mrs. Stanmer told yer, eh?"

"Fred," I said, "I know that she's my mother, so lets stop playing games, that's gone on long enough. Now what the hell happened?"

He looked a bit sheepish.

"Well, she just up and left me, been gone more'n a fortnight. I begged 'er to come back but no, she's got this bloke she's living with. She reckons she's in love with 'im and all that . . . Bloody stupid woman! She don't know when she's well off."

"Who is he, where do they live, do you know?"

"Yeah, I know 'im, name's Tommy. You remember the Brighton Trunk murder, when we lived on Park Crescent Terrace, 'e was the cab driver."

Who could ever forget? It happened just a few doors from us.

"Yeah, he drove a cab then 'cause there was no work about, but 'e's a tool-and-die maker by trade, pretty good one too. Got a real good job now doin' war work."

"Where do they live? I repeated.

"Oh, they live out in Hove, got a furnished basement flat. I wen'out there last week, tried ter get 'er to come 'ome. But she wouldn't."

"Damn! I really wanted to see her," I said, trying not to sound overly anxious.

"Well, we can go and see 'er, it's my day off, I'll take ya, maybe you can persuade 'er to come back. I really do need 'er; I'm lost without 'er. Will you do that for me eh?"

And he was crying!

"Come on Fred," I said, "Pull yourself together, it's a quarter to three now, how long would it take us to get there?"

"Oh, we can make it in 'alf an hour easy, I know all the right buses," he said.

Since he was a Bus Conductor he would know the quickest route.

"Well, if we go" I said, "I'd want to talk to her on my own."

"Of course, I'll go in the Coffee shop and wait for yer, there's one just down the Street."

For the entire thirty-five minute journey he continued to moan and groan, at times, near to tears. About how difficult life was "without my Nance" about how she was such a good housewife and always had a good meal ready for him no matter what shift he was on. At last we reached the coffee shop. He stopped and pointed.

"See them green railings down there 'cross the Street, the ones next to the f'sale sign?"

"Yes"

"Well, that's the one, number 54, go down the steps."

"Right," I said. "Now, are you going to stay in the coffee shop all the time? I've no idea how long I'll be."

"That's all right, don't you worry 'bout me. I'll be in 'ere when you get back. Now you take yer time and do yer best to persuade 'er to come 'ome. Tell 'er not to worry, I'll forgive everything. Tell 'er I love 'er."

He was weeping again and I felt pity for him.

I jaywalked across the busy street and, approaching the green railings, my heart started to pound. Pull yourself together, I said to myself. You're going to meet your own mother. Boy! Is she gonna be surprised when she finds out I know every damn thing about her since she was a child?

I descended the steps to the front door and knocked hard with my knuckles, there being no doorknocker or bell. It was one of those doors with frosted glass at the top, and with me being in uniform she guessed who it was before opening the door. I say that because she showed no surprise at all.

"Well, what brings you here? I suppose Fred told you where I was, is he with you?"

"No he's not, I came to see you, I've got something I want to discuss."

"Oh . . . Well, you better come in then."

She directed me into the front room and who should be there but Tommy himself, in his bloody dressing gown too, at three-thirty in the afternoon, what the hell?

"I'd like you to meet Tommy," she said. "He's a very dear friend, and if Fred sent you here to interfere, you're wasting your time. I'm very happy and I intend to stay."

Tommy offered his hand but I ignored it, I was so bloody mad. Not only was he here in his housecoat, which really pissed me off, but it would be impossible to do what I'd come to do. But I was determined.

"I've come to talk to my mother, I would like a word in private if you don't mind." And with as much sarcasm as I could muster, "and it has nothing to do with Fred. I couldn't care less who she lives with or where. I have an important matter to discuss, so if you wouldn't mind?"

I could see he was annoyed, but he turned on his heel.

"Oh, all right, I'll go in the bedroom."

I waited until he'd closed the door.

"Wish there were somewhere we could talk with more privacy," I said, "I don't want the whole world to hear what I have to say."

She motioned me toward the bay window, so that we were as far away from the door as possible.

"You can say all you want to say here, just keep your voice down."

As she moved to the window I noticed a marked change in her appearance. It was over two years since I had seen her; she'd put on weight. It suited her; she had a contented look about her that was missing before. But she looked older than the image I had and there were dark rings under her eyes. I now knew she was forty-two and she looked it. How could I have found her attractive back then, I wondered.

Keeping my voice as low as I could I said,

"I went to visit the Masons last week-end and I was told the truth about my parents. Everything."

I was full of pent up anger and frustration and in a hoarse whisper I almost spat out the words.

"I know that you are my mother, and when I was sixteen you took me to your bed. And we had sex, not just once but, FOUR times, FOUR times! If you'd had your way we'd have carried on with your crazy sex games. How could you do that with your own son?"

She went pale, opening her mouth to speak but I charged on.

"That was incest, a criminal offense. Have you ever thought what the consequences would be if anyone ever found out? What the hell were you thinking about to do such a thing, you must be crazy. Why the hell didn't you leave me with the Buntons where I was happy?"

There was anger in her eyes as she replied.

"Now listen to me and listen carefully. Tommy works nights and I have to get his dinner so there isn't much time. You were not like a son to me. The first time I ever set eyes on you was in Epping when you were almost six years old."

Cutting words, how could a mother admit such a thing?

"And, no matter what you have been told, I had nothing to do with your being taken away from the Buntons. If I'd had my way you would have stayed there."

She came closer to me and she was glaring.

"Yes, we did go to bed and we did have sex. But, you were all for it. You could have said no if you'd wanted to, but you didn't, you loved every minute of it, so don't come here on your high horse with me. Certainly it was wicked, I told you so at the time but you wouldn't have it. I've regretted what I did ever since and I suppose I'll have to answer for it one day. But, as I told you before, it happened, you can't change that, it's over and done with. I've put it out of my mind and you should do the same."

She blew her nose, tears welling in her eyes but I had no sympathy. I wanted to say more, to make her feel some of the pain I'd felt these last few days. But she is my mother, must remember that. I glanced at the door thinking I'd heard movement?

"Just one question," I said, "and for once in your life, for Christ sake tell the truth. Is Frank Bunton really my father?"

She buried her head in her hankie.

"Yes," she said with a half-sob.

I wasn't convinced. With that there was a knock at the door, and `himself' entered.

"I'm sorry to intrude," he said, "but I have to go to work, and I haven't eaten yet."

I felt even more angry, I had been denied my day in court, as it were. It had turned out nothing like I had intended and I felt cheated.

"All right," I said, "I'll leave now. By the way, Fred did ask me to try to persuade you to go back to him. He's like a fish out of water, but he'll get over it."

She showed me to the door with a very cool, "Good-bye."

I staggered up the steps her words ringing in my ears. Then walked to the house next door and leaned against the railings, unlike the green ones they were a sickly gray, matching my mood. I had to think a moment, sort myself out mentally, not knowing whether to laugh or cry.

She had said, "You could have said no." Christ, does she think I wouldn't have, had I known she was my mother? She thinks I'm as bad as she is. Then she said, "You loved every minute of it." Of course I did, that was the whole purpose of the exercise. Bloody crazy woman! She said, "You were all for it." I wasn't, I was shaking like a leaf when she came on to me, and I didn't know what to do until she told me to relax and showed me. What the hell! She's crazy.

Better get back to Fred I suppose. I was angry, hadn't said half what I wanted to. God! I'd like to go back and have another go, but it's no good, might as well forget it. I walked toward the coffee shop and angrily kicked what appeared to be an empty cigarette package on the sidewalk. Turned out to be almost full and broken cigarettes flew all over the place.

Fred was waiting patiently and seeing me put down the Racing Guide. "Well, what's the verdict?" he said anxiously.

"I'm sorry Fred, she won't take any notice of me. She's staying. Come on, let's get out of here."

We rode home in silence. Each time I looked at him I thought he would burst into tears, it was pitiful. I wanted to get the hell out of Brighton as quickly as I could, but when we got off the bus at St. Saviour's Church he said,

"I've 'ad nothin' to eat all day. Don't feel much like eatin', but I must. 'Ow 'bout you? I'll cook bacon 'n eggs. Then maybe we could go for a drink, 'ow 'bout it Frank, eh?"

He was pleading and I wanted to say no. I was angry and he, more than anyone, was responsible for what happened to me as a child. He should have told my mother to go to hell on his wedding day. We'd have all been happy then. But I hadn't the heart.

"Yeah, OK."

Strangely enough I enjoyed the meal. Perhaps what I had done that afternoon had helped after all. I knew nothing more could be done with my mother. I also realized that Tommy Kay was on night shift and had probably just got up when I arrived. But I still resented him being there; sick at the thought he may have overheard our conversation.

Fred continued whining about the loss of his wife. We were in the Pub now and after a couple of drinks he had begun to mellow. He asked how I learned that Nance was my mother. I told him most of what Annie had told me.

Much of it was news to him, especially that my mother had, prior to my inception, given birth to a stillborn child. He couldn't believe I was delivered by cesarean section, and his conviction was so forceful, I found myself having doubts. I began to question the truth of her story, as told by Annie. I recalled Annie's words about my mother being a "consummate liar."

If the story were false, what was the truth? Does anybody know? I wondered. Would I ever know the whole truth? My bitterness and loathing for her was growing and it bothered me. Did I have the right to judge my mother this way? Perhaps in time I would feel less confused.

Fred drank two to my one, and by now was feeling no pain. He rambled on about his sexual inhibitions, about being "small made." He knew, he said, that he was hopelessly inadequate as a lover. He also admitted knowing Nance had been unfaithful; that what I had told him on our long walk those many years before was true.

"But I just didn't wanna face it, pretended it didn't 'appen; afraid of losin' 'er."

He also told me the real reason he went through with the wedding back in

1925. It had little to do with love, he said. Certainly he was fond of her but it was embarrassment that finally persuaded him.

"All those wedding presents," he said, "Over two hundred pounds worth."

Then there was his family; some had come from as far away as Coventry and North Wales. He just could not bear to tell them the truth, didn't want them to see he'd been duped. And they were all so impressed with Nance.

Thus they had all joined in the conspiracy. He could see now, he said, how wrong it was; that he very much regretted it and hoped I could forgive. The drink talking I thought, but was reminded of an old saying, "A drunken tongue speaks a sober mind," and I felt some small consolation. He went on about how I had been robbed of a normal childhood but at the time he thought he was doing the right thing. I couldn't help wondering, for whom?

He spoke of noticing a marked change in Nance following my sixteenth birthday. She was miserable, he said, sullen and always naggin' me to do somethin' about yer behaviour. I wondered what he'd say if he knew the truth. I was tempted to tell him and to hell with the consequences. But the Landlord shouted, "Time Gentlemen please." We made our way home and I thought better of it.

I asked Fred where they kept their important documents. Was there by any chance a birth certificate for me anywhere around?

"Should be," he said.

From a cupboard beside the chimney he removed a cardboard box containing two large envelopes. Removing the contents of one of them, there was his birth certificate, then hers, their marriage certificate and a copy of a poem by the Penge Poet about his father's tragic death. Finally the last document and there it was, my birth certificate.

It wasn't the original, but a copy dated 25 July 1925, five months after their marriage and less than three months before I went to live with them. Obviously she had sent for it in anticipation of registering me at school, all part of the scheme as described by Annie. I couldn't help wondering what happened to the original? I also wondered when the box was put there; it was never there when I was around.

It contained no other surprises; the place of birth was shown as 47 Shaftsbury Road, Romford just as Annie had described. I mentioned to Fred that a mistake had been made, but he didn't believe it. He was sure, he said, that I was born in Granddad Keeling's house.

So, if Fred were right I could not have been delivered by cesarean section. He'd already said he didn't believe that. I pressed him for more information but all he would say was,

"Well, that ain't what they told me."

But one must remember he'd had a lot to drink.

What was I to believe? I decided not to dwell on it for the time being. Perhaps Fred was mistaken. Somehow I would solve the mystery but for now it would have to wait.

The next day Fred was on late shift so I just wandered around. First looking to see if by chance Reg was on leave, but no such luck. Dave, my ex college buddy was also away. Then I went to Mary's house, looked longingly at it and moved on. In the evening I went to a movie and walked out half way through, just not in the mood.

Thursday morning I caught an early train to London and went to see Auntie Edie. Again I was thwarted in the main purpose of my visit, they had company. I did manage to tell her I knew all about my family, but all she would say was,

"I'm sure we'll have another opportunity to discuss it."

I caught the train to Bury St. Edmunds arriving about eleven fifteen. As I walked to the barracks I smoked my last cigarette. Damn! Can't buy any, there's no where open and the NAAFI doesn't open until ten in the morning; I'll have to borrow some. But I was in for another surprise.

Seventeen

The Price Of Cigarettes

I slept a lot better, perhaps it was sheer exhaustion or had the confrontation with my mother cleared my mind? Anyhow, I woke feeling refreshed and hungry but most of all in need of a cigarette.

Whenever I ran out and had that dreadful craving I made up my mind to quit. Following a huge increase in the price, I threw my cigarette case to the ground, stomped on it with my army boot and stopped for one whole week. Then the army decided to issue us a hundred a week . . . Free! I really should have quit because the price I paid for the next pack was incalculable.

I hated borrowing cigarettes, some guys did it all the time, that's how they became known as "Freemans." I asked my roommate to sell me five till the NAAFI opened, his reply was quite to the point.

"No I won't, I'll give you one for now, then you can go to the sports pavilion and buy some."

"What d'ya mean? What are you talking about?"

He went on to tell me of an auxiliary canteen now operating in the pavilion, run by a couple of A.T.S girls and open whenever the NAAFI was closed.

"That's a bloody good idea, thanks" I said.

And after breakfast paid a visit to this new source of supply, I should have stayed in bed.

The sports pavilion was a locker room. On the ground floor there was a large open area at the entrance with changing rooms at either end for opposing teams. I opened the main door and the transformation was unbelievable. A row of tables had been set up at one end and there was everything one could possibly need, including two nice looking girls. Now don't get me wrong, I went in there for a packet of cigarettes, nothing else . . . Honest!

As I walked to the counter, the more mature, that's a nice way of saying older, of the two girls asked,

"'Morning Corporal, what can I do for you?"

The other girl was busy stacking things for display away from the action.

"Well, I really only came in for twenty Player's, but you've got such a display here I might need something else."

She told me to take my time and recited everything that was for sale.

"We have cigarettes, chocolate bars, fresh fruit, chewing gum, soap, razor blades . . . "on and on she went.

I settled for my cigarettes and a packet of razor blades. Paid my money and as I was about to leave, opened my big mouth.

"You know, this is wonderful, no longer having to rely on the NAAFI. You've saved my life and I feel I owe you more than just money. Maybe I should take you out to dinner or something. Trouble is there isn't a decent restaurant in this one-horse town but . . ."

She held up her hand.

"That's very nice of you Corporal but you're wasting your time, I'm married."

"Damn it, foiled again" I joked, emphasizing that everything I had said was purely in jest anyway.

As I opened the door to leave the other girl piped up.

"You can take me out if you like and you don't have to buy me dinner either."

This girl wasn't as pretty as the other one but she was pleasant-looking, younger, nice figure, what you might call wholesome looking. I didn't want anything to do with women at this point though. What I'd been through these last few days put me right off. But being an old softy and not wanting to hurt the girl's feelings, you know how it is, I agreed.

"How about we meet outside the gate at seven o'clock?" She suggested.

Shit! I thought, I don't really want to go out with this girl or anybody else for that matter. Why the hell don't I keep my bloody mouth shut? Notwithstanding I said,

"Yeah! OK, see yer then."

But I had no intention whatsoever of keeping that date. What a rotten bastard I am, I thought.

After supper my roommate suggested we go for a walk in Abbey Gardens and a pint at our favourite pub then back early ready for another day of this bloody course. God! We couldn't wait for it to end. As we walked out the gate the clock on the little tower of the Service Station opposite struck the half-hour, six-thirty that is. We had a nice walk in the gardens, browsed through the ruins of old Saint Edmund's original Abbey, almost 2,000 years old. I couldn't help wondering what war was like in those days?

We went in the Playhouse Bar for a drink. In the days of live theatre, it was the lounge where patrons flocked during intermission. In the thirties the theatre had been converted to a cinema and the lounge to a pub. It was not, however, your average, rowdy wartime establishment. Its clientele consisted mainly of business types, lawyers and local gentry. Flossie, the barmaid, was her usual cordial self.

We had two drinks and having lots of time, took the long way back, along Kings Road and down the hill to the barrack gates. To my everlasting shame, that A.T.S. gal was standing there and she saw me as I saw her. Damn, there was no way out.

I went up to her all innocent like and said,

"Well, where were you at seven o'clock?"

"Where was I? Where were you y' mean? I've been waiting here since five to seven. What on earth happened?"

I glanced at that same clock on the little tower of the service station and the hands told me she had been waiting for two hours and fifty minutes. God! Did I ever feel bad? Gotta make up for this somehow, I thought.

"Well, I don't have a watch but I'm sure it was close to seven when I came out," I lied. "I looked around and couldn't see you anywhere so I went for a walk in Abbey Gardens with my friend. I'm terribly sorry about this, have you really been waiting all this time?"

"Yes I have," she said, "And I must have seen at least a thousand servicemen over the last three hours."

"And you didn't see anyone you liked more than me?"

She gave me a coy look but said nothing.

In the early days of war we were subject to curfew. Monday to Friday it was eleven, weekends midnight. Since this was Friday I had just about an hour left, more than enough for me. She looked very young even in uniform, probably no more than eighteen. Bet she just joined up.

"Well we haven't much time. How can I make up for what happened tonight, what would you like to do?" I asked.

"Hmm! Well, I have to be in at eleven too. I live on Hospital Road it would be nice if you would walk me home."

"Where on Hospital Road do you live? That's quite a long road."

"Do you know the Pub?"

"Yes I do, I've been in there a couple of times."

"Well my father is an employee of the Brewery and we live next door."

"Oh, well that's not too far so we have lots of time," I said, wishing I'd made some excuse about having to retire early in preparation for a busy day.

During war time every day was a working day, no such thing as week-ends or holidays although we did get ten days leave every three months, if you were in England that is. Sometimes we got a Saturday or a Sunday off and occasionally a whole weekend. But in addition to our regular duties there was Air Raid Precaution (ARP) patrol, Anti Aircraft (AA) duty on top of the Tower of the Keep, guard duty about once a week and Orderly Corporal about the same. So it was a busy life and I didn't want to complicate it.

Seems a nice girl though, wonder if she can cook. Bloody Army grub's awful. I was reminded of dear old mum, "The way to a man's heart is via his stomach.

We walked casually toward her home. She told me her name was Rose and that she had joined the A.T.S in May of that year as soon as she turned eighteen. I told her I was Frank by name and frank by nature and my . . . she interrupted me.

"I know your last name."

"How?"

"Oh, just asked around."

Hmm! This girl really is serious, pretty determined too.

"Been in the Army since June, '37", I said. "I'll be twenty in November."

"Oh really, have you got a girlfriend?"

"No I haven't."

"That's surprising. Good looking, no girl friend, I can't believe it."

"Well it's true."

"You must have had girl friends though, eh?"

"Yeah, but not for a couple of years."

I knew at once that I shouldn't have said it.

"Oh what happened, did you have a row or something?"

"Yes we did" I said, and wished she wouldn't ask awkward questions.

For some peculiar reason I was using the affair with my mother as my last girl friend. This could be difficult if I'm not careful. Damn the woman, that affair will haunt me for the rest of my bloody life.

How ironic, I thought. Most men think lovingly of their mother all their lives. I'd read about men in the last throes of death on the battlefield crying out in agony for their mother. Me, I'm doing my best to forget mine.

We had walked for a while in silence; me wrapped up in that painful thought, she I think, waiting for me to say more about the ending of my last affair.

Then she said,

"For a moment there you looked miles away and quite sad, was it that bad? . . . If you'd rather not talk about it I'll understand."

She put her arm through mine squeezing it as if genuinely concerned about my feelings. For a moment I was carried away with the closeness of this person. It was rather nice to have someone interested in me who cared. Oh come on, I said to myself, I've only known her for five minutes, what the hell?

"Well it's all over now," I said. "It was a long time ago and I'd rather forget it so let's talk about something else shall we?"

We had walked down the hill and turned left on Hospital Road. There was about an acre of vacant land on the corner then a high brick wall on the south and west sides of the property. Several feet of the wall were exposed on the west side before it disappeared into thick undergrowth. About a hundred yards from her home she moved off the sidewalk into the seclusion of the west wall and leaned her back against it.

"We're nearly there, I'd like to stop here for a minute if you don't mind, there's always so many people around the pub."

As she was speaking she took my two hands into hers and pulled me a little closer.

"The moment I saw you in the pavilion this morning I liked you, having met you I like you even more. I get the feeling you have suffered some kind of tragedy, there's a sad look in your eyes. Am I right?"

She certainly is perceptive I thought, an uncanny remark for one so young.

"Well, sort of" I said. "I just returned from compassionate leave. My mother and stepfather split up after fourteen years of marriage. I went home to try and sort things out but it didn't work."

Again I thought, why the hell am I saying all this to a stranger? Somehow though it was a relief to talk about it and besides, I rather like this girl.

"That's a shame," she said, "I know what it's like when something happens to a parent. My father has been in a nursing home for the last ten years; he suffers with neurasthenia, a sort of nervous disorder caused by the last war. It's been very difficult without him. What happened to your father?"

I was sick and tired of lies and deception but there was no way I could tell the whole truth.

"Well it's a long story, but the truth is, he just didn't want to marry my mother. He was a young artist, only eighteen and, you know, artists can be odd sometimes."

She looked at me a little strained as if she wanted to laugh but was afraid she might hurt my feelings.

"Ah well, not to worry, we're both in the same boat. I think you and I have a lot in common," she said.

I thought that was a bit presumptuous but didn't say anything. More to the point, I'd only known this girl half-an-hour and here I was telling her everything. But somehow I was enjoying it; she seemed more mature than her eighteen years. I really think she cares about me, I told myself and that made me feel better than I'd felt in a long time.

There was a street lamp on the opposite side of the road, dark and sombre, a grim reminder of war and a blackout in force. But it was a clear night and a full moon so she could see her watch without any difficulty.

"Oh! It's twenty-five to eleven and you've got to walk back. Look, I know we've only just met but I've really enjoyed being with you. 'Gone With the Wind' is on at the Odeon, I'd love to see it. They say it's a wonderful picture and I think it might be good for you."

"Well, I went to the pictures Wednesday night in Brighton, walked out half way through. Couldn't stand it somehow. But you could be right, yeah! OK, where shall we meet?"

"Brighton eh! Is that where you're from?"

"Yes it is."

"Oh that's nice, anyway we'd better get going. How about we meet under the Town Hall clock about three tomorrow afternoon?"

"Sounds good to me."

"Would you walk me to the corner? Then you just turn left up the hill, it'll be quicker for you."

She pulled me toward her and gave me a little peck on the cheek and I walked her to the corner.

"I was really mad about that long wait," she said. "But it was worth it. 'Night, see you at three, don't be late!"

"'Night," I said. "I'm glad, and no I won't be late."

She walked to a door at the far end of the pub and entered, disappearing from sight.

I walked briskly, thinking I really should get a new watch, the old one never did work after I wore it in the shower that time. Now, I gotta think. This girl is pretty serious; she found out my name and waited nearly three hours. Unbelievable! I must never do that again.

Her father hadn't been at home for ten years. So, she'd had him till she was eight. That's rough, especially for a girl. Funny how she thought I was sad, wasn't far wrong was she. Another thing, she wasn't bad looking, smelled nice too. I noticed she had thickset jaws, according to my intelligence training that indicated a strong will, knew what she wanted and went for it. That's not a bad thing. She had nice eyes too and a very kissable mouth, just enough lipstick. Not like some girls who used too much.

The thing I liked most though was she seemed genuinely interested in me, as if she cared. Nah, can't be, she's only just met me! She certainly was mature for her age though. Most girls were flighty, fickle or silly; you know what I mean. Did I really want to get serious? I asked myself. No, I haven't got over my mother yet. What a stupid thing to be saying at my age. But there are so many things to reconcile in my mind. Why the hell can't I forget . . . I would have to, can't go through the rest of my life like this, I'll go stark raving mad. But how do you get over having sex with your own mother?

Sure would be nice if I could just talk it over with somebody. The only person I'd talked to was the M.O., wonder if I should go and see him again? He did say I should if I felt the need, but I didn't fancy going over every little detail with him again. Can't really imagine myself telling anybody. Wonder what would happen if somebody like Fred found out and took me to court; wonder if anybody would believe me? Incest is a pretty serious crime, maximum penalty fourteen years! I shuddered. It would be five years before I told anyone else. I never did tell Rose, she went to her grave at a very young age not knowing.

By the time I reached the barracks I had made up my mind. I would see this girl the next day but I would not get too involved. Above all, I'm not going to tell her anymore than I already have. I was sort of looking forward to tomorrow though, nice to have somebody to share life with, to feel somebody out there really likes me and is interested in me. And to think, all this started because I needed a packet of cigarettes.

Apart from military personnel, no one had shown the slightest interest in me for years, I told myself. But deep down I knew I wasn't being honest, there had been others but I'd been too pre-occupied with my own selfish thoughts. Now I come to think of it, I'd been wallowing in self-pity all this time. Ever since that last night with my mother I'd shut people out of my life, couldn't bring myself to be serious about anything or anybody. Bloody fool!

Lights out was at ten so I undressed in the dark. With the blackout, thick black screens had to be placed over every window so it was pitch dark. I had a habit of getting into bed, lighting a last cigarette and just lying there relaxed and enjoying the sense of satisfaction as I inhaled and the smoke hit the back of my throat; I would dwell a while on the day's events.

Today had been quite a day, the fickle finger of fate as Sergeant George

Ruggles, my good friend, mentor and First World War veteran would say. I took a cigarette and lit it, only one left. I'm smoking twenty a day, too much, gotta cut down. Then I made one last decision.

I would write a letter to everybody involved in what happened to me as a child. I would tell 'em all what I thought of them, make them suffer a bit like I had. Then that would be the end of it and I could put the whole darn thing out of my mind. On second thought, I won't do that, what's the good? I can't be like that anyway but I will write to them just to get it off my chest. I stubbed out my cigarette and slept well.

Saturday I only had to work until eleven-fifteen. I pressed my pants to look my best for my date. Long time since I'd had a date and I found myself looking forward to it. At least this girl was taking my mind off other things.

Whenever we went into town we were expected to look smart. There was a Guard Commander at the gate to give you the once over and if you weren't properly dressed, send you back. The town was also alive with military police whose job it was to see law and order maintained and traditional military standards of dress and behaviour upheld. So, at one hundred and twenty paces to the minute it would take me no more than ten minutes to reach the Town Hall. I left at twenty to three anyway. Didn't want to keep this girl waiting again.

As I walked toward town I told myself again not to get too involved. I'd said too much already and don't need more complications. I would just be my usual cool self and tell the truth but not all of it. There was no way I wanted to lie; I'd had enough of that.

Half way up Risbygate Street I bumped into Sergeant Ruggles and his wife. I told them about my date and they cautioned me in a kindly, parental sort of way to be wary of wartime affairs. They'd seen some tragic failures in the last one. When I mentioned she was one of the girls in the Auxiliary Canteen, George said he knew her. Before being recalled for duty he too had worked at the Brewery, knew her father well and had met the family.

"Isn't he in a nursing home in Ipswich?" I asked.

George nodded. They wished me well and I left.

I carried on to the Town Hall. It was still only five-to- three and she wasn't there, just a very attractive girl in civvies. I looked at her, turned away, looked again. It was her! I couldn't believe it, how come she's in civvies? She looked a totally different person. I had only seen her in uniform which hardly did any girl justice and wasn't terribly feminine. But, here was this girl in a beautiful looking outfit that you could tell wasn't off the rack and did she ever look smart?

She spotted me and approached all smiles, recognizing my astonishment. I saluted her, the proper thing for a man in uniform to do when meeting a lady. Not the longest way up shortest way down military type of salute, just a slow casual touching of the cap with the fingers and thumb together. She noticed.

"Ah, the perfect gentleman . . . that's nice, thank you."

"Are you allowed to wear civvies?" I asked.

"Well I was only called up ten days ago so this is the first time I've tried it.

Nobody said I couldn't, so until I'm told otherwise I'll just do it."

"Well I must say, you look absolutely stunning."

She put her arm in mine and gently guided me toward the High Street.

"Thank you, that's the best compliment I've had today and coming from you, it means a great deal to me."

"Where're we going?" I asked.

"Oh, well, I was just in the store where I used to work. I told them about you and they insist I take you to meet them, do you mind?"

"Well . . . No . . . I suppose not."

And so we walked down High Street past the Playhouse bar where Flossie the barmaid worked, to the most exclusive women's clothing store in town. As we turned to go in I said,

"You used to work here?"

"Four years, almost to the day."

I did some quick arithmetic; she must have started here when she was fourteen. No that couldn't be right, must have misunderstood her last night.

I was introduced first to the manager, a very charming and extremely well spoken lady in her mid fifties, and then two other staff, much younger but equally well spoken. In fact, I was very impressed by the way they spoke. I suddenly realized this girl Rose doesn't talk a bit like the locals, so her four years here had served her well.

I was pleased about that because I found the local brogue very irritating. "Oi say where you now go-wan oi say? . . . 'e say, Oi go-wan dow-an tow-an t'due sum sharr-pan, 'e say, an oi gotta gue t'the Pust Arfuss." Believe it or not, that's Post Office. Honestly, that's how they talk in Suffolk.

Rose seemed well liked but we had things to do. Outside I asked her about how long she had been working, was I mistaken? No, she said, it was true. She had started work just after leaving school at fourteen. It was a necessity as her older sisters were married and all she and her mother had to live on was a small pension from the brewery and taking in lodgers, so she had no option. I felt sorry for her, remembering my own struggle and that of millions of other Britons during the depression years.

We spent the next hour in a nearby restaurant getting to know each other. Despite all my good intentions, I found myself telling her my life story, all except the sex part, of course. That would always have to remain a secret. I ended by confirming my efforts to reconcile my mother's marriage. I didn't want her to think I had lied last night.

She told me more about her family; she had two sisters, Norma who lived in London, and Helen, married with two children living near Sudbury, just a short bus ride from Bury St. Edmunds. She also explained that her mother was visiting her father that day in Ipswich as she did every other Saturday.

The two sisters took turns visiting him on the alternate Saturdays. Normally, she would have a weeks holiday the last week in September and would visit him. She had always worked on Saturdays so couldn't join her mother. This year she wouldn't get the usual holiday and her mother had suggested she go with her that day, but she had declined saying she had to work.

"In fact," she said, "I didn't want to miss my date with you. I'll go and see him the first Saturday you're on duty."

I chided her in a friendly way for neglecting her father for me.

"Well . . . You've become very important to me," she said.

We enjoyed Gone with the Wind, despite seeing the end of the film first because of the long line up. I hated that usually but with this classic it was well worth it.

I took her for a drink at the Playhouse Bar just four doors from the store where she worked, she knew Flossie well. The pub was just closing as we arrived home so to avoid the crowd we continued to the end of the wall where we had lingered the previous night.

It had been a pleasant afternoon and evening, I really enjoyed myself and felt free of the mental anguish. I also liked Rose, she reminded me of Mary. Our good night consisted of more than a peck on the cheek but nothing untoward. For the remainder of that week every free moment was spent together and there were times when passions were aroused.

My Instructors course was finished; recruits would arrive on the following Thursday so we both had the weekend off. On Friday she suggested I pick her up the next afternoon at her home. She wasn't ready when I arrived so she ushered me into their front room. There I came face to face with her mother and she wasn't interested in introductions.

She hit me with,

"I don't like this situation at all, Rose has been going with a very nice boy, Geoffrey for three years and we're all very fond of him."

Rose was as stunned as I was. My first inclination was to tell her mother to get stuffed, that I didn't have to take this kind of crap. And I should have but wanted to avoid embarrassment.

"Well Madam," I said, " I'm sorry you feel like that about your daughter's choice of companionship. But surely she is old enough to make her own decisions. I wish I could say it was nice meeting you."

And with that, I stalked out of the room to the front door never expecting to see her again. Meanwhile Rose was yelling at her mother.

"Mother, how could you be so rude, I've told you it's all over between Geoff and me and I'm going with Frank whether you like it or not."

She ran after me crying and begging me to ignore her mother's outburst. I felt sorry for her.

"Ah, forget it" I said, "It's you I'm going with not your mother."

She kept on though, fearing this would affect our relationship. Foolishly, after knowing her for only ten days I started making commitments. I should have known better.

A few days later while walking in the country her conversation took a more intimate turn. First she asked if I'd ever had sex. I said yes. She said she had too and hoped it wouldn't make any difference.

"Of course not," I said.

She emphasized there had only been one man; I presumed it was Geoffrey. Had there been more than one for me? Absolutely not! Was it the girl I had left two years ago? Yes. How had I "gone without" for so long? I told her it was important I knew and cared for someone before I could indulge in such activities.

On the Thursday afternoon Rose said she would like me to meet her in the pub for a drink. Her mother would join us because she wanted to apologize. I asked what had caused the change of heart, Rose said her mother now realized she was serious about me and would have left Geoff anyway. I wasn't impressed but agreed to go along with the request.

The pub was a cozy little place. We went into the Lounge, the more refined part that most women preferred. Mother came shortly afterwards and half-heartedly apologized, more for Rose's sake, I felt. I asked what she would like to drink and she requested a Suffolk Nip, a more potent brew than other beers, more expensive but cheaper than liquor. I was surprised at how many she drank with no apparent effect. I mentioned this to Rose, she said her father used to get free beer every day at work and mother had developed the capacity to keep pace with him. I would witness this talent many times during the months that followed.

The next day Rose said mother had very much enjoyed my company and I was welcome at their house any time. In fact, mother was going to Ipswich on Saturday as usual and I was invited to spend the day there. Rose would demonstrate her culinary skills by providing a nice home cooked dinner. Naturally, this was appealing since army food wasn't the best.

I found myself alone with Rose from about eleven in the morning. She had asked me to come as early as possible so that we could, "Make a nice long day of it." She did prepare an excellent meal and I was careful to compliment her.

Following the meal we enjoyed a leisurely cigarette then did the dishes after which Rose said she would like to change. She went upstairs and after a few minutes called to me to join her. I wasn't at all surprised when I saw her wearing nothing but a very sexy and provocative slip.

I had suppressed my urges until now but could no longer resist. It was a mutually gratifying encounter and incredibly, she was every bit as skilled and experienced as my mother but younger and much more attractive. I was hooked.

Eighteen

Marry In Haste

Guard duty in those early days of the war was not a particularly onerous task. As Guard Commander the primary task was to see that sentries were changed every two hours. There were other routine responsibilities but the one advantage was that during the night one could catch up on letter writing.

After meeting Rose I decided to write to those involved in taking me from the Bunton family as a child, it still bothered me. Except for my mother, they could never know the full impact of their actions and the whole affair could so easily have been avoided.

I wrote first to the Masons, Uncle George had played the major roll; he had been the go between and raised the issue of my existence on the wedding day. "He thought it was a great idea," mum had said. He should have kept his mouth shut from the very beginning. And his reaction on learning that Annie had told me everything really ticked me off.

It was a scathing letter, no exaggeration or untruths, just about the trauma and the hurt I suffered because of their insensitivity and indifference to the plight of a defenseless little five-year-old. I ended the letter by saying, while I appreciated the kindness they had shown me over the years, I wanted nothing more to do with them.

The day before my twentieth birthday I received a reply from Annie in which she said they very much regretted my decision but would continue to send my usual birthday gift, a Postal Order for two shillings and sixpence. My first impulse was to send it back but upon reflection, decided to cash it and donate it to the Salvation Army or "Sally Ann" as it was affectionately known.

I also wrote a long letter to Jessie, not a pleasant task because she had always been my favourite sister but I felt it had to be done. I expressed surprise and disappointment that I had been given up so easily and to complete strangers, without warning, preparation or orientation.

I never did write to mum, she was aware of my feelings. My letter to Auntie Edie was never answered. Her position was that they'd done what seemed best at the time and she felt no remorse. I didn't write to my mother either; there were no words I could risk putting on paper that would adequately describe my sentiments. That she was my biological mother left me confused and at a loss to know what to say or how to say it. She was out of sight and therefore out of mind, at least for the time being.

On my twentieth birthday Rose and I had our first serious quarrel, one of many that should have convinced me we were unsuited. On Sundays the pubs closed from two-thirty till five then opened till ten. I was on duty all day but arrived at our pub about seven; my birthday party had obviously been in progress since opening time. Also, two army friends, Frank and Tom had been invited. Rose wore a rather revealing dress, chosen specifically for the occasion she insisted.

A neighbour was playing the accordion and I was asked to lead the throng in the customary singalong. I was in good voice then and made a point of learning the lyrics to all the latest songs. The only drawback was, as with the musician, there was little time to drink.

When the pub closed at ten everybody was in a jolly mood and loathe to quit. Rose persuaded her mother who was feeling no pain, to invite us into her house to continue the celebration. They bought a supply of booze including her mother's favourite Suffolk Nip and we all adjourned to the living room. I had consumed less than the others and was stone cold sober. I was expected to play host and, returning to the living room laden with glasses, saw Rose sitting on Tom's lap. There weren't enough chairs and so not wanting to be a party pooper I said nothing.

Standing by the door and over the babble of conversation, I heard Tom shout.

"Hey Frank," meaning me, "look at this."

And he proceeded to slobber all over Rose kissing her full on the mouth. She offered no resistance and I was informed it was just to make me jealous. In fact, I found it revolting. Tom was a married man, somewhat lacking in personal hygiene and very drunk.

I decided discretion was the better part of valour and thought if I ignored them it would stop. But it wasn't long before the other Frank demanded his turn and she slid onto his lap to oblige. I suggested that since we'd all had our little bit of fun maybe it was time to quit. They ignored me.

I could never stomach a drunken man slobbering over a woman. In this case it involved two men and my girl friend. None of them seemed to understand my distaste, least of all, Rose who continued to flaunt herself. So I walked out.

I hadn't gone far before the other Frank came staggering after me, berating me for being so sensitive and a spoil sport; it was all meant in good fun, he insisted. Rose was crying and upset, could I not overlook it and return to the party? He too, was very drunk and I thought it better not to argue so I returned. But the atmosphere was uncomfortable and we all left shortly after.

The following day, in the presence of her mother and both sober, I told Rose that if our relationship was to continue, such behaviour was unacceptable. She agreed and apologized but her mother was quite belligerent, saying Rose could do as she wished and I had no right to chastise her.

"Who do you think you are?" she snapped.

It was a sign of things to come. As time passed I would reflect on this incident and realize I should have kept on walking.

Since I was now twenty and medical category A1, it was only a matter of time before I would be posted to a more active status. Only those who were too old, too young or who had some disability remained in Bury St. Edmunds. It was as much this fact as anything, I think, that prompted Rose to raise the question of commitment early in January 1940. It came more in the form of an ultimatum. Mother was away in Ipswich and we had just enjoyed one of our Saturday afternoon lovemaking sessions.

"Do you realize we've been having sex for almost four months?" she began.

"Yes," and without thinking, "and you get better all the time."

"Well I deserve more of a commitment, I think we should at least get engaged?"

To tell the truth, I had never given the subject the slightest consideration and felt guilty. Of course, she was absolutely right. Here I was enjoying all the benefits without formally accepting any of the responsibilities.

So without thinking and not realizing the implications of what I was doing, I said, "Yes, of course, why don't we go and choose the ring this afternoon?"

Naturally she was thrilled and no time was wasted. The ring was purchased, it fit perfectly and she was wearing it that same afternoon. We were in the pub celebrating when mother returned from Ipswich. Rose and I had to carry her to her bed that night! She waved her forefinger at thin air, swayed on her feet a little and said,

"I" . . . gulp . . . "Shoul'nt jrrink on an emchy shtomach."

And was soon lost in a drunken sleep.

Winter gave way to spring, March went out like a lion and so did I. We had another quarrel, this time because of her mother's domineering attitude, dictating what we should and should not do. She was forever interfering with our lives and criticizing my every action. She was particularly incensed at our sexual activities; she had learned somehow that we were "doing it," as she put it.

I would say to her, "Jealousy will get you nowhere," which only made her more irate.

Anyway, I walked out again and stayed away for a couple of days but being engaged, it soon blew over and things were back to normal.

Saturday April 6, 1940, mother was home when I arrived and I knew I'd been under discussion; she blushed profusely and looked away from me as I greeted her. Uh, huh, wonder what I've done wrong now?

As we walked toward town Rose dropped a bombshell.

"Mum and I have been talking things over and I think it would be nice if we got married on June 22nd. That's a Saturday, what do you think?"

Prior to the outbreak of war engagements were long, years sometimes. Now that had changed but it still meant you were betrothed, a solemn commitment to eventual marriage. It was not uncommon in those days for men to be sued for breach of promise if, without just cause, they didn't fulfill their obligation. I had not realized at the time the full implication of what I was doing and was now taken completely off guard. There had been no previous discussion about marriage and for a moment I was speechless. She noticed my hesitancy and before I could make any response.

"Well, you don't seem very enthusiastic, what's the matter. Sometimes I think all you want me for is what you get out of me." She lowered her head looking hurt.

"There's nothing the matter," I said. "It's just so sudden, you caught me by surprise. But if that's what you'd like, that's fine." As an afterthought I said, "Being under twenty-one I'll have to get my Commanding Officer's permission, but that's no problem."

"Oh! I'm glad you agree" she said, "I'm so afraid you'll get posted overseas and I'll be left alone. There's so many girls getting left like that these days. Mum thinks we should contact your mother and I agree, I'd like to meet her; we've been going together for seven months now and she doesn't even know we're engaged, does she? Mum thinks it's terrible the way you treat your mother. Of course, she doesn't know what happened when you were little and I don't think we should tell her do you?"

"No I don't," I said, wishing I hadn't told her anything either.

God! I wish her mother would mind her own business.

"Well, let's think about that a bit more" I said. "I'm not even sure of her address. I suppose I could get in touch with her through Fred but I'm not fussy about it."

There the matter was left for the moment and Rose went on about what she intended to wear.

"I won't wear white. Mum's old fashioned and she knows I'm not a virgin."

Who would be invited? Just the immediate family she thought, did I agree? Before I could answer she said,

"You know, we really must get your mother here for the wedding, that's the least we can do."

Although not keen on the idea I could appreciate their concern. I realized it would be difficult for them to understand my lack of enthusiasm, not knowing all the sordid details. I was determined not to disclose anything more about my past so I made plans to contact my mother.

Why would I want to renew this relationship one might ask? And what happened to all that anger and disgust that was so overwhelming less than a year ago? I have asked myself the same question many times. I cannot explain it, I can only describe how I felt at the time. Rose and her mother persuaded me to re-establish contact, whether I would have done so without their intervention I don't know. In any case it would not have been so soon. In retrospect, perhaps I wanted a mother so badly that anything was better than nothing. And while my feelings toward her were mixed to say the least, there was this inner compulsion to develop some sort of relationship. Anyway, back to my story.

I couldn't, for the life of me, remember the name of the street where I had visited her the previous September. I knew it was Number 54 but that was all. The only thing to do was contact Fred. I knew it was no use writing to him, he would either take too long to reply or ignore my letter completely.

I knew when I left him in September he was on a late shift, so with the aid of an old 1939 calendar I worked out when he would be on an early shift and determined the next one started Sunday, April 14.

None of us had phones but we all knew the number of the pay phone on Ditchling Road and by prior arrangement, used it for years.

On the Saturday I followed the standard procedure and sent Fred a telegram asking him to be at the telephone kiosk at 6 PM the following day for an "urgent message." At the appointed hour, Rose and I went into my Company Office and I made the call at His Majesty's expense, strictly illegal, of course, but a common practice. Rose was allowed to accompany me because she was in uniform and well known as a Clerk in the A.T.S. Company Head Quarters. The Auxiliary Canteen had long since closed; something to do with legal positions in relation to the NAAFI.

The phone made the familiar English double ring, once, twice, "Oh! God! Don't tell me he's not there," I said.

In the middle of the third ring I heard this very pleasant female voice say, "Hello!"

I jumped because I immediately recognized the voice, my mother!

"Oh, hello," I said, "I didn't expect to hear you on the other end of the line, what's happened?"

"Well It's a long story, I'm back with Fred, since January. Poor devil he couldn't survive without me. Anyway, what's the urgent message?"

I said it was her I'd wanted to contact anyway, then broke the news that I was to be married on June 22nd, and would like her to meet the bride-to-be. She wanted to know how long I had known "this girl" and said it was all very sudden and didn't I think we were rushing things a bit?

I pointed out that I might very well be posted overseas any day and we wanted to take the plunge before that happened.

"Well, you're old enough to know what you're doing but you know the old saying, `Marry in haste, repent at leisure' I'd hate to see you make a mistake."

More out of ego than anything I assured her it was no mistake and we went on to arrange for the two of us to visit them the next weekend. Rose and my mother had a brief conversation before we hung up the phone.

Rose was thrilled at the thought of at last meeting my family and couldn't wait to get home to tell mum. For my part, I was amazed at the cool, calm and collected way my mother had talked on the phone, almost as if we had never been apart or that anything untoward had ever happened between us. There was certainly none of the acrimony of our last meeting.

I took Rose to Brighton the next weekend to meet my parents. Rose had written to her sister Norma in London telling her the news and the train we were catching. So when we reached the barrier at Liverpool Street Station, her sister and husband Frank Borden were there.

I was introduced and they insisted we go to their home in North London for the night and go on to Brighton the next morning. I politely said there was no way we could do that; my mother was expecting us in a couple of hours and there was no way I could advise her of any change in plans. Besides, we only had until

Sunday night.

I promised we'd spend the next available weekend with them. Norma was livid; she could not understand why we couldn't just do that little thing for her. I had made an enemy in the family and would suffer the consequences.

It was an intriguing weekend spent with my mother and Fred. At first I felt awkward, looking at my mother every now and then and revisiting all that had happened between us. She played the part of the dutiful mother as if it were the most natural thing in the world for her. I was amazed at the casual, effortless way she conducted herself the entire time. She and Rose went out shopping together and I learned later the nature of at least some of their conversation.

We saw very little of Fred on the Friday and Saturday. His early shift started on the Sunday and we had left to return to Bury St. Edmunds before he got home.

While my mother and Rose went shopping I went round to Reg's house on the off-chance he might be on leave but no, he had been home two weeks earlier. I returned home and sat in solitude of that very same room where, almost four-and-a-half years ago, it had all begun.

I felt the anger and bitterness again and wanted to get as far away as possible. I regretted the visit and vowed never to return. I hated everything and everybody, including Rose. Then I started feeling guilty again. It was my fault, I could have said no, why the hell didn't I? At the time I knew it was adultery, I knew it was wrong, why did I do it? And why do I keep tormenting myself?

I've been through this a hundred times and gotten over it, now it's rearing its ugly head again. All Rose's fault, I told myself, but for her I wouldn't be here, I wouldn't be going through all this again, to hell with all women! When they returned I had great difficulty composing myself.

As the evening wore on the hostility subsided. Watching the ease with which my mother conducted herself made me realize I too must put the past behind me and stop tormenting myself over something that could not be undone. Once the toothpaste is out of the tube you can't put it back. I was only sixteen, seduced by an older woman who should have known better, I rationalized. The same thing almost happened between a young married woman and me on Ladysmith Road, I recalled. But on second thoughts, that would have been just adultery not incest. My only consolation, like Oedipus, I was totally unaware this woman was my mother. By the time we retired to our separate beds I had overcome my despair.

On the Sunday morning while Rose was upstairs I had a brief conversation with my mother; what had happened to the affair with Tommy? I asked. Because of the specialized nature of his work, she explained, he was moved to a number of cities within a short period. She couldn't face the constant upheaval and decided to return to Fred who welcomed her with open arms.

I asked if this meant the end of that relationship, her response was that the period spent with Tommy had been the happiest of her life. He was trying to get a permanent position somewhere but his choices were limited. She concluded by saying,

"I didn't want to come back to Fred but there was no one else I could turn to; I hadn't a friend in the world. Anyway, who knows what the future may hold."

It was obvious she was a lonely, unhappy and unsettled woman and I felt pity rather than animosity.

When it came time to leave she surprised me by insisting she accompany us to Brighton Station. When we arrived, Rose had to go to the toilet to fix her French panties, the most fashionable underwear of the day. They had two buttons on the side, one had come off previously and now the second had given way under the strain. Hope she's not pregnant, I mused. Finding ourselves alone again my mother asked for the second time,

"How long did you say you've known her?"

"Oh, six, seven months. In fact, now I come to think of it, I met her the day after I got back from visiting you last September."

"You're not in love with her are you."

"Love . . . what the hell's that?" I said. "I've never had much success with love have I. As a child I dearly loved the Buntons and was robbed of that. And remember Mary? I really did love her. I was in love with you once too . . . "

"Now I suppose you hate me" she interrupted with a tinge of bitterness.

For one fleeting moment the acrimony and disgust I had felt as recently as the previous day came rushing back but I banished it from my mind. I knew she was suffering, perhaps more than I.

"No I don't hate you. I'll never get over what happened but I harbour no hatred . . . You seem so lonely and so unhappy and believe it or not, that bothers me."

She gave my arm an appreciative squeeze and changed the subject.

"You two are not at all well suited you know. I'm sure the attraction is purely physical."

"Oh! I don't know, I like her, we get along pretty good . . . She's very good to me in many ways."

"Maybe so, but that's hardly enough on which to base a marriage. I wish you wouldn't rush into things. Remember what I said about marrying in haste."

Rose came back and the conversation ended, but I would hear that refrain repeatedly, much sooner than expected.

We had a compartment to ourselves and as the electric train sped on it's way to London, Rose rambled on about our visit. She liked my mother she said, especially the free and easy way she talked about intimate things, and she had no hang-ups about pre-marital sex. They had openly discussed the subject and she concluded by saying it was hard to believe I had only recently learned she was my mother.

"She acted as if she'd been a mother to you all your life, I still don't understand the whole story."

So I was forced to go over it again, something I've found myself doing repeatedly over the years.

Back in barracks, I made up my mind to write my mother, thank her for her hospitality and reassure her we weren't rushing things. I thought it might lead to an ongoing correspondence, but somehow I never got around to it.

I was walking toward our Company Office, it's Wednesday tomorrow, I thought, first of May. Frank and Tom, the two characters that had helped celebrate my birthday had been posted to France. It was only a matter of time before I would follow. My thoughts were interrupted; I saw, Rose hurrying toward me with a slip of paper in her hand. My mother had phoned and the operator, knowing Rose and I were engaged, gave her the message, "Please phone this evening at eight o'clock."

She must have been inside the call box when I phoned because she picked up the reciever before the end of the first ring. Sounding apprehensive, she asked me to be patient and to bear with her. She needed help but I should not feel obligated, if I declined she would understand.

"Why don't you just go ahead and tell me what's on your mind?" I said.

"Thank you dear," she said, "I appreciate that. Anyway, Tommy has got himself a job in Bury St. Edmunds of all places; he starts there next Monday the sixth. I'm leaving Fred again on Saturday . . . Poor old Fred, I feel sorry for him but I just can't stand it any longer. He'll be on early shift so I'm meeting Tommy at the station at eleven. Our train gets into Bury at four fifty-five and we were wondering if you could find us somewhere to stay for a night or two, till we find a place?"

I was about to reply but she went on.

"I know you must think I'm awful treating Fred like this, but you know, it's no life with him. He only needs me as a housekeeper. I feel more like a skivvy everyday and I'm so unhappy."

I heard the break in her voice.

"Of course we'll help" I said, "I'm sure Rose or her mum will know somewhere where you could stay. Tell you what, we'll meet you at the station on Saturday and by then we'll have something arranged."

She thanked me for being "Such a treasure" a term she had used only once before. She talked with Rose for a few moments then terminated the call.

Back at Rose's house I related what had happened. I had to go into some detail for her mother's sake; explaining why my mother had left her husband yet again. She fully understood, she said and, what's more, she knew someone who had a nice little furnished house for rent on Whiting Street. The next day it was all arranged, I paid the first weeks rent and on the Friday we bought a few groceries. Rose added the feminine touch by producing a bunch of daffodils.

We met them at the railway station and Tommy was a bit cool. The off-handish way I had treated him when we first met obviously bothered him. But when they saw the house they were thrilled and most appreciative. It contained everything they needed and they stayed there for eighteen months.

On the Sunday, my mother met Rose's mum, Tommy didn't come, too busy getting ready for his new job we were told; and that's the way it continued. Only once did we go for a drink with the two of them together. He was invited to the wedding but declined at the last minute because of work which caused quite a problem.

Thursday May 9, at seven-thirty in the evening Rose and I met with the

Vicar of St. Mary's church and arrangements for our marriage on June 22 were finalized. Had we not done so the marriage would probably never have taken place. On the following day, the world as we had known it changed forever. Nothing, including my relationship with Rose, would ever be the same.

It was on Friday May 10, 1940, that Hitler launched his Blitzkrieg in Europe and the phony war was over. Luxembourg fell the same day, Holland five days later and despite the allied efforts, Belgium was overrun by May 28. But before that, on May 26, the miracle of Dunkirk began to unfold. From the moment it all started, life for us was turned up side down. We all matured a great deal in those early days and we would soon age before our time.

The threat of invasion on the south coast of England was very real. I became involved in the defense of some strategic positions and facilities in East Anglia. I was away for days on end and returned so exhausted I had little time or energy for anything. This, of course, did not sit well with Rose. She couldn't understand why it was always me being sent on these assignments. I tried to explain to her that it was because of previous training but she wasn't convinced and neither was her mother.

Once France fell the air raids began and Bury St. Edmunds was an early target. It's hard to believe now, but it was bombed several times because it had a large sugarbeet factory. German Intelligence was convinced the morale of the British population would suffer if sugar supplies were destroyed. And so it was, that the powers-that-be decided we would work by night and sleep by day. This played havoc with everyone's social life, but there was a war on, so we all took it in our stride . . . Except Rose.

In the days immediately prior to my marriage, Murphy's law prevailed, everything that could go wrong, did. We received a letter from the Vicar, asking us to attend a pre-marriage counseling session on Thursday evening, June 20. The letter ended by saying, "Perhaps you (me that is) would be good enough to bring along the document certifying that the banns of marriage have been read at St. Saviours Church in Brighton," my home parish.

I had a heck of a job to make the meeting and had to tell the Vicar I knew nothing about having to have banns read in Brighton. I hadn't lived there for three years, I told him. He tutt! tutted, shook his head and for a moment I thought he was going to say the wedding couldn't take place. But after a pause he said that he would see to it that the banns called in St. Mary's Church would suffice for both of us.

On the night before the wedding there was a heavy air raid and I spent the entire night on top of the tower of the Keep in charge of an-anti aircraft crew. We didn't fire a shot; our weapons were too small to have any effect on the Luftwaffe anyway. We did, however, play an important role in that particular raid.

From our perch atop the tower we could see for miles. As wave after wave of aircraft droned overhead I saw a light flashing about two miles out in the country. I placed a rifle in a stand and removed the bolt. I then aligned the flashing light inside the barrel and clamped the rifle firmly in place. Looking through the barrel at dawn it clearly outlined a farmhouse. The military police were notified and later we were informed that five people had been arrested and illegal equipment seized.

I also recall some friendly banter from a couple of my colleagues about my marriage later in the day. It continued throughout the night. It made for a laugh and passed the time away.

Since we were working nights and sleeping during the day, no one was allowed to leave Barracks until after four, but I was to be married at three. Len Keeble, my best man, and myself managed to persuade the Company Sergeant Major to give us our passes the night before and about eleven thirty in the morning when everyone was sleeping, we squeezed through a gap in the fence at the bottom of the football pitch. And so I had to be AWOL (absent without leave) to get married, not a good way to start, I thought.

I had seen my mother several times in the weeks leading up to this day and every time she expressed misgivings about the marriage.

"You are totally unsuited," she said, "I see nothing but problems for this marriage, it is doomed to failure. Why don't you face up to it? You know I'm right."

After leaving the Barracks I took a circuitous route so as to avoid detection and visited her on my way to Rose's house. Again she pleaded with me to back out of it. "It's not too late," she said. "I'll go and tell them if you like. It grieves me to see you make such a fool of yourself." But I wouldn't listen.

"Nah! Can't do that," I said, "All those presents and all the people coming, gotta go through with it now."

I left and standing at the corner, watched as a drama unfolded overhead. A single Spitfire made several breathtaking maneuvers and blew a lone German bomber clear out of the skies. Then did a victory roll as he returned to his base at Mildenhall.

When it was all over, I couldn't help thinking about my mother's warning. Deep down I knew what I was about to do was foolish. I was marrying for all the wrong reasons but hadn't the guts to back out of it. Ah! What the hell, I thought, there's a war on, who knows what's gonna happen, live for to day and to hell with tomorrow.

Just as I had done for months, I knocked, opened the front door and walked in. I shouldn't have, because Rose was in the hallway and unable to escape before our eyes met.

"On the day of the wedding," her mother intoned, "the groom should never set eyes on the bride until at the altar. It's bad luck," she insisted.

Following the ceremony, a colleague and professional photographer in civilian life, went to work. He had refused payment so was invited to the reception. Tommy, my mother's partner, couldn't make it so there were thirteen at the head table. A heated argument ensued between the mothers of bride and groom as to who should sit elsewhere.

According to Murphy's law, my mother was right!

Nineteen

Repent At Leisure

Regrettably, the celebrations following our wedding turned into a bit of a drunken orgy, something to do with the pressure of the times perhaps. France had fallen, our fighting forces were in disarray and England stood very much alone. Invasion was on everyone's lips, seemingly just a matter of time.

I had bought liquor and a good supply of bottled beer, including mother-in-law's favourite Suffolk Nip. Then the Brewery donated a Firkin of their very best draft ale, a gift to the daughter of an employee on the occasion of her marriage. Now a Firkin is nine gallons and only thirteen of the invited guests could attend. Mind you, we had issued an open invitation to any of my compatriots in Camp who might wish to drop by . . . And they did, in force!

Once again my mother-in-law had to be carried early to her bed. I have to say that there were times when her drinking became a problem. For example, she would purchase a supply of booze Sunday night to help her through the weekly wash Monday morning. She got sloshed as she washed, as it were. Sometimes she became belligerent and downright hostile toward me. After a while it began to place a strain on our marriage and I suggested to Rose we move to a place of our own. But to her, that made little sense because, as she put it, "You'll likely be posted any day."

We had no honeymoon and spent all day Sunday cleaning up the mess. Her mother was completely incapacitated.

The following Saturday, Rose and I went to Ipswich to visit her father. It was only twenty-six miles and I was looking forward to meeting him. Once seated on the train, Rose told me that her father was, in fact, in a mental institution.

This was quite a shock to me and I was annoyed at being deceived, I criticized her for being less than forthright but she brushed it off saying his disorder was of a minor nature and would have no hereditary effect, "If that's what you're worried about," she snarled. It is interesting to note, however, that her sister, Norma spent the last ten years of her life in a mental institution. Some of the incidents leading to her committal were bizarre in the extreme.

At Heathlands Mental Institution we were directed to a visitors lounge. I was immediately struck by how normal the old man seemed. His general demeanor was that of a perfectly ordinary human being. He was a simple man with little more than a grade six education but was able to conduct an intelligent conversation.

He was timid at first; not surprising after being incarcerated that long, but he soon relaxed and opened up. He was fond of horses and had driven the Brewer's Dray delivering beer for over ten years prior to his committal. His description of the two horses reminded me of the pair next door to us in Ongar and I told him about them.

Following our two-hour visit I suggested to Rose we talk to his doctor. I'd heard of people in the old days being committed simply for being a nuisance in their community, others that had acquired a mental disorder solely as a result of their incarceration. Surprisingly, the doctor said he could have been released long ago but his wife refused to sign him out. I offered to do so and plans for his release began. His wife wasn't very pleased but said little. It didn't work out though; I wasn't twenty-one and could not, therefore, legally take responsibility so my signature was invalid. On her next visit mother signed and he came home two weeks later.

The doctor had told us that alcohol was a contributing factor in the old man's debility and that caution should be exercised in the future. Despite the warning it wasn't long before, encouraged by his wife, he was in the pub drinking heavily. Having been partially involved in his release I had a personal interest. Foolishly, I expressed my concern to my mother-in-law, which led to a terrible row. She accused me of meddling in their personal affairs and trying to dominate their lives, I got no support from Rose.

On July 6, 1940, I was promoted to Sergeant and shortly thereafter, relieved of my duties as an instructor. I was put in charge of constructing a defense system against both air and ground attack for the entire area occupied by the Military. It included Britannia Barracks, a huge facility known as Blenheim Camp that had just become operative and a small airfield adjacent to the Camp.

It was a major task and had to be completed as soon as possible. Britain had adopted double summer time; the clocks were put forward two hours instead of one. Thus it was light until well after ten and we took full advantage but it placed an even greater strain on my marriage. I would leave home before seven in the morning and wouldn't return until late at night. This went on every day for a couple of weeks.

On the odd occasion when I did get an evening off I would go to the Sergeants' Mess and drink at the bar rather than go home because of the constant nagging. I take full responsibility for the consequences, it was a thoughtless and foolish thing to do because it aggravated an already tenuous situation. Rose would don her uniform and come to the back door of the Mess demanding I come home. This, of course, was the ultimate embarrassment; wives just didn't do that sort of thing in wartime. The first seeds of discontent were sown.

Things came to a head on Saturday, August 31. It was a rare day off so we joined Edna, Rose's maid of honour and Len my best man, for a long walk in the country. They later married and lived out their lives in Bury St. Edmunds. Anyway, at some point Rose and I withdrew to a secluded spot where we could enjoy a little privacy. We were just about to make love when I heard the unmistakable sound of the general alarm, so did Len. We knew this had to be serious, maybe an invasion. Rose refused to believe there was any urgency and was outraged when Len and I left and ran all the way back to barracks. Edna chided her for being so childish.

When we arrived, it was obvious something dramatic was happening. The defense positions I had worked on were fully manned and huge trees had been felled blocking the main road. We later learned that German ships had sailed from Terschelling and were headed toward the Norfolk coast. The supposed invasion proved to be nothing and at four in the morning the order was given to stand down.

I crawled into bed shortly before five, had three hours sleep and was back on duty at nine, Rose was still sleeping when I left. I got home just after four in the afternoon, she was in a foul mood, refusing to speak and unwilling to prepare a meal. I wasn't in a good mood either and her attitude was just too much. I blew my stack, we had one hell of a row and I stormed off back to camp. This is not the way it is supposed to be, I thought.

My mother-in-law also proved difficult. The old man, although grateful for my part in his release, was too scared to say a word. In the five weeks we'd been married Rose had become a totally different person. She was domineering, unreasonable and seldom satisfied. As the old saying goes, she was "Everything by turns and nothing long." Above all, she simply could not accept the fact that war meant my duty to the military took precedence over everything, including her.

I spent the night in Camp in the bed of a colleague who was on leave and was deeply troubled as I settled down for the night. Again, I was reminded of my mother's warning, "Marry in haste, repent at leisure." I had certainly married in haste and, what with Rose's change of attitude and her mother's frequent hostility toward me, everything pointed to a leisurely repentance.

Battalion orders next day included a request for volunteers for the Colonial Forces. The pay was more than double that of the Regular British army and there were other very attractive benefits. My army records will show that I volunteered; I was gonna be posted soon anyway so what the heck! I didn't tell Rose what I had done. We settled our differences and I returned home but things got worse.

Two days later, I was told in strictest confidence that the Company Sergeant Major and myself were being posted to Dover. We were to be involved in defense activities prior to a possible invasion of the continent by the Allies. I couldn't tell Rose but in any case my secondment to the Colonial Forces came through first.

On Friday September 6, we both started ten days leave and on the Monday afternoon went to the Odeon cinema. Just got seated, lights dimmed and about to enjoy a good film when the Usher came sweeping her flashlight along each row. Learning my identity she informed me I was wanted outside immediately. A colleague advised me I had been posted to Africa and was to report to the Hotel Great Central in London the next morning.

Rose was devastated, I felt guilty that I had not prepared her. At my request she went home and packed my things. I went back to Barracks, was issued additional equipment and completed all the necessary documentation.

It was well after seven when I got home. We spent an hour in the pub, bidding farewell to friends and neighbours and then to bed for the last time in a very long while. We threw caution to the wind and had sex. Two days before sailing to Africa, Rose wrote saying the doctor had confirmed her pregnancy.

The Hotel Great Central was located at the corner of Great Central Street and Marylebone Road, a few blocks west of Madam Tussauds Wax Museum. It had been expropriated by the Military. To all outward appearances it was just an army transit camp but, in fact, was much more. The second floor had been taken over by MI 6 the branch of British intelligence responsible for secret agents operating in continental Europe. They also had an office at number 64 Baker Street.

I spent an interesting evening with one of the occupants of the second floor. It took place in a pub just off Baker Street. He had just come from Bletchley Park, or "BP" as it was referred to then, fifty miles northwest of London. After the war we learned this was where Germany's secret codes were broken using the famous ENIGMA machine.

There was a heavy air raid in progress so I had sought refuge in the pub. The bartender, a tall, graying man, mid fifties, stood with arms outstretched, hands resting lightly on the bar like a preacher about to deliver a sermon. I ordered my usual pint of mild and bitter and glanced around. The place was empty save for a young, well dressed gentleman who I felt sure ought to be in uniform sitting at one end of the bar, and at the opposite end, perched cross-legged on a high bar stool, a lady of the night. She was dressed in a beautiful scarlet evening gown with plunging neckline and a tantalizingly smooth, white thigh exposed almost to the waist. She sat nonchalantly reading the Evening Standard completely oblivious to the sound and furor going on overhead.

I made conversation with the young man and learned he too was billeted at the Hotel Great Central, on the second floor no less. We talked for a couple of hours then made our way back to the hotel. Eight years later our paths would cross again but under very different circumstances.

When we first arrived at the hotel, a Sergeant, whose name escapes me, greeted us. He had been the front desk manager for years before the hotel was expropriated, at which time he was conscripted into the army, appointed to the rank of Sergeant and continued in the same role. He became quite famous and was well known by all the "Patrons" of the hotel. He was also mentioned in several post war books about the secret service activities at Bletchley Park, the Baker Street office and the Hotel Great Central.

A southwest corner suite on the fifth floor was my home for the next seven plus weeks. On Saturday, September 7 1940, the Germans had launched the first mass air raid on the city of London. Every night for the remainder of our stay we were subjected to similar attacks.

I feel compelled to comment briefly on the seven weeks of sheer hell that was commonly referred to as "The Blitz." I can say without hesitation that of all my wartime experiences it was the most appalling and the most debilitating. It continued until January of 1941, long after I had left.

Every night about five o'clock the adrenaline would flow as we listened to the undulating wail of the siren signaling another massive air raid. Hour after hour, usually until about seven in the morning waves of Heinkel HE 111 heavy bombers would fly over the Greater London area dropping thousands of tons of high explosive and incendiary bombs. The devastation and carnage heaped upon the civilian population is indescribable. To this day I marvel that I survived the ordeal almost without a scratch. The stories of bravery and heroism are legion; I'm sure there were more acts of bravery during that short period of time than in many a battle fought in later years.

A few incidents remain to this day impregnated on my mind. A young Dutch refugee girl, unable to speak a word of English, alone in a cellar, bombs dropping all round, giving birth to an unwanted child. She was no more than sixteen. A friend had left her to seek help, I stayed with her and did what I could to comfort her until that help arrived, by which time the baby's head was almost in my hands.

A friend with whom I had served for years inviting me to join him on a visit to a long lost Aunt. She greeted us with the usual cockney hospitality, apologizing that she hadn't a drink to offer us. We volunteered to go to the Pub on the corner just two blocks away to get some. As we entered the Pub there was the most horrific explosion, the ground shook like an earthquake and plaster fell from the ceiling. Obviously a "big one" had dropped nearby. When we returned to the end of Auntie's road it was no longer there! The houses on both sides for an entire block were nothing but a pile of rubble.

I stood at the top of Brixton Hill the night the Germans set fire to the London docks and watched in awe as a continuous wall of flame stretching for miles rose hundreds of feet into the air. It was an eerie sensation. Instead of the pitch black of night, it was like a summer's day. And seeing hundreds of London Firemen risking life and limb in a losing battle, trying to prevent the fire from spreading. But most impressive was the Salvation Army right in the thick of things handing out "Char and wads" (Tea and cakes). No matter how bad things were or what time of day or night an emergency arose, one could always rely on "Sally Ann" to be there with a "Cuppa."

Finally, returning at dawn from an overnight visit to Rose's sister and husband, being ordered to assist firemen and rescue personnel, digging out survivors from a six story building that had received a direct hit. I was to witness pain and suffering by women and little children the like of which I never again want to see.

From the beginning we had expected our stay at the Hotel Great Central to be short. As the weeks dragged on, with little to do but draw tropical clothing and equipment, a process seemingly dragged out by issuing a bit today and a bit tomorrow, we became restless and curious about the delay. Eventually we learned the boat that was to take us to Africa had been sunk on its way into Liverpool. We had to wait for another one to be assigned. We also learned the ship carrying the previous draft to Africa had been sunk in mid Atlantic with the loss of over three thousand lives, we were the replacements. What a comforting thought!

It wasn't all doom and gloom though, even in the midst of chaos there were lighter moments. Four of us shared the hotel room. As well as myself, there was Jimmy Hinton who was also from Bury St. Edmunds. Then there was Freddie Palmer who got married the day we left and spent his wedding night on a troop train en route to Glasgow. And, last but not least, Sgt. Robert L. Caruso, so close to Robinson Crusoe, Daniel Defoe's famous character that we immediately dubbed him our man "Friday."

As the nightly bombing continued we became close friends. One night, after some idle chatter about our respective family backgrounds, Friday mentioned that in civilian life he had worked for a heraldry company somewhere in Surrey; I think it was in Guildford but I'm not sure. He was fascinated with the story of my ancestry and offered to help verify what uncle George Wright had told me back in 1929.

We went to Somerset House, which at the time was the main office of the Registrar of Births Deaths and Marriages. But it only opened from ten till four Monday to Friday and we had great difficulty getting out of the Hotel during those hours. We did make it out one afternoon about two-thirty but by the time we got there we had less than an hour for research.

Normally we used the subway because I knew it like the back of my hand but for some reason we decided to take the bus. As we lurched through the streets on the top deck, making endless detours because of bomb craters, I became aware of the extent of the destruction. I felt enraged and bitter at what the Germans were doing. It had absolutely nothing to do with military tactics and everything to do with the cold-blooded murder of women and children and the destruction of civilian property. It was designed solely to destroy the moral of the population and I longed for the day when we could retaliate. Little did I know that eight years later I would fly over Berlin and witness destruction a thousand times worse. After what I had seen in London I felt no remorse.

I was also concerned at having to tell Friday about my illegitimate birth, it still carried some stigma in those days. When we arrived, a very charming young lady greeted us at the desk and, in a low sexy voice, asked how she could help us. Boy! If she only knew! After I explained our mission, she described the layout of the archives and how the system worked then directed me to where I should begin my search.

There were rows of leather-bound binders on at least two if not three levels. One reached the appropriate level by ascending a little circular iron staircase then proceeding along a narrow catwalk to the relevant alphabetic binder. Friday was so busy trying to charm the pants off our cute little archivist that by the time he joined me I was already back to Grandfather Albert George Keeling, born August 7, 1868.

We laboured through a series of ledgers until closing time making little progress but hoping to return the next day. It was several days, however, before we made it back only to be told at the end of the day that the next area of search was not open to the public. It involved large underground vaults and searches could only be conducted by staff for what was then a substantial fee, depending upon how far back one desired to go; also, there was a long waiting list. Friday thought it was nothing but a racket and said he could do better through his old company.

So I gave him five pounds sterling and several months later received via the army post office (APO. 101), a very large and impressive looking document, which I was assured was, indeed, my family tree. It did go back to a William George Keeling born in 1578, died in 1620, and whose occupation was listed as "Ships Master."

Perhaps Uncle George Wright's story of my maternal ancestry really was valid. Unfortunately, this document was among other personal effects that I lost on the return journey from Africa in 1942.

Monday, October 28, there was a flurry of activity. Obviously our time had come. We were confined to the Hotel for twenty-four hours and all but our personal effects were loaded on trucks which disappeared we knew not where, nor did we care. The strain of the bombing night after night had left us with a feeling of total indifference. To us it was a case of eat, drink and be merry for who knows what the hell might happen tomorrow.

We were allowed out until 2359hrs., on the 29th., and three of us decided to have one last fling, Freddie Palmer was getting married. We took advantage of a little-known law. By moving from one borough of London to another it was possible to legally obtain a drink in a pub for all but one of the twenty-four hours a day. The pubs opened for shift workers in the various markets: Smithfield for meat, Billingsgate, fish and Covent Garden for produce.

Somehow we ended up in Hammersmith about one in the morning feeling no pain. Walking boisterously along the High Street we badly needed to relieve ourselves. There was no Public Toilet around so we all lurched into the doorway of a bombed-out shop. It had been a large double-fronted store with display windows on both sides of a corridor leading to the entrance, so we were well back from the sidewalk.

We didn't realize it but we were right opposite the Hammersmith Police Station. A London Bobbie hearing the commotion decided to investigate. We were all arrested and charged with various breaches of London County Council bylaws relating to what one could and could not do in a public place. We were placed in cells in the basement of the Police Station.

After a while the Officer in Charge interviewed us. We explained that we were off to Africa that day and this had been our final celebration before leaving. He phoned the Hotel Great Central, confirmed our story, all charges were dropped and a constable drove us back to the Hotel. We arrived about three in the morning just in time to see our mates standing at attention in the main hall ready to move out to the railway station on the first leg of a long and eventful journey.

We dashed to our room, grabbed our gear and only just made it for roll call, then to waiting trucks that took us to Kings Cross Railway Station. The most heartrending sight was the sobbing wife of Freddie Palmer standing on the sidewalk determined to get one last glimpse of her husband. They had been married just twelve hours. I thought of my own marriage and wondered about its future. If a leisurely repentance was to be my fate this was but the beginning.

Twenty

A New Beginning

I spent my twenty-first birthday on a rusty, overcrowded old tub the "Almanzora." She was ploughing through rough seas in the middle of the Atlantic Ocean with nearly three thousand troops aboard, far beyond her normal capacity. The lucky ones found space enough to sling a hammock but most slept on or under the mess tables and on the bench seats. In a few days we would reach tropical waters and could sleep on deck. Sleep? What the hell's that?

Because we were part of a convoy, we went no faster than the slowest freighter, which wasn't very fast. Jimmy Hinton and I were leaning on the ship's rail on the port side bemoaning the ordeals of wartime travel that had dogged us since leaving the Hotel Great Central. And to add insult to injury, there was nothing stronger than vinegar on board to celebrate the most important birthday of my life. I was now legally an adult.

As we gazed toward the sharp end of the ship, the rope on a davit attached to one end of a lifeboat snapped. It dropped like a stone into a perpendicular position then briefly swung pendulum like on the side of the ship. The strain proved too much for the rope on the other end and it too gave way. We watched in dismay as the lifeboat crashed into the sea breaking in what can only be described as a bundle of kindling. Jimmy, with his usual dry humour said,

"I see no ships, only hardships."

And that just about sums up life for the next two years. In the first four months of my tour of duty in Africa I was sent on assignment to three different countries. I learned what it was like to hack my way through virgin jungle with nothing but a compass for guidance. I patrolled miles of crocodile-infested rivers and traversed swamps that could literally swallow a truck. I learned too what it was like, because of the stupidity of a junior officer, to be hopelessly lost for thirty-six hours without food or water, three hundred miles deep into the jungle. At the time I was the only white Commander of a reconnaissance patrol consisting of eight heavily armed black troops who knew I was lost and sensed my despair. Every jungle creature God made save the tiger, there are none in Africa, also confronted me.

One creature that took an instant liking to me was the female species of the mosquito. For the first four months of my contract, I was repeatedly stricken with a very serious type of malaria known as Malignant Tertian (M.T). This is a disease that, to this day, kills millions of people. I was based in Kintampo when it first struck. This was a Godforsaken place in Ghana or, the Gold Coast as it was called then. It was nothing but a clearing in the jungle and a few mud huts, or Ghiddas. It is about two hundred and fifty miles into the jungle north of the Atlantic coast and about twenty miles from the eastern border of the neighbouring country of Ivory Coast.

Kintampo was notorious at the time for two reasons. First, it is in the heart of the Tsetse fly belt. This insect, like the mosquito carries deadly parasites but instead of malaria, the tsetse parasites cause trypano'sorniasis or mid-African sleepy sickness. It looks very similar to the ordinary housefly except that when it comes to rest the wings are crossed whereas the housefly's wings remain side by side.

Bouncing along a jungle trail in a small truck one day, I felt a sting on my arm and sure enough it was a tsetse fly. On my return to base I was required to report the incident and give a blood sample.

Kintampo's second claim to fame was a most unlikely character named Saunders. He was a sandy-headed Scottish professor who had spent twenty-one years there studying the tsetse fly and it's effect on man and beast. He provided us with instant lab services and my test proved negative. Obviously it was papa fly and not mamma that had bitten me. I mention this incident only because it had some amusing consequences many months later.

It was also in Kintampo that I received news of the birth of my daughter. We had an old gasoline operated generator that provided power for a radio, strictly for the transmission of military communications. It was our only means of contact with the outside world. I received this simple message transmitted from Military H.Q. in Accra. DAUGHTER BORN 26 MAY 1941 STOP MOTHER AND CHILD WELL STOP.

Since she was born on Queen Mary's birthday, that's the wife of King George V, my mother-in-law insisted she be given the name Mary, and Rose after herself and her daughter. I was happy to go along with the names.

Life in the jungle was hard at the best of times, suffering with recurrent malaria merely added to my discomfort. I spent a lot of time in the sick bay, which provided much opportunity for reflection. The news that I was now a father made me think long and hard about life during the past couple of years. Especially the realization that I now had additional responsibilities, it was no longer just Rose and me.

In the solitude of the African jungle I concluded that life at home wasn't so bad after all. In these circumstances we tend to forget the bad times and think only of the good. And I pledged to myself that if I got through this rotten war, I would do everything in my power to make a success of married life and provide a good home for my family. When I get home, I told myself, it would be a new beginning.

Shortly after this I suffered my third bout of the recurrent malaria in two months and was declared unfit for active service. I was transferred to H.Q. in Accra, the capital city of Ghana. It was located on the coast, where I was to be reassigned. The speculation was that the more moderate coastal climate would help. In between the recurrent malaria I was healthy and fully capable of hard work.

A new two hundred-bed hospital had just been constructed on the outskirts of Accra and there was a desperate shortage of medical personnel. I spent the next five months in Number 36 General Military Hospital. When I was fit enough to work, I would assist in the ward and when sick, I would be confined to a bed. The first aid training I received in the Boys' Brigade proved very helpful.

It was hard work but very rewarding and, although I didn't appreciate it at the time, the experience was invaluable. Along with my Intelligence training it served me well in civilian life. Unfortunately I continued to be plagued with the malaria. Research into an effective vaccine for this deadly disease continues to this day. At the time, Quinine was the only preventive drug available, I was a guinea pig for two experimental drugs, Atabrine and Mepacrine, and I do believe they helped. Each time I had a relapse I lost weight and by February 1942, I was a shadow of my former self.

It reached the point where I was declared medically unfit for further duty. The Chief Surgeon told me I probably wouldn't live more than five years. He also said I wouldn't have to worry about contraception for a long time. The amount of Quinine and other drugs that had been pumped into me would, he said, definitely make me sterile.

I was subsequently returned to England on medical grounds and for a time, my military career was in jeopardy. I boarded a Naval Patrol vessel that took me from Takoradi to Freetown in Sierra Leone. There I was transferred to the MV Letitia; the last refugee ship to have left Singapore before it fell to the Japanese. There were six hundred women and children aboard. During the month-long voyage two baby girls were born, they were both named Letitia.

It was a perilous journey with all the dangers associated with U-boat warfare. After three days in harbour waiting for a convoy to assemble, we sailed out of Freetown at the usual slow convoy speed. But the Letitia was a fast boat, capable of twenty-eight knots, and so after three days we took off alone. I shall never forget the sight as we sailed from the rear of the convoy, right through the centre, finally leaving it far behind in our wake. Also, it was the only time I ever saw the end of a rainbow and, contrary to ancient legend, I found no pot of gold. I was on deck and had observed the rainbow for several minutes, then watched fascinated as we sailed right through it, the colours reflecting off the ship's deck for its full length.

Although I was not in the best of health, I had to take my turn on watch. Two days after leaving the convoy I was on the bridge to starboard, scanning the sea. It was a beautiful day, clear blue skies and a calm sea. Suddenly, for a split second, I thought I was dreaming. There, not more than thirty feet from the ship's side, I saw a submarine lying motionless just below the surface parallel to our ship. As we slid smoothly past this barely submerged monster, I could see quite plainly the conning tower and the cables running from the tower to both ends of the vessel. For a moment I was sure we would scrape its side we were so close. It was a German U-boat. The First Officer, standing beside me saw it simultaneously and quickly gave the order, "Hard to port, full ahead."

The Captain was informed and immediately joined us on the Bridge. All the watertight doors were closed and the ship vibrated as every ounce of speed was coaxed out of her engines. We maintained the customary zigzag course and all able-bodied men were on standby in case the worst happened. We maintained maximum speed for the next eighteen hours and there was no sleep that night. The well being of the women and children on board was uppermost in our minds. But we saw nothing more of the U-boat and the journey continued without further incident. It was all a little anti-climactic.

After that I came down with a severe bout of malaria. For five days I was confined to the sick bay and cared little whether I lived or died. There were times when the Chief Surgeon's projected five-year life span entered my mind. But I survived and as I lay recuperating I thought of the childhood dream I'd expressed in Wales so many years before, to live to see the year two thousand. I was determined to see that dream fulfilled.

As well, I realized how precious life really was. And my thoughts turned to home and what lay ahead. My resolve for a new beginning grew stronger as each day we neared our destination.

We docked at Greenock early on the morning of Sunday, 15 March 1942, and for several hours the women and children disembarked. There were dozens of volunteers there to assist them. Many had left England years before and some had never seen their homeland. For them it was a traumatic experience.

As the day wore on and the other military personnel disembarked I began to feel very much alone; I was the last person on board save for the crew. Finally the Railway Transport Officer (R.T.O) came aboard and confessed he didn't know what to do with me. I had no papers; they had been forwarded by army mail after my departure. He suggested I be admitted to hospital in Glasgow but I had no desire for that. I told him I felt fit enough to travel and would prefer to be returned to my parent unit in Bury St. Edmunds where excellent hospital facilities were available. I made no mention that I had a wife and child there, I thought that might be pushing my luck.

Eventually he agreed, issued me the necessary travel warrant and at long last I descended the gangplank. For the first time in over a month my feet touched terra firma. The first thing I did was to send a telegram to, Rose advising the time of my arrival the following day. She had no idea I was on my way because we were not allowed to divulge our movements at any time during the war.

It was then I learnt one of my trunks was missing, it didn't get transferred to the Letitia. I could never get official confirmation, but I believe the naval vessel that had carried me to Freetown, and that still contained my trunk, was sunk while escorting the convoy across the Atlantic. It was heart breaking because most of my personal things were in it.

I traveled all night by train to Bury St. Edmunds via London. Arriving about eleven in the morning, I left the Railway Station feeling excited at the thought of seeing Rose again and my daughter Mary for the first time. But my excitement was tempered somewhat because as I waited for a cab I met, Flossie the barmaid from the Playhouse bar and she had something on her mind.

She expressed concern at my physical appearance then, "The last thing I want to do is spoil your home coming but there is something I simply have to tell you."

I sensed her discomfort.

"I feel," she continued, "better it come from me than from others who may not have all the facts."

She said that Rose and her mother had, for a long time, been banned from the Playhouse lounge. They had made a habit of entering by the back lane leaving the baby in her pram. The baby would wake up screaming but Rose simply ignored it and other patrons had complained. Despite several warnings the practice continued, resulting in the ban.

Flossie was careful to emphasize that her mother always accompanied Rose. She apologized again for being the bearer of such news, but expressed the opinion that now that I was home, things were bound to change. At that point my cab arrived and I proceeded to the barracks, reporting to the Orderly Room.

My papers still hadn't arrived so I was granted twenty-eight days disembarkation leave but subject to immediate recall. As was the procedure, I remained on the payroll of the Colonial Forces until 12 April 1942. I had to wait for the paymaster to get paid and for my pass, so I sorted through what was left of my luggage and had a meal in the Sergeants Mess.

I then had a few moments to myself and time to reflect on what Flossie had told me. I decided to dismiss the whole thing from my mind and forget about it. I had to realize, I told myself, I had been gone for sixteen months and could hardly expect Rose to lead the life of a nun. But I did feel her behaviour was less than ideal and not what I would have expected.

I arrived home mid afternoon and everyone was horrified at my gaunt appearance. Mary was eleven months old and I was deeply moved by her beauty. I took her into my arms and she screamed her head off. It took several days before she got used to me and then I was gone again.

This was a price families had to pay in wartime. Most children were denied a nurturing relationship with their father because of long absences on military duty; and for the same reason the father was also disenfranchised. This caused inestimable harm to, and in some cases literally destroyed, many family relationships following war's end.

We spent an hour in the pub that evening and I was overwhelmed with good wishes and welcome home. But by now I was feeling the effects of my long journey, the change in climate, the different food and the strong English beer. I expressed a desire to get to bed, which Rose interpreted as an urge for sex. But I was unable to perform and she showed little understanding; the next night things were different.

I was determined my homecoming would, indeed, signal a new beginning.

Over the next three days I did my utmost to bring this about but it proved more difficult than I had expected. There were harsh words with my mother-in-law over money. Rose was well provided for financially during my absence, almost double what she would have received as the wife of a Sergeant in the regular British army. But her mother insisted that, not only had she and the baby lived with her rent free, but that she had subsidized her in other ways. This was ridiculous, of course, and I told her so in no uncertain terms. In fact, Rose ought to have saved money and eventually admitted to not being prudent with her money. All told, the atmosphere was anything but cordial.

On the Thursday afternoon, I received word to report to the Medical Officer the following morning. It was the same M.O. that I had seen prior to the confrontation with my mother two-and-a-half years earlier. My medical documents had arrived from Africa and after examining me, he insisted I be admitted to the base hospital. And there I stayed until the following Monday, Rose didn't visit me at all. Then I was transferred to a large military hospital in Colchester and was there for seven weeks. She visited me once for three hours. Her mother looked after the baby.

When she walked into the ward I was shocked at her drab appearance; she'd gained weight and had little to wear. I got permission to go into town, withdrew money from my Post Office savings account and bought her a new outfit. It was an, off-white, three-quarter-length jacket with red lapels, red trim on the pockets and a red pleated skirt to match. It fitted perfectly so she tossed her old attire in a bag and wore it for the rest of the visit.

The amusing consequences about the tsetse fly bite referred to earlier, occurred when I was admitted to the hospital in Colchester. I was ordered to bed and slept continuously. They would wake me for a meal but after eating I would fall asleep again. This went on for two days and the medical staff didn't know what to make of it. Some were convinced I was suffering from narcolepsy, an inability to resist the urge to sleep. They tried sitting me in an armchair in the centre of the large, old-fashioned military ward. A nurse was instructed to jog my arm each time she passed to ensure I stayed awake but it didn't work.

Next they insisted I walk in the grounds. I found a nice shady tree, lay down and promptly fell asleep. I didn't realize I'd wandered outside the hospital boundary and when I hadn't returned within the allotted time, the whole staff was out frantically searching for me.

One young doctor reviewing my medical records was convinced I was suffering from Sleepy Sickness because of my encounter with the tsetse fly. He ordered blood samples to be sent to the Hospital for Tropical Diseases in Liverpool and was quite put out when they told him by 'phone to stop wasting their time.

Their conclusion was I suffered nothing more than complete exhaustion. With rest, healthy diet and temperate climate I soon made a full recovery. I spent the last ten days of my hospital stay playing tennis all day, and I never did have another full blown episode of malaria, just the occasional rigor at night.

I returned to Bury St. Edmunds feeling almost my old self. I had regained much of the lost weight and was feeling full of energy. I hadn't felt this good in years. After only three days, Rose took me aside and informed me she was pregnant. I expressed surprise, quoting the Senior Surgeon in Accra about the likelihood of me being sterile. She had been to the doctor she replied and he had confirmed the pregnancy. So much for one doctor's opinion on sterility, I thought.

I was re-appointed to the Staff as an Instructor and medically classified C2, which meant I was not eligible for overseas or active service. I could, therefore, look forward to a more stable life in the same place for the foreseeable future.

This was just what we needed for our fresh start. I also knew the only way we could succeed was to get a place of our own. Rose agreed and we rented two large rooms plus kitchen on St. Andrew's Street South.

From the beginning we had problems. Rose had become so reliant on her mother to take care of everything including the baby, that she had little desire for housekeeping. There were other problems too, but suffice it to say that within a month we were served notice to vacate. Her mother was furious and went to see our landlady demanding an explanation. Apparently she was not very tactful and was told precisely what the problems were and she left with her tail between her legs. We found a second floor flat on Risbygate Street, the main road leading from town to the Barracks, just three blocks away.

Shortly after moving in, we were surprised to get a visit from her father; he was alone too, which was even more surprising. It was the first time we had been alone with him since our visit with him in Ipswich shortly after we were married. His wife had told him the reasons we had been evicted from our previous accommodation. He then proceeded to chastise Rose unmercifully for all her shortcomings as a wife, mother and tenant, as described by our previous landlady.

I was absolutely flabbergasted, I never thought the old man had it in him to do such a thing, and with such fervor. He seemed to enjoy playing the role of a dutiful father correcting an errant child; it was all quite touching. Rose didn't challenge his criticism at all, simply promised to do better in the future. She did too, but only for a week or two, then gradually slipped back into her old ways.

In fairness to Rose it must be said that she was, in many ways, a very warm and capable person. It is my belief that, at the time we met anyway, she was thoroughly spoilt by her mother. She was the youngest of three girls, the other two being much older so she was somewhat pampered from birth. When life as a spouse, mother and homemaker got difficult, it was all too easy to turn to, and become reliant on a willing mother that was near at hand. It is interesting to note that when she eventually moved away, she became a much more self-reliant individual. But then, she had a sister living next door. In other words, from the very beginning there was always a close relative of hers interfering in our daily lives.

Summer drifted into fall, and the only good news in those otherwise dark days was the unconditional surrender of Italy. Rose was heavy with child and for her it brought no joy. Indeed it was a burden that made life difficult for everybody. She spent more and more time at her mothers which, of course, caused more heated arguments.

There was a large corner house opposite our flat; expropriated by the Army it housed about twenty A.T.S. girls. I suggested Rose invite some of them over in the evenings when I was on duty to keep her company. She did so and several thoroughly enjoyed visiting her and later the newborn baby, it was a welcome break for them. A couple of them would baby sit occasionally, allowing us to go to the cinema or a function at the Mess. Refusing payment, they would bring their knitting or sewing and listen to the radio, sometimes they would just sit and talk girl talk. They called it their "stitch and bitch night."

My pay wasn't as much now that I was back in the Regular Army but I was living at home and paid a daily ration allowance. In addition, three food items were issued in kind, meat tea and sugar. All things considered then, we had the makings of a relatively good life, better than many in those difficult war-torn days. As Rose expanded her circle of friends, things improved. But it didn't last long, her mother complained of being neglected.

Named after his paternal great-grandfather, Albert George was born on December 13, 1942; he was delivered at home under the watchful eye of a very good midwife, the doctor arriving just in time. He was a healthy child and Rose quickly recovered.

There was a New Year's Eve party in the Sergeants' Mess that year which Rose and I attended. After a few drinks she made a spectacle of herself to the embarrassment of everyone present. We left immediately and I told her she would never be invited to the Mess again. From that point on things really began to deteriorate.

In early June, I was granted ten days leave and took Rose and the children to her sister's in London. By this time the Luftwaffe had been basically destroyed and the VI's and V2's had not yet been introduced, so London was relatively quiet.

Upon our return, Rose expressed dissatisfaction with life and demanded time to herself. She wanted one evening out alone, "completely away from everything." She concluded by saying there was a long neglected friendship she wanted to renew.

So each Friday evening, the only convenient night for her friend, she would leave home around six-thirty and return sometime after ten. If I were on duty, I would swap for a Saturday or Sunday. There was always someone eager to free up a weekend. Mary was two years old and Albert almost eight months, so they were no trouble and I enjoyed my weekly baby-sitting task.

Friday, August 6, 1943, we were on double summer time so it was still light when, just after ten, I realized I was out of cigarettes. The children were sleeping peacefully, there was a Pub on the corner just a hundred feet from our front door, so I decided to nip out and buy a packet. As I entered the "Off License" as it was called, I glanced up the side street and saw an American Airman, his back toward me and a female companion leaning against the wall.

I paid little attention, it was a common sight. A huge American Airforce base had been built at Rougham, five miles outside Bury St. Edmunds. It was the home of the so-called "Murderous `A' Squadron." After the war, the film "Twelve O'clock High," a black and white classic starring Gregory Peck was produced on location. It was based on the history of this illustrious squadron and later, serialized on Television.

I made my purchase, left the pub and again glanced up the side street. The airman had changed position so that now I could clearly see his companion. Although her back was to the wall, I recognized the outfit she was wearing. It was an off-white, three-quarter length jacket with red lapels, red trim on the pockets and a red pleated skirt to match.

Twenty-One

A Soldier Of Misfortune

We had returned from our holiday in London on Sunday, June 13 and it would be the following Wednesday when Rose first mentioned her dissatisfaction with life and a need for time to herself. I was surprised because she spent most afternoons at her mothers, had one or two of the girls from across the street visit her a couple of times a week, and I was home much of the time. But listening to her I could not, in all fairness, disagree.

She pointed out that I spent the odd hour in the Mess, not like the old days of course, but occasionally. Also, Sunday mornings if I wasn't on duty Rose would dress Mary in a cute little outfit and I would walk her up to the Mess and have a beer before dinner. All my compatriots would make a fuss of her, she was such a pretty child.

She always got a chocolate bar which was a luxury item then and she would sit in a big black leather arm chair all wide eyed at what was going on around her. Usually her nice clean dress would be soiled and I'd get heck when we got home. Anyway, I could see Rose's point, being around two small children all the time could be a strain.

When she mentioned wanting to renew the friendship with Vera I asked her.

"Who is this Vera, do I know her?" I couldn't remember any such person.

"Of course you do. I don't think you've seen her since you've been back from Africa. I used to take Mary to see her a lot when you were away."

"Well I don't remember" I said. "Anyway, where does she live?"

"Oh, you must remember, in Abbey Gardens, just after we were married. We bumped into her . . . She congratulated us and admired my engagement ring . . . You don't remember that?"

"Yeah! I think so, that was a long time ago though, is she married?"

"No . . . Not Vera, she's not the marrying kind. Nice girl though, you'll like her when you get to know her.

"O.K." I said.

And there the matter was left until about a week later; we were eating supper.

"By the way" she said, "I saw Vera to-day, just for a few minutes at her work. Friday is the only night convenient for her. So I said I'd see her this Friday about seven, at her place . . . I hope that's all right with you?"

"Well, yeah! I s'pose. O.K.," I said.

And so they got together on the Friday that would be six weeks ago. God how time flies! She got home about ten-fifteen and they thoroughly enjoyed their evening, she said. I asked what they'd done.

"Oh! Just sat around and talked . . . You know . . . Girl talk! . . . Had a glass of wine . . . I feel so much better for the break."

It all sounded so innocent.

On subsequent Fridays it was, "We just went for a walk in Abbey Gardens," or "we decided to go to the cinema to see a movie." Until now it had always been referred to as "going to the pictures."

"Really, what was it like? I asked.

"Not a bad show, not your kind of film though."

Cinema, movie, show, film? She was beginning to sound like a bloody American. I wondered where she got it all from. Six weeks later, here she was in the arms of an American airman! Now I knew where she got it.

When I first recognized her I was about to step off the sidewalk, then quickly retreated, hugging the wall so as not to be conspicuous. My heart was pounding and I was livid. What the hell was she doing? All kinds of things flashed through my mind. If she would do a thing like this when I'm home what might she have done when I was away for sixteen months in Africa? I remembered my meeting with Flossie the day I arrived back and the more I watched the angrier I became.

She had her back to the wall, her hands on HIS hips; he was facing her, standing too bloody close for my liking. His body was pressed close to hers and his hands were resting on her forearms as if poised to wander somewhere else, and in broad daylight. Well, not exactly daylight, it was beginning to get dark, but anybody could see them. Blokes walking back to camp, many of them knowing both of us. They weren't doing anything indecent mind you but she was looking into his eyes talking away. They looked as if at any moment they would be smooching and then what? Boy! That really made me mad.

Should I just stand there and see what they do? Did I really want to find out? No!

I strode toward them having great difficulty containing myself. My first impulse was to put my fist between his eyes but that would have done little for international relations and solved nothing. Then she saw me and quickly pushed him away. Blushing profusely and almost in a whisper she sheepishly said,

"Er! This is my husband."

He looked startled and well he might, he could sense my anger.

"I think it would be better if you just left." I said.

"Yes Sir," he said with emphasis on the sir, and turning quickly, disappeared around the corner.

I grabbed her arm propelling her hurriedly across the street to our front door.

"What the hell do you think you're doing?" I hissed, not wanting to make a scene in public.

I could see passers-by staring at us and as we mounted the front steps, I saw Charlie our Storeman out of the corner of my eye.

Through the front door we went and I could smell liquor on her breath, up the stairs and into the living room. I couldn't raise my voice, the children were sleeping in the next room and downstairs our elderly landlady wasn't in the best of health.

I felt a mixture of anger, hurt, betrayal and bewilderment. I mean, it wouldn't have been so bad if she was just standing there talking to him. And I could have accepted him walking her home. I wouldn't like it much, it would set too many tongues wagging, but I could've lived with it. But no, there she was in his bloody arms, gazing into his eyes like some love struck teenager.

"Why would you do such a thing?" I demanded, trying to control myself. "What the hell were you thinking of, out there in broad daylight showing yourself up, haven't you got any pride?"

"It wasn't broad daylight, don't exaggerate. Anyway, I wasn't gonna let him do anything wrong."

"Why did you go up the side street then? Why not stay on Risbygate? And why were you in his arms letting him press up against you like that? If that's not wrong for a married woman I don't know what is."

There is little to be gained by detailing the terrible quarrel that ensued. Rose died of cancer at a very young age, is not able to defend herself and I have no wish to say more than necessary. I threatened to confront Vera, blaming her for what had happened. But she tearfully conceded Vera had nothing to do with it. She admitted to going dancing and drinking with the American but insisted nothing improper had transpired. In my anger I didn't know whether to believe her or not, and suddenly I didn't care! I packed my bags and moved back to camp. She showed no remorse for what she'd done and little concern at my departure. What was I to make of it all?

Once it became known I was no longer living at home there were plenty of people eager to tell tales about what they had seen, including Charlie the storeman. He recounted how he had followed Rose and the American all the way from town that night and was surprised when he saw me come on the scene. He also said he had seen them together on a previous Friday night, she was sitting on his lap in the crowded bar of a pub next door to the Odeon Cinema.

It was arrogance I suppose, but I really thought my leaving might bring Rose to her senses and at some point we would get back together if only for the children's sake. But it was not to be. In the loneliness of my room I felt a sense of failure and was reminded of my mother's warning about marrying in haste. Then another strange thought came to mind. It was my need of cigarettes that had brought us together in September 1939. Now, a month short of our fourth anniversary we were separating for the same reason. But, I kept asking myself, what would have happened had I not run out of cigarettes on this occasion?

That first night I lay sleepless and chain smoking wondering what made her do it. I had tried my best to make things work. Surely it couldn't be sex. She had always been sexually assertive, insisting on it every other night. Occasionally I would come home for lunch and she would coax me into the bedroom and I would always oblige. What the hell was it then? Perhaps I was being punished for past sins? . . . I gave up.

The next day being Saturday, I spent a couple of hours sorting out my gear and making my room as comfortable as possible. The hut held the thirty men that constituted my platoon. My room was at the far end, about eight by sixteen with it's own little pot-bellied stove for warmth in the winter. Until now it had been used as an office and coffee room. A dartboard hung on the back of the door and we played darts during slack periods. How long would it be my home this time I wondered?

For a few months we had lived together as a family, an opportunity for me to be a real father and for my children to get to know me. The nurturing relationship I spoke of earlier, all this had come to a grinding halt. Thousands of couples would have given anything for such an opportunity.

Like most young people we rented the flat on a weekly basis. Following Pay Parade each Friday I would pay the rent from my ration allowance. That would cease now that I was no longer living at home but Rose could afford the rent from her Army Allowance. A shelter allowance was included in the rates paid to a spouse plus an amount for each child and a portion of my pay went to her.

But I had to think about the children, what was best for them. I could visualize Rose getting the girls across the street to baby-sit while she went dancing and God knows what else. The thought made me shudder, had I done the right thing? Should I have stayed?

I wrote to Frank Borden, her sister's husband in London. He worked for a large corporation that, among other things, managed large housing estates; the Company managed the house in which he lived. Perhaps he could find a house for Rose and the children? That would get them away from the influence of her mother and the problems inherent in such a massive concentration of military personnel that was now Bury St. Edmunds. Unfortunately, he never received the letter. Many years later I learned that his wife had intercepted it.

I felt the need to get away from it all and decided to take a stroll through town to the Abbey Gardens. On that beautiful August day it seemed that every inhabitant of Bury and the thousands of military were all out shopping. Back in 1937, when I first arrived, it was a quiet little market town with less than two hundred soldiers in the Barracks.

I walked past the Corn Exchange and that made me angry again. The door was open, there was some kind of charitable function in progress and I found myself drawn into the place. I meandered around totally disinterested in what was going on. It was the scene of the crime, as it were, and I was curious. I talked to the caretaker about the Friday night dances, he spoke of their popularity, especially with the Americans. That made me even angrier.

Feeling frustrated I walked in Abbey Gardens then had fish and chips in a coffee shop on Angel Hill. I had no desire to return to the loneliness of my room so came to the conclusion that a drink was in order. Not in my favourite watering hole though, Flossie would ask questions; not tonight, I thought. And so, for the first time ever, I went to that pub next door to the Odeon Cinema. The bar was crowded as usual so I went into the lounge it was much nicer. Upon entering I spotted a young Corporal from my Company sitting alone. Seeing me he beckoned me to join him.

As we sat sipping our beer I noticed another Corporal sitting with an attractive, well-dressed woman. From our vantage point both seemed to be thoroughly enjoying themselves. Just to make conversation I said to my companion,

"Look at old what's-his-name, he's your room mate isn't he? Seems to be enjoying himself."

"Yeah! We're `roomies' . . . Tells me all his problems. She's married . . . Her old man's been overseas ever since war started . . . Some kind of classified work . . . He's been going with her for a fortnight . . . Can't get to first base."

"Oh! Really!"

"Won't let him do a thing, he's getting fed up . . . Said if he can't make it with her tonight she's had it!"

"Crude bugger" I said.

"Yeah! Well, with a war on that's the way it is these days."

Our conversation turned to other things.

Later I went to the toilet; it was the old fashioned type with one long urinal. The Corporal who had been the subject of our earlier discussion entered and stood beside me and to my left.

"Hello Sarge, how yer doing?"

"Oh! Fine." I said, and took a furtive glance to my left.

He had the biggest penis I'd ever seen. No wonder he couldn't get to first base, I thought, wouldn't blame anyone for avoiding that. He complained about the quality of beer these days to which I agreed, bade him farewell and dismissed the episode from my mind.

Sunday morning it was Church Parade then a leisurely afternoon preparing for work Monday and trying to get used to my new way of life. Went to tea at four-thirty and was just finishing when the waiter came to our table and said I was wanted at the front entrance. I had visions of Rose being there and moved reluctantly to the door. To my surprise it was one of the A.T.S. girls from the big house opposite our flat looking very worried.

"Rose asked me to come and tell you that your landlady died late last night, natural causes apparently. Rose didn't want to stay in the house so she's gone to her mothers."

"Oh! God," I said, "Did Rose find her?"

"No . . . As I understand it, the old girl was in bad shape earlier in the evening when a neighbour popped in to see her. She sent for the doctor but the old gal passed away before he got there."

I thanked her and headed back to my room wondering what the hell to do. Rose and the children were all right at her mother's; I didn't want to go there. I felt sure Rose would not have told her parents what really happened on Friday and no doubt I was being blamed for everything.

If the old girl had died of natural causes there'd be no inquest or anything. The Undertaker would lay her out in the front room, as was the custom. I'll do nothing for the time being, I decided. Maybe I'll take a walk down there to-morrow after work; which is exactly what I did.

Approaching the house I noticed our drapes and those of our neighbours were drawn. I quietly unlocked the door and, out of respect for the deceased, tiptoed quietly down the hall. Before reaching the stairs leading to our flat I was confronted by a charming young lady, mid twenties I would guess. She introduced herself as a niece of the deceased and sole heir to the estate. She lived in London she said, and had taken a week off work. She further informed me the funeral was to be held on Thursday morning.

I expressed my condolences and mentioned about paying the rent the next Friday. She said a lawyer, the Executor of the Estate, would be there Friday afternoon about three. Would it be possible for me to meet him? I agreed and told her we would avoid the house on Thursday because of the funeral. She thanked me for my understanding and I climbed the stairs; why, I wasn't quite sure. The place held little but unpleasant memories.

The rest of that week was very difficult, I neither heard nor saw anything of Rose and the children and life seemed terribly empty. I wondered if Rose would get her mother to baby-sit Friday night and go dancing at the Corn Exchange. And that damned American came to mind.

It wasn't jealousy, just anger; and my ego had suffered a severe blow. There and then I realized that Rose and I had little in common. When we first met the war had just begun and our to-morrows were uncertain. We were impulsive teenagers eager and excited to be together. But that, I concluded, was only because it always ended in intimacy. We had lots of fun but obviously were not really happy. As well, there was a sense of insecurity about our relationship that was definitely more than just the strain of wartime conditions.

I got off work at three on the Friday afternoon arriving at the house about ten past. To my surprise Rose and the children were there but we had little time to ourselves. Hearing me arrive, the lawyer knocked on our door and introduced himself in the superior manner common to an upper class member of the English legal profession. I took an instant disliking to the man. In a clipped monotone he informed us the new owner of the house had already left and that the house was to be sold forthwith. We were, therefore, given one week's notice in writing to vacate.

I was about to protest when Rose said,

"Oh well, to hell with it. I'll just pack the rest of my things and stay with my mother, I don't care."

That was music to his ears. He smiled, thanked us for our co-operation and pounded down the stairs.

After what had happened between us I saw little point in arguing. So, I thought, the die is cast. The new beginning I had dreamed about so long ago in the depths of the African jungle had been completely destroyed.

Then there was another surprise. Rose said she was going to spend the night at the flat. After supper she would pack the last of the things and her dad would move everything to her parent's place on the Brewer's dray, so there was nothing for me to worry about. Obviously, it was all pre-arranged. I subsequently learned she had spoken with the heir to the estate earlier in the day so she knew exactly what was going to happen.

I was determined to spend the evening with the children and, as Rose busied herself with the packing, I made Albert a Choo! Choo! train out of an empty cocoa tin and bits of wood and cardboard that were lying around. The wheels came from a broken toy long since discarded. I remember solving the problem of the chimney by using the cork from a Stevens Ink bottle. I just made a hole in the top of the tin and stuck the cork in . . . perfect. As I left, I placed the toy in his crib, kissed Mary and with a casual good-bye to Rose, I was gone. It was Friday the 13th!

I walked slowly back to camp overwhelmed by a feeling of despair. Haven't had much luck lately, I told myself. I am not by nature a superstitious person so I refused to believe that the day and date in any way shaped my destiny. But I did recall the story of mediaeval soldiers who would fight with any army regardless of the cause. They were referred to as men who lived by their wits and called "Soldiers of Fortune". As for me, I was at a loss to know what to do. I was at my wit's end . . . Hm! . . . I was a Soldier of misfortune . . . Obviously!

Three months later, in January 1944, Rose and the children moved into the house next door to her sister in London. Norma took credit for arranging everything with no reference whatsoever to the letter I had previously written to her husband. But by then, it was of no consequence.

Twenty-two

A Brief Encounter

In 1940, the concern on everyone's mind was the possible invasion of England by the Nazis. Now, three years later the talk was of a second front, the return of Allied forces to the Continent. The Russians were clamouring for it and the Americans were raring to go. The winds of war, for so long blowing against the Allies were now turning in their favour. So every able bodied man and some not so able, was being posted to combat units. Training of recruits had been elevated to an unprecedented level and for the first time that I could remember there was no shortage of arms and equipment.

One by one, buddies with whom I had served for years were being posted to the First Battalion, by this time based in the north of Scotland. They were busy practising beach landings on the shores of the Moray Firth. I was not eligible for such rigorous assignments but before long that would change. First though, there was my "affair du Coeur." You could have fooled me; I would never have believed it.

For the preceding six weeks I had begged and sometimes bribed colleagues to swap duties from a Friday to a weekend to accommodate Rose's night out. Now I was doing the opposite, I needed my weekends free. I refused to go to my mother-in-law's house, which meant I could see the children only by appointment. So Rose and I made an unusual arrangement.

She was friendly with an A.T.S. girl across the street named Dela; an escapee from Nazi occupied Poland. She worked for the Company Quarter-Master-Sergeant. Rose would inform Dela when she was going to the Park or Abbey Gardens, she would tell me and I would meet them. Then, on August 23, the communication became more direct because I was promoted to acting C.Q.M.S., so Dela was my secretary.

Time with Rose and the children on these occasions was limited to little more than an hour on Sunday afternoons. If I complained I was told to stop being so stubborn and visit them at mother's house. I couldn't do it, not yet anyway. But there came a time when the weather forced me to have a change of heart.

Our first two meetings in Abbey Gardens were awkward and less than congenial. I enjoyed being with the children but Rose was sullen, irritable and argumentative. Any discussion about the future resulted in recrimination and she seemed more concerned about her financial security than anything else. She showed no remorse and was quite content to be once again living with her mother.

Obviously, life was so much easier for her there. Little or no housework or cooking and help with the children. The bickering continued each time we met and she showed little interest in how or what I was doing. I didn't ask her what she was doing either, because I no longer cared. The marriage, it seemed, was over. But the children's future had to be considered. I would do nothing hasty I thought, just let things rest awhile . . . See what happens.

My promotion included a number of secondary benefits. Gone were all those irritating extra curricular activities like guard duty and Orderly Sergeant. Except for about four days a month it was a nine to five job. At first it was wonderful, but there was little to do other than sit alone in my room or go to the Mess and drink or play cards. After a while it became boring.

As an Instructor I had three assistants, one Corporal and two Lance Corporals, as a C.Q.M.S. I had one secretary, Dela. I had no desire to go out with her; she was too close to Rose, and besides, she had a boyfriend. I'd had enough of women anyway, I told myself. So when Bob Chalmers, a former assistant, suggested I join him for a bike ride one evening I readily agreed.

It was Wednesday August 25, a beautiful summer evening and we went for a ride way out into the country. It was good to get away from all the military hustle and bustle. The English countryside was at it's tranquil best at this time of year. To this day I recall sitting on the bank at the side of a deserted country lane enjoying a cigarette with nothing to disturb us but the sounds of nature.

Eventually, feeling hungry we headed into Bury for fish and chips, one of the few things not rationed. Although, in a way it was because the shops weren't open every day. For the best in town we went to a shop on St. Andrew's Street, just off Risbygate. On arrival there was a huge line up.

"Ah, to hell with this I'm goin' to the NAAFI," Bob said.

He wheeled his bike around and headed off toward Camp. I was about to follow when this lady, leaving the fish shop almost dropped her large order of fish and chips. She had a sling bag over one shoulder and it started to slip. As she reached to grab it the newspaper in which her order was wrapped started to unfold and there would have been a major disaster had I not come to her rescue.

It turned out to be the person I had seen in the Pub with that Corporal, you know the one . . . The one with the big, you know what! She wouldn't "Let him get to first base," I recalled. I wondered if he had carried out his threat to leave her if he, "Didn't make it with her that night." I bet he did.

She thanked me for my help and recalled seeing me in the pub. She had to get home she said, the fish and chips were for mother, who was visiting from out of town, a local girlfriend and herself.

For some reason, I felt drawn to this woman and ignoring my hunger, offered to walk her home. It must be remembered there were literally thousands of military personnel in town, many just prowling around with less than honourable intentions.

She introduced herself as Marion and was happy to have me accompany her.

Surprisingly, she lived only a short distance away in a house that I passed every day when living with my mother-in-law. There was a store nearby where I frequently bought cigarettes and other necessities on my way home. I knew the owner and his wife well.

Marion also knew them and had lived in Bury St. Edmunds for seven years. She said she knew Rose and that we were married. She went on to say she bought most of her clothes from the store where Rose used to work. She also knew Flossie the barmaid at the Playhouse. The office where she worked was in the same downtown area and they often met at lunchtime or coffee break.

We had moved a little way down the lane so as not to be too conspicuous. I told her Rose and I were no longer living together, that things didn't work out. Her reply was that it was regrettable, especially when children were involved. But somehow, I got the impression that she already knew what had happened and perhaps more.

Then she told me about her husband; he was abroad, had been since the beginning of the war. I knew that, of course. I remarked about it being almost four years and how difficult it must be.

"At first I was devastated," she said, "and missed him a great deal but now I'm resigned to it . . . We've both had to adjust to the realities of war."

She went on to explain that she had a circle of friends whose company she enjoyed, played a lot of tennis in the summer and belonged to a club that offered recreational activities in the winter. It was only just recently she had gone out with another man and said it had not been an enjoyable experience. Since I knew the identity of her escort, I fully understood.

She told me that some months previously her husband had written informing her that he was keeping company with a lady friend. He hoped she would understand and would accept her doing the same if she were so inclined. She felt the only adult thing to do was to accept the inevitability of the situation given the extraordinary circumstances. This was a most unusual arrangement I thought, requiring a lot of courage and understanding.

After about fifteen minutes she decided she should go. Her guests would be wondering what on earth had happened and the fish and chips were getting cold. I was sorry to end the conversation and sensed she was too so I expressed the hope we might meet again. I was pleasantly surprised when she said her mother was leaving at noon on the Friday and invited me to dinner at her place about seven. With Army food the way it was how could I possibly refuse?

I rode my bike back to Camp and began to question what I'd done. Here I was, after just twelve days making a date with another man's wife. Was this any different to what Rose had done? Well, I felt it was different because Rose and I were separated and I wasn't deceiving anyone. Marion's husband was doing the same and had invited her to do likewise.

Rose had shown no interest in what I was doing; if ever she asked I would tell her. I had no idea what she was doing but, after the affair with the American, I felt sure she wasn't living a life of seclusion. It wouldn't bother me if Rose knew what I was contemplating and, in any case, it would be a purely platonic friendship. Nothing more could possibly come of it . . . I would make sure of that . . . Of course I would, and quickly dismissed the feeling of guilt.

I spent a most enjoyable evening with Marion on the Friday. Despite food rationing she made a very nice meal. As we sipped on a glass of Port wine she wanted to know more about me. I felt completely at ease and I suppose it was inevitable that I should start with the breakdown of my marriage. Having explained what happened I asked her, from a woman's point of view if she thought I was wrong? Was I too hasty in leaving Rose?

"Oh! Frank, you're the only person that can possibly know the answer to that. You're the only one with all the details. In particular what your feelings are toward Rose. You obviously felt deceived; could you trust her in the future or would you forever be plagued with doubt?"

There was silence for a moment then,

"While I can't possibly judge whether what you did was right or wrong, I do understand . . . Completely."

I was watching her intently as she replied and now I felt sure she knew more, much more about my situation.

I had mentioned in passing that I was a Regular Soldier, joining the Army before the war, she was curious to know why. I went back to the earliest days of my childhood and told her everything . . . Everything except the affair with my mother, couldn't tell anyone about that could I.

I watched her closely as I described how, at the tender age of five, I was given over to strangers . . . How the identity of my mother was hidden from me until I was almost twenty.

"How could a mother do such a thing?" She said with a break in her voice.

She was obviously moved by it all and made little attempt to hide her tears. Feeling guilty, I apologised and insisted we change the subject.

She told me more about herself, that she was an only child, her parents were farmers so she was a country person at heart.

"That makes two of us," I said.

She had attended Business College and her first job was as a secretary but she was now working in a key position. This placed her in a "Reserved Occupation" and could not be called up for military service.

She had been married over five years but had enjoyed little more than a year with her husband before he was sent overseas. He was highly skilled, with rare qualifications and was doing some kind of classified research overseas. And finally, as if to ensure that I would feel comfortable as a friend, she read me an extract from the letter from her husband regarding his female companion.

I left with only ten minutes to spare before curfew and as I did so she said how much she had enjoyed my company, that she would like very much to be a friend. I could have sworn that her eyes were moist as she said,

"You've had a terribly hard life Frank, I think you deserve better."

I wasn't going to argue and we arranged to meet again the following afternoon. I was so determined to be the perfect gentleman that I actually shook hands with her as I left. In the days and weeks that followed we found ourselves looking back with amusement at that little gesture.

Over the next three weeks we saw a great deal of each other. She had a comfortably furnished three-bedroom home, nothing lavish but everything of high quality. It was the kind of home I had always dreamed of, and gradually Marion made me feel more and more a part of it. And I realised how much I missed a nice home and all it could offer.

She had a piano and was an accomplished pianist. We spent many an evening singing the latest hits especially those of Vera Lynn, "White Cliffs of Dover" and "Now Is The Hour" were favourites. At other times we would just sit and talk, she was a most interesting person. We played tennis together both singles and doubles, including a tournament between the Senior N.C.Os' (Non Commissioned Officers) and the Officers Mess. In this way she came to know, and was accepted by, many of my colleagues.

We enjoyed the occasional bike ride through the surrounding countryside. On one such ride we stopped at the bridge on the old road to Newmarket about a mile out of town, the one that crossed the main railway line to London. We leaned on the wall in the centre of the bridge and gazed at the steel rails. I remarked about the illusion of their merging and then disappearing in the direction of London. We crossed the road and looked toward Bury St. Edmunds station where a train had just arrived.

I recalled doing this in Epping following Annie Mason's dramatic disclosure regarding my heritage. I reminded Marion of the story and mentioned a similar scene had greeted me following that traumatic event. We stood for a moment in silence and again I was reminded of the whole sordid affair with my mother. Marion sensed the emotional impact of what was happening and although no word was spoken, her very closeness brought succour to my troubled soul. Then the silence was shattered as the London train roared toward us and under the bridge and we were engulfed in smoke. That moment in time lingered long in both our memories and the bridge would haunt us yet again before the year was out.

We also went for long walks in the country, at first all very formal, we didn't even hold hands. But there came a time when that just didn't seem right. The first time she rather tentatively put her arm in mine I offered no resistance; in fact, I gave it a reassuring squeeze. Then she asked if I was worried about being seen in public with her. I assured her that, indeed, I was not, that I had no intention of sneaking around hiding our relationship.

From that time on we walked freely about town arm in arm making no secret of our friendship. I did not tell Rose because she didn't ask and I wasn't sure how she would react. Perhaps she didn't care, but in any case, might react out of spite if she met us in public. I was fully prepared for such an event. I'm not sure if she ever found out, I think she must have. If she did she never mentioned it.

Following a tennis match one Saturday afternoon all the participants were invited to the Sergeants Mess for tea and refreshments. Later we retired to the lounge and as soon as it became known Marion could play the piano she was persuaded to perform. As a result she became one of the more popular guests and we spent many enjoyable evenings having the traditional British singalong. We became an excepted couple by my compatriots and their wives; all knew I was married to Rose but no longer living together. There was some gossip behind our backs but we didn't care.

One of the first to welcome Marion was my old friend Sergeant George Ruggles and his wife. George wasn't at all surprised that my marriage had failed he thought we were totally unsuited. He also recalled the conversation we had the first time I was going to meet Rose. I had mentioned about her father being in a Nursing Home. He had known all along that he was in a Mental Institution and now regretted not telling me. He also said there were those who thought her sister Norma was a little "peculiar" too. This, of course, proved prophetic.

George also talked from first hand experience about servicemen following the end of the First World War. How, despite many political promises of a land fit for heroes, hundreds of thousands were released back into civilian life with no help whatsoever. All they had to look forward to was unemployment lines and soup kitchens. I realised my period of Regular service expired the following year and decided to re-enlist for another five years as soon as I was medically upgraded to A1.

Shortly after we met, Marion wrote to her husband about our friendship. She insisted on reading all the letters to me and I was surprised at her sincerity and frankness. It was strange listening to her description of some of our activities. Later, she would read his replies and again I was amazed at how he accepted my friendship with his wife. In time, more details came to light providing a better understanding.

She wrote to her parents and told them about me and I was invited for a delightful weekend at their country home. It was a large cottage with thatched roof, leaded windows, low beamed ceilings and the most beautiful English country garden. It was all very proper, of course, I slept in the guest room and Marion in her old room. But something happened that weekend. Marion was such a fun person to be with, a bubbly sort of personality, liked by everybody, loved by most.

We went for long walks then stood around the piano singing the old favourites in the cool of the evening. It was the kind of weekend made for the young at heart, the kind that would stir young people to plan for the future. But in wartime there was, for us, no future. Tomorrow's ground was uncertain, hopes and dreams all too often shattered by the ravages of war. Besides, we had an agreement didn't we? There could be no long-term future for us.

That's right, from the very beginning we agreed nothing permanent could come of our friendship. Despite the long separation from her husband and what had happened, Marion was still deeply in love with him. He was her first love and nothing could change that, she said.

In the beginning, we were very formal. Gradually, though we didn't realise it, desires were being awakened. It began innocently enough, just walking arm in arm, then holding hands. Nothing wrong with that surely? It doesn't mean we own each other. Then our goodnights became more than just a peck on the cheek. But, what the heck, kisses aren't commitments! Birthdays came and we exchanged gifts but we knew that presents weren't promises. We were "keeping company," so what? Neither of us was looking for security.

About every fourth month there would be a weeks break between recruit intakes. My colleagues used the time to review training techniques. Being the C.Q.M.S., I was spared such tasks. Marion had Wednesday afternoons off so on September 22, I got permission to take off at noon.

It was hot and sultry with thunderclouds gathering overhead, there'd be a storm soon. Marion was upstairs when I arrived and as usual I removed my shoes and jacket. Battle Dress could be so uncomfortable in hot weather. Hearing me she ran downstairs. We embraced as usual but somehow today was different and we both knew it.

I hesitated.

"Suppose you were to get pregnant?"

She pulled me closer assuring me she had finished her period just yesterday, so it was unlikely. But what would her husband think? We were standing next to the dresser where she kept her writing materials. She leaned over and from the drawer removed a sheet of blue writing paper; I recognised the handwriting. She handed it to me.

"I think it's time you knew the whole truth."

I heard her footsteps on the stairs as I read the contents of both sides of the page. The confession to an extra marital affair included intimacy, it was all perfectly clear now. She returned wearing nothing but a flimsy, transparent nighty. She looked so seductive and once again embracing me she said,

"Now, wouldn't you like to make love to me?"

It was now October, the weather wet and cold. To see the children I had to swallow my pride and go to my mother-in-law's house. The reception was cool but to my surprise she showed no animosity. My father-in-law said little but I sensed he was deeply troubled that Rose and I had parted. Although I didn't know it at the time, she and the children would soon take up residence in London and I never saw the old man to speak to again. It was hard for him because I was responsible for his release from the institution. He was well aware that, but for me, he might have spent the rest of his life there.

From that time on I would spend only part of my leave with Rose and the children. We never again lived together as a couple and except for one unfortunate occasion we were never intimate. Instead, I would spend more and more time visiting the home of my mother's sister Edie in Romford.

I had discussed with her the role she played in the conspiracy of silence regarding my parents and accepted her explanation that she had to go along with it or lose a sister. She had already lost two brothers to unknown foster homes she said, and Nance was the only surviving relative. When I asked her why she never visited granddad Keeling, she replied that it was a family disagreement that went back many years and she was not prepared to discuss it. Now, her son Desmond was nineteen and in the Forces so we had much in common and a kind of affinity developed between us.

My favourite cousin Paula had become, like her mother, quite heavy and as a result had little social life. As so often happens her peers teased her unmercifully at school. I felt sorry for her and went out of my way to entertain her whenever I was there. Then there was ten year old James, he lived in awe of anything in uniform. Older brother Desmond and I were his heroes.

I was feeling good now with no sign of malaria, playing tennis all summer and now soccer. Having gained back most of the lost weight, I realised a posting was imminent; Marion was apprehensive. It would bring to an end what had become a very close and caring relationship. So we made a deal; we would set aside our fears for the future and make the most of every moment we were together.

My birthday, November 5, was on a Friday. Knowing it probably would be the last we would spend together we made the most of it. It was candlelight and wine and Marion's gift to me was a beautiful silver cigarette case with glowing terms of endearment engraved on the inside.

On the Sunday evening we sat by the fire reminiscing. The weekend spent with her parents was often the topic of discussion. I expressed the wish that I had parents like hers so that I might offer her a similar holiday; she surprised me.

"You know Frank, I would dearly love to meet your mother, just to see what kind of woman she really is. And I've never been to Brighton."

I wondered what she would say if she knew the whole truth.

"Well you surprise me, I can't imagine why you'd want to meet her but if that's what you would like we can easily arrange it."

And I took Marion to Brighton the next weekend.

I contacted my mother in the usual way and told her a little about Marion; that she was married and her husband was abroad. I stressed that our friendship was sincere but could never become anything more, and ended by saying she came from fine old English stock. Mother was impressed and said how much she looked forward to our visit.

"But she'll have to sleep in the middle room and you in your room, you know Fred wouldn't allow anything else."

"Of course mother" I replied, "I wouldn't dream of any other arrangement."

"Hm . . . I'm sure! Anyway we'll expect you about nine thirty Friday night . . . 'Bye."

We got away early on the Friday afternoon. I wore my navy blue Dress Uniform for a change, much more comfortable. Made from the finest Worcester material and the three bar chevron with crown mounted above, indicating my rank, were gold with red trim. Very smart, I had bought it for my wedding back in 1940.

We were to catch the five fifteen train to London. I arrived to pick up Marion around four-thirty, she had never seen me in "Blues" before and was very impressed, but I was in for an even bigger surprise.

"I'm all ready" she said excitedly, "Just got to put my coat on, you can help me with it."

"It", turned out to be a luxurious fur coat.

We boarded the train, packed as usual with troops of all nationalities. Walking down the centre isle of the coach to the Restaurant Car for dinner caused quite a stir.

"Jealousy will get them nowhere," I said.

Marion chuckled, clearly very happy. I was too, but the knowledge that time was not on our side made it a bittersweet occasion.

Mother greeted us in the hallway and immediately raved about the fur coat. Marion invited her to try it on and she pranced around the house with a sweeping motion just like Betty Grable. Fred was his usual simple self but had obviously been warned to be on his best behaviour.

After she'd calmed down my mother said,

"Come Marion dear, I'll show you up stairs, the guest room is all ready."

It was always the "middle room" to us, simply because of its location between the other two. Most disturbing though, this was the same room and the same bed in which I had lain with my mother. She and Fred now slept in the front bedroom. The thought of Marion sleeping in that bed was sickening but what could I do? I would have to live with this sort of thing for the rest of my life.

One thing about my mother, she sure knew how to put on the airs and graces, as we used to say. She and Marion found lots to talk about or perhaps I should say, mother did. And they were still at it when Fred and I retired.

I showed Marion the sights of Brighton the next day, including a walk on the famous promenade. It was chilly but otherwise a nice sunny day and she thoroughly enjoyed her whirlwind tour. We spotted a gentleman's wristwatch in a Pawnbroker's shop on Western Road that I admired. Without a word, Marion marched in the store and bought it for me.

She took us all out to dinner that night and refused any assistance with the bill. It was a good meal considering the times and a very nice restaurant. Everything was first class with Marion; the sheer luxury of pheasant and port wine remained with me for a long time.

Mother was quick to recognise all this and, perhaps it was the wine, but she proceeded to dote over me as if I was the prodigal son. I felt humiliated and was relieved when the visit ended. We left early on the Sunday, glad to be alone again. My mother was quite demonstrative as we said our good-byes and again, to me it was all so pretentious.

As the electric train sped toward London I said to Marion,

"Well, what do you think now that you've met her?"

She was not the type of person that would denounce anybody. Her philosophy was, if you can't speak well of someone don't speak at all. And so I wasn't surprised when she snuggled up to me and imitated Royalty that so often talk in the first person plural.

"We are not amused." Then in a more serious note.

"She's your mother so let's not criticise. She struck me as a rather tragic figure."

Tuesday, November 23, the news came. Another Sergeant, a Scotsman, and myself were to be posted to Scotland on the Thursday. He was quite happy; for the first time in years he would be stationed in the land of his birth.

This was the news we had both feared. I was saddened to be leaving Marion but glad that I would be playing a more meaningful role in fighting the war. I phoned Marion at her office, heard a gasp as I relayed the details and a distinct catch in her voice as she hung up the phone. It was a long, sad evening that we spent together.

The last hours before a posting are always hectic. I had to hand over the duties of C.Q.M.S., then draw additional equipment and pack my kit bag. One sad task was to remove the Crown above the three stripes on my Battle Dress; I would now revert to the rank of Sergeant. In those days, to retain a specific rank permanently one had to hold it continuously for one full year. I was penalised three times by this ordinance during the war.

I spent a couple of hours at my mother-in-law's house with Rose and the children. Mary was two-and-a-half and Albert just three weeks short of his first birthday neither understood the significance of my departure. Rose expressed concern but was otherwise cool; our goodbye was affectionate but not amorous. I knew it would be many months before I'd see them again and from somewhere in the depths of my mind, the fleeting thought that it might be never. But seldom does the universe unfold as we think it should.

The last hours before curfew were spent with Marion, a sad and difficult time for both of us. Our friendship had been short yet so meaningful. But we knew from the very beginning didn't we that it could only be ephemeral, two ships passing in the night. I know for my part, had the right word been spoken this could have changed. I am certain Marion felt the same but we both held our peace, thus the future was decided. It was long after mid-night when I finally eased myself from the arms of a grieving paramour and made my way back to Camp. Of one thing I was certain, having spent this all-too brief time with Marion, I could never go back to a life with Rose.

My travel orders were to leave Bury St. Edmunds by train at 0815 hours., arriving in Edinburgh the same evening. Next, an over-night train to Aberdeen arriving around dawn followed by a two-hour wait, then on to Inverness. The remainder of the journey was by bus.

Marion insisted she would ride her bike to the station for a few precious moments of final farewell then go to work. Imagine my surprise as, seated beside the driver of the truck taking us to the station, I saw Marion pedalling furiously along Risbygate Street in the opposite direction. I wondered where on earth she could be going? Wherever it is she'll have to hurry to make the train, I thought.

We made our way through the tunnel, up the steps and on to the platform. There to be greeted by the sight of Rose standing a few feet from the Waiting Room with the children in the pram. It would have been nice if she was there to bid me bon voyage but I knew her appearance was born out of curiosity. To see whom else might be there.

I knew then that she was aware of my affair with Marion but she made no mention of it. Instead, all bright and breezy she said,

"I thought it would be nice to bring the children to say good-bye."

"Oh! . . . How thoughtful of you," I replied.

But by this time the train had pulled into the station and it was all hustle and bustle. Finding a seat, getting my kit bag up on the rack and removing all my equipment in preparation for the long journey. Thus, there was little time for good-byes before the train was on its way.

Seeing Rose on the station platform I knew at once where Marion was headed. I went out into the corridor, opened the nearest window and hung out. Sure enough, there was Marion in the centre of that very same bridge frantically waving a white handkerchief. As the train passed under the bridge she crossed to the other side, I turned and continued to wave until she was lost from view.

She and I would be alone only once more in our lives and then under very different circumstances. She would explain to me how that morning, she had seen Rose heading for the railway station and decided to make for "Our bridge." She also saw me in the truck.

"I just knew you would realise where I was headed," she said.

There were no wild promises about writing every day or keeping in touch, just one simple but tearful request.

"Drop me a line when you have time . . . Just to let me know you arrived safely" and after a long pause, "Would you ask your mother . . . if anything . . . were to happen . . . I mean . . . serious . . . to please let me know?"

I did write, just before Christmas. No sloppy love stuff mind you, just a nice, warm, friendly letter telling of my new surroundings and friendships. And of course, Seasons Greetings . . . ended with, "Affectionately Yours, Frank". Nothing suggestive, nothing incriminating . . . Well, that was the way it was supposed to be wasn't it? There had been no commitments, no promises; each laid no claim to the other. We knew it had to end and the time was now.

I didn't contact my mother either; what the heck, nothing's gonna happen to me.

Twenty-three

And A Drunken Sailor

The north of Scotland can be a harsh and unforgiving land and the banks of the Moray Firth in the dead of winter are no exception. 1943-44 was, according to the locals, one of the worst winters in living memory. Those bitter north east winds were cold enough to freeze the balls off a brass monkey. The only redeeming factor was the kindness and hospitality of the good folks in Nairn and the tiny village of Ardersier.

I corresponded regularly with Rose and was kept informed of the childrens' progress. In mid-January she wrote to say her sister had kindly found them a house "right next door" and that she had moved in already. Again, no reference to the letter I'd written to my brother-in-law so many months earlier.

I visited her at the new home in London and during this visit she asked me not to say anything to sister Norma or husband Frank about us being separated.

"It's none of their business" she said "and besides, who knows what the future might bring."

She went on to say her parents didn't know either. I had a feeling she was thinking about reconciliation but said nothing.

The new home was the typical three bedroom, terraced house with a small front garden and a larger one at the back. It had been built just after the turn of the century but had been well maintained. I inspected the back garden and at the far end came face to face with a young sailor in the garden immediately behind ours, he was also on leave. We chatted and finding we were both soccer fans, decided to go to White Hart Lane that afternoon to watch Tottenham play. After the game we agreed to get together on the Monday morning for a drink.

Just before the ten o'clock opening time we took a bus to the Angel Hotel, a pub located on the border between Edmonton and Tottenham. There was at least one pub at every intersection between the Angel and the Cock Inn, just around the corner from where we both lived. Some idiot challenged us to drink one pint of beer in each pub and survive. Full of bravado we accepted the challenge.

It was a stupid and irresponsible thing to attempt and long before we reached home we were both very much the worst for wear. I am ashamed to say I have never been so drunk in all my life. It took me days to recover and I recall little of what transpired. In fact, to this day I have no recollection of taking that long train journey from Northern Scotland to London for that leave. I do recall, however, taking Rose and the children boating on Edmonton Lake on the Thursday. "Oh! What do we do with a drunken sailor?" After this fiasco I had some very strong feelings as to what we should do.

On the Friday the sailor and I went our separate ways, he to his ship in Portsmouth and me for a quick visit to Auntie Edie and Paula. I returned to Scotland on the Monday.

By this time rumours of the impending invasion of the continent were rampant. Letters from loved ones began to express concern and apprehension as well as admiration and encouragement. I was the recipient of one such letter from Marion, the only one she ever wrote. It wasn't just a letter to me, it was a tribute to all those serving their country. It also described the feelings of those like Marion, left behind to wait and wonder. And it was written with such tenderness and understanding that grown men with whom I shared some of her comments were moved almost to tears.

The allied invasion of the continent took place on June 6, 1944. It was not the text book operation that many would have us believe and there are simply no words to describe the horror of it all. But as I have already indicated, that is "grist for another mill."

In mid June I found myself in hospital back in Scotland. I was there for five weeks. The last two were spent in occupational therapy on a farm, haymaking with a horse and cart. It was great rehabilitation and reminded me very much of life in Ongar.

Marion learned that I was in hospital through a mutual acquaintance back in Bury St. Edmunds. She immediately took an overnight train and made straight for the hospital. Told only relatives could visit at that hour, she promptly became my sister-in-law. She could only stay for the weekend but it was good of her to go to so much trouble and expense and I thoroughly enjoyed her stay. She was my only visitor.

The most disturbing thing while in hospital came in the form of a letter from Rose telling me she was pregnant. My first reaction was, so what? "Happened when you were on leave in February," the letter went on. I remembered the drunken episode with my sailor friend but that wasn't February.

The hospital had its own weekly newsletter run by patients, another form of occupational therapy. A quick check of their records revealed that Tottenham played at home on Saturday, March 31, 1944. For a moment I felt a little smug, but then began to wonder. Was it possible? Surely not . . . When I've had that much to drink I'm absolutely useless, could never rise to the occasion as it were. I've always been like that. Anyway, I would have remembered . . . of course I would. No, it just could not be! . . . But it was.

I was discharged from hospital on July 21, and spent the next week in a Transit Camp in Colchester. Monday August 31, I was sent to London, to the Hotel Great Central again. That brought back a flood of memories.

By this time hundreds of pilotless planes loaded with explosives, officially known as V1's, we called them "Doodle Bugs" and rocket-propelled missiles,

V2's were being aimed at London every day. Between June 13, 1944, and March 29, 1945, almost three thousand flying bombs fell on London. Sixteen thousand people were killed, another eighteen thousand injured and twenty-three thousand homes destroyed. But this was minor compared to the "blitz" of 1940.

A large Army facility housing sensitive documents had been severely damaged and I was in charge of a group of men responsible for the salvage of the material. I was there until August 28, a little over a month. Several times I thought about visiting Rose but kept making excuses, I knew it would be an ordeal. Besides, we were working long hours, six and sometimes seven days a week. I was always so tired; just didn't feel up to it. But now it was September 3, and I was going on my first leave since April. No more excuses, tomorrow morning I would be on my way to face Rose.

That first discussion was surprisingly civil. My "February" leave was again mentioned and I corrected her.

"Oh, February . . . March . . . Whatever," she irritably replied.

"I have no recollection of any such incident," I insisted.

But no matter, the deed was done and that was that. There was nothing more to be discussed as far as Rose was concerned.

I asked when the baby was due.

"Oh . . . about December the 18th., the doctor says," and then she rather smugly added, "It'll all be over nicely before Christmas."

I dropped the subject; Rose's Army allowance would increase with the arrival of the child so why worry? What the hell! . . . Who cares? There's a war on, life's too bloody short to worry.

The following afternoon I went downtown alone. When I returned there was a telegram from Colchester. RETURN TO UNIT IMMEDIATELY STOP was all it said. Damn my hide, first bloody leave since last April and look where that got me. Now this, can't win can I. Gathering my belongings I bade the family a hasty farewell and was on my way.

At this point in the war thousands of Germans were being taken prisoner daily. Prisoner of War (POW) Camps were springing up all over the British Isles. It was to one such Camp in Staffordshire that I was posted.

Because I could speak the language I was appointed to a position with the unlikely title of "Cage Master." This meant that I spent all my time inside the compound co-ordinating the administration and security of some three-hundred-and- eighty prisoners. Many of them were high-ranking officers. Strangely, my predecessor was a full Lieutenant but rest assured it was nothing like "Hogan's Heroes."

Shortly after my arrival the locals put on a dance for the troops. I went with a buddy and during the course of the evening had one dance with a young girl from a neighbouring village. After the dance she was waiting for me outside.

"Cindy," for obvious reasons not her real name said,

"I wasn't able to dance much this evening because I've just come out of hospital after a minor surgery but would very much like to be a friend."

"Well," I said, "I'm married with two children and another on the way. So nothing much can come of any friendship."

"Oh, that's all right," she replied, "I know it's a lonely life up there at the Camp, I'd just like to offer a little company."

This was not uncommon in those days; families would often adopt a soldier and provide a few home comforts. So I finished up walking the three miles to her home.

As we walked I told her a little about my background and let slip that I was separated. I then had to explain the episode with the drunken sailor, thus accounting for my wife's latest pregnancy.

Within days I was invited to her home, met her parents and was a frequent visitor. I was on duty on Christmas Day so they arranged their special meal a day early so as to share it with me. This hospitality continued until the day I left.

From the beginning, she asked me not to tell her parents I was married.

"They wouldn't approve," she said.

It wasn't long before I learned she had been sexually active for some time and I was encouraged to participate; I accepted.

I took her into a nearby town to the cinema and while waiting for a bus for the return journey we browsed through a jewelry store. She admired an attractive little ring, it was relatively inexpensive so I bought it for her but emphasized it was nothing more than a friendship ring. I also made sure her parents understood the nature of the gift. They expressed disappointment that it was not an engagement ring because, they said,

"We have grown very fond of you."

I told them it was much too soon for such talk.

Then I got a forty-eight hour pass and decided to go to Brighton in the hopes of renewing my friendship with my friend Reg, I hadn't seen him in years. Cindy expressed disappointment that I would be away so, much to her surprise, I invited her to come with me.

We stayed with my mother, Cindy sleeping in the middle room and me in my old room. As we already know, Fred would have it no other way. We did, however, make love on the couch in the living room one afternoon; trouble was my mother returned unexpectedly from a shopping trip and caught us in the act. Her reaction was mild to say the least, she simply apologised and beat a hasty retreat. I met Reg too, we bumped into him in the line up at a cinema, retired to the nearest pub and had a most enjoyable reunion.

Late in the afternoon of November 6, I received a phone message that Rose had given birth to a daughter. This was followed two days later by a letter in which she informed me that Angela had been born prematurely. She wrote that, the night before, she and sister Norma, "Drank almost a full bottle of Creme de Menthe between us." She was sure this had caused the premature birth.

In accordance with Army procedure I notified the Company Office of the date, place of birth and given names, for publication in Part II Orders. Thus the Army Records office and the Paymaster would be informed. Five weeks later, in mid December, I went on leave again and saw Angela for the first time. She was a beautiful baby with fair hair and blue eyes.

During my stay I drank no alcohol and slept on the couch downstairs, for as Cicero put it, "To stumble twice against the same stone is a proverbial disgrace." I also reminded Rose she should have received an increase in her Army allowance by now and to let me know if she didn't get it within the next week or two. I heard nothing more and assumed the increase was being paid.

Three years later while working at Infantry Records Office in Warwick, I persuaded one of the staff to let me look at my records, strictly forbidden under normal circumstances. I found no record of the birth of Angela and Rose had never received the additional allowance. She had, for reasons known only to herself, chosen not to pursue the matter. To this day only Mary and Albert appear on my Army records.

I must say I was ill prepared for what occurred on the second evening of my leave. Again, it gives me no pleasure to recount what happened and I do so only because it ended what had been, up to that point, a very tenuous relationship.

She had made up her mind we were going to have sex and I was just as determined we weren't. She seemed obsessed with the notion that I couldn't resist her and despite my insistence that I could, she continued her advances. I pleaded with her not to humiliate herself, that regretfully I no longer found her attractive and wanted nothing to do with her proposal. Despite this, she slowly and deliberately removed every item of clothing until completely naked. Meanwhile, she repeatedly challenged me to deny that she was attractive and pleaded with me to make love to her.

All this took place in the living room and I have never been so embarrassed in my entire life. I finally brushed her aside and left the room; she stormed upstairs in a dreadful rage. I say in all sincerity that I would have given anything for it not to have happened.

The following morning I said a hasty farewell to the children and left, the last time I would see them for a very long time. I spent the remainder of this leave in Romford.

Returning to my unit, Cindy said she had obtained my home address and had written to me. I expressed my annoyance that someone would divulge this information, to do so was strictly forbidden. But I had seen no such letter so dismissed the matter from my mind. It wasn't long before I got a letter from Rose telling me that her sister Norma, on one of her frequent visits while I was on leave, had picked the letter off the floor in the hallway. She kept it until the day I left then gave it to, Rose saying the writing looked feminine. This was the second time Norma had interfered with my mail, a criminal offense. I could have taken legal action but just didn't care anymore.

The letter from Cindy was filled with terms of endearment and of how much I was missed. Norma was informed that I had admitted to an affair but it was all over now. Rose concluded her letter by chastising me for "giving this slut my address."

Shortly after Christmas 1944, I was posted to another POW Camp in

Northern Ireland, to the small town of Markethill in County Armagh. This was just a few miles from the border with the South, which had remained neutral throughout the war. It became an attractive refuge for prisoners-of-war bent on escape to a neutral country.

I took my quarterly ten days leave of absence from the first to the eleventh of March 1945. Being in Northern Ireland we were allowed an extra day travel time.

After what happened in December there was no way I was going to visit Rose. I spent the entire leave with the Wright family in Romford. But this particular visit would set off a chain of events that, although frustrating at times, would have the most profound effect on the rest of my life.

The overnight ferry trip across a very rough Irish sea from Belfast to Heysham was dreadful. And there was still the long and tedious train journey to London. When I arrived at Auntie Edie's house I was exhausted. This, however, was the one place I could be assured of a quiet and restful visit. As well, she and Paula always made a fuss of me, but this time everything turned out very different.

Twenty-four

Joy To The World

Being a frequent visitor to the Wright household I didn't have to await permission to enter, I simply rang the bell, walked in and announced myself. This time I sensed something was wrong the moment I opened the door.

"Hello! . . . Anybody home? . . . It's me . . . Frank."

And usually, depending on the time of day, there would be a rush of excitement and a fond greeting. Paula called out from upstairs.

"We're up here Frank, come on up."

Everyone, including Uncle George was in James' room.

"Scarlet Fever, doctor came this afternoon," auntie Edie said, looking grim.

James wasn't feeling up to visitors so I expressed my regrets, hoped he would soon recover and we all went downstairs for a cup of tea.

Uncle George explained that three days earlier, James had started vomiting, developed a high fever and sore throat so they called the doctor. It was a relatively mild attack, not serious enough for hospitalisation but the doctor would return the next day for further assessment. He insisted everyone take precautions because it was highly contagious. Paula was to be kept away from school for the next ten days.

I had left Markethill after lunch the previous day and was absolutely exhausted, so I was relieved when auntie Edie said I could stay if I wished. I would pay a price for my decision but in a most unusual way.

James was eleven and not a good patient. He was the baby of the family, a bit spoilt and had everyone running ragged. But despite everything we had some enjoyable moments. Paula celebrated her fourteenth birthday on the 9th., and we made the most of it. When I left, James was well on the way to recovery but Paula looked a little pale and complained of stomach pains.

We had a small Medical Centre in Camp staffed by a Sergeant in the Royal Army Medical Corps. When he learned I'd been exposed to scarlet fever he put me in quarantine saying I would be putting hundreds of men at risk. I was stuck in that tiny isolation room for ten days.

I was due to return to my regular job as Cage Master at 0800 hours, Thursday, March 22, but to my astonishment, found myself detailed for guard duty. I complained bitterly but was told there was to be a rotation of staff. When I asked why I was given the stock answer, "Yours is not to reason why, yours is to do or die." I expressed my displeasure in typical army terms but to no avail.

I loathed guard duty; hadn't done it for years, but what was most objectionable, in Markethill anyway, was that it was a twenty-four hour stint commencing at four in the afternoon. Thus two consecutive evenings were ruined, the one on duty and the one following, when you were too tired to do anything. Not that there was much to do in Markethill, it was just a small village, one main street and a few Council Houses at the far end. It did have a village hall and we arranged a dance once; had a hell of a job finding enough females.

Anyway, I decided since I had nothing to do all morning I would take a stroll down to the village and have a pint at the local. It was strictly forbidden, of course, but what the heck, I deserved a little freedom after being cooped up in isolation for ten days.

It's surprising how time flies when you're relaxed and doing something you enjoy. There I was all by myself just sipping away, a little idle chatter now and then with the landlord or the barmaid. Suddenly I felt very tired; don't know why, slept good last night. Haven't done a darn thing for three weeks, first my leave and then that bloody isolation, what an idiot that Sergeant was to do that to me. Totally unnecessary, I knew I wouldn't get scarlet fever.

I looked at the clock. Blimey! It's gone twelve. Half an hours walk back to camp, I'll miss dinner. So I decided to phone my buddy the Motor Transport (MT) Sergeant, he'd send a truck to pick me up. I'd done him lots of favours.

The switchboard operator answered before the completion of the customary double ring.

"MT office please," I said.

"One moment, I'll put you through."

A single ring this time, then a voice I didn't recognise.

"MT Office"

"Oh, is Tommy there?"

"No he isn't . . . lunch."

"Oh, yeah 'course he would be, well this is Sergeant Keeling, I'm down the village . . . In the pub . . . Don't feel like rushing . . . I'll miss dinner, so send a truck down for me will yer? . . . He won't mind . . . you know the place . . . the one on the right . . . bottom of the hill."

The voice at the other end made an inaudible comment and hung up but I knew they'd do that little thing for me, so I decided to have another pint while I waited.

The door of the pub was wide open so I could see the road from my barstool. I hadn't got half way down my glass before there was a screeching of brakes and a truck pulled up right outside the door.

Jeez! I thought, that was quick. Good blokes these MT types. Ah, but what's this? It's the MT Officer himself and for one brief moment I thought how nice of him to come himself, just to pick me up. But the stern look on his face, in fact, his whole demeanour, told me there was something very, very wrong.

"What the hell do you think you're doing here Keeling? Drinking at this time of the day and you're on guard duty at 1600. You know this is not allowed."

Ah, now I recognised the voice that had answered the phone.

"Yes, sir," I replied, "But you know Sir I've been cooped up in Camp in isolation for ten days."

"Yes I know that and it's a good job you've got three stripes on your arm or you'd be cooped up for another ten. You're on a charge, now get in the truck."

Rotten bastard I thought, but I didn't say anything except, "Yes Sir" and we drove back to Camp in silence.

When we arrived, things went from bad to worse. My high falutin chauffeur said I wasn't in a fit state to perform guard duty, ordered me to my room and told me to report to the CO's office at nine o'clock the next morning.

I didn't stay in my room. I just had a sleep for a couple of hours then went to the pub again and to hell with all of 'em. I even passed the Regimental Sergeant Major (RSM) on my way out of camp. He didn't say a word, not even his usual "evenin' Sar'nt." Ah well, who cares anyway?

At 0855 hours the following morning, Friday the 23rd., I presented myself outside the Orderly Room where the CO's office was located. There were three of us, two Privates and myself due to appear for various misdemeanours. As the senior person I would be dealt with first.

We were inspected by the RSM and then told to stand at ease. The Adjutant came out and stood talking to him. Shortly afterward, the RAMC Sergeant arrived with a file under his arm. He saluted the Adjutant and handed him the file, as he did so I caught a glimpse of the name and regimental number printed in the top right hand corner. It was mine!

So, I thought, the old man has asked for my Medical Records. Why would he do that I wonder? . . . Probably to do with my stint in isolation . . . Yeah, of course, what else? Shortly thereafter I was marched in and the charge was read.

"Conduct prejudice to good order and Military discipline" etcetera, etcetera.

The Motor Transport Officer (MTO) gave his evidence.

". . . . Sitting alone in the MT Office at 1217 hours on the 22nd., instant" . . . "the phone rang and the accused requested transportation from the pub in Markethill" . . . "sounded inebriated" . . . "to avoid embarrassment to the unit I complied" . . . "considered the accused unfit for guard duty" . . . "ordered him to his room and placed him on a charge . . . Sir!"

With all the solemnity of the occasion you'd have thought I'd committed first degree murder . . . At least!

The CO quietly acknowledged the evidence given saying,

"Thank you Geoffrey, that'll be all."

He slowly raised his head and looked at me.

"I've always looked upon you as one of my best NCOs' Keeling," he said, "What went wrong?"

"Well sir," I replied, "I'd been stuck in that ten by twelve room in the Medical Centre for ten days, wasn't even allowed out for meals. Then I thought I was going back to my old job as of yesterday but found myself detailed for guard duty. I was upset about that, it was a beautiful morning, I didn't have anything to do and I just felt I had to get away for a while. It was a foolish thing to do and I apologise Sir. And I only had two beers so I'm quite sure I could have handled my duties as Guard Commander, Sir."

"Hm . . . This isolation, how did that come about?"

"Sir, I went on leave to my Aunt's and my young cousin came down with scarlet fever while I was there, when I returned the RAMC Sergeant insisted I be quarantined Sir."

He looked down at my records, turned a page.

"You're married?"

"Yes Sir."

"Two children?"

"Three Sir."

"Oh . . . Didn't you go and see them?"

"No Sir, we're separated."

"Oh . . . I see . . . How long?"

"Er . . . Eighteen months Sir." Again he looked down at my records and turned a page. Wish he'd get it over with.

"Did no one tell you why your duties had been changed?"

"No Sir."

"Did you ask?"

"Yes Sir."

"And what were you told?"

"I was told it was not for me to question Sir"

"Hm . . . Well I ordered the change. You'd been doing that job continuously since last September. That's enough for anybody, stuck in that cage eight to ten hours a day or more, weren't you feeling the pressure? The Adjutant thought you were."

"Well Sir," I said, "it can be a strain at times but with leave every three months it's manageable."

"Yes well, I've been looking at your Medical Records, you shouldn't have been assigned to this kind of work in the first place . . . The case is dismissed, Sar'nt Major."

"Sir," snapped the RSM.

"This NCO is to be placed on light duties until further notice. That'll be all. Thank you!"

"About . . . turn . . . quick March" barked the RSM and I marched out of there feeling pretty lucky to have such an understanding CO. Once outside the Sar'nt Major told me to fall out and take it easy, he'd be in touch.

I had the rest of the weekend off much to the chagrin of my colleagues, and on the Monday and Tuesday afternoons I was given a most unusual task. The unit had been presented with six silver bugles, where they came from no one knew. Anyway, five men with limited experience were assigned to form a bugle band. It was my job to take them to the furthermost corner of the compound and teach them all the military bugle calls.

Tuesday March 27th., returning from a session I bumped into the Company Commander. I saluted and he stopped dead in his tracks.

"Keeling you lucky bugger, do you know where you're going?"

"No Sir."

"Well" he growled, "You're going to Broadstairs, the most beautiful seaside resort in the British Isles and I'm bloody envious!" And he stalked off.

The rest of the day I packed, bade farewell to friends and by noon the next day I was in Belfast. Leaving my kit bag at a cafe, I toured the city.

The overnight ferry to Heysham wasn't as rough as the previous trip but the train journey to Broadstairs via London was long, tedious and boring. By suppertime I was glad to be settled in a private house which, like most others in the area had been expropriated by the Army for the duration of hostilities.

I was billeted in a middle class neighbourhood. The house was unfurnished except for the regular army cot and footlocker. It was located just a block from Victoria Parade and the Band Shell. The unit was a huge Transit Camp for personnel awaiting reassignment.

My roommate gave me a quick orientation and informed me the Commanding Officer was a creep who insisted one had to be there for a month before qualifying for a weekend pass. Rotten bastard, I thought. Sits on his parsimonious butt dreaming up ways to make life miserable for us peasants. "Colonel Blimps" we used to call them; few had seen combat and most spoke with that exaggerated English accent.

The following morning, March 30, was Good Friday and after the usual paperwork and kit inspection, I was told to take the rest of the day off. Ah well, maybe it wasn't so bad after all. Went to dinner at noon then back to my billet and lay on my bed. Must have dozed off because the next thing I know this bloke is shaking me.

"You Sergeant Keeling? He says.

And I, still half-asleep just grunt.

"Well this is for you then."

And he hands me a telegram. I hated receiving these darn things, always seemed ominous . . . probably from my mother . . . or Rose . . . something wrong with one of the children . . . better open the bloody thing . . . no good looking at it is it! I ripped open the envelope and nearly fell off my bed then read it a second time. Blimey! What a shocker!

PAULA CRITICALLY ILL STOP ROMFORD COTTAGE HOSPITAL STOP ASKING FOR YOU STOP PLEASE COME STOP EDIE STOP.

I had become quite close to Paula. Although more than eleven years her senior I was more like a big brother than a cousin and the news bothered me. I remembered her complaining of stomach pains when I was there maybe it was appendicitis? . . . No, that wouldn't be critical, not unless there were complications but you never know. Anyway, no good sitting here speculating, better do something. It was twenty minutes past three; I'd slept two hours.

The Company Office was closed but a Lance Corporal stood outside.

"Where's the Orderly Sergeant?" I wanted to know.

"Oh, he's married and lives out, won't be back till four-thirty."

"Any idea where I could find the Company Commander?"

"God no! He's gone till Tuesday."

"Sargeant Major?"

"He's gone too."

"What about the Orderly Officer, any idea where I could find him?"

"Well he was around the dining hall at dinner time, lots of complaints; bloody swags and mash was awful . . . "

"Listen Corporal," I interrupted, "I've got an emergency, I'm not interested in the culinary problems of this military establishment. Where the hell is the Orderly Room?"

"Oh, sorry Sarge, well, let me think . . . it's on . . . I think it's on . . . er! . . ."

"Oh, never mind I'll find it," I said somewhat exasperated and turned on my heel wondering what the hell the army was coming to.

It wasn't the same anymore. Within six weeks the war would officially end but everyone knew it was all over. Attitudes were changing, we hadn't had a Good Friday or an Easter Monday off in six years and now half the unit was missing at four o'clock in the afternoon. After walking a block I saw an officer approaching, I saluted.

"Excuse me Sir, I have an emergency and I'm looking for the Orderly Officer." Before I could say more he replied.

" 'Fraid I can't be of much help Sergeant. I'm not stationed here I'm just on leave but I think your Orderly Room is on Westcliff Road, I've passed it a couple of times. You go down here, take the second on your right, then the second on your left, that's Granville Road. Go down there take the second on your left again, that's Granville Avenue and it's just across the street.

"Thank you, Sir," and as I saluted again I jokingly said, "If I can't find it, I'll come back and ask you again."

He gave me a sickly smirk as if I were stupid or something. Trouble with these officers . . . No sense of humour!

I'd just turned onto Granville Road when I saw my room mate with a very attractive woman on his arm. Turned out it was his wife visiting for the Easter weekend.

"So, where're you off to, Frank?"

I told him about the telegram and that I was looking for the Orderly room.

"I'd like to try and get some compassionate leave, this girl is more like a sister to me," I said.

"Well you're going in the wrong direction."

"Oh!" I cut in, "An officer just told me it was on Westcliffe Road."

"No way, that's the RASC Office, come on I'll show you, it's not far."

"Sure you don't mind? I don't want to take you out of your way."

"No problem, we can get where we're going that way too."

We did a complete turn around and walked for about five minutes.

"There y'are, Frank," my room mate said, "Lukem yu bakagen."

He'd been to Africa too and that's Pidgin English for "see you later." I thanked him and made my way up the steps and through the main door.

Over the first door on the left was a sign "ORDERLY ROOM," progress at last. I explained the purpose of my visit to the clerk and she disappeared through another door. The clock on the wall indicated it had been almost an hour since I got the telegram. A female Warrant Officer appeared.

"Hello Sergeant," she said "I'm Warrant Officer Manning, everybody calls me `WO', I hear you've had some bad news."

I handed her the telegram.

"What relationship is Paula to you?"

"Cousin," I said, "but she's more like a sister. I lived most of my life with my Aunt" . . .That's not a lie, think about it!

"Well they don't normally grant compassionate leave for a cousin but I'll take it to the Adjutant. I'll have to hurry they'll both be leaving any minute."

"Thanks," I said, and presumed she was talking about the CO.

Another five minutes went by then the phone on the Receptionist's desk rang. "Looks like you're just in time, he's agreed to see you."

I was ushered into a waiting room and after listening to the shuffling of paper, this tall, fair haired, toffee nosed officer with an Oxford accent irritably said,

"All right, come in Sergeant."

I walked into his office, stood to attention and saluted. Most officers would pleasantly tell you to stand at ease, this creep looked at his watch and growled.

"All right, all right. Now, you want leave for a sick cousin, we don't accept that relationship as compassionate grounds."

I dragged up everything that had happened in the last two years, a real sob story but I sensed I was getting nowhere. Then fate took a hand, "Himself" came out of another door.

"Are you nearly ready, oh? . . . What's the problem?"

The Adjutant told the CO about my request and pleaded my case better than I had, obviously feeling it necessary to justify the time he'd spent with me. Anyway, the CO asked what time had I received the telegram? Why hadn't I gone to my Company Commander? But before I could answer, said to the Adjutant.

"Oh! Give him a forty-eight, hurry up, let's go."

"Very good Sir. I'll just be a moment, come with me Sergeant."

He signed the blank pass telling WO Manning to fill in the details: After duty March 30 to 2359 hours April 1, 1945. Can't get away from that damned April Fool's day can I. She stamped the pass, filled in the stub and handed it to me. The next train I could catch would get me into Romford in the middle of the night so I decided to go early the next morning. WO Manning wished me luck and I was out of there.

The rest of the evening I meandered around feeling lost and worried about Paula. On High Street I heard music and decided to investigate. It was the regular Friday night dance, I watched the action for a few minutes. There were several ATS girls there, one nice looking blonde, a very good dancer too. I was in no mood for dancing though, so went back to my billet and to bed.

Arriving at Romford Cottage Hospital about three-thirty Saturday afternoon, I learned Paula was gravely ill with peritonitis. Everything that could be done had been done, I was told. I spent fifteen minutes at her bedside, tried talking to her then left, not knowing whether she recognised me. My Aunt was beside herself with grief when I arrived at the house. The doctors had said nothing more could be done and the best thing the family could do was to, "Go home, get some rest and pray!"

I did my best to comfort her and we all visited Paula in the evening, there was little change. The next twenty-four hours would be crucial we were told. We talked till one in the morning, none of us feeling like sleep.

Cousin Jean and I visited Paula Sunday morning, Auntie Edie and Uncle George in the afternoon. Jean took James out for a walk and I had a sleep then got ready to leave. I"d have to leave Romford about six-thirty to get back to Broadstairs by midnight.

When my Aunt and Uncle returned from the hospital they were in high spirits. Paula had taken a turn for the better, was alert and quite lucid. She vaguely remembered me being at her bedside and expressed the hope that I could visit her before leaving. I mentioned to Uncle George about the time of the train I would have to catch and he made a suggestion.

There was, he said, a mail train that left London Bridge Station at two-fifteen in the morning arriving in Broadstairs at six. I could catch an all-night bus just across the street from their house at eleven-thirty, which would take me directly to the station. The only drawback, I would have a two-hour wait in London. I didn't mind that and decided to go for it. I would sneak into my billet before most people were up and no one would be the wiser.

After an hours visit in the evening Paula was tiring but the worst was over and I was glad I'd stayed. Back at the Wright's house I realised my pass would expire before reaching London and there would be lots of military police (Red Caps) around. I examined the pass. WO Manning's writing, like her, was diminutive. The figure one following the word April was quite small; I could easily alter it to a 2, giving me an extra twenty-four hours. Once in Broadstairs I would tear the pass up, place it in the nearest garbage can and say I'd lost it.

The little bottle of Stevens ink was a lighter blue than the bulk ink supplied to the Army but after going over it a couple of times it looked reasonable. Anyway, it'll be dark so it won't be so obvious. Pleased with my handiwork and oblivious to any thought of failure I spent the rest of the evening drinking tea and chatting with the family.

Just as one should "Beware the Ides of March," I should have been more concerned about April fools' day. I was at London Bridge Station; everything had gone according to plan. There was an all night Canteen on the lower level and I can picture it to this day. A wide metal staircase with an iron handrail down the middle. I descended, looking forward to a nice cuppa tea, and as the lower floor came into full view I came face to face with a Red Cap. I felt a surge of adrenaline, he was only a Lance Corporal but there was no turning back now.

"Eve'nin Sar'nt," he said.

"Good evening, Corporal."

Trying to sound friendly and nonchalant, I emphasised the "Good" then made my way to the counter. So far so good, but he might quiz me on my way out, I'll have to have a good story ready. I mean, why would a person with a pass valid until Monday midnight, be wandering around London Bridge Station at two a.m Monday morning?

There was a copy of the Evening Standard beside an empty table so I spent the next hour hiding behind it, drinking tea and hatching my story. Wasn't that difficult really, just needed a little imagination. It went like this.

I was given compassionate leave to visit a critically ill relative in Romford Cottage Hospital. Her condition had been upgraded yesterday afternoon and she was now out of danger. He could verify those facts. I had decided to visit my parents in Brighton, hadn't seen them for a long time.

Brighton? Then why was I at London Bridge Station and not Victoria? Simple, the all night bus took me from right outside the door in Romford, directly to London Bridge; there was no similar bus to Victoria. And by the way, it was the last bus I could catch to make the first train to Brighton. I would end my story by saying that after visiting my parents I would take the Southern Railway train back to Broadstairs via Eastbourne, Hastings and Ashford.

Where was I off to now then? Well I was just going to walk around, being a bit stiff after sitting here all that time. Then I would check the Destination Board for the time of the first train and make my way to the appropriate platform. See, I'd thought of everything hadn't I, and that's why the eventual outcome was so inconceivable. There's no such thing as the perfect crime.

A couple of minutes before two, three Privates descended the stairs into the canteen and the Red Cap decided to check their credentials. Perfect I thought, now's my chance. I strode casually up the stairs, the Red Cap gave me a fleeting glance, I was home free.

The train was already at the platform, the engine making that gentle hissing sound as it got up steam. The only other sound to break the silence of the night was the clank of the Fireman's shovel as he fed the coal into the firebox.

The nights in London were strangely quiet now. Allied troops, nearing the River Elbe in eastern Germany had finally captured all the V1 and V2 launch sites and the last "Doodle Bug" had fallen on the City the previous Thursday, March 29. But it was an eerie silence. Because of gasoline rationing the once constant roar of traffic was but a memory and after five long, war-weary years Londoners could sleep in peace.

I found an empty compartment, stretched out on the seat and totally exhausted, immediately fell asleep. For the next two hours and forty-five minutes I was vaguely aware of strange noises and the occasional murmur of voices. The clickatty! clack! of the wheels was like a sedative and I drifted in and out of a deep but restless sleep.

Suddenly everything was different. The swaying had stopped; there were voices, lots of them, then the slamming of doors. I opened my eyes, the sun was shining and it was not only broad daylight it was Broadstairs. I jumped up still half asleep, grabbed my haversack from the luggage rack and made a hasty exit, convinced any moment the train would start moving again.

Once on the platform, I noticed several young Privates running up the grass bank at the far end of the platform and climbing over a high fence. Why on earth are they doing that? Silly young buggers.

I walked through the door into the waiting room and straight into a Red Cap. Now I knew why those silly young buggers were doing that. Before I had time to think he said.

"Your pass please Sergeant?"

Without thinking, I took my AB 64 (Personal Identification) out of my breast pocket and opening it, started to retrieve my pass from the inside pocket. Then it hit me - I'd altered the bloody thing hadn't I? What the hell was I thinking about? But it was too late; he had spotted the corner of that familiar Army form, for which men stole, lied, bribed and fought and which I had illegally altered. I looked pleadingly at him . . . His hand was outstretched . . . I was trapped. For one fleeting moment I wondered if my forgery would go undetected but no such luck.

It was Easter Monday, a time for rejoicing, or so we were told. But there was nothing for me to sing about; they threw the book at me. Absent without leave, in possession of a document purporting me to be on leave when, in fact, I was an absentee. Misuse of a Government document; conduct prejudice to good order and military discipline. And a host of other charges.

I was brought before the CO at nine o'clock, remanded for a Summary of Evidence, the precursor to a Court Martial and placed under close arrest. This meant house arrest and being accompanied by another Sergeant twenty-four hours a day. He was personally responsible for seeing that I didn't escape or do anything stupid.

Following the hearing, Sergeant "Smudger" Smith my first escort, decided we should go for a coffee. All Smiths are called "Smudger," because traditionally, blacksmiths smudged their invoices with their dirty hands. We found a quaint little restaurant, "The Tea Caddy," on the corner of High Street and Vere Road. It's now a Real Estate Office. Anyway, we went in, ordered coffee and took our seats. In the opposite corner there were two ATS girls. One a very attractive young blonde the other a very plain and much older looking brunette.

"The beauty and the beast" I joked to Smudger, keeping my voice low so as not to be overheard.

The blonde was facing me and for one fleeting moment our eyes met; but for the time being I had no interest in women, I had more important things on my mind.

We drank our coffee and left. As we walked down the hill, Smudger dawdled, waving repeatedly to the girls who had followed us out of the restaurant. I was impatient, wanting to get back to my Room and relax.

"Come on, Smudger," I said, "you're too old for them."

He kept waving till we reached Belvedere Road, I weakened and gave a half hearted wave then turned the corner dismissing the incident from my mind.

After lunch I lay on my bed still wondering how I, a relatively old soldier with lots of experience and two years of Intelligence training, could have been so stupid as to get caught. I recalled instances where men had purloined blank passes filled them in and got someone else to provide a signature. One bloke had a whole book full of blank passes and he would sell them to any willing buyer. They even had an old stamp and they would twist it just as it hit the paper so that it was smudged but looked authentic. They didn't get caught!

So, I'd committed a serious crime in the eyes of the Army and would have to face the music. No good worrying about it, there's nothing I can do now. If found guilty I would be reduced to Private, no doubt about that. But that wasn't the end of the world; it wasn't all beer and skittles being a Sergeant and I'd been one for almost five years.

The immediate problem was, while under close arrest I would receive no pay and it could be weeks before my case came to trial. I had no money in my savings account either. Ah well, I'd have to sell something if worse came to worst. I had a little left from last payday but not much, my trip to Romford had been expensive. My mind wandered idly; Rose and the children would be all right financially, my situation didn't affect their income at all.

Wonder how Paula is today? I wouldn't tell them what had happened, no point in worrying them or making them feel guilty.

Smudger was talking. He was much older than me and had a very prominent middle-age spread. Not a bad old stick though, a bit doddery at times which got on my nerves but I was stuck with him for the foreseeable future.

"Know what, Frank?" he was saying, "it's a beautiful afternoon and there's a Military Band playing down on Victoria Parade, first one since before the war. Let's go and listen to it."

"Oh no, Smudger," I said, "I hate military bands, besides I'm tired, didn't get much sleep last night, sooner just lay here and have a snooze."

But he was adamant and I knew that if we were to get along I'd have to compromise. So I reluctantly joined him in a leisurely stroll to the Band Shell.

The band was in full swing and we stood on the path right against the fence on the west side of the enclosure. Smudger was obviously in his glory, giving it the old "boompa! doompa! . . . doompa! doompa! doompa! . . . dah! dah!" as the band blared out its rendition of Colonel Bogey. Me, totally bored, thinking of a million things I'd rather be doing and a hundred places I'd rather be.

It was Easter Monday and it was April. My thoughts drifted back to Ongar and my childhood. I could see clusters of bright yellow primroses on a carpet of lush green grass. Hear childish laughter as the first bouquet of spring flowers was eagerly gathered for mum. Oh my! . . . Whatever happened to Jack? I felt lonely, empty and sad. And the music did nothing to soothe my savage breast.

Then a ray of sunshine came into my life in the form of that girl with the golden hair I'd seen in the Tea Caddy. She was walking toward us with the same companion. What a contrast, almost as different as Smudger and me. They hadn't seen us yet, giving me time to study the blonde as they came closer.

She had a neat figure and an open smiling face. Most striking though was her hair. It was the colour of golden corn, rolled up on her head with ringlets falling down each side of her face. As she drew nearer I felt somehow that destiny demanded I learn more about this lovely person. Suddenly I felt as if relieved of a heavy burden and my troubles forgotten, I threw caution to the wind.

"Well, hello! Blondie, how are you?"

She blushed lightly saying; "I'm fine . . . enjoying the music?"

"No I'm not" I said, I'm not fond of Military Bands"

"Neither am I . . . My friend is though' . . . so I agreed to walk down here with her."

By this time her friend was talking to Smudger and both were obviously enjoying the music. I found myself studying this girl again; she's nice I thought. Obviously a little shy, a pleasant change from some of the brazen females one met in the Forces these days. And again, that lovely long, blonde hair sparkling in the sunlight . . . I recalled it being said that a woman's hair is her Crowning Glory. It was longer than regulations allowed and she wasn't wearing a hat, also against regulations. But with hair like that who could blame her? Besides, the ATS hat wasn't at all attractive.

During the intermission the four of us decided to walk down onto the beach. We could still hear the music but it wasn't so crowded. Then it was time for introductions.

"This is Sergeant Smith," I said. "Like all Smiths he's known as `Smudger', I'm Frank by name and frank by nature." There was a chuckle.

"This is Alice," said the blonde, "my name's Joyce, everybody calls me Joy."

"Ah! . . . So you're Joy to the World," I said. "Now we know who it is they all sing about at Christmas."

Everybody laughed and the ice was broken.

We spent the rest of the afternoon and evening together as a foursome and had great fun. I learned that Joy and Alice were posted to Broadstairs to operate a military Tailor's shop, Joy having learned the trade in civilian life. I also learned that because she was such a good cook she had worked as the head Chef in the Officers' Mess for a period of her army career. I jokingly reminded her that, "The way to a man's heart was via his stomach." She promised to keep that in mind.

I felt compelled to explain my situation. About Cousin Paula and her critical illness the compassionate leave I had been granted and the terrible crime I had committed. I also explained the ramifications of being under close arrest including no pay and the enforced companionship of Smudger.

I had no regular duties now, just a couple of meetings with my Defending Officer and an appearance at the Summary of Evidence. I had much time on my hands and all my activities were subject to the agreement of my escort. On the plus side, however, we were billeted in civilian houses and thus free to come and go with very little interference.

Smudger, old enough to be my father, was not an ideal escort and to talk of a generation gap would be an understatement. And so I was very pleased when, the day after meeting, Joy another Sergeant was assigned to the job. He was about my age with red hair so naturally we called him Ginger. He was a conscript with little time for military protocol so that from the moment of his arrival, life under close arrest became much more tolerable.

As soon as he knew I was seeing a girl friend he suggested the three of us meet in some secluded spot. He would leave to pursue his own activities and we would meet again at the same spot just before curfew. The one condition being, Joy and I could not be seen alone in public, but we did manage several trips to the Cinema.

The day following our meeting a complication arose. Without prior warning we were moved to Cliftonville, half way between Broadstairs and Margate. There was no way to advise Joy so I was unable to meet her as arranged. But again, fate took a hand.

My new billet was opposite Montrose school on Northdown Park Road, one of the main streets leading into Margate. Joy, hearing of our move decided, along with Alice, to walk around the general area in which we were concentrated hoping to find us. By sheer coincidence I decided to sit on the wall in the front garden. I couldn't believe my eyes when I saw the two of them approaching, nor could I believe how excited I was to see her. I knew then that this girl meant more to me than just a friend.

Over the next three weeks we saw much of each other and feelings grew stronger with each passing day. She was fun to be with, uncomplicated, sincere and down-to-earth. She was also very kind to me. Knowing that I received no pay, she brought me a packet of cigarettes every day and the occasional bottle of beer.

Her tailors' shop was on Northdown Avenue in a three-story house with large bay windows. Ginger and I spent most of each day there and I had the best fitting uniform in the entire unit. Our evenings were spent walking in the surrounding countryside, very enjoyable, very romantic. There was no better place in all of England to go acourting.

But all was not well; I was married and I hadn't told her yet. We'd been seeing each other now for almost two weeks and she had admitted being fond of me the previous evening.

Reluctant to part and waxing a trifle poetic, I said,

"Do you think in the course of many moons you could learn to love me?"

She looked at me as if I was stringing her a line, but when she realised I was serious she responded saying, while this was a little sudden,

"I have become very fond of you."

I expressed my pleasure and there the matter was left.

Now it was time to come clean and I made up my mind to tell her that evening. I didn't know what to expect and wasn't looking forward to it. I knew it might end the relationship but it had to be done, it wasn't fair to deceive this girl any longer.

Ginger left us as usual and we were walking down Elmwood Avenue beside the North Foreland Golf course. Suddenly she stopped in the middle of the sidewalk, looked at me with a pained expression.

"I have something I must tell you," she said.

She looked pale and all sorts of things flashed through my mind but I don't think I was really prepared for what came next.

"I'm married," she said, looking as if it were the end of the world.

I just burst out laughing, I couldn't help myself. And there, in broad daylight I took her into my arms.

"So am I, and I've been tormenting myself about not telling you before and had made up my mind to tell you tonight."

Then we both laughed!

As we continued our walk, Joy explained she had married only five months earlier. As with thousands of young people, she was caught up in the expediency of war and drifted into marriage to a man discharged from the army on medical grounds.

On only her second visit to his home she learned that he and his entire family were chronic epileptics and, to make matters worse, it became obvious he was an alcoholic. She made up her mind there and then to end the marriage.

So, I thought, we had both been deceived, she about epilepsy and me about mental illness. Joy later told me the marriage had hardly been consummated. She being a virgin and neither of them having any experience, the wedding night was a fumbling, bumbling disaster. There had never been any further attempts so there were no children involved.

It took much longer for me to tell my story. I touched briefly on my childhood, about being given over to strangers at an early age and the conspiracy surrounding my parents. I told of the way in which I'd been manoeuvred into marriage, its initial breakdown and of my subsequent volunteering for service in Africa. I also told of my efforts at a new beginning and how it too had failed.

I told her about the children, including the birth of Angela following the episode with the drunken sailor. That their existence notwithstanding, I had decided almost two years previously that I couldn't face a lifetime with Rose. I mentioned that I had only visited them for a few days of each leave during that period; that since the previous December I had not seen them at all and the reason why. I assured her they were well provided for by what, in those days, was a relatively generous Army allowance.

Then, for some reason I felt compelled to tell her everything. I had no idea what the future might hold but if there was to be a future, I wanted no skeletons. With all the courage I could muster I explained the sordid affair with my mother. It was the first time I had told anyone since talking to the MO back in September 1939. I described the torment of having to harbour such a dreadful secret and of the terrible guilt I felt.

Joy was shocked and disgusted that a mother would do such a thing but didn't blame me. I was overwhelmed with the depth and sincerity of her compassion, of her understanding and felt a great sense of relief and gratitude. The subject was not mentioned for another forty-seven years.

I told Joy about my affair with Marion and for the first time, showed her the inscription inside my cigarette case. It was obvious the terms of endearment bothered her so I put the case away. Shortly afterwards I disposed of it altogether.

For the next two weeks we spent many hours talking about our situation and what lie ahead. Every conceivable angle was explored and every time we came to the same conclusion. We wanted very much to make a life together. We also knew how difficult it would be. But as I said then, and have said many times since, "Omnia vincit amor" Love conquers all things.

Twenty-five

Second Time Around

My trial by Field General court-martial took place in an old theatre on Monday April 23rd, 1945, and what a farce. Talk about a Kangaroo Court! The Judge, prosecuting officer, defending officer and Clerk of the Court sat on stage, witnesses in the isle seats, while the accused and escorts sat in the balcony. There were about twenty on trial, the entire proceedings resembled an assembly line and took less than a day.

It was impossible to hear what was being said and only by seeing my defending officer on stage, was I aware that my case was being heard. No plea, no witnesses, nothing; just the Prosecutor reading the charges, presenting the exhibits, followed by my defence counsel making his pitch, it took all of ten minutes.

Ginger, my escort, disgusted with this so-called military justice, urged me to write to my Member of Parliament insisting that the matter be raised in the House. He offered support but I declined. It was unlikely to change anything and I wasn't prepared to face the delay. I knew that with my experience and skills I wouldn't be a Private long.

The sentence was handed down on Thursday, April 26, and as expected, I was found guilty and reduced to the rank of Private.

"Well at least," I joked, "Joy and I are now on equal terms, I can no longer pull rank."

She cut the stripes off my sleeves with a razor blade and we stuffed them down a drain. Then the three of us, Ginger, Joy and I, went to our favourite pub and celebrated my freedom. Joy missed curfew, staggered out of a taxi minus her hat, right into the arms of WO Manning. She was placed on a charge and sentenced to seven days CB (Confined to Barracks). But it had little effect on our lives because she still had to go to work and she worked lots of overtime for the next seven days.

I was assigned to the armourer's shop repairing various types of weaponry and other military paraphernalia. It was located opposite Joy's shop so we saw more of each other than before and I quite enjoyed the work.

She insisted I meet her family before making any final commitment. So on

Friday, May 4th., we spent the week-end with her parents in Ipswich, in the County of Suffolk. On the train Joy insisted that her's was an ordinary working class family, her father a carpenter and joiner. I told her that Paddy Bunton, the only father I'd ever known was the same. I also pointed out that J.C.'s father was too, so not only did we have much in common, we were in the best of company. After a while I had to explain that J.C. was Jesus Christ.

I was well received by the family including ninety-year old William Elliston, Joy's maternal grandfather. On the Sunday morning Dad and Gyp, the family dog, joined us for a walk across country to Nacton Shores then home to roast beef and Yorkshire pudding. I knew then why Joy was such a good cook, she had a great tutor.

We told her parents of our intentions and they were fully supportive. They pledged to help in any way they could and thanks in large part to them, we survived.

On the journey back to Broadstairs we finalized our plans. At the time, divorce was difficult if not impossible for the ordinary working class. It was costly and time consuming so we decided to live common-law. Not as acceptable then as it is now but we didn't care. It was the second time around for both of us, we were on cloud nine, very much in love and full of youthful confidence.

Joy was twenty-three and I was twenty-five and the subject of family arose. A soldier's pay wasn't very much in those days so we decided to have two children and have them close together so they would be company for each other. Joy would be discharged from the army as soon as her pregnancy was confirmed. She would live with her parents and confident of getting her old job back, work as long as possible.

The first thing I did was to phone Rose. She expressed little surprise or concern save for her financial security. I assured her she would continue to draw her army allowance and if she wanted a divorce I would co-operate in every way.

At her request I confirmed everything in writing and the letter was couched in terms that would facilitate a simple and speedy divorce. I said nothing detrimental and made no mention of her affair with the American airman, to have done so would jeopodize any divorce proceedings. I ended the letter by accepting full responsibility for the breakdown of the marriage. I would live to regret writing that letter and others. They were incomplete, not entirely factual and left too many false impressions that I was never able to correct. Above all, they proved unnecessary.

A year later Rose filed for divorce and her lawyer requested sworn affidavits admitting adultery. In June 1947, he phoned saying the divorce was proceeding that Rose was marrying someone she had known for "Some considerable time," and was I prepared to pay the costs? He listened carefully as I outlined my financial commitments then told me not to worry, "It'll all be taken care of."

One year after that conversation Rose was jilted and the suit dropped. It would be another six years before we gained our freedom under a new, less stringent divorce law.

Meanwhile, Joy and I spent an enjoyable couple of months in Broadstairs. We celebrated VE (Victory in Europe) day, Tuesday, May 8th, along with thousands of jubilant members of the Armed Forces. On Saturday the 12th., after much searching, I found an attractive gold wedding band, gold was hard to come by in those days. Without pomp or ceremony I slipped it on Joy's finger and from that day forth she was Mrs. Keeling. The following Monday I changed my army records listing Joy as my next of kin. All that remained was to consummate the relationship, something that under the circumstances, proved easier said than done.

We sought shelter from the rain in a concrete air raid shelter on the sea front one evening, not the most romantic setting. In the darkness of that long abandoned bunker I leaned against the wall not realising it was covered with graffiti, written with white chalk. I walked home with the back of my battle dress covered with it, much to the amusement of my compatriots. And nothing had happened!

Saturday May 19 was a beautiful warm sunny day. We toured Kingsgate Castle, a perfect setting and one steeped in history; we were about to add to that history. In a nearby field surrounded by a high wooden fence with nothing but the wind whispering through the grass and a burst of song from a pair of meadowlarks, we made love. Joy missed her next period.

Within a couple of weeks I took Joy to meet my mother and while two bedrooms were empty, we paid for Bed and Breakfast accommodation rather than surrender to Fred's pious attitude toward our common-law relationship. It proved ideal, we were free to come and go at will and had a large comfortable bed in which to make love. After which we would lay together in the glow of the late September evenings savouring the moment. It was the perfect honeymoon and for the first time in years we felt absolute contentment.

My mother was courteous but impassive toward, Joy. She always felt I should have pursued Marion despite our insistence that nothing could come of that relationship.

During this same visit an interesting conversation took place, one never to be forgotten. We were all comfortably seated in the living room, a bright, pleasant room facing west. The furniture was a mixture of early Victorian, inherited from grandma Ince and more modern pieces purchased at great sacrifice since their marriage in 1925. There were also a couple of pieces I had hand crafted as a teenager during a brief flirtation with the art of woodworking.

I directed the conversation toward my childhood so as to corroborate what I had told Joy. She could then bear witness to the validity of my life story. My mother showed little emotion and made no attempt to challenge or contradict anything I said. Fred, on the other hand, was visibly moved.

"Jeez! You should write a bloody book," he said, as I ended my commentary.

"I fully intend to one of these days," I replied.

"What will you call it?" he asked.

"The Sins Of The Father," I said without hesitation.

"Hmm! Sins Of The Father eh? Well you're damn right there."

My mother appeared startled by the tenor of the conversation. Drawing herself up sharply and making no attempt to hide her irritation she said,

"Why on earth would you call it that?"

"I think the reason is obvious," I said.

There was an awkward silence and the conversation ended.

When it came time to write my memoirs, a book entitled "The Sins Of The Father" had already been copyrighted.

By July 8, Joy had missed a second period so there was no doubt she was pregnant. She admitted to being a little scared but on a long, enjoyable coach ride to Dover, Folkeston and Dungeness I put her mind at rest.

The next day she visited the Medical Officer and subsequently the pregnancy was confirmed. Tuesday July 31, 1945, her Military career ended. She was demobilised at Canterbury not far from the famous cathedral. She received nothing more than twenty-eight days paid leave in return for her three and a half years of faithful war service. They even failed to send her the medals to which she was entitled but in those days we didn't care much about medals.

Seldom does the universe unfold as expected. Joy's return to the family was most welcome but she was unable to work. Her mother was diagnosed with breast cancer and just before Christmas, 1945 Gramma Borret, as she was fondly known, had a mastectomy.

And so it was that Joy assumed the task of head cook and general factotum. In addition to mum and dad there was Granddad Elliston, Thelma, the youngest sister and Francis her only brother. I paid for Joy's keep out of my army pay and although it was a bit of a struggle, we managed.

To subsidise our income I played the horses. For years as a youngster I had listened to Fred as he explained the intricacies of horse racing. About the owner, the breed and the trainer; the horse's age, the distance, the going, the weight and the skill of the jockey; all this was common to me.

As well, Bury St. Edmunds where I spent so much of my military career was only fourteen miles from Newmarket, a famous and popular racecourse. During the war, both experienced and apprentice jockeys were drafted and sent to us for training. Also Bob Chalmers who, it will be recalled, was one of my assistants, lived in Newmarket and often invited me to his home for a weekend. Thus we moved in the right circles, close to the horses mouth you might say.

So occasionally, either on the basis of form or, in some cases, nothing more than sentiment or coincidence I would have a little flutter. I clearly recall and so did, Joy a horse called Herringbone winning a big race, we'd had herrings for supper the previous evening. In 1946, I was on a course at the Airborne Records Office in Edinburgh, when Airborne won the Derby at fifty to one. Walking down Risbygate Street in Bury St. Edmunds one day I watched a Spitfire destroy a German Bomber and as the pilot returned to base at Mildenhall he did the traditional victory roll. The next day Victory Roll won at six to one.

The Borrett family didn't own a lawn mower and their front lawn was so long we set fire to it, the next day Burnt Grass won a feature race. The day I arrived back from Berlin in 1949, Russian Hero won the Grand National at thirty to one. We were out of coal when Coal Scuttle won us a handsome sum. These are but a few examples of our successes; we didn't always win though.

Following her discharge from the army Joy visited me in Broadstairs but the journey became too much. So, imagine our excitement when I was posted back to Bury St. Edmunds, only twenty six miles from her home in Ipswich.

I arrived on August 27, 1945, and appeared before the CO. Reviewing my records he opined that for me to be a mere Private was a shocking waste of talent. He promoted me to Lance Corporal and assigned me to a research project in the Orderly Room. I said I wouldn't be a Private long didn't I. Four months later I passed the test for a Tradesman Clerk and was promoted to Corporal. On April 26, 1946, a year to the day after being "busted" I was promoted to Sergeant.

Joy and I spent Christmas 1945, together at her home and for the first time in six years there was peace on earth. But sad to say, the goodwill toward men had declined since war's end. It was a difficult time with everything still severely rationed. Even beer and liquor, although not officially rationed, was in short supply and many times a pub would run dry before closing time. We would join in an irreverent rendition of The First Noel. "No ale, no beer no stout, sold out; we'll go to bed with our tongues hanging out." This was very amusing but not to the innkeepers.

Granmma Borrett was discharged from hospital and I was determined we'd have fowl for Christmas dinner. I hitchhiked from Bury St. Edmunds to Ipswich stopping at every village and farm where chickens might be raised.

I reached Claydon on the outskirts of Ipswich before an elderly couple took pity on me. They kept half a dozen chickens in their back yard. I told them of my mother-in-law's illness and my desire to surprise the family with a bird for Christmas dinner. Such was the shortage of food in those days and what's more, it took me almost all the daylight hours to make that twenty-six mile journey.

There was more cause for celebration that Christmas. A vacancy arose for a Sergeant Clerk in the Orderly Room. The CO offered me the position on an acting basis with the rank of Corporal. Then, as previously stated, I was promoted to Sergeant the following April. The additional pay was a godsend. Another privilege I enjoyed was the use of a truck to drive home every night. It was like having a nine to five job most of the time. Joy was still not working because mother was not sufficiently recovered from her illness.

Meanwhile, we were busy preparing for the birth of our son. Everyone was knitting furiously and a horse whose identity_escapes me paid for a handsome crib and a beautiful baby carriage.

Dennis Edward, his father's second name and maternal grandfather's second name, arrived hale and hearty just as the bugler was sounding reveille on Thursday February 21, 1946. A midwife delivered him assisted by Doctor Wiener the family doctor. I've often wondered if his colleagues roasted him when he retired. Pardon the pun.

Arriving at work, the CO sent for me and read a complimentary letter from the War Office regarding the Manpower study we had produced. It was this assignment that first brought me in contact with a comprehensive study of health care produced back in 1942. It had the ungainly title of "The Social Insurance and Allied Services Report," we called it the "Beveridge Report" after it's author. It later formed the basis of the British National Health System.

I also learned about the World Health Organisation and its Charter. Doctor Brock Chisholm a Canadian, played a leading roll in its development. The preamble to the Charter clearly defines "health" as being, "Not only the absence of disease but a state of complete physical, mental and social well-being." As well, it unequivocally designates health care as a right of citizenship. Sixteen nations, including Canada and the United States signed it in 1946. Those opposed too, or who advocate major changes to our present system in Canada should be mindful of this document.

The Commanding Officer ended the interview by thanking me for my contribution, congratulated me on becoming a father and told me to take the rest of the week off.

It was now four years since I had left Africa and still no malaria but I was plagued with another painful legacy. During the first few months in Africa, I was frequently sent on reconnaissance missions that might take days, much of it through dense virgin jungle. We would live off the land but the lack of water and its quality created problems. It was so precious that in a desperate attempt to conserve, we would forego the luxury of cleaning our teeth. Instead, we followed the example of the natives and chewed on the root of a plant. For me, it didn't work and in early 1942, I developed Vincent's Angina otherwise known as trench mouth, a very painful gum disease.

I had been receiving treatment for almost five years without success. The Army Dental Specialist said the only way it could be cured was to remove all my teeth. This was a blow because I had lost only one tooth and the others were in perfect condition. But the Army had no mercy, once the decision was made all thirty-one teeth were removed in just two sittings. A full set of upper and lower dentures, a replica of my own teeth, was also inserted at the same time. The disease was eventually cured but what a price to pay! Years later I had to have tissue taken from the roof of my mouth to rebuild the lower gum.

Another sad event occurred around this time. I have repeatedly mentioned my love for soccer. While playing for my unit in a Southern Command play-off game, I received a severe injury to my left leg just above the ankle. I was hospitalised and it was diagnosed as a blood clot that had become infected. Fortunately it was treated early enough to avoid permanent damage or worse. It ended my playing career but I eventually became a, Federation of International Football Association (FIFA} certified Referee. FIFA was the governing body for world soccer. I continued until 1964 and handled many games, including one international match at Taylor Field in Regina.

As a Sergeant I subsequently filled the position of Assistant Chief Clerk. In October the same year I was transferred to a similar position but with a Brigade Unit in Colchester, just nineteen miles the other side of Ipswich.

There, not having a truck at my disposal I could only get home twice a week. But I did enjoy a better railway service and a much better highway on which to hitchhike home when short of cash. That was quite often, a British soldier's pay wasn't much in those days. But we managed and it wasn't long before Joy was once again with child.

On a Saturday afternoon early in January 1947, I was on duty when I received a message that my daughter Mary had been admitted to an Isolation Hospital in London with diphtheria. At first I thought it was a ploy by Rose to get me to London and refused to go. After a while it was confirmed that indeed she was critically ill and they feared for her life; I left immediately. It was a very stressful week as we continuously watched over her but she pulled through and made a complete recovery.

Michael Frederick, the latter being my stepfather's name was another Thursday child, born March 20, 1947. We had hoped for a girl but were more than happy to accept another bonny, fair-haired, blue-eyed boy and just thirteen months after Dennis. So as far as we were concerned our family was complete.

There was just nowhere for young people to live in those days. Not nearly enough houses were being built to replace those destroyed by enemy bombing. The hundreds of thousands that were requisitioned were all too slowly being repaired and returned to the housing market. And the war had been over for two years. An added problem was that daily, tens of thousands of men were being demobilized from the armed forces. So not only was there a shortage of living accommodation, there was a shortage of jobs. Signing on for a further five years service proved another wise decision.

The Borrett family lived in a modest three bedroom council house on Nacton Road in Ipswich. By now, in addition to mum, dad and Granddad Elliston, there was Phyllis, husband Jim and baby Carol; Thelma, Joy's youngest sister and her only brother Francis. Then, of course, there was Joy, our two boys and me, so there were seven adults, two teenagers and three small pre-school children as well as Gyp the dog and a cat whose name escapes me. But I do remember it learned how to use the doorknocker by standing on his hind legs and hitting it with his front paw. Granmma Borrett had a fit the first time she answered the door to find nobody but the cat waiting to come in.

In June of 1947, everything seemed to fall into place, it was like living in paradise. I was transferred to Fornham Park just outside Bury St. Edmunds, a lovely old Georgian Mansion in the midst of hundreds of acres of beautiful parkland. It had been converted into a Prisoner of War Camp for senior German Officers who, for various reasons, were being detained in the UK. I was posted there as Chief Clerk with an increase in pay and a living out pass, which meant I was paid an additional daily food allowance.

We could now afford to share a new Council house with Eileen and Eddy Cullen, long time friends of Joy's. It was a great thrill to furnish our first home albeit with the barest of necessities and all purchased on credit.

Under normal circumstances the daily journey to and from work would be long and difficult. Fornham was further into the country and somewhat off the beaten track but again I was lucky. An Ipswich contractor was involved in a large housing development just a mile from my office.

Key personnel were transported night and morning to and from the job site and for the entire period I was there I never missed a ride. Another nine-to-five job with all weekends free. In addition, the Sergeants' Mess developed it's own vegetable garden with volunteer prisoners doing most of the work. Every day throughout that summer I took home fresh vegetables. Then, Rose's lawyer phoned and assured us the divorce was going ahead so we could soon look forward to wedding bells. This was, indeed, a wonderful time.

Shortly after my arrival I had to go into Bury St. Edmunds on business. While crossing a busy street I caught a glimpse of Marion pushing a pram and gleefully playing peek-a-boo with the baby. She had turned the corner and was walking away from me so I made no attempt to make my presence known. Obviously her husband had returned from overseas, ending his army career. No doubt they were enjoying life making up for lost time; that's the way it should be, I said to myself.

It was June 19, 1948; we had enjoyed almost a full year of what can only be described as marital bliss. I had a wonderful wife, two handsome young boys and for a few brief months we were an extremely happy family. We had a nice house and although we had to share it, we got along very well with our upstairs neighbours. I went to work each morning and returned home at night just like a civilian. Only a little more than a year to serve and I was sure I would finish my term under these ideal conditions. But the fates decreed otherwise.

We woke that morning to the news on Radio that the Russians had blockaded the City of Berlin. This was a serious act of aggression and a violation of the peace agreement between the Allies. Nobody knew what the future might hold but heeding Winston Churchill's warning about the threat of communism, nobody took the action lightly. There was even talk of this being the start of World War Three.

To set the scene: Germany was divided into east and west. The east was occupied entirely by the Russians, the West jointly by the Western Allies. Thus we had the American zone, the British zone and the French zone. Similarly, the City of Berlin had been divided into American, British, French and Russian Sectors.

There was a narrow transportation corridor linking Berlin with West Germany. It was this corridor that the Russians blockaded denying the Allies access to that part of Berlin, which was theirs to administer under the terms of the armistice.

The Russians resented the Allied presence in Berlin and assumed their action would force them to leave but we stood firm. An airlift of goods and services on a scale hitherto unknown was immediately organised. Everything needed for the survival of three million people was delivered by air.

It was this vast Allied military operation that ended our perfect lifestyle and brought everything crumbling down around us.

Twenty-six

Paradise Lost

The war had been over for three years and although things were not completely back to normal the military had relaxed many of it's regulations. Thus I had been allowed a living out pass despite my home being thirty miles from base. With the Berlin Blockade all this changed. Within days I had to relinquish my pass and remain in Camp at night. I could still go home on weekends but it was the loss of the daily ration allowance that was our undoing.

I pleaded for more time on the grounds I would have to relocate my family and was granted a reprieve till the end of July. I clung to the hope that by then the blockade would be lifted but it was not to be. In fact, tensions were heightened, as the Russians became more belligerent.

And so we were forced to give up our first home. My meagre army pay wasn't enough to cover rent, payments on the furniture and living expenses. To add to our troubles, Joy and the children couldn't go back to live with her parents. By this time her sister Pearl who was pregnant and husband André were living there. The house just wouldn't hold anymore. And so reluctantly, I turned to my mother.

I had helped her in 1940 when she and Tommy Kay were homeless. Now she was back with Fred and they had two bedrooms not being used. She had never done anything to help us and so it didn't seem too much to ask. She readily agreed and on Friday, July 30, 1948, we solemnly watched as the few chattels we had striven so hard to acquire were loaded onto a horse-drawn wagon, sold for a fraction of what we had originally paid. It was but a sample of future heartbreaking events, including the news that Rose had been jilted and the divorce proceedings dropped. It was, without doubt, a case of "Paradise Lost."

I took Joy and the children to Brighton, staying for two days. My mother appeared happy with the situation and I left feeling the family was in good hands. It wouldn't be for long, I told myself, and things would soon be back to normal. Again, it was not to be.

Back at Fornham Park I was to experience a strange phenomenon. One that, to this day, has me baffled. I have never believed in the supernatural. Being from England I've heard many ghost stories and, "A Christmas Carol" starring Alistair Sim has always been a family favourite. So we're familiar with Jacob Marley and don't believe a word.

Nevertheless, on my way from the mansion to my hut one night and stone cold sober, I saw this ghost like figure in what appeared to be a white translucent shroud. I stood transfixed as it floated noiselessly the length of the garden disappearing near the compost heap.

Must be the lights of a car coming up the long driveway from the main road, I told myself. But there was no sign of any vehicle. Besides, the lights of a car coming up the drive would shine on the row of trees and shrubs to my right. I saw no such reflection, the object was definitely separate and apart from anything else.

I looked at the windows of the mansion, all were in darkness, no reflection from there. Could it have been headlights from a car on the main road? Regardless of the direction a vehicle might approach the entrance to the Park, it would be going away from the garden because the entrance was on a bend. My apparition caused such a stir in the camp that the Motor Transport staff tried their damnedest to replicate the phenomenon without the slightest success.

Those among us who believed in the paranormal took the incident very seriously. Every possible theory was put forth but there simply was no logical explanation. I was teased unmercifully by the cynics but I know what I saw and to this day it bothers me because I don't want to believe it was anything but an apparition.

Throughout the controversy I noticed one member of the staff remained strangely quiet, a big burly Sergeant Major. The day I left I was about to board the truck for the Railway Station when he sidled up to me and, with his hand partially covering his mouth, quietly bade me bon voyage.

"Good luck Frank," he said, "And by the way, I saw that bloody ghost too! Scared the hell out'er me. Buggered if I know what ter make of it."

With that he was gone and like me, is probably still bothered by it.

Looking back, it's difficult to comprehend the workings of the military mind. I had but twelve months to serve and Army Council Instructions decreed I be entitled to spend the last six months in England. Also, I was Medical Category B1 HS, the HS meaning "Home Stations."

In theory then, I could not be sent overseas. Imagine my shock when, on September 27, I was ordered to report to Berlin within forty-eight hours. I protested to the highest authorities because of my home station classification only to be told that West Germany, including Berlin was, for military purposes, classified as a home station. Only the moguls of Whitehall could possibly dream that one up.

I had a brief visit with Joy and the children before embarking on the overnight ferry from Harwich to the Hook of Holland. Then by train to Buckeberg where I spent the night. The following morning I flew into Berlin in a Halifax Bomber loaded with coal. I would make that hazardous journey several times during the next few months. Having been on the receiving end of the "Blitz" in 1940, I felt no remorse as I flew over mile after mile of utter destruction. It was also on that first flight that I renewed the acquaintance of the secret agent I'd first met in the Baker Street pub back in 1940. He was still in civilian clothes and operating under cover in Berlin. What a small world!

I won't dwell on my tour of duty in that beleaguered city except to say that after a short period of orientation I was transferred to a Royal Army Service Corp (RASC) unit. It was based in the Northwest corner of the huge Spandau Prison complex where the notorious war criminals were incarcerated. For most of the time I was directly involved in the operation of the airlift.

Two weeks before Christmas Joy wrote saying she had been invited to spend the holidays with her family and needed additional money for the train fare. I sold my one and only civilian outfit, sports jacket and flannels to raise the extra funds.

The blockade was lifted on Thursday, May 12, 1949. I left on the first train departing Charlottenburg station at 1700 hrs. When we reached the checkpoint at Helmstedt, the border between East and West Germany, we were confronted by a heavily armed band of Russian troops. The news that the blockade had been lifted hadn't filtered down from Moscow. For four hours they lined each side of the train with Browning automatic rifles at the ready refusing to allow us to proceed. I had but four months left to serve and at one time during the ordeal wondered if I would make it.

Joy and the children never did return to my mother's after the Christmas vacation. Her sister Phyllis and family were allocated a council house so there was room for them. Later, Joy told me the real reason she never went back. From the moment I left my mother started treating them in the same impersonal and overbearing way she had originally treated me. I was horrified and chided her for not telling me at the time; she felt I had enough to worry about.

On arrival at her mother's she put twenty-month old Michael to bed with what she thought was a nasty cold. A short time later her sister Pearl took a peek at him. He had turned completely blue. It was subsequently determined he had pneumonia, no doubt brought on by my mother's refusal to supply adequate heat during that very bitter winter.

On a lighter note, though not amusing at the time, Dennis decided to explore the world outside the confines of Granmma's garden. Nacton Road was a busy road so the garden was well fenced with a sturdy latch on the gate. Dennis found out how to undo it and off he went.

There was panic when it was discovered he was missing. The Police were called and it was several hours before they received a phone call from the Vicarage of a church more than a mile away. The Vicar's wife saw Dennis wandering aimlessly along the road, took him in, fed him milk and biscuits and called the police. He was just three years old and not the least concerned at the anxiety he had caused. He did say though that he missed his mum.

I returned for the last time to Bury St. Edmunds in May, had ten days leave and was kicking my heels awaiting discharge to Class Z Reserve. For the next ten years I was subject to recall. My release date was September 20, but I was demobilised on Friday August 19th. The last twenty-eight days being paid leave.

That weekend I was Orderly Sergeant on the Sunday so couldn't go home. Saturday evening two of us decided to go for a beer. Purely by coincidence we found ourselves in a Pub close to where Marion lived. I had long since dismissed that affair from my mind so when the owner of the nearby convenience store walked into the pub I thought little of it. I greeted him with the usual handshake and enquired after the family. He said they were well, then shattered me with,

'Spose you heard Marion died?"

"When?"

"A year ago," he said, "terrible tragedy."

I wanted to know more but we were abruptly interrupted by a business acquaintance and they left. Visibly shaken, I returned to my table and my companion was curious. I said I'd just been told about the death of a very dear friend. It was difficult to regain my composure in the noisy pub so I left saying, I simply had to get out of there.

"That's OK Frank I understand," said my friend.

I wandered slowly back to Barracks hardly able to believe what I had been told. A year ago; she would be just thirty-two, what could possibly have happened? I recalled it was two years almost to the day that I had seen her with the baby in the pram, she was obviously a very happy woman then. Why would such a thing happen? Why Marion? Such a loveable person, so young! It just didn't make sense.

As I approached the gates I heard a train heading toward Cambridge, sounding it's whistle as it neared the level crossing at Beeton's Footpath. Another mile and it would pass under that bridge . . . I was filled with a deep sense of sorrow. A multitude of thoughts flooded my mind, among them the weekend I had spent at her parents home. Should I contact them and express my condolences? No, it was too late for that. They were probably over the worst of their grief by now and besides, it wouldn't be appropriate. I never did find out the cause of death, only that it was sudden, how sad.

I'd have been less than human had I not felt shock and sorrow at the news of Marion's death. During the war years, the death of comrades in battle, of friends or relatives in air raids had become commonplace and one became resolved to the inevitability of it all. But the war had been over for four years, these things weren't supposed to happen anymore.

It had been five years since our brief encounter, much had happened in that time. I now had a wife and children so my grief although sincere was short-lived. I had my own life to live and a future fraught with uncertainty. I would soon enter civilian life after more than twelve years and I was about to learn first-hand the truth regarding this land fit for heroes about which I had heard so much.

The Army had several programmes designed to assist people being "demobbed". Having proven myself as an Instructor my thoughts turned to a teaching career. It would mean going to a Teaching College for three years so what kind of assistance could I expect from the Army? It turned out that, as with all courses, it was less than half my existing pay and allowances. Completely out of the question.

In August I was granted compassionate leave because in less than three weeks I would be leaving the service and still no job. I went to the Ipswich

"Employment Exchange" as it was called and they were quick to tell me my supervisory experience, clerical trade classification and Intelligence training would mean little to a civilian employer. And if I wanted to pursue an administrative career I should be prepared to start at the bottom.

They did, however, advise me of an opening at Crane Limited, a large factory on the outskirts of town fifteen minutes walk from the Borrett household. I was interviewed and offered the position of Production Planning Technician to commence work Monday August 22, 1949. The pay wasn't very good but at least it was a job so I accepted.

Those last few weeks were the most frustrating of my entire military career. The Depot was no longer used for training recruits, an activity long since transferred to Colchester as a Brigade rather than a Battalion function. Thus the place was empty save for us few awaiting discharge and a handful of staff. Among the latter an RSM who took an instant disliking to me and went out of his way to make life as miserable as possible.

The only noteworthy thing was our preparation for the upcoming celebration of Minden Day. This was a battle honour earned in the mid fifteen hundreds. It was celebrated annually on the first Sunday in August, a reunion that is carried on to this day. I mention it only because I was in the gymnasium atop a stepladder hanging bunting; I fell, pulling a muscle in my back and was crippled for weeks.

Despite my discomfort and a chit from the MO saying I should be given light duties only, that bloody RSM gave me a dogs' life until the day I left. But I got my revenge.

On the Saturday before Minden day we had a cricket match, the Depot versus a local team. I was forced to "volunteer" as Umpire. Now this RSM fancied himself as a cricket player and when it was his turn to bat, he faced a particularly ruthless fast bowler. The very first ball thundered down that twenty-two yard pitch like a streak of lightning, he moved slightly to his right to address the ball, missed, and there was no mistaking that sickly sounding smack as the ball brushed off his pad. As is customary under such circumstances there was the usual chorus of "How's that." I, with as much solemnity as I could muster raised my hand, finger pointing ominously skyward, denoting he was out "Leg before wicket"(LBW).

As he passed me stonefaced on that long embarrassing walk back to the pavilion I murmured, "Bad luck Sir." There was a barely audible grunt for he knew, as I did, his leg was at least six inches outside the stump. But he was out for a "Duck" and revenge was sweet. My action made no difference to the outcome of the game, a far superior Bury St. Edmunds side soundly defeated us.

Thursday afternoon about four o'clock on August 18, 1949, I was handed my travel documents for Guildford and walked out the Barrack gates for the last time in uniform. Thirty-nine years would pass before I would enter those gates again and then as an "Old Comrade" with my wife of forty-three years on my arm. We spent seven weeks in the summer of 1988 retracing my military adventures.

I spent the night in Ipswich, then off to Guildford the next morning. I had a compartment to myself for the journey to Liverpool Street in London. It was the end of an era and I found myself once again in a reminiscent mood.

It had been a tumultuous twelve years and the ravages of war had effected me. I felt much older than my years, had witnessed death and destruction on a scale hitherto unknown and felt both the horror of defeat and the joy of victory. I had savoured the luxury of pheasant and port wine and endured the pangs of near starvation. I'd enjoyed the adulation of an adoring public in times of war, and suffered the disdain to which peace time soldiers were all too often exposed.

For some reason I recalled the quiet of Armistice days as they were called, prior to World War Two when, at the eleventh hour on the eleventh day of the eleventh month our entire world stood still.

We only had the day off if it fell on a Sunday. Most people worked at least half day on Saturdays so it was work as usual. But with a blast from an old steam horn or the boom of an artillery field gun, everyone downed tools; all traffic pulled to the side of the road and came to a halt. Pedestrians stopped in their tracks and for two minutes there would be absolute silence broken only by the howl of a canine frightened by the deathly calm. Meantime, an entire population with heads unashamedly bowed paid homage to the fallen. This is a far cry from the contemporary Remembrance day; just another statutory holiday for an ever growing body of the populace. We would do well to heed the words of Herman Wouk the esteemed author who wrote, "The beginning of the end of war lies in remembrance."

I remembered the day I first joined the Army; how I slammed the front door just to show my Aunt I didn't give a damn. My Aunt, oh my! But I'd made up my mind to forget that sordid affair; and that dreadful afternoon I spent with Annie Mason as she intoned the shocking story of my heritage. Problem is, there is much truth to the old maxim, "The things we remember best are those better forgotten."

The memory of such a deed is never lost, it gets different but it never gets better. It differs over time as you suffer through varying phases. First fear then guilt, then shame followed by disgust and perhaps hatred, then back to fear again.

I thought of flying over the Island of Malta in a RAF Sunderland Flying Boat based at Kalafrana. Our purpose was first, to study that gallant little Island from the air then sail around it in the pride of the British navy, the battle cruiser HMS Repulse, to examine it from the viewpoint of an enemy. And finally, being issued with bicycles in order to travel its entire length and breadth.

All of this so that we might enhance its defences against a formidable enemy under whose ghastly and persistent attacks it never did surrender. I remembered my jubilation when His Majesty King George VI, awarded this jewel of the Mediterranean the George Cross for the gallantry of its defenders and the fortitude of its inhabitants. And felt just a little pride in the small role I had played.

I remembered too when the entire Intelligence Section returning by motor launch from an assignment on the nearby island of Gozo, was shipwrecked on

St. Paul's Island. The very same where, so it is written, the good saint himself had been shipwrecked back in biblical times.

In the years following World War One, the Suffolk Regiment had built a road from St. George's Barracks where we were based to another part of the Island. To somewhat belatedly commemorate this undertaking, young Elm trees were sent from England to be planted down each side of the road. The young saplings were fragile and had to be staked. The men planting the trees cut the stakes from a cluster of nearby bushes. Years later I enquired as to the progress of those trees only to be told that within a year all the trees had died but the stakes started to sprout leaves. I was never able to confirm the story.

I remembered too, Chamberlain's ill-fated "Peace in our time" document upon his return from Munich in September of 1938. I also remembered the sense of relief we felt as he made his declaration of war speech on radio a year later. At last we were going to do something about this tyrant who was threatening to overrun all of Europe. Little did we realise the enormity of the task that lay ahead.

I arrived at Liverpool Street and had to make my way by Underground to Waterloo where I would catch the train to Guildford. There was the usual huge crowd milling around and I was reminded of an incident at St. Pancras Station, another large London terminal, in September 1944.

I had accompanied a colleague to the station on a Friday evening around five. We were to meet his fiancee, visiting from Luton in Bedfordshire. The station was packed with thousands of people, many paying a week-end visit, some just passing through and still others returning home from work in the suburbs. Suddenly, there was the nerve-wracking sound of a flying bomb, the engine stopped indicating it's immediate descent. In a matter of seconds the terminus was all but deserted. I've never seen so many people disappear so quickly in all my life.

I have a lingering memory of a young father who moments before had been greeted by his wife and two young children. He threw his arms around the three of them and as he forced them to the ground, I heard him say,

"It's all right, it's all right, if we have to go we'll all go together."

I shall never forget the look of absolute terror on the faces of those two little children. The bomb dropped a few hundred yards from the station, did little damage and caused few casualties.

I thought of crossing crocodile infested rivers deep in the jungles of Africa. In particular, one gruesome episode when we lost an African RSM to the wily creatures. Of shoals of flying fish as we crossed the Atlantic, something I always thought existed only in the land of fairy tales. I thought also of the six hundred women and children aboard the MV Letitia, how many I wondered were now widows and orphans?

My mind wandered aimlessly from one thought to another, nothing orderly, nothing cohesive; not the way I had been trained to use my powers of retrospection; how strange I thought. I realised also that I'd been gazing out the window at the English countryside as the train sped on its way, yet I had seen nothing. Suddenly I was conscious of telephone poles flashing by, the wires strung between them rose and fell, up down, up down and up again. I knew there were other people in the compartment on this leg of the journey but was completely unaware of their presence.

We were travelling at high speed now, there was a swish as we passed under a bridge and I was lost in my thoughts again.

I dwelt long on the carnage of D-Day. In my mind I recited the familiar names of comrades with whom I had served for seven years and who paid the supreme price on that fateful day. I knew many of their wives and children and felt a mixture of sorrow and anger at the futility of it all. I also found myself wondering why I had survived. In fact, there were, and still are times when I feel guilty because I survived. What strange mortals we are.

I was also painfully aware of the many so-called experts who wrote books about the Normandy Landings. Some were critical of my Regiment and others because of our failure to achieve all the major objectives on the first day. We failed because the overnight bombing did not initiate the crucial breakthroughs on the ground that had been anticipated.

I remembered learning first hand about the many acts of bravery and self-sacrifice and the awards that followed, most of them well deserved. But there was much cynicism among the ranks at some of the decorations, especially on the home front. Relatively minor acts, many out of self-preservation rather than bravery were rewarded while others far more courageous went unrecognised. As well, many splendid men went unnoticed because there was no one left to tell their story. It was often said decorations were handed out like the rations, so that every command got its fair share. A couple of incidents come to mind, which illustrate the point.

A significant part of a recruit's training involved the use of the Mills Bomb better known as a hand grenade. A short distance outside Bury St. Edmunds there was an area set aside for recruits to practice throwing live grenades. It consisted of a wall of sandbags about five feet high behind which, each man stood to throw his grenade. Nothing more than a small mound of earth surrounded the area where the grenades exploded. Otherwise the whole area was wide open and had the appearance of something resembling the moon. Thousands of grenades were exploded there during the course of the war.

Recruits were given training with dummies before handling live grenades and usually, but not always an Officer would be in charge of the latter. A section of eight men would assemble behind the wall and one by one they would hurl their missile in the manner in which they'd been taught. Occasionally things would go wrong.

Pulling the safety pin with ones teeth is reserved strictly for Hollywood. That is not the way it's done. For a right handed person the grenade is gripped firmly in the right hand holding down the lever controlling the firing pin. The forefinger of the left hand is placed through the ring of the safety pin and the grenade placed on the right hip. The pin is removed by straightening the right arm. In other words, the grenade is removed from the pin rather than the reverse. It is then lobbed overhand much like a cricket player bowling a ball. In one case, as a recruit straightened his right arm, his hand came in contact with his web equipment. He dropped the grenade at the feet of the Platoon Sergeant who scooped it up and threw it underhand. It exploded without causing harm.

The Officer in charge reported the incident in accordance with regulations. For his actions, none other than His Majesty King George VI awarded the Sergeant the OBE (Order of the British Empire) at Buckingham Palace even. Now to me, that's not an act of bravery it's a case of self-preservation. The bomb had a five second fuse, what else would he do, stand there and watch it explode?

In the second incident everything was the same except there was no officer present, a Platoon Sergeant was in charge. And this time it involved a grenade that failed to explode. Every grenade had to be accounted for because it was not uncommon for children to play in the area when not in use and civilians used it as a short cut.

It was anticipated that a subsequent grenade would explode the faulty one but the last man hurled his grenade and still no double explosion. The Sergeant had to go out and deal with it. To me that takes a lot of courage, the danger to life and limb was obvious. He had time to deliberate on what had to be done and the risks involved. This was no spontaneous reaction to an emergency. Self-preservation played no part in this situation but rather it was the lives of others that were at stake. He could leave the damn thing there and hope it was a dud or perhaps it would explode when the next platoon came. None of these thoughts entered his mind, he knew what he as the senior person present had to do.

He strode deliberately but calmly across that piece of moon like real estate picking his way carefully through the myriad of shell holes that were so close together that sometimes the walls collapsed under the weight of his tread. He had almost reached the furthermost hole when, behind him and slightly to his left he heard the unmistakable hiss of a fuse. The plunger had finally come free and struck the detonator. He had but five seconds to decide his next move. He shouted "Down" to warn his platoon of the pending explosion. All save the Platoon Corporal dropped to a crouching position behind the sandbag wall. He was determined to watch the entire episode, he had served with this Sergeant for a long time. They were close friends and he was concerned for his comrade's well being.

The Sergeant, realising there was no time to run, dropped into the nearest shell hole and crouched, pulling his tin hat tight over his head. The explosion rocked the ground and with a whoosh! dirt, rocks and shrapnel flew skyward. He couldn't resist taking a glance upward and watched the debris as it rose fountain like into the air. By some miracle he emerged unscathed and there was a loud cheer from the men who realised what had happened and a sigh of relief from the Corporal as his Sergeant rejoined the men.

It was a conversation piece in Camp for weeks among the rank and file. All the details were duly reported in writing to the Company Commander, complete with signed statements by witnesses as required by regulations. Officially, no mention was ever made of the event, not a "Thank you" or "Well done," nothing! One caustic remark was to the effect that next time he should try something simple, like Russian Roulette.

I was suddenly brought back to reality. The train had pulled into Guildford station and I made my way with hundreds of others to the Great Hall where the last act would take place. It was a memorable occasion, thousands of square feet of men's clothing. Not "Saville Row" quality mind you but not bad either. I selected a navy blue pin striped suit. Then, handing in most of my military paraphernalia was issued one months pay and a travel warrant back to Ipswich.

I have never felt so self-conscious in all my life, for some reason I felt as if everyone was staring at me. They weren't of course it was just my awkwardness. Anybody would think I'd never worn civvies before. In fact, it was less than a year since I had sold them in Berlin.

That night we celebrated my permanent homecoming in our favourite pub, The Golden Hind, just across the street from the Borrett household at 439 Nacton Road. It was here that I spent the next months adapting to life in the real world.

I commenced work at Crane Limited on the Monday and took an instant disliking to it. Although an office job I spent much time in the foundry. A dirty, noisy, unhealthy place it was stifling and oppressive and the pay was lousy. The only way I could begin to make ends meet was by working overtime evenings and weekends. I was working close to sixty hours a week and still not earning a great wage. It was all work and no play making Jack a very dull boy and with little time for the family.

Christmas, 1949 came and food rationing was still with us albeit a little more generous. The big day was a Sunday that year so we had a nice long weekend. There was another surprise too; as each employee was handed his or her pay cheque on the Friday night, we were handed a cardboard box containing canned food. Gifts from our Crane co-workers in Canada. They had been doing this every year since the beginning of hostilities. There were canned peaches, pears, hams, and many things we hadn't seen for years. All very much appreciated by the whole family.

And so it was that the turbulent forties came to a close. Life was hard but we made the most of it and wondered what the fifties would bring. New Year's Eve was celebrated quietly by the whole Borrett family. It was the end of one of the most appalling decades in the history of mankind. As well, the future was fraught with uncertainty because by this time an "Iron Curtain" had descended upon Eastern Europe. The "Cold War" had begun.

Twenty-seven

A Period Of Adjustment

In the seven years following my discharge from the army I had twelve jobs, several lasting only a few weeks. Things were little better than after the First World War, the body Politic had obviously learned nothing and one was reminded of the old saying, "He who ignores history is destined to relive it."

According to "The Statesman's Year Book" for 1946-47, by the end of World War Two, there were 2,950,800 men and women in the British Army, 760,000 in the Air Force and 492,800 in the Navy, not including the Merchant Marine, for a total of 4,202,800.

The Government had set the total strength of post war service personnel at 190,000. Therefore, slightly more than four million were to be demobilised. They weren't all "demobbed" at once, of course. Each person was allocated a number based on his or her length of service, first in first out. But the numbers entering the private sector every day placed an impossible burden on an economy geared solely to the production of war goods.

Also, after six years of war England was in a state of virtual bankruptcy. All the assets of the once mighty Empire had been liquidated to finance the war and the country was heavily in debt. Factories were antiquated and the infrastructure crumbling. The need for massive rebuilding and modernisation of its industrial base was obvious, but the short-sighted industrialists and financiers were slow to invest in new and modern plants and machinery. And the Politicians lacked the vision and the fortitude to recognise let alone meet post-war needs.

Thus we saw the gradual erosion of the once prosperous manufacturing base that had served England so well for centuries. Those countries defeated in war now became victorious in peace because their industries had been virtually destroyed and they had to rebuild from scratch. And finally, it is probably true to say that whether out of pride, politics or just plain British pig headedness, more aid was given to old enemies than to old allies.

My demobb number was 20 with a suffix DR (Deferred Regular). A colleague and close friend with whom I had served in Colchester had the same number. He was discharged in September 1946, as I would have been. He was older than me, had been a Chief Clerk in a Brigade Unit for years and had four years of post Secondary Education, whereas I had been credited with just two. The only job he could find was as a Special Police Constable on Southampton docks working the graveyard shift.

He did eventually develope a career in the Regular Police Force and was a detective in the Criminal Investigation Division (C.I.D) at the time of his retirement. But those early years were painfully frugal. Shortly after his discharge he wrote to me expressing his disillusionment with civilian life in this so called, "land fit for heroes" and advised me to stay in the Army as long as possible. Three years later when I joined the ranks of a somewhat disenchanted civilian population things had not improved. In fact, by this time, so many more had been discharged it was even more difficult.

As previously stated, we were forced to live with Joy's parents at first but in early 1951, were allocated a Council house on Rushmere Road. I'd been working at Crane's for sixteen months but hadn't been able to save and so again, we had to go into hock for the bare necessities of furniture. Shortly after moving into the house we finally heard from a lawyer representing Joy's husband, he was suing for divorce. We provided all the legal documents then sat back and watched the wheels of an antiquated judicial system grind exceeding slow. Our excitement was tempered somewhat by the experience we'd had with my divorce.

I hadn't been happy at Crane's from the beginning and things got progressively worse. So in February, Johnny Haines, another disgruntled employee, and myself decided to try our hands as entrepreneurs. Management expressed disappointment saying, with my organisational abilities they had hoped for great things from me. But I dismissed their overtures as idle talk.

Gasoline had been rationed since the outbreak of war but now the supply had been increased and there were more vehicles on the road. John and I saw the need for a car wash facility. We had no capital so is it any wonder our venture into the world of business was short lived?

We tried raising a line of credit through the bank, approaching them full of enthusiasm and lots of facts and figures to support our endeavour. We even had letters of recommendation from a couple of prominent businessmen, but the bank wanted so much collateral that if we'd had that much we wouldn't need them. Mark Twain had it right when he wrote, "A Banker is one who will lend you his umbrella, then when it rains demand its immediate return." But we tried.

Following this setback, John got himself a job with the Gas Division of the British Power Corporation and was to be based in Epping of all places. He needed room and board for a while so I referred him to the Mason's. I hadn't kept in touch but thought they might be willing to assist and at the same time help themselves with a little extra income.

The following weekend he told me his visit to the Mason household had been anything but cordial. A housekeeper who was looking after Annie told him that Uncle George had died the previous October. That Annie had suffered a debilitating stroke shortly thereafter and they could be of no help.

Then I started job number three with a company that for hundreds of years had produced top quality antique furniture. They had hitherto hand crafted all their reproductions and there was a huge market in North America but price was a crucial factor. They decided to switch to a system of mass production.

I was hired because of my experience with similar production techniques at Crane's and was promised handsome bonuses when the new system became operative. After three months of hard work and long hours the system was introduced and was a huge success. The weekly production of some items quadrupled. Owners and management alike were delighted with the success, but in a dispute over their failure to pay the promised bonuses my immediate superior, the Senior Accountant was fired and I quit in disgust.

On a lighter note, I remember the first Christmas in our own home. We were hard up as usual and so it was somewhat austere. The back garden hadn't been properly landscaped so the young lad next door and myself made Dennis and Michael pint-size wheelbarrows as their main Christmas present. The idea being, they could amuse themselves moving soil thus helping in what was quite a major task and have great fun doing it.

The boys had other ideas; Christmas afternoon they took their wheelbarrows out in the back garden but instead of moving soil, they decided to race them around the garden in opposite directions like cars on a racetrack. And, of course, there had to be the inevitable head-on crash. Imagine my horror and disappointment when, glancing out the window, I saw them gleefully gazing down at what could only be described as a pile of kindling. I could have wept, so much TLC had gone into the making of those toys. Ah well, boys will be boys.

Within days I started job number four, an office job in the Regional Office of a multi-national oil company. Again, the pay wasn't very good but in those days employers always insisted there were "Extraordinary opportunities for advancement." I had only worked a couple of weeks when I found that the Regional Manager's Secretary was also his mistress. I'm sure he was old enough to be her grandfather. Anyhow, I didn't take kindly to having to answer to a very inexperienced and very arrogant eighteen year old girl as well as a boss. And so after less than a month I quit.

By this time I was thoroughly fed up with these low paying jobs and living from pay cheque to pay cheque. I came to the conclusion that, for a time at least; I would simply have to make considerably more money. The reason for our financial difficulties was that besides keeping Joy and the children I was paying maintenance to Rose.

I heard that big money could be made working for a Contractor relaying railway track on the main Ipswich to London line. It was hard work, especially for one not used to that kind of physical activity and long hours too. With travel time to and from the job site it meant fourteen hour days, but since the pay was more than double anything I had earned hitherto I decided to give it a whirl, at least until I got on my feet. Job five.

The safety and working conditions were atrocious and it wasn't long before the men on the gangs began to grumble. At our one and only meal break we would sit on the railway bank and discuss our grievances. It reached the point where it was agreed something had to be done. Everyone insisted I had a better command of the English language than the average navvy employed on the job and so I was unanimously elected spokesperson.

This, it must be emphasised, was the main line to London and express trains were hurtling down the track at frequent intervals twenty-four hours a day. The old rails, including the ballast would be removed; we would then lay new ties, install new rails and replace the ballast. It was all done manually, we had none of the heavy-duty machinery of modern times.

Everything had to be co-ordinated with the running of the trains. They would have to slow down while travelling through the work area but to have one stop completely would be unprecedented. Having removed a nice long section of track, we downed tools and refused to budge until our grievances were addressed.

The Foreman agreed, subject to the approval of his superiors. He hopped the next train to London and upon his return said all our demands had been met. I was the hero of the day but my popularity was short-lived. As I left the bus that night I was handed my pay packet and told, in no uncertain terms, my services were no longer required. Ah well, I had the satisfaction of knowing that henceforth those men would have much improved working conditions. But never again would I be the spokesperson no matter how just the cause.

The town of Ipswich is located on the River Orwell about ten miles from the North Sea. Being a small port it had a couple of silos wherein grain was stored. A new one was to be built using a technique developed in Sweden. Instead of erecting scaffolding, forms were slowly raised by hydraulic lifts. Once it started at ground level it couldn't stop until it reached its ultimate height of two hundred feet. Then the lifts were halted and the roof was poured in the normal way; this was the first time the process had been used in England.

This new silo was to contain four bins, so in addition to the four outside walls there were two more dividing the silo into four. An awful lot of concrete had to be poured and it was a twenty-four hour operation. This was job number six and lasted a couple of months. The pay was even better than the railroad and all I had to do was wheel a specially designed barrow full of concrete from a huge mixer.

With the roof poured the forms had to be dismantled and it was during this process that a terrible accident occurred. The bins had a hatch leading to the roof through which we lowered the dismantled forms. Following a coffee break, a carpenter with whom I was working lost his balance and plunged the two hundred feet to his death. I had witnessed death and destruction during the war but nothing equalled the horror I felt watching helplessly as my fellow worker plunged, without a sound, to his death. He had become the proud father of a baby boy, his first-born just two weeks earlier.

Shortly after this tragic event the job was completed and I moved on to job number seven but I didn't have to move very far. With the completion of the new silo its owners needed more staff; a neighbour and I were offered jobs. The money was good and my job was to operate a small crane, hauling sacks of various types of grain up to the top floor of another building where it was mixed and ground into different kinds of animal feed. It was easy work but boring, the hours were long and it involved shift work, something I hated.

I also began to realise that I had been doing this kind of donkeywork for far too long. Now I could fully understand the disillusionment expressed by my army friend. I also felt there was a danger I might be lulled into a state of indifference about a more desirable vocation. But this was just a period of adjustment I told myself; soon everything would fall into place.

With this in mind, I redoubled my efforts to find more meaningful work. The best money, it was said, was in sales. It was now January 1952, the war had been over for almost seven years and most rationing was over. But many goods were still in short supply and it was a seller's market.

This was particularly true in the food industry. The English people had for so long been starved of little delicacies that to day we take for granted. This is where I decided that perhaps my future lie and to that end enrolled in a correspondence course with The London School of Salesmanship. Many sales executives, it was claimed, owed their success to this most prestigious institution so although the fees were substantial we considered it worthwhile.

Around this time we received a most unexpected but exciting piece of news. A letter from a London solicitor advised us that my on again off again divorce proceedings were on again. They had all the information they needed so there was nothing for us to do but wait and what a long wait it turned out to be.

Glancing through the Daily Telegraph shortly after this event, there was an advertisement for personnel with office experience to sell Office Supplies. The potential Employer was a very prestigious national company with Head Office and factory in London. They had a Branch office in Ipswich but particularly appealing, was their offer of a comprehensive training programme for successful applicants.

Since I had been a Chief Clerk in a Brigade Office that consisted of five large departments and a total staff of seventy people, I considered myself qualified. But as previously mentioned few employers recognised experience gained in the armed forces.

I applied for the position and was interviewed by the Regional Manager. He had been a Captain in the Army and had held the positions of both Intelligence Officer and Adjutant and fully appreciated my training and experience. I got the job and started training on Monday, January 14, 1952.

The course was held in London and apart from a small subsidy for room and board, I had to cover all expenses including travel back to Ipswich on weekends. But it was one of the best courses I ever attended and the most comprehensive. So began my career in sales. I was, as the British like to call it, a Commercial Traveller.

One evening, while attending the course, I realised I was only half an hour by bus from the Wright family in Romford and decided to pay them a visit. I hadn't seen them for almost seven years and felt guilty. I only intended to stay for an hour but there was so much to talk about I ended up staying the night.

I was greeted with the same cordial enthusiasm as always even though I had neglected them for so long. Uncle George answered the door and hardly recognised me in my business suit.

When I explained what I was doing in London he, with his usual dry humour said,

"Can you name the greatest salesman of all time?"

"No" I replied.

"Why, Christopher Columbus of course."

"Really! How come?"

"Well, when he left he didn't know where he was going, when he got there he didn't know where he was, when he got back he didn't know where he had been and he did it all on borrowed money and then got a repeat order."

We all had a good laugh.

Then we sat around the dining room table and I was brought up to date with all the family news; Desmond had met and married a Yorkshire lass while serving in the armed forces and was now living in her home town. Incidentally, he fought in the battle to relieve the Airborne Forces at Arnhem, had a terrible time. Jean was married and lived in Ilford; her husband was Produce Manager in a Supermarket. James, although only eighteen on January 11, had been called up for his National Service. Every young person reaching the age of eighteen was required to serve for two years in the Forces. Conscientious Objectors worked in the coal mines. So the only one still at home was Paula. She would be twenty-one in March and operated a very popular Cigar Stand on the main street of Romford.

I told them all my news; about the failure of my first marriage, which didn't surprise them; about Joy and the two boys and they insisted we must all get together as soon as possible. They assumed I was divorced and remarried so I said nothing. Then the subject of my heritage came up when Auntie Edie asked, was I still in touch with the Masons?

"No," I said, "I haven't seen or heard from them since the day Annie told me her story. But a friend told me that Uncle George had died in October 1950. And that Annie had suffered a stroke and was being cared for by a housekeeper."

They were aware of Uncle George's death but not of Annie's stroke.

Now that the subject had been raised, both Edie and George were curious about what Annie had told me way back in September 1939; up to that point the subject had always been taboo. So I briefly related the main points. Edie had quite a different version of my mother's affair with her employer. She insisted it was not the old man, but his son that was involved and went on to tell a more titillating story.

"That's what Nance told me," she concluded, "and I believe her. I know her well enough that she would never have an affair with a man that old. He was old enough to be her grandfather for God's sake!"

In fact, he was fifty-four she was twenty-two.

When this conversation took place, I was convinced Annie's story the more plausible. Edie's version was, I thought, another of my mother's fabrications. It was the first time a son had been mentioned and Annie had described the old man in detail as the person involved. Also, Edie's story was one of returning World War One heroes, romance and high society; of traditional English barriers between the classes, the son of a Banker and a servant girl, falling by the wayside. It sounded like an excerpt from George Bernard Shaw's play, "Arms and The Man."

It is only as I write that confirmation of a son has come to light. The old man's death certificate dated 3 July 1953 lists a daughter-in-law of 14 Vicarage Road, Coopersale, Epping, Essex as the informant. Amazingly, this is across the street from where Jessie lived. Despite contact with government offices, local libraries, newspapers and funeral directors, I have been unable to find any further information on this person. Nevertheless, I still believe Annie's version to be correct.

Paula had remained silent through most of the conversation; this was the first time she had heard many of the details and was obviously moved by the whole story. For the first time the significance of the Keeling name dawned upon her, she said.

"It's never been a household word; somewhere in the back of my mind I knew mum was a Keeling but it was something we never discussed. You lived with Auntie Nance whose last name was Ince so I never really thought of you as a Keeling."

After a pause she went on.

"Grandma Keeling died long before I was born and for as long as I can remember anyway, grandpa Keeling hasn't been a part of our family. We've always had grandma and grandpa Wright, dad's parents and quite frankly I've never given much thought to the others."

As if to add weight to Paula's rationale Auntie Edie said,

"Yes, we've had little or nothing to do with grandpa Keeling for years. He remarried; woman named Mullett who had six kids so he's had his hands full."

"Maybe you should go and see him Frank," Paula said.

"Yeah! Maybe I should."

But I never did, didn't like to intrude. Besides, he probably couldn't or wouldn't tell me anything I didn't already know.

Then, well after midnight the inevitable question arose.

"Well, are you a Bunton or not?" Paula innocently asked.

Edie and George immediately dismissed the thought as impossible. To them I was too intellectual and sophisticated to be of such humble stock. I told them their comments were both pretentious and unkind. Surely, I reasoned, Mrs. Bunton must have seen something to convince her I was her grandson. What other reason was there unless I was kin? They had seven mouths to feed, times were hard and Mr. Bunton must have been convinced too. Suddenly Edie exclaimed

"It's one o'clock."

And my question was never addressed. We all retired to bed, I had to be up at six to catch a bus back to my digs.

The course ended and I spent all of Monday, February 4 in the Ipswich Branch Office for orientation. On the Tuesday the Branch Manager accompanied me, demonstrating just how it should be done although he didn't make a single sale. On Wednesday the 6th., we travelled the forty miles by train to Frinton-On-Sea, a charming little seaside town of about five thousand, mainly well-to-do retirees. It was while walking down Connaught Avenue, the main street, that he decided it was time for me to make my first sale completely alone.

We stood on the sidewalk opposite a large office building.

"Now go in there" he said, "and show some of that initiative that served you so well in the armed forces. Let's see you come out with a nice big order."

"I'll certainly do my best" I replied and made my way across the street.

As soon as I entered the building I knew something was wrong. Everybody was rushing around putting on their coats and making for the exit. For a moment I thought there must be a fire. A young staff member, seeing me standing there with my briefcase said,

"Oh haven't you heard? His Majesty the King died early this morning, it just came through on the wireless, we're all closing down out of respect."

"Oh . . . No, I didn't know, sorry," I said, and beat a hasty retreat.

As I crossed the road to rejoin my boss I could see the look of consternation on his face, I had been gone less than two minutes. He looked as if he might explode.

"Well," I said, "so much for my first solo effort, the King died this morning and all businesses are closing for the rest of the day out of respect."

He looked at me in disbelief but then, glancing down the main street, we could clearly see all the shops drawing their blinds and closing. We made our way to the station and returned to Ipswich, a bit of an anti-climax.

Despite the somewhat inauspicious start, I did enjoy reasonable success in my first venture into the world of commerce. But I quickly learned that the field I had chosen was not an easy one. My territory was huge, stretching from Aldeburgh, Suffolk in the North to Clacton-On-Sea, Essex, in the south. I had no vehicle so had to rely on public transport that, in the rural areas, was not good and the company paid no travel expenses.

In time I got to know Travellers representing other companies, many of them provided with a Company car and they would offer me a ride. They were unanimous that I had chosen a most difficult field and was not likely to make a fortune.

"Frank," they would say, "you've got to get into the food business, it's the only way to go. People have had to put up with rationing for so long they're just clamouring for all these pre-war goodies."

They also insisted there was no way a person could succeed without a vehicle.

In October, while walking along the main street of Ipswich I bumped into the accountant who had been fired over the bonus issue at the furniture factory.

He was now selling accounting machines for Remmington Rand. He referred me to his Regional Manager who offered me a position in their Office Supplies Division with better pay and vastly improved conditions; in particular, all travel expenses were paid. I accepted the offer and started job number nine. It was better than my previous position but still not totally satisfactory. The constant strain of travelling by public transport in England's foul weather, over such a large area was getting to me.

On Monday, November 3, 1952, I had barely sat at my desk when Joy arrived bearing a letter from my mother marked "URGENT." The Postman had delivered it a few minutes after my departure. And as she said, "It looked awfully important," so she decided to bring it to the office. It was to inform me that Annie Mason had died on November 1 and that the funeral was on my birthday, the 5th. Mother felt strongly that I should attend, "Just in case . . . You never know," she had written. It was common knowledge that at one time I was the sole heir to the estate.

She was arriving in Epping later that day and we would meet at the Mason's place. After some discussion with Joy it was decided I should go. I had to get an advance of ten shillings to cover expenses, that's how hard up we were in those days.

On arrival at the Mason household, I was greeted by a Mr. Pat McClean and his wife "Dori" They had, they informed me, been renting from Annie for several years. She had the main bedroom to herself; the rest of the house was shared. I could see now why they couldn't help Johnny Haines with room and board.

Annie had been confined to a wheelchair for two years and was almost completely paralysed. The Housekeeper, I was told, had faithfully tended her every wish and whim since the day she had been stricken.

Mother arrived later. She and I went out for a meal and she bought me a black tie saying the one I was wearing was "Too gaudy for a funeral." During the meal she admitted that she had known all along about the McCleans living with Annie and I got the impression that she had been quite friendly with them.

On the Tuesday there was much to do. Annie's personal effects had to be collected from the Hospital where she had died; a visit to the lawyer's Office and to the Undertaker; all dutifully carried out by Pat. I accompanied him at his invitation but at each venue was asked to wait in the car. He was completely in charge of everything and no wonder, it turned out he was the Executor of Annie's Will.

Following the funeral we all gathered in the Mason living room, that very same room where, back in September 1939 Annie had poured out the shocking story of my heritage. My mind flashed back to that afternoon and I remembered well the contempt and animosity I had felt later toward the deceased and even more toward poor old Uncle George. I felt a little guilty, God knows why.

My thoughts were interrupted; Pat was standing beside the fireplace with his left elbow resting on the mantelpiece. His hands were clasped and as he spoke he slowly twiddled his thumbs, I found it most irritating. He spoke without variation in tone or cadence, a cold and callous discourse completely bereft of any kind of emotion. We were simply informed that the lawyer was unable to attend that day but it made no difference because everything had been left to Annie's housekeeper. There was nothing to question nothing to discuss and, as far as Pat was concerned, that was that.

I glanced at my Mother, she was visibly upset but all she said was,

"Is there not one little keepsake for me or for Frank?"

"No there is not," we were brusquely informed.

I could see that she was about to break into tears, more out of anger than sorrow I suspect. As for me, I saw the whole thing as an ironic joke. In my mind's eye I could picture Annie looking down from the heavens at the gathering and feeling very smug about it all. Personally I didn't give a shit! They could all go to hell as far as I was concerned. I grabbed my Mother's arm.

"Come on, let's get out of here."

She gathered her things and we left without another word. We travelled together as far as Liverpool Street where she left for the Underground and on to Brighton. During the familiar train journey that I had taken so often as a child, she rambled on about the unfairness of it all. About how much she had done for the Masons', her mother's sister and her guardians, especially during the thirteen weeks prior to Lizzie's death in 1927.

"This would never have happened were Uncle George alive," she said. "He must be turning over in his grave. I know he would never have treated me like this, or you. That damned Annie Bunyon, she was eaten up with jealousy when George married Lizzie and the poor woman was hardly cold in her grave before she was pestering him to marry her."

"Oh, come on," I said, "Don't carry on so, who cares anyway?"

"Well, I do!" She snarled, with the emphasis on the do.

And for a while she sat expressionless, seemingly with all the troubles in the world on her shoulders.

When we reached Liverpool Street Station, I offered to walk her to the Underground but she declined.

"You have a much longer journey than I . . . don't worry I'll be fine."

I caught the next train back to Ipswich and we made the best of what remained of my birthday. Many years later I was told the housekeeper sent my mother eighty pounds sterling, about three hundred and twenty dollars in those days, guilt I suppose. I must admit I was never able to confirm the story but I'm sure it's true.

Shortly after this, I learned that a good friend Roy Davis had joined a well-known company in the food industry. He would be based in Bury St. Edmunds. It seems I just can't get away from that little town, I thought. They supplied a car and all other expenses were paid. Their products were in great demand and the salary and commission was excellent. I was somewhat envious, but not for long.

In February 1953, an advertisement appeared in the Daily Telegraph for a Representative to cover the County of Essex for the same Company. The successful candidate would be based in Colchester.

I was interviewed and hired on the spot. During the interview the Regional Manager said, "If you can do as well as Mr. Davis has done we shall be very happy."

I later learned that upon receipt of my application they had questioned Roy about my abilities as a Salesman. Being a good friend he had responded in glowing terms for which I was most grateful. I also learned that what impressed management most and was largely responsible for my being hired, was the formal training I had received, both from my first employer in sales and with the London School of Salesmanship. So our investment in the tuition fees proved worthwhile.

Monday March 2nd., I took the train to Colchester and met the person covering the territory. He was an older man, had not been in the service during the war and was apologetic because of it. I put him at ease by reminding him of the terrible hardship suffered by the civilian population, especially in London during the "Blitz." He was fascinated by my wartime escapades and would often question me about them, expressing admiration sometimes to the point of embarrassment.

My territory was divided into four geographical routes. Each route or journey as it was called took four days to service. Fridays were devoted to clerical and administrative tasks. My colleague was to stay with me for one complete cycle. He had a new 1953 Hilman Minx, a beautiful little car and it was a pleasure to travel the countryside in such comparative luxury. He had been with the company for about thirty years and knew all there was to know about its products and how to sell them and he taught me well.

Journey four was the Colchester area so there was little travelling involved. Also, as previously mentioned, most businesses closed Wednesday afternoons, so on the fourth Wednesday I travelled to the head office in Cricklewood, North London to pick up my car. I would start working alone the following Monday.

On arrival the Transport Manager said he had not been advised of my need for a car and there was nothing available. Reminding him I was to start selling on the Monday he agreed to see what could be done. I had visions of getting a brand new car, perhaps a Hilman Minx like my colleague but it was not to be. We walked around a huge lot that must have contained fifty cars; they were all, he said, cars that were no longer fit to drive. Some of them certainly looked in rough shape.

We would approach a vehicle, he would refer to a list and say, "No, not that one," and then go on to explain why. Up and down the lines of cars we went still nothing suitable. At one point we came across an almost new Ford Prefect, it couldn't have been more than a year old.

"What about this one?" I asked somewhat excitedly.

"No, that one was vandalised, has to have a new engine installed."

Finally, we came to a gray Hilman, not a bad looking car, about a 1946. But of course it had been driven hard every day of the week for over seven years.

"This is about the best I can do," he said, consulting his list. "The brakes will have to be relined as soon as possible but apart from that it's not bad."

"Well," I replied, I was taught to drive in the army so I use the gears as a brake most of the time."

"Well that's good, let's take it for a run."

He drove around the block then stopped.

"Well, I don't know about this," he said. "Brakes shot, steering's not so good, transmission . . . hm!" And his voice trailed away to nothing.

He sat for a moment staring into space then took a deep breath and turned toward me. "Frank, I'm sorry about this, somebody goofed. I knew nothing about you coming, this is the best I can do and if you want to take it you can. You could get it into a garage in Colchester tomorrow and get it fixed."

"What's the alternative?" I asked.

"Well you'd just have to go back to Colchester and wait till I can fix something up."

"Well actually, I live in Ipswich but how long would that take?"

"Oh, could be next Tuesday or Wednesday."

I knew my colleague was committed to start his new territory on the Monday and I didn't want to start two or three days late.

"D'you think this car's safe to drive?"

"Oh yeah! It's safe, as long as you get those brakes fixed tomorrow, don't leave it any longer. That's the only thing I'd worry about, should be all right otherwise. And I'll get another car down to you as soon as I can that's a promise."

And so I agreed to take the damn thing. We completed the paper work and I was about to open the trunk to put my brief case away.

"Oh by the way," he said, don't put anything in there, it leaks."

I opened it anyway and sure enough there was a long narrow hole in the floor, rust had eaten right through. You could see where the wheels had churned up the mud and splattered all over the trunk. I turned to him and shook my head in disbelief. He just grinned, turned on his heel and left.

I took it easy at first, on to the M5, turned east to the A12 and then headed north. Once out in the country I opened it up a bit, wasn't too bad. The brakes certainly had to be fixed, there was a lot of play in the steering wheel and the gears were well worn. I had a job to find third to begin with but soon got used to it.

I eventually made it to Ipswich, had a bite to eat and then took Joy and the two boys for a ride out into the country. They were thrilled and all the neighbours gawked. Nobody else in the neighbourhood had a car. I didn't say anything about the car's deficiencies, didn't want to worry anybody.

Next morning I drove the nineteen miles to Colchester and met my colleague for the last time. He lived in Cambridge, had spent Monday to Friday in a hotel in Colchester for years and was now looking forward to a nine-to-five stint.

"Morning Frank, how's the car? Looks pretty good."

I told him the whole story and that I had to get it in the garage right away to get the brakes fixed at least.

"Gimme the keys," he said, "I wanna take it for a drive round the block" and off he went. As he drove away I noticed it had a distinct list to starboard, obviously the right rear shock absorber was shot.

He returned in less than five minutes, opened the passenger side door and motioned me to get in.

"Where we going?" I asked.

"To my garage. I think I can get my mechanic to do the brakes and check this bloody thing out completely. You know Frank, if I'd 'a been you I'd have refused to accept this bloody thing, it's a heap . . . bloody disgrace."

"Well, the Transport Manager said this was the best he could do, otherwise I'd have to wait until middle of next week. Didn't want to do that."

We arrived at his garage; he introduced me to his mechanic who was, of course, anxious to get all my service work and agreed to do the brakes at least. He would check out the rest of the car, he said, but could make no commitment. Anyhow, it wouldn't be ready until five.

We finished the day's work around four-thirty. I knew my colleague was anxious to get going, he had a long drive ahead of him.

"Just drop me off at the garage, that'll be fine."

"Are you sure, I'm a bit worried about that damn car."

"It'll be OK, not to worry."

And so he dropped me off and with a firm handshake wished me well and said how much he had enjoyed my company for the past month. I thanked him and we promised to keep in touch.

"Don't forget Frank," he said, and I was moved by his obvious sincerity, "if there is ever anything I can do for you, if you ever need help just phone me. You've got my number, now don't forget." And with that he was gone.

I would seek his counsel much sooner than either of us could have imagined.

I was pleasantly surprised to find the car was ready. The mechanic, who was also the owner of the Service Station wasn't around; called away I was told. The young man left in charge knew nothing except that the brakes had been relined and my signature was required on the work order. I told myself there couldn't be anything else wrong with the car or there would be some comment on the work order. I drove back to Ipswich and there was a noticeable difference with the brakes but apart from that everything seemed the same.

Joy's youngest sister Thelma had, by this time, married an American airman stationed at Bentwaters just a few miles out of Ipswich and they were living with Joy's parents. On the Saturday he invited us to an evening of entertainment at the Base. We had a few beers but by no stretch of the imagination were we inebriated.

The Base was located on a narrow winding road off the A12. I knew it well having hitch-hiked through the area en route to Aldeburgh on my first sales job. There was a particularly sharp bend just before the A12 and it was here that I lost control of the vehicle. There was no skidding, no squealing of tyres; the steering wheel just would not respond. It was rather like watching a movie in slow motion.

I had slowed as we approached the bend, but by the time I realised something was wrong we had crossed to the wrong side of the road and the car was going up a guy wire supporting a telephone pole. I watched in utter disbelief as the car reared like a lion rampant, twisted as it lost momentum and struck the pole with little more than a thud. The pole snapped about two feet from the ground, more from the weight of the car on the guy wire than anything else I believe. The car then slowly and gracefully rolled over on its side and, in the still of the midnight English countryside, we became entangled in a mass of telephone wires.

My first concern, was anyone hurt?

"Everybody OK?" I asked.

Don insisted they were fine and proceeded to exit the car, Joy wasn't so lucky. She had struck her chin on the dashboard and bit her tongue and had somehow bruised her knee but she was more scared than hurt. As for me I was completely unscathed, only my pride was hurt. I had, over the years, driven everything from a motor cycle to a five ton Troop Carrier, to a Bren Gun Carrier and this was my first accident. It was a severe blow to my ego. I also feared for my future as a Commercial Traveller, how would the company react, I wondered.

A quick examination of the car indicated little damage but some oil was beginning to seep into the ground. By this time two carloads of American airmen from the base had stopped to offer assistance. Together we decided to first get the car upright. There was no reason to suppose it wasn't driveable.

We all surrounded the car and gave it the old heave ho, with no thought whatsoever as to how or where it would land. To my horror it came to rest with the front axle solidly embedded in the splintered stump of the pole. We made gallant efforts to lift it off but to no avail. We tried backing it off but the ground was mostly sand and the back wheels just spun. After a while we gave up. Don, Thelma and Joy got a ride home and agreed to send a tow truck to lift the car off. It never did arrive and I sat for what seemed like hours disconsolately pondering my future.

After about two hours a local policeman rode up on his bicycle. A passing motorist had reported a car off the road and perched up on the stump of a telephone pole, he said. And his Sergeant had received numerous complaints of telephones being out of order.

He circled the vehicle giving it little more than a cursory glance I was relieved. Then he walked up and down the road shining his flashlight here and there looking for skid marks no doubt. Finding nothing he returned demanding to know what had happened. Fearing for my job, I was reluctant to implicate the Company in any kind of negligence, so I said nothing about the mechanical state of the car or that I had only had it a couple of days. Instead, I said I wasn't familiar with the road and was probably going a bit too fast and failed to negotiate the turn. He accepted my confession. I was charged with driving without due care and attention and ordered to appear before a Magistrate in Woodbridge, Monday, April 20.

About four in the morning I hitched a ride back to Ipswich and after a couple of hours sleep got the local garage to drive out to the scene, hoist the car off the stump and, with great caution, drove it back to the garage. There was more damage to the front end than I had thought but it was mainly superficial. Nevertheless, it was considered unfit to drive, not because of the damage sustained in the accident but rather, the general mechanical condition of the vehicle.

Later in the day I phoned my colleague in Cambridge. He immediately put my mind at rest, the Regional Manager had phoned him late on Friday evening he said, and he told him about the shocking state of my car. The Manager was furious, saying that Head Office had been given ample notice of my needs and he would be on the phone to them first thing Monday morning.

"Don't you worry Frank," he concluded, "Phone George right now and tell him exactly what happened." I thanked him and still a little apprehensive made the call to my boss.

He too was most understanding his main concern was that no one was seriously hurt. He expressed his annoyance that I had received, "Such shabby treatment." He told me not to worry, that there would be another vehicle delivered to my house sometime late the next day. He would personally see to it he said. I slept a lot better that night.

True to his word, another Hilman was delivered the next day; it was the same make and model as the previous one but in excellent condition. I thought it strange that they could produce this vehicle at such short notice. My conclusion was it belonged to someone who had a large city territory that could be covered, at least temporarily on foot. I went to work the following day and soon made up for lost time.

The old car was in such bad shape that the company sold it to the garage owner for parts. A few weeks later I was driving on the highway out of Marks Tey when in the distance I recognised the old gray Hilman. The damage had been repaired, it had been given a coat of paint and sold to a young, unsuspecting business woman. "Caveat Emptor," I thought, as I overtook her with a grin. But the most amazing thing was, it still had that list to starboard!

Twenty-eight

Let Them Eat Cake (or Cookies)

We hustled the boys off to school early that Monday morning and drove the few miles to the little town of Woodbridge in typical April weather. Puffy white clouds swept impatiently across an otherwise blue sky. Now and then a grey, murky looking cloud would cover the sun followed by another downpour. This was spring, nature's world was astir, England was at its best and it was good to be alive.

The town is beautifully located on the estuary of the River Deben. Its narrow streets lined with medieval houses including an array of interesting olde English shops. But it wasn't a shopping spree that brought us to this quaint little corner of pastoral East Anglia. I had a date with the local magistrate who looked for all the world like a character out of Charles Dickens.

Driving without due care and attention the charge read maximum fine five pounds. That's not bad, a first offender was rarely fined the maximum. Besides, maybe I'll get away with it. In hindsight I should have if only on a technicality.

The charge was read, I took the oath and the Prosecution handed out eight by fourteen blowups of the approach to the scene of the accident. In the centre of the photograph there appeared this hideously disproportionate SLOW sign painted in the middle of the narrow road.

But most galling was that the picture had obviously been taken in broad daylight on a beautiful sunny day. The scene as depicted, bore absolutely no relationship to the moonless, pitch-dark midnight conditions under which the accident occurred. Surely this was false and misleading evidence and ought never to have been permitted. I should have objected immediately and demanded the case be dismissed. Instead, I said nothing and proceeded to call Joy as the one and only witness for my defence.

She took the oath and I proceeded to question her about my driving habits and things that might prove me innocent. At the same time avoiding any reference to the mechanical state of the vehicle. The Magistrate constantly told me to stop putting words in Joy's mouth and finally, unable to hide his irritation told me to sit down and proceeded to question her himself.

I was found guilty and fined two pounds, that wasn't so bad. As we drove back to Ipswich we were almost involved in a much more serious accident. During a particularly heavy downpour and with visibility limited, I was about to pass a cyclist when he swerved to avoid a pothole. Somehow I avoided him and proceeded on to Ipswich. We had lunch then I went back to work.

Over the next three years everything seemed to fall into place. Things were so good I wondered if it could last.

Shortly after my day in court I received a phone call from a Mr. Sidney Cook in London who introduced himself as the other man in Rose's life. The divorce was expected shortly and they were contemplating marriage. He would like to meet with me to discuss the division of assets and the children's' future. I expressed concern that such a meeting might be construed as collusion but agreed to drive up to London on the following Wednesday.

I parked the car at Rose's house and he and I retired to a pub just around the corner. He was older than Rose, a widower with married children and a good job. He was a very congenial person and in the couple of hours we spent together I was impressed by his sincerity. I answered his questions truthfully with no exaggeration and without apportioning blame. I also made no reference to Rose's affair with the American airman. After a couple of hours Rose joined us, we talked of mundane things for a while then returned to my car. As I was about to bid them goodnight, Sid began to denounce Rose most disparagingly.

Apparently, my answers to his questions differed from the version he had been given. She made no attempt to deny or challenge the validity of what I had told Sid. Instead, she apologised profusely and begged him to forgive her for having misled him. He was very angry and started to walk away threatening never to return. Rose became hysterical, clinging to him and again begging him not to forsake her "after all this time."

It was a most unpleasant and embarrassing scene. I stood there stunned by Sid's sudden and intense outburst. I began to realise the divorce proceedings might be in jeopardy and I was worried. Finally he came back, grabbed her by the shoulders and angrily expressed his displeasure.

"You have lied to me, he said. "I've spent two hours alone with Frank and he is nothing like the person you described, he is a very decent person."

Again, Rose begged forgiveness and clung to him screaming that she couldn't live without him. Embarrassed, I jumped in the car and drove off. As I did so I saw Sid break free and stride defiantly away.

I drove the long journey back to Colchester convinced the divorce proceedings would again be dropped. Nevertheless, I felt a sense of satisfaction. Obviously my reputation had been tarnished but the record had now been set straight. To this day I am convinced that neither Sid nor the children of my first marriage were ever told anything resembling the truth about me as a person or my relationship with their mother..

As it turned out, it wasn't long before Rose was granted a decree nisi. The decree absolute came six months later in October. So I was now a free man but we had heard nothing more about Joy's divorce. Then, the day after my birthday, her decree nisi came through. After eight years of inactivity and frustration everything was happening at once. Six months and we would be free to marry.

It was three-and-a-half years since I had left the Army. Dennis was seven,

Michael six and all that time I'd worked every hour of overtime I could. Six sometimes seven days a week just to make ends meet so the family was often neglected, especially the two boys. Now all that was to change. At last I had a job that would pay me a good wage with all weekends free except for the occasional sales meeting.

The company was in the top five of its class, producing the best in biscuits and cake. The British public had been starved of such luxuries since before the war and it was a seller's market. We supplied everyone from the small corner store to Butlins' Holiday Camp in Clacton-On-Sea, who used a truckload of our products every month. The one minor drawback was that much of the territory was seasonal. But Christmas specials, particularly the decorated tins of biscuits, helped offset the winter doldrums. Many of those tins are now valuable collectors' items and fetch a price far beyond their original valuc.

Life for Dennis and Michael had not, up to this point, been as rewarding as one might have hoped. That is not to say they were in anyway neglected. They always had a good home and were well provided with the necessities of life, and throughout their entire childhood their mother was always at home. Joy and I had agreed, no matter how difficult it might be she would not work while raising the children. Parenting to us was a full time job.

Now we had a home, a well-paid and secure job and we could add to our meagre possessions. We had a car which very few enjoyed and it wasn't long before we had a family dog. He came to us through Joy's Aunt in Long Melford. The only thing missing was a little girl. Joy and I had often talked about it but economically, it had been out of the question. Now all that had changed so we threw caution to the wind and waited and hoped, but nothing happened!

Almost every weekend for the next three years and on our annual holidays, we travelled all over the southern half of England. We visited every seaside resort on the Southeast coast. I took the family to Brighton to visit my mother; she showed little interest in her grandchildren. We received a much warmer welcome from her sister, Auntie Edie.

I took them to Ongar several times where first, we met Evelyn. It was then I learned that mum had died on May 5, 1952 of a heart attack at age seventy-four. I was deeply saddened. I had failed to keep in touch so nobody could inform me.

During this visit our two boys were invited to play in the back garden. Forty years later Evelyn told us how they took her bread knife off the counter, cut every cabbage from the vegetable patch then sat and chopped them up into little pieces so that they were good for nothing. Claude, her husband, was furious and vowed they would never be welcome in his house again; we were most embarrassed. When reminded of the episode, Michael remembered it and was filled with remorse.

Next, we were guests of Charlie and Olive for a weekend during which we spent some time with Frank Bunton. He was very kind and attentive to the boys. There came a time when Joy would confess to seeing a likeness between us.

"And like you," she said, "he doesn't have earlobes and that's unusual."

We visited Jessie and family in Coopersale on the edge of Epping Forest and thoroughly enjoyed our visit. Dennis and Michael had great fun playing in the forest with Jessie's two boys, Trevor and David. On a sad note, Jessie died of a heart attack in 1965 at the age of fifty-one. I later learned that Lena also died of heart problems.

We went to Cambridge several times to see Joy's sister Pearl and family, often taking Granmma and Grandpa Borrett. In fact, we took Joy's mum and dad on many of our trips just to make life a little more interesting for them. Pearl and André later moved to St. Athan in South Wales and we spent a week with her, taking Joy's youngest sister, Thelma with us. The journey was most interesting, especially a whirlwind tour of the ancient City of Bath.

We crossed the River Seven over the famous suspension bridge and saw the beautiful City of Bristol so heavily damaged by bombs during the war. I could go on and on about the many and varied journeys we made into the English countryside but enough is enough. I will conclude by saying that eventually we made it to the famous Whipsnade Zoo which, at the time was one of the largest in the world.

Early in 1954 I was given a brand new Ford Prefect, not as nice as the Hilman Minx but much appreciated. I have a feeling the company wanted to make up for the shabby treatment I received initially. They had a policy whereby we could purchase our old vehicles at a reasonable price; I couldn't afford to buy the old Hilman but had high hopes for the Ford, if and when it became available.

In April we moved to Colchester. The name means, "Castle on the Hill." This is where Julius Caesar set up his first stronghold when he invaded ancient Britain. A Norman castle now stands on those ruins. We lived on Mill Road on the outskirts of town in what was part of the old warehouse where flour from the mill was stored, and cattle grazed in the adjacent meadows.

Occasionally, a cow would force its way through the hedge into our garden in search of a change of diet. One morning Joy went downstairs and I heard a piercing scream. She had taken a curtain in each hand and thrust them wide open as always. Normally she would pause for a moment and enjoy the early morning beauty of our garden; it was alive now with spring flowers. Later in the year she would be greeted by the sight of hollyhocks and roses, Colchester was famous for the latter.

But this morning she would be greeted by something quite different. As she opened the curtains an enormous cow confronted her, its nose pressed firmly on the windowpane, large brown eyes looking straight into hers. I ran into the garden clad only in pyjamas and firmly coaxed the beast back to its pasture while cursing it for trampling on our flowerbeds.

On June 11, 1954, we received notice of Joy's decree absolute. I went immediately to the local Registry Office and following the mandatory three-week waiting period our wedding was set for Saturday July 3, 1954.

It was an unusual wedding. We hadn't told the boys we weren't married, and knowing from personal experience how cruel children can be saw no point in doing so. Dennis was eight and friendly with a charming little blonde girl named Jennifer. We all fell in love with her and vowed that if we ever had a little girl, Jennifer would be her name.

Both our parents were invited to the wedding and Joy's mum and dad took the bus to Colchester, spending the day with us. My mother declined our invitation but sent bed linen as a wedding gift. Johnny, my partner in the ill-fated car wash business was best man and his wife, Jean was Joy's maid of honour. The ceremony took place at eleven in the morning. Joy's parents kept an eye on the children, they were told the four of us were going "shopping." And they were quite happy to stay home and play in the surrounding fields.

Our wedding banquet consisted of good old roast beef and Yorkshire pudding followed by fresh strawberries and cream. After dinner we introduced everyone to our good neighbours John and Leah. John took the wedding pictures of bride and groom and a family group standing amidst a great display of hollyhocks, pictures treasured to this day. John and his wife were unaware that it was our wedding day.

Joy's parents caught an early bus back to Ipswich. We drove Johnny and Jean back there after a modest celebration in the local pub. Driving back to Colchester around midnight, we saw ahead of us a young man on a motor bike plough into the back of a truck parked without lights on the side of the road. In the glare of my headlights I saw his body thrown like a rag doll up in the air and into a ditch on the opposite side of the road. I insisted Joy stay in the car, not wanting her to see what might be an ugly scene. He was wedged firmly in the narrow ditch, unconscious with several broken bones. Others arrived and gave what comfort they could while we raced to Dedham to summon police and Ambulance. We finally got to our marriage bed about three in the morning. Well at least it was different!

Later that summer I parked the car in the drive and found, Joy talking to a young Gypsy woman peddling handmade lace. For some reason I took pity on her and gave her one pound sterling for her lace. She thanked me profusely and proceeded to tell my fortune.

"Within two years," she insisted, "you will travel a great ocean to live in a new land where you will one day become very rich."

After she left I scoffed at the suggestion that I would ever leave my beloved homeland, the country for which I had sacrificed six years of my life and faced untold hardship, death and destruction. The idea was simply preposterous! As for the bit about being rich, well we could all dream couldn't we.

Come fall, another milestone in our newlywed life. We bought our first house on King George Road, taking possession a few days before Christmas. Aware of this, Auntie Edie invited us to her home for the holiday. We took our cat and it ran up the chimney the moment we arrived thank goodness there was no fire.

In the spring of 1955 I took part in an event few working people would encounter in a lifetime. The company held its annual convention at the world famous Savoy Hotel in London. I stayed, along with my friend and colleague Roy in the Russell Hotel. At the banquet we enjoyed a sumptuous meal culminating with brandy and a Havana cigar that would have done justice to Winston himself. And all served by liveried waiters. Oh to see and enjoy, just for one brief evening how the other half lives.

Shortly after that I received yet another phone call from Sid. He and Rose were to be married shortly and they wanted to discuss the future with both Joy and me. In our previous meeting Sid had expressed views about my relationship with the children which, he said, I should think about.

"When I marry Rose," he said, "I don't fancy the idea of you popping up here every now and then to see the children or them going to Colchester to visit you. They have seen so little of you during the past eight years any change might be disruptive."

I felt this was harsh but didn't argue.

On Saturday May 28, 1955 I took the family to London. As we approached the front door Mary, now fourteen emerged. Showing no signs of recognition, I asked her if she knew who I was.

"Yes I do," she said, then hurried away.

Everything was well planned. Albert and Angela were absent and following introductions Rose suggested our two boys play in the garden. Obviously she didn't want the children involved but she did have a girlfriend there. Sid was friendly throughout, Rose was indifferent making several snide remarks. Sid became irritated and quickly silenced her especially when she brought up the past, reminding her of, "What we agreed to earlier."

Then, presumably for Joy's benefit, he repeated his previous comments to me. He said quite bluntly it had been eight years since I'd had any meaningful contact with the children, I meant little to them and to revive the relationship could be disruptive.

"Yes, and they're very fond of Sid," Rose added.

I'd heard all this before, but listening to him one would think I was the villain in the whole affair. While I made no claim to perfection or to being completely blameless for what had transpired I felt his remarks were unreasonable.

I was tempted to set the record straight, there being so much he and the children didn't know but I held my peace. Sid insisted that since he had not served in the war, had a good job and was financially secure he wanted no money from me. The only thing required of me was agreement that Rose retains ownership of everything in the house.

I wanted nothing but an African teak chest I'd had made in Kintampo, in Ghana. It was a beautiful piece of workmanship. Rose curtly informed me she had sold it to her brother-in-law. My first impulse was to go next door and demand its return but concluded it wasn't worth it. Then, much to everyone's' relief it was over, we said our good-byes and left. That was the last we saw of them and thirty-three years would pass before we saw the children again.

Back in Colchester I continued to prosper in the Cake and Cookie business. We had so many free samples all the children in the neighbourhood as well as visitors enjoyed the fruits of my labour; pardon the pun. When the boys complained of hunger between meals it was "Oh let 'em eat cake, or cookies."

For two years we had hoped for a daughter but Joy was now thirty-four and we had long since ceased talking about it. Six weeks after our trip to Whipsnade Zoo Joy's pregnancy was confirmed. The animal kingdom had worked another miracle. My first reaction was disbelief then elation, then apprehension. The boys were ambivalent.

The usual prenatal activities were pursued with a vengeance. There was never any question in our minds that the new-born would be anything but a girl and her name would be Jennifer. Anne with an "e" was chosen as a second name just to give an added touch of Olde English charm and the spelling preferred by my mother.

By fall Joy's heir was very much apparent. The boys were at school all day so she would often accompany me, sitting in the car knitting. Most of my territory was rural, with miles of delightful countryside between clients. We would spend much of our lunch hour exploring old churches and graveyards. Some of them dating as far back as the twelfth and thirteenth century. I recall reading about an ancient font dug from the sand at low tide at West Mersea, famous for its oysters. It was eight hundred years old and would enter our lives again some ten years later.

The glories of autumn gave way to the stark but no less imposing solitude of winter. And with it the damp, raw cold that seemed to eat into your very bones. Thus it was that I bought Joy her first fur coat, a long grey fur. But after a few days she didn't like it so we changed it for a beautiful Persian Lamb.

Just before Christmas we received a 'phone call from Joy's sister Phyllis. It originated in Ipswich, a surprise because the family had emigrated to Canada two years previously. Her stay was indefinite because there was some kind of problem in Canada.

We met with Phyllis and family and I was particularly interested in her description of Canada and its opportunities. Some of her stories of accomplishment, prosperity and wealth were extraordinary. Her description of educational advancement, especially for ex-servicemen were also impressive. A far cry from what Britain had offered and I felt a twinge of envy.

Nineteen fifty-six arrived and with it growing tension in the middle east. The Suez Canal was the vital link through which Persian Gulf oil made its way to Europe via the Mediterranean. Without it, massive oil tankers would have to take the long, costly and perilous journey around the Cape. A worrying time, but Joy and I had more important things on our mind.

About this time I met Nigel a middle-aged philanthropist, deeply religious and dedicated to charitable work. In particular, the purchase of a large residence to accommodate unwed mothers. Colchester, being a garrison town had more than its share of these unfortunates. He was also unswerving in his belief in the healing power of prayer.

We became close friends and he got me involved in some of his charitable activities. I told him about the ancient churches I had discovered on my journeys and on a couple of occasions he asked to join me, he was thrilled with what he saw.

Just as the Middle East was having its problems so too was Europe. France was changing governments with the seasons and Italy every other week. In Britain, unemployment was high and there was a general feeling of discontent throughout the nation. Winston Churchill resigned in favour of Anthony Eden the former Foreign Secretary in the hope that he could better deal with the crisis in the Middle East. But he was doing little for the domestic front and thousands of people were emigrating to other countries. The political upheaval was beginning to take its toll on business and commerce.

In April we had another phone call from Phyllis. Whatever problem there had been in Canada was now resolved and she was going back. It was about this time that Joy's Dad was admitted to hospital with cancer and half his stomach had to be removed. We drove to Ipswich to see him; he was never the same after that.

Nigel invited me on a trip to Newmarket the famous racecourse near Bury St. Edmunds. Although deeply religious, he saw nothing wrong with playing the horses so we had something in common, he was also very well connected.

He drove a 1948 Pontiac that was originally a United States Embassy vehicle in London. It had been modified to right hand drive. It was a huge car by English standards completely streamlined and heads turned as we drove the narrow streets of England. Nigel hated driving and often asked me to drive.

We took a side trip near the village of Stoke-By-Nayland and discovered a six hundred-year-old church. At the entrance, under a glass case there were architectural drawings of the original building including the surrounding scenery. It included carts with solid wooden wheels drawn by oxen and several monks engaged in some aspect of the building process.

The inside although in need of repair was equally fascinating. The isles were the resting place of Noblemen and their Ladies going back hundreds of years. Also, there was a prayer printed on the walls in gilded Olde English script. It began at one side of the massive oak entrance, traversed the four walls, with the last word ending on the other side of the door.

Saturday April 21, 1956, was a dull dreary day. Joy was heavy with child so I wouldn't leave her alone for long. The boys were restless, same old story, nothing to do. Sometimes we went to the cinema but there was nothing on that appealed to us. It would be too uncomfortable for Joy anyway.

So I decided to take the family for a ride into the country and what better place than the old church at Thorington. None of them had seen it and I knew they would find it interesting. The countryside looked bleak and sorrowful but it was a short ride.

We looked around the graveyard then went inside. I pointed out the prayer, the beautiful stained glass windows and the ancient beams that had supported the roof for centuries. I drew the boy's attention to the tombs. There were Lords,

Dukes, Bishops and Squires, each with a unique epitaph inscribed upon the tombstone. Then I noticed Joy sitting motionless, completely relaxed, obviously enjoying the peacefulness of this ancient sanctuary. She looked even more attractive in her pregnancy, I thought; a sort of maternal glow. I leaned down to whisper to her but she had something on her mind.

"I think we'd better make for home," she said quietly, "I just had my first pain."

We wasted no time getting back to Colchester.

Twenty-nine

The End Of An Era

We were well prepared this time, Joy was to be admitted to St. Mary's Hospital and we had long since bought all the necessities, Nigel insisted on buying the baby carriage. It was eleven o'clock before Joy decided it was time to be driven to the hospital. In those days fathers were not allowed anywhere near the delivery room so I had nothing to do but go home and try to sleep. Daylight saving time started around two in the morning so I put all the clocks forward an hour and went to bed. After what seemed hours of tossing and turning, I dozed off.

The phone was ringing! I was redecorating the dining room so it was empty save for the desk upon which the phone sat, this made it sound even more shrill. Who on earth would be phoning at this time of night? I've only just got to bed. Then my head cleared, it was the hospital. Yes, of course, I had taken Joy there last night and we're having a baby!

I flew down stairs worried that I might not get there before the caller hung up. What stupid things go through one's mind at a time like this. I glanced at the clock, six o'clock precisely, didn't seem like I'd been in bed that long.

"Colchester 4570," I said huskily.

"Mr. Keeling?"

"Yes"

"St. Mary's maternity - congratulations - baby girl, six pounds twelve ounces, five o'clock this morning. Both doing quite well, Mrs. Keeling's sleeping now, visiting hours are from two till eight O.K?"

"Oh! Yes, thank you, thank you very much, I . . ." Hmm! The dial tone, I was talking to a dead phone. I couldn't help thinking how bloody cold and indifferent these people were. Nothing like the individual care, the warmth and sincerity of the midwife at a home birth. Years later, when it was too late to do anything about it, Joy told me just how callous they were during the entire delivery. But for now all I could think about was, it's a little girl, wow! I've never been so excited in all my life.

Out of curiosity I rechecked the two calendars to establish a possible conception date. Exactly two hundred and eighty days had elapsed since that trip to Whipsnade Zoo. She was a Sunday's child too, just like her mother. The old folklore had lots of good things to say about a child born on the Sabbath didn't it.

It was only a little after six but I had lots to do. For the next week I would be looking after the boys so I had arranged to take a week of my holiday. Later that morning I would phone Eric Fordham, my relief, to take over. Must get my Journey Book and Order Forms from the car and make a few notes for him. The boys were still sleeping so I decided to do that first.

Being a Sunday, all was peace and quiet as I worked. And I found myself reflecting on how difficult things had become. The Russians had marched into Hungary creating waves of refugees across Europe. The British economy was sluggish and my sales had suffered accordingly. There was lots of competition from the junk food industry and they were making inroads into the market. Even Christmas had been slow and the company's experiment of separating the cake and biscuit divisions, using cheap advertising and forcing us to abandon our small shopkeepers was a disaster. There was talk of layoffs and amalgamating territories. The only bright spot was that finally and officially, after eleven long years following the war, meat rationing ended.

But again, I forced the negative thoughts from my mind and went about the business of caring for the family, especially our new-born daughter. I visited her that afternoon and was enchanted by the loveliness of this six pound twelve ounce bundle of joy, pardon the pun. Joy looked radiant despite the rigours of childbirth. They were both released from hospital on the Friday and greeted with a welcoming cup of tea by our kindly neighbour, Lily Harding who insisted she hold Jennifer.

With two big brothers and doting parents it soon became obvious Jennifer would be spoiled. I even found myself thinking that maybe she should have a little sister. The only set back in those early days was Joy's breast milk. The quantity was adequate but the quality was found wanting, so Jennifer had to be put on a formulae. This was a disappointment but not uncommon during and after the war. I must hasten to add, she wasn't given the popular, subsidised brand known as "`National." Nothing but the best was good enough for our Jennifer.

Also, there was at that time a large body of opinion that insisted anyone with a family history of breast cancer should not breast feed. We didn't know much about genetics then but Joy's mum had a mastectomy so perhaps it was all for the good.

Thursday, July 26, 1956 the proverbial hit the fan in the Middle East. The President of Egypt, Gamal Abdul Nasser unilaterally nationalised the Suez Canal. France had spent ten long years from 1859 to 1869, suffering the most terrible hardships to finance and build the canal with a lesser contribution by Egypt. In 1875, Britain had purchased all Egypt's shares, so for seventy-five years these two countries had shared the burden of operating and maintaining the facility and were not about to relinquish ownership lightly. That same day Anthony Eden declared a state of emergency, troops were mobilised and gasoline was once again rationed. It looked very much as if England would again be plunged into war.

The company was quick to react. With gasoline rationing they immediately laid off about a third of the Sales Force, which included myself and my good friend Roy Davis. He covered the adjoining territory. The following day I was instructed to deliver the car to a garage near Colchester Railway Station, someone would pick it up from the regional depot shortly thereafter.

Also on that day, all other company materials were handed over to Eric Fordham who would be covering three territories. Obviously, this was the end of my career as a Commercial Traveller but somehow I wasn't sorry. I never could envisage myself pursuing this as a lifelong vocation. I knew there had to be something better but where and when I knew not.

President Nasser did eventually close the Suez Canal - he sunk two massive freighters right in the middle of it. On October 29, 1956, Israel landed troops and on November 5-6 Britain and France invaded Egypt. However, on December 22, the United Nations ordered them to withdraw. It was an election year in the United States so they got no support from that quarter. Eden was eventually forced to resign and in 1957, Harold McMillan became England's fifth Prime Minister since the end of World War Two.

Overnight business and commerce had been plunged into a state of near chaos. Real Estate sales ground to a halt and you couldn't give a car away. Nobody was hiring so what on earth was I to do? For the time being, I would have to go on the Dole.

On the Saturday, Nigel phoned and I told him of my plight.

"Well, I could certainly use some help," he said.

I was on the point of saying that I couldn't afford to work full-time for charity but he had other ideas.

"How much did you earn selling biscuits and cake?"

"Oh, on average fourteen pounds a week."

"Hm! I'll pay you fifteen pounds a week plus all expenses if you'll come and work with me until my secretary gets back to work, shouldn't be more than a couple of months now."

"What exactly would I be doing?"

With a chuckle he replied, "Oh, there's lots to do. First thing, get my books in order they're in a mess. There's several letters need typing and I'm in the middle of negotiations for a beautiful piece of property." And with obvious glee he continued, "Yes, Frank, at last I've found the perfect property for the Sanctuary but the blighters are asking the moon, maybe you can help me with that."

"Well, the bottom has dropped out of the Real Estate market"

I said, "So you shouldn't have much trouble now, surely?"

He thought for a moment, "Yes, you're right there, so what do you say?"

"When do I start?"

"Come up to the house Monday morning; oh you don't have a car now do you. OK I'll pick you up about nine-thirty, how's that?"

"Fine," I said, and there the conversation ended.

I told Joy, she was dumbfounded. Neither of us could have possibly imagined me working for Nigel and being paid a salary. But we were both relieved that our immediate needs would be met.

Thus it was for the next eleven weeks I would be employed in a most unusual job. For Income Tax and Unemployment Insurance purposes my official title was "Personal Assistant," but I found myself performing all kinds of odd jobs. Nigel would always introduce me as his "Friend and Adviser" but there were times when I was flying by the seat of my pants. I was not used to moving in such high circles.

Throughout my career as a salesperson I had always worn the traditional dark gray suit, blue shirt with detachable stiff white collar, very English, very proper. But this didn't suit Nigel.

"I feel," he said, "As if I'm continuously in the company of the local Vicar."

He, being the Country Gentleman wore nothing but expensive tweeds. On the Monday, the first thing he did was to introduce me to his personal tailor and order something less formal. It was a green and brown chequered tweed jacket with greyish green pants to match, an outfit that immediately met with his approval.

"Just put it on my account," he said as we left the Tailor's Shop. Thank God for that I thought, I had no idea what it cost but knew it was far out of my reach; that outfit served me well for many years.

Working for Nigel was a challenge. I typed letters, sorted out his books, sat in on numerous business deals and drove him to all the famous race meetings, including Newmarket and Ascot. Often in the Silver Ring we were in close proximity to members of the Royal Family, the Queen herself even. I also helped with his charitable activities. Watching him on some of his visits to the terminally ill was very moving. He would spend hours at their bedside bringing them peace and serenity in their final hours and ensuring they died with dignity.

There were times too, when he would insist I stay at home and he would take Joy to one of his favourite places of worship, a break from her daily routine. Thus it was that we found ourselves drifting back to the church and a religion long since abandoned.

In August of that year, The Suffolk Regiment with whom I had served for so many years returned from Cyprus and was stationed in Colchester. Princess Margaret was their Colonel-In-Chief and she was to present the Regiment with new Colours. I was invited along with Joy to attend the ceremony. As Chairman, I was to represent the local chapter of the Old Comrades Association, an organisation of retired members of the Suffolk Regiment living in the Colchester area. It meant a new outfit for Joy, a delightful lilac coloured two piece suit. As for me, the new outfit Nigel had provided was good enough for this occasion but I had to buy a new set of dress medals because I had allowed the two boys to cut their teeth on the originals.

It was a beautiful day so with Lily Harding baby-sitting Jennifer, we walked the half-mile to the Barracks. The entire Regiment including Band and Drums was assembled in typical military fashion on the parade ground. The high-ranking dignitaries and we lesser mortals were placed to one side. Following the ceremony we were to line up in the Sergeants Mess where we would be presented to Her Royal Highness, Joy had practised her curtsey for days.

Many of the ladies were dressed in the most delicate summer wear. A murmur went through the assembled throng as it was reported that the Royal cavalcade had passed a certain checkpoint, a few minutes and all the pomp and ceremony could commence. The "Royal watchers" and the Press were all set to bask in the glory of this great occasion but Mother Nature had other ideas.

As so often happens in Britain at that time of the year, a black cloud appeared from nowhere and the heavens just opened. It poured so hard it was difficult to see the far side of the parade ground. We were hustled into the corridor of a Barrack Room to watch the proceedings. The Princess Margaret arrived, made a hasty tour down the front rank under an enormous umbrella held aloft by an Aide, jumped back into her car and was whisked off to the Officers' Mess. We caught a fleeting glimpse of her figure from the hemline down.

Early September saw Nigel's dream become a reality. The property to be known as "The Sanctuary" was his. The political uncertainty of the times had, as I had predicted, worked in favour of the buyer. It was a beautiful piece of Real Estate, two storeys Tudor style in immaculate condition and large enough for the seven occupants that Nigel visualised as the first tenants. The grounds too were large and well kept, it even had a tennis court complete with a Pavilion for players and distinguished guests.

Joy and I spent many hours with Nigel in the first couple of weeks helping decide on the interior decor and the multitude of detail involved in operating the facility. There was a small opening ceremony and the Vicar of Marks Tey was pleased, for a handsome fee, of course, to wander throughout each room reciting a form of blessing designed especially for this type of facility.

In those early days, the Sanctuary became an obsession with Nigel to the exclusion of all else. Efforts to direct his attention to other pressing matters went unheeded. On what proved to be our last visit to Newmarket we both won a substantial amount of money. He had a habit of simply stuffing his winnings in his jacket pocket, an open invitation to the highly skilled pickpockets that roamed through the crowd.

On this occasion, as we descended the steps from the stand, I noticed his jacket pocket bulging and a large wad of banknotes in full view. I kept close behind him as the crowd swarmed toward the exit. Once outside I dared to chastise him for his continued disregard for security. He was obviously irritated and told me to mind my own business. A week later he went to another race meeting alone. A little after five in the afternoon the phone rang, it was Nigel. He had been relieved of more than fifty pounds, his entire winnings for the day and was most upset because the Police had told him there was nothing they could do.

By this time I was becoming somewhat frustrated with the way things were going. The Middle East situation was deteriorating, unemployment rates were soaring and hundreds of thousands were leaving the country. I began to despair and wasn't at all sorry when, on Wednesday October 10, Nigel informed me that his secretary would return to work on the following Monday and my services were no longer required. He did ask me to continue helping him in any way I could, voluntarily of course.

At least now I had to do something, I could no longer just drift along hoping for something to turn up. As a temporary measure, I got a job as a Photographer's Agent in the Greater London area. It meant travelling to London by train every working day but at least it was a job and Christmas was coming.

It was November 6, 1956, the day following my thirty-seventh birthday and the second day of the invasion of Egypt by British and French forces. But all this paled by comparison to what eventually transpired. I caught the early train to London and it was a typical English November day, thick fog, what we called a "Pea-souper."

My business was in Westminster, the very heart of the City of London. The train was an hour late because of the fog and I took the Underground from Liverpool Street to Westminster. Emerging from the depths of the Subway opposite Big Ben I couldn't even see the enormous structure. It struck the half-hour, ten that is, as I stood staring into the mist. It was an eerie sensation but I had often been in London under similar conditions. I had no intention of groping around trying to find a strange business on a side street with which I was not familiar.

Westminster Abbey was but a stone's throw from where I stood so I decided to go in there and sit a while waiting for the fog to lift. I mounted the steps and made my entry through the massive doorway and was confronted by at least a hundred school children obviously there on a field trip.

I was in no mood for childish banter so I made my way to a small side chapel, St. Faith's. It was completely dark save for the two large candles burning on the altar, I relaxed and began to take stock. Yesterday I had celebrated my thirty-seventh birthday, in biblical terms I was more than half way through my three score years and ten. I had a wife and three children to support, had wasted my time in dead-end jobs and now something drastic had to be done.

I reflected upon my education, training and background and felt cheated. First by the circumstances of my birth and early childhood and then by the war. I thought of that Army Council Instruction that said "Every Regular Soldier shall spend his last six months in England to prepare him/herself for civilian life." I had been stuck in Berlin till mid May, the last twenty-eight days of that six month period was mandated as paid leave which had left me less than half the designated time to plan a civilian career. But not to worry, I was going to be a teacher, I was going to Teaching College wasn't I.? The Army was going to pay my way weren't they? Wishful thinking, I told myself. All this seemed a lifetime away yet it was a mere eight years.

Excuses, excuses, I had to admit. All that had transpired was entirely my own doing; I knew from the beginning that I was capable of better things. I could see now that I had given up too easily following that initial setback. I recalled the interview in the Employment Office in Ipswich. They had told me my experience in the Armed Forces would count for nothing; that I would have to start right from the bottom, but they were talking about a clerical career. The Army had taught me a great deal more than that.

It had taught me about planning and organising, about logistics and assembling resources. I had learned much about personnel supervision, directing, co-ordinating, motivating and communicating. My Intelligence training had taught me how to gather and evaluate information, how to exercise judgement based on facts, the art of decision making and more. I thought about the medical training I'd had, with its humble beginnings in the Boys Brigade and reaching its peak in 36 General Military Hospital during the most vital period of the North African campaign. For the first time I began to realise just how much I had to offer.

From somewhere in the depths of my mind I recalled a military lecture. The speaker, to emphasise a point had quoted Napoleon, "Ability is of little account without opportunity," he had intoned. So, was that my problem? Looking back I realised there hadn't been many opportunities. But on the other hand I had to admit I hadn't looked very hard. I'd just moved from one job to another, always in a hurry, always looking for the biggest buck. Why? Because for me so much time had been lost by military service, I had so much catching up to do.

We had just received a letter from Phyllis saying how well things were going. Jim had two jobs, they had a house and a car. Although she missed her family everything else was fabulous. Maybe it was divine guidance because of my location but in a flash I knew what I had to do. I hurried out, pausing only to buy a picture postcard of the Abbey. This was a turning point and I wanted to preserve the moment for posterity. Then I recalled the gypsy's prediction, but I still don't believe in fortune-tellers. Outside the fog had lifted, there was bright sunshine and a red double-decker bus headed for Trafalgar square arrived. In five minutes Nelson's column was in full view.

At Canada House I was directed to the appropriate office. Told of my desire to emigrate to Canada and my family connections in Saskatchewan, the kindly bureaucrat suggested I go to Saskatchewan House. There, another civil servant tried to discourage me saying that being British I would find the climate in British Columbia much more to my liking. I declined his advice so he sent me to yet another government Office that dealt only with the immigration process.

There were long lines at every wicket and from the moment I joined the queue it seemed everything and everybody was determined to make the task as difficult as possible. It took ages to reach the counter only to be told there was a three-month backlog. Undeterred, I got the necessary documents and left for Colchester. On the train I looked at the literature and was even more convinced I was doing the right thing. I decided not to say anything to the boys just in case it didn't materialise. I also decided that the next day I'd better attend to business.

With the boys in bed I told Joy what I had been up to all day. At first she was stunned, but the more we discussed the pros and cons the more enthusiastic she became. Although a little apprehensive she said it would certainly be an adventure, her sister being there made it easier of course.

I wrote to Phyllis enlisting any help she could offer. I told her we expected to have about two thousand dollars and hoped that it would be enough to give us a good start. In less than two weeks she replied. Thrilled by our decision, she offered accommodation in her house until we could find a place. As well, her brother-in-law Bill, who operated a business, had made an offer of employment. She also assured us that two thousand dollars would be adequate, confessing that they had started with nothing. Armed with this new information I went to the Immigration Office immediately. They told me that with a guarantee of employment and accommodation there was no doubt my application would be approved.

Over the next six weeks there was a flurry of activity, filling out forms, getting passports, medical exams for the whole family, including X-rays and a host of other detail. Working in London was a big help, I could respond to the multitude of demands on a daily basis. As a result I became friendly with some of the staff.

Having been assured my application would be approved we immediately put the house up for sale and booked a cabin on the motor vessel "Seven Seas." It was to sail from Southampton on March 2, 1957, the journey would take six days. We told the boys and they were thrilled.

The house hadn't sold by this time so I applied for an assisted passage from the Canadian government. The initial loan was for a thousand dollars, the cost of the sea voyage and rail travel from Halifax to Regina. I had no qualms about doing this because of the equity we had in the house. We had made several improvements up to that point and I intended to do more.

Christmas came and all the presents consisted of clothing more appropriate for the harsh climate of the Canadian prairies. Joy had her Persian lamb coat and boots; I bought myself a fur lined parka and for the boys, heavy duffel coats and fur-lined boots. It was becoming more expensive than I had anticipated and we had still not sold the house. I had continued to help Nigel as and when I could and in return he helped by paying the ten- percent deposit for the fares.

At year's end, after a heated argument about travelling expenses I quit the photography business and went on the dole, there were just nine weeks left before we were due to sail. I had paid Unemployment Insurance for well over seven years and had used it very little so didn't feel at all guilty.

I immediately started remodelling the kitchen and redecorating much of the house in the hope that it would expedite a sale but to no avail. Then another set back. I received a letter from Immigration saying that my application had been rejected because Saskatchewan only wanted skilled tradesmen. I travelled up to London at once and talked to one of the friendly staff, telling him I was a tradesman, a plumber, in fact. I gave him the address and phone number of the company in Brighton with whom I had worked before the war and hoped for the best. I was told not to worry my application would be approved. We all breathed a sigh of relief.

We then started to sell our furniture and bit by bit the house began to resemble the morgue. We worked out a deal with a second-hand furniture dealer that would allow us to keep the bare necessities until the day we left so it wasn't too bad.

Dennis was eleven on Thursday February 21. Normally it would be quite a day and would include a trip to the cinema after school. On this occasion we were all so busy and so excited about our upcoming adventure that we completely forgot about poor old Dennis' birthday but we made up for it eventually.

On the Friday we received another letter saying Saskatchewan had refused our application because plumbers were not needed in March. Eight days from sailing, everything we owned sold and a hot prospect for the house. What on earth was I to do? I decided this called for drastic action. I phoned the Member of Parliament for Colchester, told him of our plight and pleaded ministerial intervention. It was Friday afternoon and he agreed to do what he could. We spent a very uneasy weekend.

Monday morning just after nine the phone rang. I was told to present myself at the Immigration office as soon as possible but was given no hint as to the decision. I left immediately, arriving at the office mid afternoon. I was greeted with, what I can only describe as V.I.P treatment. Obviously there had been discussions in high places. In any event, there were apologies all round for less than ideal treatment and blame was placed at the feet of an inexperienced junior clerk. All that mattered was our application had been approved. I left with all the documents duly signed and stamped. This time it was for real, there would be no turning back.

I had written to Joy's parents and my mother asking them if they could possibly visit us to say our goodbyes. We no longer had a car and to travel as a family by train, especially on the Underground, would be so much more difficult for us than for them. Joy's parents came by bus and spent a pleasant day with us on the Wednesday. We were shocked at her dad's appearance after his surgery; he looked but a shadow of his former self.

It was a tearful farewell at the end of the day; the last of the Borrett children was leaving for foreign lands. Phyllis and family were already in Canada. Pearl and family were living in Amiens, France, although they did return to England to live some months later; Thelma was living in Pennsylvania, USA, the home of her husband; and Francis, with his rapidly growing family was in Germany; he later emigrated to Australia.

We heard nothing from my mother . . . nothing!

The prospective buyer for the house failed to obtain the necessary financing and so with less than seventy-two hours in which to make a deal, we signed power of attorney to a lawyer and hoped for the best.

Thirty

The Seven Seas

Saturday, March 2, 1957 dawned bright and sunny and unusually mild. Our feelings were a mixture of excitement and sadness. On the one hand the thrill of adventure, on the other, the thought of leaving behind all we had worked so hard to accomplish. For me, leaving the land of my birth, the land I loved and for which I had sacrificed so much was overwhelming. It's all for the best I kept telling myself.

I read my favourite newspaper for the last time and found comfort in one item. Harold McMillan was now Prime Minister. He reminded me of an old Basset hound; sagging jowls, big ears and large, brown sorrowful eyes and he was the epitome of English upper class snobbery. A reporter asked him if the enormous exodus of people emigrating from the British Isles concerned him in any way.

"Not at all," he replied, "they'll all be back. The British people have never had it so good."

Completely out of touch with reality and his disdain for the common folk was rivaled only by that of Marie Antoinette.

Just before two in the afternoon I closed the front door of 16 King George Road for the last time. The keys were left inside for the real estate agent so there was no going back. We sat on a large trunk on the sidewalk waiting for the taxi that would take us to the station for the first leg of what was to prove a long and stressful journey.

We caught the two-thirty train from Colchester to Liverpool Street, then by cab to Waterloo for the train to Southampton. Before boarding the train Joy fed Jennifer the last of her baby food. Phyllis had travelled the Atlantic and assured us that the boat would supply similar food so we hadn't bought anymore.

At six-thirty that same evening we walked up the gangplank and boarded the ship to rousing music by a local band. Female members of the crew greeted us and were eager to help. Most of the ship's company was German so my knowledge of the language would prove valuable. Once in our cabin they insisted we go for a meal while they looked after Jennifer. We were reluctant to leave her with strangers but when we returned she was quite happy.

At ten o'clock the ship gently eased away from the dockside. Jennifer was sleeping and the boys were in their bunks so, Joy and I went on deck to take one last look at our homeland. We stood by the rail hand in hand listening as the last strains of Auld Lang Syne gently faded in the distance, then lingered a while to watch as the lights of Southampton slowly disappeared into the gloom of a moonless night.

The ship would soon turn west into the Solent, that strip of water between the mainland and the Isle of White, then head out to sea into the broad Atlantic. But there was a chill in the air and we decided to retire to the warmth of our cabin and we found ourselves wondering. Wondering what lie ahead.

We had an outside cabin on the port side, second deck, half way between midships and stern. There were four bunks, two up, two down with Jennifer's crib in one corner and our baggage in the other.

The first night was smooth sailing, just took a while to get used to the throbbing of the ship's engine and the vibration. The dining facilities were excellent for adults but, contrary to what we had been told, they did not supply special food for babies. Fortunately, Jennifer had been on some solids for a while so we improvised.

The weather on the first day was glorious. I sat on a hatch stripped to the waist basking in the sunshine; it felt more like a Caribbean Cruise than an Atlantic crossing. But this proved to be very much the calm before the storm. We also met some of our fellow passengers. A few English, Dutch and German families but the majority were refugees from Hungary. Many had escaped the ravages of the civil uprising in their homeland with nothing but the clothes on their back.

The countries of Western Europe had given them asylum, fed and clothed them and they were now on their way to Canada to start a new life. The tragedy that had befallen them was readily apparent in their eyes. Many seemed timid and shy some a little frightened others just overwhelmed with all that was happening. We felt especially sorry for the little children and did whatever we could to befriend them; Dennis and Michael quickly made friends. But there were a few young men in their late teens or early twenties who were sullen and unfriendly, resentful that the western world had not come to the aid of their country.

Come the dawn of day two things were totally different. The moment I woke it was obvious we were at sea. Along with the throb of the engines and the vibration there was now a distinct swell. An empty pop bottle rolled, first to one side and then the other on the empty promenade deck above, something that happened repeatedly and would prove most irritating throughout the rest of the journey. A glance out the porthole revealed a dark, angry looking sky and a sea whipped by gale force winds. We all staggered like drunken sailors to the dining room; Dennis was the first to decline food.

Our daily routine was simple. After breakfast we would bundle Jennifer up in her carrycot which, with the twist of a couple of butterfly nuts was then fixed to the chassis of her baby carriage. This was quite a unique design and one that proved invaluable in the years to come. We would then walk around the deck for exercise, weather permitting. When the weather was too bad we would spend our time in the lounge. Jennifer, much to the amusement of fellow passengers, would hitch on her bum from one side to the other; she never did crawl.

As the second day wore on the pitch and roll of the ship became more violent. Jennifer lay in her crib sliding back and forth with the movement of the ship, somehow sleeping through it all. The third day was even worse. We struggled up on deck simply out of a desire for fresh air, it was so stuffy in the cabin.

By now few people could eat, the dining room was almost deserted at meal times. The sight and sound of people overcome with seasickness became commonplace. I told the family not to think about the queasy feeling in their stomach, convinced from experience it was mind over matter. Eventually they all succumbed to the malady. I was the only one able to enjoy food.

We stood on deck and watched, as time and again, the boat would sink into an immense trough. Although being equivalent to seven stories high, we saw only this huge wall of water that looked as if it would completely engulf us. It would heave up to the crest of another gigantic wave, another glimpse of sky then plunge even further it seemed to new depths. This and the violent roll from side to side were enough to test the metal of the hardiest of mariners.

On one occasion, as the boat rose from the depths of a huge gully, we caught sight of a merchant vessel no more than half a mile off our port bow. We watched in awe as its giant propellers came clear out of the water like a bucking bronco. Before long our ship did the same with an unpleasant burrrr, as the spinning screws met no resistance.

The seas were so rough, ropes were tied across the lounge so that passengers could claw their way hand over hand from one side to the other. On one occasion as we entered the lounge from the outer deck, the boat gave one enormous heave forcing Dennis to run into the rope catching him at throat level, I thought he was going to choke.

All that day and night the storm continued to rage. The Captain was quoted, as saying this was the worst Atlantic crossing he had experienced in his thirty-six year career. I had sailed the Bay of Biscay and the Irish Sea several times, which were said to be the roughest waters in the world at certain times of the year. I had experienced both at their worst but I had encountered nothing to equal what we were going through now.

It all ended on the morning of the fourth day. Only two more days we told ourselves, and it looked as if the rest would be plain sailing. The sea was relatively calm, a gentle breeze and a clear blue sky. Everybody was moving briskly around the ship again and at meal times the dining room was filled to capacity. We all breathed a sigh of relief but not for long.

Suddenly the throb of engines ceased, no more vibration and the ship slowly came to a stop. Throughout, there was an uncanny silence, passengers and crew looked questioningly at one another. What was wrong? Just some minor malfunction we thought, not to worry, soon the engines would start up again and we would hear that familiar throb.

During the first hours rumours were rampant. It's amazing how fertile the human mind under these circumstances. A young boy had fallen from a top bunk and smashed his skull on the deck. They were operating on him in the sick bay and the ship had to be kept steady for the surgeon's scalpel. A man had fallen overboard and a lifeboat would be launched to search for this unfortunate individual. The engines had failed and we were destined to flounder helplessly at the mercy of this mighty and unpredictable ocean until help arrived, and that could be days. On and on it went. But as the hours passed and still no movement, a sense of unease swept through the ship.

All that fourth day and well into the night the silence continued; the boat wallowed aimlessly moving only at the will of wind and current. It was an eerie sensation. Any question to the crew was met with a stony silence or, pretending not to speak English, a curt, "Ich wisen nicht." I don't know. When pressed in their native tongue they would simply say that their superiors had given them no explanation which, of course, was ridiculous.

Sometime during our fifth night at sea I woke with a sense of movement, albeit very, very slowly. There was no vibration, none of the throbbing of internal combustion engines; we just seemed to be gliding noiselessly through the night. I glanced out the porthole, it was a clear moonlight night and I could see quite plainly that we were, indeed, moving. Progress I thought and tried to get back to sleep; but sleep did not come easy, I was concerned at the delay in our sailing time.

The sixth day, the day we should have disembarked in Halifax, came and went and still no explanation. Everybody was getting on edge; we felt we had a right to know. On the seventh day, groups of passengers were allowed to visit the bridge, I was determined to be among them and equally determined to use my knowledge of German to get some answers.

The line of passengers filed slowly from the starboard entrance to the bridge, past the helmsman at the wheel and out again through the door on the port side. Along the main bulkhead there hung a series of photographs of the MV Seven Seas in various stages of construction and post-war reconstruction. It was originally built as a merchant vessel and saw service as such through much of World War Two. At some point it was sunk in shallow water in Kiel harbour. After the war it was raised and converted to a fairly comfortable cruise ship.

The picture of the vessel lying fully submerged, obviously taken from the air, brought forth many caustic remarks related to its slow progress and the air of secrecy surrounding it. The crew ignored the remarks or pretended not to hear, but as I said, I was determined. I dropped out of the line and approached a smartly dressed officer with lots of gold braid on his sleeves and cap.

"Entschul'digen bitte," Excuse me, I said.

"Ja" Yes, said my officer.

"Warum geht das schiff so langsem?" Why is the ship going so slowly?

"Ich wisen nicht," I don't know, he said somewhat offhandedly.

"Das est ansseror'dentlich, scherzen sie." That is extraordinary, you must be joking?

"Nein, Ich scherzen nicht." No, I'm not joking.

"Ich denken sie liegen." I think you lie. At this he became quite irritated.

"Ich scherzen nicht, Ich liegen nicht, Ich wisen nicht, bitte." I'm not joking, I'm not lying, I don't know, please! And he took my arm and gently but firmly guided me back to the line and the exit, so much for my language skills.

We continued at a snail's pace for the rest of Saturday, day seven and still nobody knew why. The latest rumour was that the engines had completely broken down, the Captain was going to radio Halifax for a tug to tow us in but a search of the passenger list had indicated that a marine engineer was on board. He had been consulted and had found a way to start one engine, hence our slow pace. He was rewarded by having the entire cost of his journey refunded. But we were never able to confirm any of this or learn the true reason.

On Sunday, two days behind schedule land was sighted. We were all on deck, suddenly a flurry of excitement and all eyes turned toward the starboard bow. There at last a large black land mass soaring skyward. Cheers echoed throughout the ship but it would be several hours before we docked.

I gathered the family together and reminded them that, there in the distance, was our new homeland. That many things would be different, people would be different. We should accept these differences I stressed. After all, we had chosen to come to Canada seeking a new life.

"Forget the old ways of doing things" I said, "accept the new and realise how fortunate we are to be given this opportunity."

Joy often recalled my little speech.

The boat finally docked but disembarkation was delayed until Monday morning, March 11, three days late. As well, the Hungarian refugees would be the first to leave, we were told. The authorities were anxious to process them and get them on their way as soon as possible and we fully understood.

There was a party in the dining lounge that evening complete with paper hats and all the usual trimmings. Later that night the boys looked after Jennifer while Joy and I went to a farewell dance. At last we were beginning to feel human again. We retired to our beds quite late, for the first time in two weeks without the pitch and roll of the ship and the noise of its engines.

Feelings were mixed as we said our goodnights, it was the end of a long and harsh journey across the Atlantic. Now, there was a finality about it all. I felt a tinge of sadness and a little guilty that we had, perhaps, deserted the land of our birth. Then excitement at the thoughts of life in a new land, apprehension for the future and finally, uncertainty as to whether we had made the right decision.

After breakfast we went on deck and watched the refugee families walk down the gangway and into a huge warehouse. There were several dignitaries on hand to greet them but we saw nothing of the ceremony.

The train to Regina via Montreal, where we were to change, left Halifax at four in the afternoon. We had lunch and then it was our turn to disembark. We walked into that large warehouse and were amazed to see isle after isle of toys. Each refugee child had received one or more upon arrival. It was difficult for the other children; Jennifer was upset that we weren't even allowed to browse.

Customs officials were polite and very proficient; they searched every inch of our trunk despite my assurance it contained nothing contraband. They asked how much money I had for the journey and insisted it wasn't enough. Then promptly gave me twenty dollars, our first taste of Canadian generosity, I thought. Weeks later I found it had been added to my account.

We had an early supper in the coffee shop on Halifax station and I was horrified when presented with a bill for seven dollars for sausage and mash for four. This was the equivalent of one pound fifteen shillings or half a day's pay. I had no idea of the relative value of money then. Before journey's end I learned not to convert to sterling and felt much better.

The train left Halifax with just enough daylight for us to catch a glimpse of our first Canadian city. The most striking difference was the bright colours of the houses and the architecture. A pleasant contrast to the monotonous row upon row of brick houses in England.

As our railroad, we had learned not to say railway by this time, journey of three days and nights continued, we began to appreciate the vastness of Canada. The train travelled for hours between towns, in England it would be only minutes. The landscape was completely different too; compared to the tiny patchwork of England's fields, here they were enormous. At first, sleep came in fits and starts and I would peek through the blind at the snow covered landscape; here and there a cluster of farm buildings standing dark and silent in the moonlight. It was both awesome and fascinating, another world.

We reached Montreal at eight o'clock Tuesday evening and with the help of a charming lady from the Department of Immigration, boarded a bus for the Canadian Pacific Station. I didn't think anybody cared, but this was all part of the immigration service and much appreciated.

The boys and me were the last to board and it was standing room only; Joy got a seat with Jennifer on her lap. I stood at the back of the bus clinging to a bag of oranges, determined the family would get its daily dose of Vitamin C for the rest of the journey. The streets were slippery and as the bus slithered down a sharp incline, the bag burst and oranges rolled one behind the other, down the isle and accumulated at the feet of a not too pleasant bus driver. He wasn't amused when, in less than perfect French, I told him he could have one for his trouble.

And so, on to the longest train we had ever seen and it had two domed coaches, we'd never seen them before. But we were in for a bit of a shock. Unlike the train from Halifax, this one had two classes and we were relegated to the lower, Tourist Class. By comparison, the seating was dreadful. Instead of two comfortable high backed, well padded seats each side of a table, we were stuck with long bench seats. There was a space between the seat and the backrest, most uncomfortable.

For sleeping purposes one was expected to stretch out on the narrow seat. With the swaying motion of the train one found oneself constantly slipping between seat and backrest, with the potential for falling on the floor. Studying their construction, I realised if one bolt were removed from each seat the backrests could be adjusted downwards forming a double sized bed.

Joy was thrilled, we could snuggle up, share our blankets and once during the journey we even made love, very discreetly, of course. When the Conductor saw what I'd done to the seats he wasn't pleased. He lectured me about damaging Railroad property, albeit the coaches were of ancient pre-war vintage. Anyway, he decided to take no action but did instruct me not to show the other passengers. Of course, they all stood and watched me that night and followed suit. He walked through the coach in the middle of the night in stony silence.

The restaurant car was too expensive for all meals, so it was soup and sandwiches from the coffee bar. For a change, we bought a few groceries from a store which the Conductor assured us was adjacent to the station at the next stop.

Not being accustomed to forty below weather I left the over heated coach in my shirtsleeves. Well, it was only across the platform wasn't it? In fact, it turned out to be two blocks from the station and when I got there, nobody was in, so I returned empty handed and frozen stiff. The Conductor apologised for his mistake saying it was the next station. He would never know what harm he'd caused; it almost cost me my life.

At three-thirty on the afternoon of Thursday, March 14 1957, twelve long, weary days after leaving Colchester, the train pulled slowly into Regina. Joy's sister Phyllis and husband Jim were there to greet us. They looked like a couple of Eskimos in their heavy parkas with fur lined hoods. We felt positively naked compared to them. But Phyllis was thrilled at the sight of Joy's Persian lamb coat. It was good to see them at last, and soon we were seated around their dining room table, there was so much to tell. The coffee was hot, the conversation intense; the laughter was light and we were among friends.

Thirty-one

Deja Vu All Over Again

To say the amenities in the Hurkett household were a cultural shock would be an understatement. It was on the south side of the tracks, the better side we were told but on the extreme western outskirts of Regina and it was non-modern. It had an outside toilet at the bottom of a long garden emptied by a visit from what was jokingly referred to as the "Honey Wagon," and the communal water tap was at the end of the block.

To use the toilet at night one had to lift a trap door in the floor, descend half a dozen steps and walk doubled over because of a lack of head room to the night bucket in the corner of the crawl space.

Each morning one of the adults would carry the bucket down the garden and sometimes, with such a large extended family it would be full to overflowing. Imagine my horror at the sight one morning of Phyllis struggling through knee deep snow, bucket slip slopping from side to side dressed in Joy's beautiful Persian Lamb coat. Because of the hospitality they had shown us I was reluctant to speak my mind but did suggest it was hardly appropriate apparel for that particular chore. Phyllis agreed she'd been thoughtless.

Unlike the sturdy, brick built privy in Ongar, this one was built of wood and it leaked like a sieve; it was enough to freeze the balls off a brass monkey. Certainly not the place one would spend more time than absolutely necessary, Sears Catalogue notwithstanding. After our nice modern home in Colchester it was almost unbelievable but there was worse to come.

We spent the Friday getting acclimatised, meeting new relatives and friends of the Hurkett family and registering the boys for school. Their orientation was made much easier because of cousins Carol, Jimmy and Allen to help and guide them; then there was Janie the baby of the family.

Over the weekend I developed a nasty cold, then it began to feel more like flu. But on the Monday morning I reported to the Employment Office as directed by Immigration. The Counsellor was most apologetic because there was no call for plumbers at that time of the year and couldn't for the life of him understand why they hadn't so advised me in London. I didn't like to tell him they had, and breathed a sigh of relief that I wouldn't be forced to work in the trade. But he did advise that natural gas was coming to Regina in the spring; a lot of money could be made in that field he assured me. In the mean time, sales was all he could offer and referred me to a sales position in the sports department at Sears.

I attended an interview that afternoon arriving home about five and feeling dreadful. Again, I was convinced it was the flu and went to bed taking aspirins and lots of fluids. As the evening wore on I became progressively worse, severe chest pains and could hardly speak. I realised it was something more serious.

We'd just disembarked from a boat where I had mingled with refugees from Eastern Europe. Who knows what kind of infection I might have picked up? I was well aware that many serious diseases begin with flu like symptoms. But we had no medical coverage so I was on the horns of a dilemma. Joy was becoming increasingly worried and persuaded Phyllis to ask her doctor to make a house call. But it had snowed continuously since our arrival and huge snowdrifts blocked all roads save for the steep hill leading from the creek.

The doctor finally arrived and told of how he had become stuck in the snow twice and that it took three attempts to make it up the hill. He only persisted he said, because we had just arrived from overseas. There was always the risk that I had developed some serious and highly contagious disease and he was duty bound to attend if humanly possible.

His diagnosis was double pneumonia and pleurisy. He told Joy, had he not come till morning as was almost the case, he would have needed only his fountain pen to sign the death certificate. He gave me a hefty shot of penicillin and told me to stay in bed. I would have been hospitalised if we'd had health insurance; as it was a month passed before I could venture from the house.

We had no source of income but rather than go on Welfare I got a further advance of a thousand dollars from the Federal Government; I now owed them two thousand. But not to worry, I should get at least five hundred pounds Sterling from the sale of our house; at four dollars to the pound that was two thousand dollars so we were still solvent.

The next problem arose over education; foolishly I had not brought proof of my formal schooling. The originals were long since lost and I hadn't needed them for years. I was advised to go to the Provincial Department of Education who would provide interim documentation. I did so only to be told that without documentary proof I could only be granted grade eleven and was given a letter to that effect.

I wrote to the Sussex County Council for proof of high school graduation and to Brighton Technical College for confirmation of attendance and standing. It took months for them to arrive.

During my illness it became painfully obvious that we could not stay long with Phyllis and Jim. Theirs was a three-bedroom cottage, far too small for four adults and seven children. And so, shortly after my recovery we moved in with Jim's sister Vera and husband Bill. They had four small boys ranging in age from one to five but their house was a lot bigger.

The problem was, life with them was even more hectic and so it was with great relief that within a few weeks we got our very own "little house on the prairie." It wasn't much but at least it was a start. I must pay tribute to our temporary hosts and fellow parishioners from their church who helped us furnish our new home.

All this time I was trying to find meaningful employment and it was deja vu all over again, just like being demobbed from the army. I worked for a janitorial company, in a paint warehouse then a paint and wallpaper store. I sold insurance and then Real Estate, a far cry from what I expected but I was encouraged by future prospects.

My optimism stemmed from an interview at the Saskatchewan Public Service Commission. A mature gentleman with many years service read my resume and I explained why I had only claimed grade eleven. He listened carefully then, using a heavy felt pen, wrote grade twelve in large Roman figures followed by a plus sign then his initials. "Only doing his job," he said, referring to the official in the education department.

He was one of the few Personnel Officers to show interest in my military training and experience. He was convinced, he said, that the combination of administrative and medical training and exposure to the British health care system should ensure a place for me in the Medical Care Plan which the Government was pledged to introduce.

"When that is established" he said, "Practical experience will be of more importance than formal education."

After a pause he continued, "Unfortunately, it is still only in the discussion stage, it will undoubtedly be an issue in the next election, probably 1960. So it will be sometime after that before there will be any hiring."

"That's three years away" I said, "I need something now, are there any openings?"

"Well yes, but only at a junior level, Clerk III for example, and the pay isn't all that good. You probably couldn't afford to enter at that level," he concluded.

Despite this, his last words were, "Don't despair, I just know that somewhere there will be a place for you, I'll be in touch."

I left feeling somewhat encouraged by his last remark but it would be a long time before we would meet again.

Then we suffered another major setback in the form of a letter from the lawyer in England responsible for the sale of our house. I could hardly believe my eyes as I read his statement showing the disposal of the property. The bottom-line was, there were insufficient funds from the sale to pay all the bills and a request for instructions as to how this was to be dealt with.

I went immediately to a lawyer in the Motherwell Building at the corner of Twelfth Avenue and Scarth Street and reviewed with him all the facts relating to the house and the statement I'd just received.

"Surely" I concluded, "This can't be right?"

For a few moments he was engrossed in the letter and his notes, then he looked up at me over the top of his old fashioned horn-rimmed glasses.

"Mr. Keeling," he said plaintively, "on the basis of what you've told me I think you've been had. There is no doubt you have a case but I must tell you it will cost you more than it's worth to fight it." He took a deep breath,

"My advice is to forget the whole thing and put it down to experience."

I was stunned and momentarily speechless. Then, sensing his desire to get on with more lucrative business thanked him for his time and left. I walked in a daze down four flights of stairs and emerged into the brilliant May sunshine. Crossing the road, I entered Victoria Park and sat on a bench gazing into space wondering what I had done to deserve all this.

After a while I convinced myself it wasn't the end of the world and made my way home on the bus. By the time we reached the end of the line on Dewdney Avenue and I'd walked the half dozen blocks to Fort Street I felt a lot better. I knew it would be hard for Joy so I made light of the setback and convinced her we would overcome. But I also knew it wouldn't be easy, we owed the Federal government two thousand dollars, not a good start to a new life in a new country. Incidentally, I never did reply to the Lawyer's letter and heard no more about outstanding bills.

I attended my first soccer match and was so appalled at the standard of refereeing that I approached an official and offered my services. My FIFA certificate was renewed and I Refereed several matches in Taylor Field over the next five years. I also trained other referees and linesmen and made some extra money on the side. Joy and Jennifer sat in the stands and enjoyed the enthusiasm of the crowds.

The school year ended on June 28th., and the boys began nine and a half weeks summer holidays, something unheard of in the old country. Dennis was eleven and had adjusted well, his first school report was most encouraging. For Michael on the other hand, it was a struggle. He was a year behind Dennis; it had been difficult for him in England and the switch to the Canadian system was overwhelming but he did his best.

We were now enjoying our first Prairie summer; we had survived snow and blowing snow, blizzards and forty below. We had marvelled at the first display of the Aurora Borealis more commonly known as the Northern Lights. We had learned quickly what it was like to walk ankle deep in prairie gumbo. Now as we walked along the main street with temperatures nearing one hundred degrees farenheit, grasshoppers in their millions squelched under foot. On the other hand, we stood and watched in awe as the sun disappeared below the prairie horizon, we had never before witnessed such glorious sunsets.

We also experienced our first prairie growing season, the ploughing and seeding then a carpet of green as far as the eye could see as the early grains somehow forced their way through the heavy soil. We watched each day as the hardy crop gradually turned to its beautiful golden hue, mile after mile of good Saskatchewan Durham wheat gently waving in the prairie breeze. Compared to the tiny farms in England it was, indeed, a sight to behold.

We bought a 1954 Pontiac, two door hard top in August, sheer luxury compared to the old one. Then just after Christmas, got a fantastic deal on a 1954 Ford Mercury, an ideal family car. We spent many weekends exploring the province; I recall a memorable trip to Moose Jaw where we saw, among other things, our first live buffalo. And equally memorable, in 1961 we visited the sight of the dam being built on the Saskatchewan river near the town of Elbow. Michael had become a rock fiend by this time; we watched in amazement as he would select a rock, give it one blow with a hammer exposing a variety of petrified fish and other ancient specimens.

We spent many a Sunday at the beach, either Regina Beach or Long Lake and over the next few years visited every place of interest in the southern half of the province. Then explored Montana and North Dakota. But the summers in Saskatchewan were all too short, it would be Exhibition time, the crops were harvested, the Roughriders began their annual training camp and another harsh winter would be upon us.

Our first Christmas in Canada was memorable for many reasons. Apart from our new car, we all had new, more appropriate clothing for the winter; we had an eight-foot Christmas tree and a sixteen-pound turkey, both luxuries hitherto unknown to the Keeling family.

We also bought, through our insurance company, a supply of Christmas cards the likes of which I had never seen before nor since. They were modest in size, about four inches by seven; the paper was black with a velvet texture, quite unusual.

A typical winter scene graced the front of the card. There was an undulating, snow-covered foreground and a narrow lane winding its way to a red, "A" frame cottage. Giant Douglas fir trees, branches heavy with snow stood sentinel like on either side of the warm and inviting home. In the middle distance there was a row of fir trees silhouetted against the dark winter skyline. Smoke drifted lazily skyward from a red brick chimney and a full moon hovered front and centre between the two huge trees. A few snowflakes drifted slowly earthward as a horse drawn sleigh carrying a warmly clad couple made its way toward the house.

On the inside, another view of the same cottage but from a different angle. With its velvet base it had the look of a hand painted masterpiece. On the opposite page, in flowing silver script, the words, "Greetings of the Season and the very best of Holiday Cheer." Underneath, in small silver print, "Joy and Frank Keeling and Family."

I had written a couple of long and interesting letters to my mother but had received nothing in return. So on the inside flap of an unsealed envelope and to reflect the spirit of the season I wrote, "Drop us a line sometime. Still love you and miss you both. Frank & Joy." Followed by four X's. I wrote in those terms because I wondered if she thought we were offended at her failure to visit us before we left England. I wanted to assure her that it was not so and hopefully rekindle what appeared to be a waning relationship. The card resurfaced thirty-one years later; it is framed and hangs on our living room wall, a gloomy reminder of an unusual family connection.

At this time there was much talk about the government's proposed universal Medical Care system. If implemented it would be the first of its kind in North America and there was a lot of opposition to it from the vested interests on both sides of the border. Because of my familiarity with, and involvement in the British system, my opinion was frequently sought. So much so, that I was urged to run for political office with the incumbent party. I was wined and dined a couple of times by influential proponents of the system but declined their overtures. I was interested in government service, especially in the health care field but lacked the appetite for politics.

In the spring of 1959, I phoned my contact in the Public Service Commission. Nothing doing yet but he begged me to be patient. I thought back to the first interview I had in the Unemployment Office, in particular the comment about money to be made in the natural gas business. I recalled my experience as a teenager in Brighton, installing gas fired appliances and my work at Cranes where many of them were manufactured. All this should be a distinct asset, I thought. I remembered a young soccer player, a native of Birmingham, England, who had worked for the Insurance Company and left just before me. He was now in the natural gas business and by all accounts was doing very well. I decided to pay him a visit.

To my surprise he was the Assistant Manager in what had become a thriving Heating Corporation. More interesting was the fact that it was an employee owned operation. After a probationary period of employment a successful employee could purchase or contribute to common shares either by cash or pay-roll deduction. He was aware of my sales ability and offered me a job.

There were four other Representatives and each month there was an attractive prize for top Salesman. Over the next few months I brought home a toaster, a pair of exclusive shoes, a fridge, cook-stove and an electric clothes dryer.

It was during this period of relative success that I finally heard from my mother. It was a strange and forbidding message and one that brought an end to our unorthodox relationship. In the three years we had been in Canada I had written to her several times and always acknowledged birthdays and sent Christmas cards. The previous month I had written a long letter describing our change in fortunes and the usual family news but never knew whether to expect a reply. What letters we had received were brief and banal. This one was bizarre.

In those days, an airmail letter consisted of a single sheet of light paper folded into four. It had pre-glued flaps on two of the quarter sides to fold over and seal before mailing. I used a paper knife to carefully open the letter and as I spread the double page before me I felt a surge of dismay and absolute disgust. It was blank save for one hand written line across the middle of the double page. I could hardly believe my eyes at what I read. "Received your letter, glad you are doing well but I'm really not interested."

There was nothing to indicate it was from her other than the Brighton postmark and her handwriting, Joy was horrified. For me it was the last straw. In my anger I set a match to it and watched as the flame slowly consumed the paper, it curled under the searing heat and turned a sickly brownish colour. I cast it into the kitchen sink and doused the last glimmer of flame with water, then watched as the remnants swirled around the drain and disappeared. It was the end of what was surely the strangest mother, son relationship ever. I never saw or heard from her again.

On Thursday, February 1st., 1962, a month before her sixty-fifth birthday she collapsed on that infamous divan in the living room and died instantly. The autopsy revealed that she died of a pulmonary embolism. It would be almost six years, however, before I learned of her death. At the same time, I was told that Frank Bunton had died of lung cancer also in 1962, what a coincidence! He was only sixty-one. To add to the irony, he never smoked or drank yet he died of this dreadful disease. At the time of his death he and the other Bunton boys had, for years, operated a painting and decorating business. Lead from the paint contributed to his demise perhaps?

For several days after receiving that final contemptuous note I felt a mixture of anger, disappointment and hurt. What kind of a mother was this? I wondered. How could she be so callous and why? What had happened to make her suddenly turn so spiteful? I could only guess. As time passed, my anger and my hurt subsided; it was time to get on with the rest of my life.

In the spring of 1960, a series of events took place that proved a turning point in my career. Up to that point I have to admit to a somewhat chequered employment record. Anyway, the Assistant Manager's wife absconded with his best friend taking his little daughter with them. For him it was the end of the world; he sought immediate release from his position, redeemed his shares and set off for Winnipeg in pursuit of his wife and child. I was offered his job.

A short time before this offer, I had made the biggest sale in the history of the Corporation, the plumbing and heating contract for two very large apartment buildings. The commission was just over two thousand dollars, a lot of money in those days. I'd already had a good month so when offered payment in the form of common stock I readily agreed. This, of course, made the offer of management all the more attractive since I would be playing an active roll in the company's fortunes.

I was also advised that if successful I could look forward to the Manager's job in the fall as the incumbent was to open another branch in Winnipeg. I accepted the position and in the fall of 1960, became General Manager.

Shortly thereafter, I suffered another indignity. We had a customer in her mid sixties, of above average means and quite active for her age. On a visit to the store to settle her account she casually mentioned she was going to England for a vacation and Romford was her main destination. I told her that was the place of my birth and that I had an Aunt living there. She offered to visit her on my behalf, I accepted and forgot about it.

Several weeks later she came into the store saying she had news for me. I asked her into my office where we could talk in private.

"Well, I went to see this Aunt of yours and I must tell you I was not at all impressed."

"Oh, really" I replied. "Did you meet my cousin Paula?"

"Yes I did, I was invited to join them for afternoon tea and she was there the entire time but had little to say."

I could tell she wasn't very comfortable in her roll as the bearer of unpleasant news but she continued.

"I told her all about you, the successful business you were operating, in fact, I gave her one of your business cards. She was amazed at your title of President and General Manager and immediately assumed you were rich."

"To cut a long story short, for the remainder of my visit she spoke of nothing but what you might do for her. Everything from fresh peaches, for which Canada was famous, as she put it, to more expensive pursuits such as a holiday in Canada at your expense. The whole conversation became quite sickening and I was glad to get out of there."

Taking a deep breath she concluded by saying, "If I were you I'd have nothing more to do with that Aunt, she thinks nothing of you other than what she might get out of you. I'm sorry but that's the unmistakable impression I got."
I expressed my disappointment, thanked her and we went on to discuss other things.

I can't say that I was completely surprised; the Auntie Edie I had known had always been somewhat mercenary. Even when we were there as a family at Christmas in 1954 and again on James' twenty-first birthday in 1955, it had been obvious. I expected to hear from her but never did and didn't bother to keep in touch. What I had been told left a nasty taste in my mouth.

There was never a dull moment at this period of our lives. I had my regular job and on the weekend, either Saturday or Sunday and sometimes on a Wednesday evening I would referee a soccer match at Taylor Field for which I was paid the princely sum of five dollars a game. Then came another challenge. There appeared in The Leader Post, Regina's major newspaper, an urgent call from The Regina Little Theatre Company for someone with an English accent to play the lead roll in "See How They Run," a play that had been enormously popular in both London and New York.

The play was due to open in three weeks; the first night's audience would include none other than the Lieutenant Governor, the Premier, the Mayor of Regina and other dignitaries. The person originally selected to play the part had been stricken by a serious illness and the Theatre Company was desperate.

Joy wasn't very keen on the idea but to me it represented a challenge. I had been on stage a few times during the war in amateurish attempts to entertain the troops; this was a chance to see if I could do something a little more professional.

I auditioned along with several other aspiring actors and was selected. For the next three weeks and with much help from, Joy I studied my lines at every spare moment. I was playing opposite Lynn Goldman, a regular with the group and a recent returnee from Hollywood. We performed an excerpt on local television for promotional purposes and the first night was well attended. I didn't set the world on fire nor was I "discovered" but the critics wrote that I "Brought a unique character to the part." It was my one and only venture into the world of theatre but it was interesting.

In the spring we moved to a three-bedroom, ranch type house on Twelfth

Avenue East. For the first time since leaving England, Jennifer and the boys had their own bedroom. As well, this was the year that Dennis graduated from grade school and he did so with excellent marks. I recall how proud Joy and I were when, on a Saturday shopping trip, we met the Principal of his school; he was full of praise for Dennis, saying that he was an outstanding student in every respect. I remember too, sitting down with Dennis in our living room and telling him of our chance meeting with the Principal and how pleased we were.

Jennifer was now four, quite the little madam. For well over a year we had talked of a little sister, we were taking no precautions but nothing happened. Dennis raised pigeons and became keenly involved in breeding. Michael was becoming well known for his rock and gem collection, it was not uncommon for adults to visit the house to observe and admire. All in all, life was pretty good; the only drawback was the long hours I was required to work.

Now that I've reached the age of wisdom I realise that the most precious thing a man can give his children is time. But in those days, like all breadwinners raising a family on a single income, I was between a rock and a hard place. Trying desperately to provide the best of everything for a young family in a world of ever-increasing materialism and at the same time be a good father.

The following year, Jennifer started Kindergarten; at first, she found it difficult to leave home and mother had to stand at the window and wave to her till she disappeared round the corner but after a while she got used to it. Then she was a guest on Romper Room at the local TV Station and with her big blue eyes and lovely long, wavy blonde hair, made a stunning debut into the world of television.

The long awaited provincial election in which Medicare was the main issue was fought and won by the incumbent party. But it would be another two years before the plan became a reality. By that time I was too busy trying to make a success of our company to bother about Medicare. In fact, I had painted myself into a corner, or perhaps a better way to put it, I was on the banker's treadmill and couldn't get off.

Things came to a head on Christmas eve 1961. During the night our store was burglarised. Every item of stock with any value was hauled away; gas furnaces, water heaters, and appliances both gas and electric and anything else of value that wasn't nailed down and we had no insurance! Talk about penny wise, pound-foolish. Amongst the rubble left behind we found an envelope containing common shares owned by the two previous managers, now operating in Winnipeg; they had been signed over to me.

They were eventually arrested on charges of theft, the only legal way to get them back into Saskatchewan. There was a trial that dragged on for months, bleeding the Company of thousands of dollars in legal fees. They were found not guilty on a technicality; the shares had been left as payment for the goods taken even though they were worthless. I learned the hard way that theft is the most difficult crime to prove. We were urged to appeal but because of the financial drain on the Company I declined.

The day following their acquittal, in consultation with the remaining shareholders, we placed the company in voluntary receivership. When the dust cleared, two of us started another company but were doomed from the start. Suppliers were reluctant to give us credit so again, we had to rely on a line of credit from the bank, backed this time by our own signatures.

At about the same time we received a very moving letter from Joy's Dad, Grandpa Borrett. He was a proud man and I know the agony he must have suffered writing such a letter. It will be recalled that when we left England he had recently had major surgery for stomach cancer. His letter indicated he had been unable to work since then, all his savings were gone and he had nothing but a reduced old age pension on which he and Granmma Borrett struggled to survive. His choice was to go on welfare or humble his pride and seek help from his children. He could not he said, bring himself to apply for welfare without first asking if we could help.

I immediately wrote a note enclosing a twenty-dollar bill and sent it special delivery. I told him we would send him two dollars every week. That doesn't sound much now but the twenty dollars was five pounds sterling; the weekly two-dollar bill was three pounds sterling a month. Granddad soon wrote back expressing his gratitude, saying that the contribution was the difference between living and existing. He told of how much he enjoyed taking the Canadian bills to the bank each week to exchange them; how, for the first time in his life he was on friendly terms with a Bank Manager and how proud he was to talk about his family overseas.

Meanwhile, after months of struggle with our new company and just as we were beginning to make progress the bank pulled the plug. The manager had loaned us his umbrella one fine day, now that it was pouring with rain he demanded its return. My partner and I were in hock for eighteen thousand dollars, nine thousand each. Stunned and disgusted with the callous and unwarranted action by the bank I declared personal bankruptcy and to hell with them! The only thing I lost out of the deal was a near new 1959 Chev.

That same year news of Grandpa Borrett's death came. So many thousands of miles away there was little we could do but grieve a while then carry on with our lives. Gramma Borrett went to live with Pearl where she stayed until her death ten years later.

I inquired about work with the government, still no vacancies but I was assured it was only a matter of time. In the months that followed I worked in refrigeration then for a weekly newspaper selling advertising. I felt like the proverbial Jack of all trades again.

As the end of 1961 approached, Joy casually mentioned she had missed her period but we thought nothing of it. After all she was forty; surely not?

Thirty-two

Politics And Passions

Joy missed another period and the doctor confirmed her pregnancy, her due date was the end of July. This was the same physician that had struggled through the snow to save my life when we first arrived in Canada. Now, after six years we were to be parents again, Joy was forty.

Jennifer was six and at first seemed excited at the news, constantly talking about a little sister. How did the boys feel about it? Well, I think it was a case of, "Oh no, not again." Dennis was sixteen and in high school, Michael, a year behind, still struggling.

Our move to the East Side proved a disaster, in the spring we moved back to the West Side on Coldwell Road. Had we moved sooner the boys would have gone to Martin High School along with their cousins and would, I think, have done much better.

I borrowed a car from my good friend Wilbur. His family had farmed for years in Lipton north east of Regina and there was an old Dodge Sedan sitting in the barn. He was in the process of establishing a Student Driving School. Joy was one of his first pupils; twice she got her learners licence but never did pursue it. "Too many maniacs on the road" she insisted.

On a Friday afternoon in early May I returned to the newspaper office where I worked to pick up my pay cheque, the publisher was no where to be found. The whole staff waited for three hours before he appeared only to say there was no money in the bank, the company was broke. In those days, unemployment insurance was not compulsory; if you earned above a certain amount you did not subscribe to the fund or receive benefits. I had always exceeded the limit.

We all remained in the office refusing to budge until we could talk to one of the directors. They were reluctant to become involved and it was not until some of the more rabid "print types" threatened to wreck the joint that one of them agreed to appear. After another couple of hours of haggling we had gained nothing. Most retired to the pub to drown their sorrows. I got twenty dollars cash because I had three children and a pregnant wife. That was enough to buy a weeks groceries.

This also was the year (1962) that Tommy Douglas the legendary preacher and politician from Weyburn, Saskatchewan saw his dream become a reality. Although now the leader of his party in Ottawa, his successor, Premier Woodrow Lloyd announced that "Medicare" would come into effect on July 1st.

The New Democratic Party, formerly the Commonwealth Co-operative Federation (CCF) had been given a clear mandate in the 1960 election to create the first publicly administered health care plan in North America but it had its opponents. First the Liberal opposition party which was to be expected. But the main opposition came from the medical fraternity. This included the Canadian Medical Association, the Saskatchewan College of Physicians and Surgeons and the Regina Medical Association. The latter being represented by a local Urologist who was also an opponent of what he and others characterised as "Socialised Medicine." The American Medical Association also got its oar in the water.

Incidentally, one of the Urologist's public pronouncements was that a doctor should run Medicare. I recall the Chairman of the Medical Care Commission responding to the press:

"I would agree to let the good doctor run Medicare" he said, "If he would agree to me performing a certain surgical procedure on him."

There were a lot of political shenanigans going on behind the scenes and the radical right wing elements carried their opposition well beyond the realm of reason or common sense. As well, there were isolated incidents of intimidation and vandalism.

On the Monday following my untimely departure from the newspaper, I sat in our living room wondering what to do next. As if to provide the answer, the phone rang; it was my contact from the Public Service Commission asking if I could attend an interview that afternoon.

"There is an immediate opening and I believe you are just the person we need" he said. "It would be a temporary position at first but I know it will lead to a permanent and more important position in the very near future. I'd rather not discuss it more than that over the phone."

An assistant to the Secretary Treasurer of the Commission interviewed me. He was sufficiently impressed with my understanding of health care administration that I was hired on the spot. He said he wished he'd known about me much sooner.

"You could have helped us a great deal," he said.

I told him my application and resume had been on file for years, he couldn't believe it.

I was introduced to the Executive Director, a former Captain in the Royal Artillery and participant in the Normandy landings. My initial position was in Public relations dealing with the mountains of correspondence and countless phone inquiries to the Premier, the Minister of Health and the Chairman of the Commission. The controversial plan had gained world-wide attention and the letters and calls were every bit as widespread. I was to have two University law students as assistants for the summer, Ed Sajonky, who would eventually become a well-known criminal lawyer and Roy Romanow. The latter had to withdraw at the last moment due to the illness of his mother. But he went on to become Attorney General and then Premier of the province a position he holds as I write.

Opposition to the proposed plan was mounting and tensions were running high. All kinds of protest groups sprung up, the most notable of which was the "Keep Our Doctors" (KOD) group. Doctors were threatening to leave en masse and to withdraw their services if the government went ahead with the plan on July 1st. There was fear and uncertainty on the part of many patients and politics and passions rose to unprecedented heights as the physicians' daily became more belligerent.

Even the Roman Catholic Church with its Liberal leanings got into the act. I recall Father Athol Murray of Notre Dame Hockey School fame, appearing on television to voice his opposition and that of the church. He came on camera wearing his dog collar and a garish flannel shirt with wide vertical stripes similar to that worn by inmates of a concentration camp. How futile it all seems now that Medicare is a much-cherished national programme that few would want to surrender.

Yet there are the revisionists who will claim the medical profession was not opposed to Medicare itself but rather, the manner in which it was imposed – "without consultation" they will say. That is simply not true, government and Commission tried to involve those representing the medical profession but they were not interested. They were philosophically opposed to a publicly administered plan and chose to play politics with the health and well being of the people.

Joy would be forty-one in September and only six more weeks before the baby was due. The threatened Doctors' strike became a source of concern but I found it difficult to believe they would resort to such unprecedented action. In any case, I told myself, it was illegal for a doctor to abandon a patient during pregnancy without proper notice and referral, so not to worry.

July 1st., 1962 was a Sunday and Monday was Dominion day, now Canada day. Normally, this would be a long weekend but the doctors carried out their threat. For the first time in medical history and to the everlasting shame of their profession, the doctors withdrew their services. As a result a small number of key people, including myself, were required to be on hand at all times in case of emergency.

The following day while home for lunch, the phone rang. It was our family doctor.

"Mr. Keeling?"

"Oh, hello doctor" I said, recognising his voice.

"Well my friend" he said, a little too haughtily for my liking, "You're on your own, I've been assigned to Moose Jaw for emergency services."

I didn't appreciate his arrogant attitude.

"Oh really" I replied, "Well I'm sure you're aware that under the Canada Health act you are required to give Joy thirty days notice and refer her to another physician acceptable to her."

"Yes, I know all about that but we're in an emergency situation."

"The only emergency situation is that brought on by your profession doctor. I work for Medicare and I am well aware of the circumstances leading to the present situation."

"Well I don't think much of your choice of vocation."

Before I could reply he said, "Look Mr. Keeling I'm the person that saved your life doesn't that mean anything to you?"

"Yes it does doctor but that has absolutely nothing to do with our present situation and your obligation to my wife. I have a meeting with the Chairman of the Commission this afternoon, it'll be interesting to see what he has to say about this."

"Well I don't think much of your choice of company, goodbye."

I hung up the phone disgusted knowing it would bring nothing but anxiety for Joy.

In the afternoon, I met with the Chairman and mentioned what had transpired.

"I wouldn't worry about it Frank" he said. "I'm sure something can be worked out."

Later, I was pressured by a senior bureaucrat in the Premier's office to launch a civil action against both the doctor and his association. This, he said, was the sort of situation they were looking for, but I declined for two reasons. First, the doctor had saved my life. Second, it would mean a great deal of publicity, in all probability nation-wide if not international, such was the furore that had been created. I had no intention of subjecting Joy to that kind of exposure.

I did attempt to find another doctor though. One by one I phoned every obstetrician listed in the yellow pages getting the same response each time.

"Oh yes, I'm sure doctor so and so will be happy to take care of your wife, I'll phone you back with an appointment."

Then within a short time they would phone back saying apologetically that the doctor wasn't able to take on any new patients. Obviously word had spread that I worked for Medicare. I was blacklisted and they were making Joy suffer; we were, indeed, very much on our own. My disgust for the Saskatchewan physicians knew no bounds. There were a few who defied their politically oriented leaders and went about their business treating patients as usual. I have nothing but praise and admiration for those who did so.

To cope with the lack of medical manpower, the government advertised in Britain and the United States for volunteer physicians to augment the emergency services provided by the profession. The response was overwhelming. I was issued with a government car and one of my jobs was to meet groups of doctors at the airport, take them to the Health building for documentation then to a hotel for the night. The following day I would drive them to Saskatoon to the College of Physicians and Surgeons to be issued a licence to practice medicine.

The media, especially television, were there from all over the world. I recall one occasion when a group of doctors was arriving at Regina airport and I had been assigned to meet them. There were at least thirty cameras set up in the airport lounge and hordes of correspondents eager to challenge the new arrivals. Sensing the possibility of intimidation I boarded the plane to alert the doctors of what they might expect. I shall never forget the scene in the airport lounge that followed. Striking doctors and their politically oriented leaders were there in full force ready to berate their volunteer colleagues and spout their opposition line to anyone who would stick a microphone under their nose.

In the days that followed the tension grew. The media, both print and television would hound us everywhere we went trying to get interviews and provoke controversy. One evening in a Saskatoon hotel I joined several doctors from England for dinner in the restaurant. A particularly obnoxious reporter from a local newspaper started to pester the doctors. Asking them how they felt being strike breakers and making other inflammatory remarks. I asked him politely to refrain, pointing out that we had been on the go since early morning and would like to eat our meal in peace.

I identified myself as a government representative and offered to make a statement after the meal. But that wasn't good enough for this uncouth imbecile and he continued to harass the doctors in a loud and boisterous manner. Finally, I sent for the manager and told him that if the harassment continued we would leave the hotel. The offensive individual eventually left but not before slinging a few insults at me. The next morning, the front page carried a story of the arrival of doctors from Britain and describing me as a "Government Henchman." Such were the times.

Joy's due date came and went and nothing happened. A few days later she got a phone call to go to Gray Nuns' hospital for a prenatal examination, unusual but under the circumstances we agreed she should attend. I drove her to the hospital but could not stay.

When I got home that evening she described what happened. She was shown into an examining room and after a long wait a very young and obviously very nervous male intern entered the room. Joy was convinced he had never examined a pregnant woman before. His hot and clammy hands trembled as they prodded and pressed randomly over her swollen abdomen. His questions and conversation were obtuse. Every few minutes he would leave her lying there and retire to a small room, presumably to consult his medical textbooks. This went on for almost an hour, at which time Joy showed her frustration by heaving exaggerated sighs. He finally quit mumbling something about the fetus being prominent. Joy was never more disgusted.

In the late afternoon of Wednesday, August 8th., the Chairman sent for me.

"Frank" he said, "There is a doctor in Prince Albert who is setting up a Community Health Centre. He is a well-known family practitioner, well liked and has lots of experience in obstetrics. He has asked for some administrative assistance for about a week or ten days. Would you be interested? You have a government car and you could take the wife and, of course, all your expenses would be covered."

"When would he like me to be there?" I asked.

"Oh, as soon as possible, tomorrow would be fine."

"Well, I don't think I could make it tomorrow, I have to make alternate arrangements for my two sons but I'm sure we could leave Friday morning."

He looked amused as he said, "OK, I'll phone him right away and tell him to expect you and the wife late Friday afternoon."

A kindly neighbour offered to look after Dennis and Michael during our absence. Early on the Friday morning, with the temperature near the one hundred degrees mark I drove Joy and Jennifer the two hundred and fifty long and tedious (for Joy) miles to Prince Albert via Saskatoon where we stopped for lunch. We went for a stroll around town after lunch to stretch our legs and give Joy some relief.

We arrived at the clinic at five o'clock that afternoon, the doctor insisted on seeing Joy immediately. He reprimanded me, in jest of course, for bringing a pregnant wife on such a long journey when she was obviously about to go into labour. He admitted her to hospital and a beautiful, blue eyed, fair-haired baby girl came into the world at five o'clock the next morning, August 11th 1962. And so it was that Michelle Josephine came into our lives, a Saturday's child. According to English legend she would have to work for a living:

Monday's child is fair of face	
Tuesday's child is full of grace	
Wednesday's child is full of woe.	That's me folks! And my mother.
Thursday's child has far to go.	Dennis & Michael.
Friday's child is loving and giving,	
Saturday's child must work for its living.	Michelle.
But a child that is born on the Sabbath day	Joy & Jennifer.
Is fair and wise, and good and gay.	

The author is unknown and the word gay is an adjective not a noun.

Joy left the hospital on the Tuesday without Michelle. There was nothing wrong, just not the policy in those days to discharge a new born so soon.

On the Wednesday as part of my work for the health centre, I accompanied one of the doctors on his regular visit to the Prince Albert Federal Penitentiary. I sat with him during the entire sick parade. It was quite an experience, first to see the inside of a maximum security prison and secondly to watch and listen as the doctor dealt with a multitude of ailments; many of them related to long periods of incarceration. The sick parade was held twice a week and usually consisted of about sixty patients. All the inmates were there for serious crimes, of course, including murder. And I recall my astonishment at the disposition of some of these hardened criminals.

Meanwhile, Joy and Jennifer strolled through the well kept grounds until a horrendous dust storm arose, then they ran for the car and sat there until the storm subsided, a frightening experience for both of them. It was always said that in the spring Saskatchewan was blown into Alberta and in the fall it was blown back again. Obviously, this was a case of an early fall.

On the Friday morning, Michelle was discharged. I bought a pink baby bathtub from a nearby hardware store, filled it with blankets and it served as a crib for the journey back to Regina. That was when we saw a glimmer of resentment on the part of Jennifer. This was not unexpected; after all she had been the centre of attraction for the last six and a half years and was a bit spoilt. Now she would have to share all that love and affection and for a little while it was difficult for her.

We had taken the number two highway from Prince Albert. Jennifer, with Michelle in her little make shift crib were on the back seat. As we approached the intersection with the Trans Canada highway east of Moose Jaw I heard a cry of anguish from Joy. Glancing around I saw that Jennifer had bitten the back of her hand so hard as to draw blood. We showed understanding and made an effort to prove to Jennifer she was still loved and that she had an even more important family role to play.

I had little time to enjoy our new daughter in the ensuing weeks, working most nights until ten dealing with all kinds of emergent situations. The government acquired the services of Lord Taylor from England as a mediator in the dispute with the medical profession. An expert in health care delivery systems he was respected by all. Ed Sojonky my assistant was appointed as his aide so at the end of the conflict I got all the inside information first hand.

The dispute ended on August 26th., 1962. The medical profession won, among other things, the right to greater representation on the Commission, the government insisted on matching political appointments so that it lost the independence so carefully contrived in the initial plan. By far the most disruptive concession, however, was the retention of the five privately operated medical plans as clearing houses for doctors' claims. Instead of one paying agency there were six, a costly and inefficient system placing an unnecessary financial burden on the plan.

Overnight a new payment system had to be designed. I was promoted and transferred to a specially created "Payments and Inquiries Branch" to develope the new system. A few months later I was transferred to the Medical Branch as Acting Assistant Director but my appointment was never confirmed.

For the remainder of that year and well into the next it was long hours and hard work, often including weekends. As a result my time with the family, including our newborn daughter, was limited. But just after Christmas we enjoyed an amazing piece of good luck; it was a case of being in the right place at the right time.

Many of the doctors from England decided to remain in Saskatchewan after the crisis ended. One of them invited me to visit a building being modified for his clinic. The place was alive with carpenters, electricians and painters. Toward the end of the tour, picking my way around a pile of rubble, I came face to face with an old acquaintance. It was the Contractor responsible for the renovations and the person with whom I had negotiated the plumbing and heating contract for the two apartment blocks years earlier. His partner operated the Real Estate end of the business; I had also worked for him when we first came to Canada. My doctor friend volunteered that I was now a "Big Shot" with Medicare and Geof was genuinely pleased that I had, at last, found my niche.

The doctor excused himself and after some idle chatter, Geof enquired about the family and where were we living?

"On Coldwell Road" I replied, "We're renting a three bedroom rancher. Not bad" I concluded, "Nice area."

"How would you like to own your own home?"

"Well, naturally I'd love to but haven't been able to save enough for a down payment yet."

"How much rent do you pay." I told him. Then, after a moments pause he came up with an astonishing proposal.

"I could put you in a beautiful house in south Regina with no down payment for little more than you're paying now" he said.

"Tell me more" I replied, "This sounds too good to be true."

He went on to explain that he had built a large split level house on the thirty-five hundred block of Wascana Street. His Real Estate colleagues had persuaded him there was a market for this type of property but after several months it had not sold. To cut a long story short, we viewed the house on Sunday, signed a deal on Monday and moved in on February 1st., 1963. It was, indeed, a beautiful house just as Geoff had described. A three level split with Cathedral Roof and within walking distance of the parliament buildings where I worked.

Joy then decided she wanted to go to church; and so it was that the whole family became regular parishioners at St. Luke's Anglican Church, a newly constructed place of worship not five minutes walk from our front door. We were told that the font in this church was the ancient one dug up in the sand at low tide in West Mersey, near Colchester, England.

In April 1964, Premier Woodrow Lloyd called a general election and his government was defeated. The furore surrounding the introduction of Medicare had taken its toll. Under the Leadership of Liberal Ross Thatcher the best health care system in the world was further eroded. This was the father of the infamous Colin Thatcher who, as I write, languishes in a federal penitentiary in Edmonton for the brutal slaying of his wife.

Against all advice Thatcher introduced user fees in his second term. They proved an absolute disaster and he and his party were thrown out in the election of 1972, never to be heard from again. He died soon after a broken man.

In 1964 tragedy struck our family. Joy's sister Phyllis was diagnosed with inoperable cancer. She had been to her family doctor a year earlier complaining of bladder problems. All the usual tests were performed but nothing was detected, she was told to return in six months for reassessment. She didn't, and a year later was rushed to emergency. Her bladder was removed but the cancer had spread.

We visited her in the Gray Nuns hospital almost daily for the next nine months and watched as she slowly and agonisingly wasted away. She died on Sunday October 10th., 1964. Although her passing was, in many ways, a happy release it was nonetheless tragic. She was but forty-five years of age and left four children; the oldest, Carol was eighteen, Janie, the youngest nine, with

Jimmy and Allen in between. We knew her condition was terminal yet when the end came it was hard, especially for Joy. She and Phyllis had been so close all their lives.

By June, I had worked at Medicare for more than two years. I had attended both medical and administrative upgrading courses and learned the Rules and Regulations governing the payment of fees for medical services rendered. I also witnessed the dawn of a new age in computer technology, third generation IBM 360. Later, I studied systems analysis and design and computer programming.

I had been acting assistant director of the medical branch for almost a year; it was interesting and challenging work. Apart from my supervisory duties I was involved, under the direction of staff physicians, in the adjudication and assessment of the most complicated of medical and surgical procedures submitted for payment by physicians. I learnt much about the practice of medicine during that period. The permanent position was advertised and I felt confident, but my confidence was misplaced.

As so often happens in the public service, the position was filled more on the basis of seniority than experience and ability. It was a severe blow from which I never fully recovered. I had worked long hours including most weekends for what, in retrospect, was a pittance. I was dedicated and enthusiastic about my work and my superiors acknowledged what they described as my "very valuable contribution to the establishment of a medical care delivery system second to none." But it was not enough.

As consolation, for want of a better term, I was asked to develope an assessment manual for personnel involved in the adjudication of the more complex claims. The importance of such a compendium was undeniable but I felt insulted. Within a short time, the successful candidate for the Assistant Director's position left and joined the federal bureaucracy.

I was given an office in a secluded part of the building and answered to a committee of senior officials from government, medical profession and technicians responsible for the system. It met every Sunday morning to review my recommendations and took almost a year.

Under this arrangement I answered to no one but the committee, worked at my own pace and my own hours; no one was concerned with my comings and goings. As long as there was fodder for the mill Sunday mornings everybody was happy. So I took advantage of the situation and enrolled in a course of Business Administration at University of Saskatchewan, Regina Campus. I successfully completed the first year but following a change of jobs, had to drop out at the end of the second. The workload was just too much to handle. I fully intended to complete the course at a later date but never did.

At about this time an Australian doctor had immigrated to Canada via England. He was working as a Staff Physician for the Commission. On a visit to the continent prior to leaving he had bought a Volkswagen "Bug" directly from the factory in West Germany which he brought to Canada as part of his settler's effects. Since England and Australia both drive on the left, it had a right hand drive.

His wife became homesick and declined to stay, he stayed to finalise their affairs. Twenty-four hours before leaving he had still not sold the vehicle. Over a farewell drink in the Hotel Saskatchewan he offered it to me for a thousand dollars, well below its market value.

"What's more" he said, "You can pay for it simply by paying the monthly premium on a life insurance policy I recently purchased."

How could I refuse such an offer?

As anyone familiar with the "Bug" will know, there was a grab bar on the dash board on the passenger side level with the steering wheel; Michelle, as a toddler, would sit on Joy's lap firmly grasping the bar in her two little hands. Imagine the surprised look of drivers coming in the opposite direction, it almost looked as if Michelle was driving.

Doctors in Saskatchewan had a special license plate for their vehicles at the time. A vehicle brought into the country as settler's effects could not be sold for one year so, although the car belonged to me, I had to drive it on the doctor's licence plates for the balance of the year. As a result there were times when I got treatment reserved only for members of the medical profession.

We came upon an accident on Pasqua Street one evening, there was a line up of cars for blocks and no one was moving. One of Regina's finest saw my licence plate and motioned me to leave the line sending me on my way with a smart salute and a courteous "This way doctor." Once out of sight we all had a good laugh.

Also in Regina at that time, people owning their home were identified in the phone book by a lower case "r" for resident, following their last initial. I was listed as Keeling F.D; somehow the space between the "D" and the "r" was omitted so that the listing read, Keeling F.Dr. So here I was, driving a car with a doctor's licence plate, listed in the phone book as Dr., and working for Medicare. I had one hell of a job convincing people I was not, in fact, a doctor. Neighbours would phone and insist on addressing me as doctor and in many cases my denial was interpreted as modesty.

Shortly after her mother's death, my niece, Carol phoned me one morning saying she had decided to drop out of high school and find work, could I help her? My first reaction was to lecture her about the importance of education and not encourage her. But she was eighteen years of age, obviously her father had tried to dissuade her and she had suffered a grievous loss, who was I to lecture? I agreed to help and would phone her back. Ten minutes later I arranged for an interview with the Director of Hospital Services that afternoon. She attended, was hired on the spot and worked there for years.

In June, almost a year to the day, I completed the Assessment manual. It was introduced with great fanfare. The entire staff of Medicare as well as dignitaries from government and the medical profession were assembled and the Chairman of the Commission made glowing remarks about my accomplishment, describing the manual as "The most comprehensive document of its kind and one of inestimable value to Medicare." Praise and congratulations came from all directions. Following the meeting I was assured of bigger and better things for the future.

My next task was to set up an Audit section. Medicare was issuing in the neighbourhood of a million cheques a year either paid directly to physicians or reimbursement to beneficiaries. Naturally, there were mistakes. The computer processed about eighty per cent of the claims with few problems but of the remainder there were human errors, some quite embarrassing.

Once the section was running smoothly and efficiently I handed it over to another individual. I was then asked to accept a temporary position in the Research Branch as Special Studies Manager. My main task was to examine the practice of physicians in general but in particular, a few who were abusing the system. As a result, a number of doctors were referred to their disciplinary committee and subsequently fined, sometimes several thousand dollars

By now, changes were taking place at home. Dennis and Michael finished High School, left home and headed for the West Coast. They had become part of what I call the, "Stop the world let me get off" generation. But with the harsh Saskatchewan winters, who could blame them?

Things were not going well at work either. I was called into the Director's office and told that while my work was important it was limited, and there was no future for me in the Research Branch. To cut a long story short, I applied for a job with the Saskatchewan Power Corporation and was the successful applicant. It meant a twenty-five dollar a month increase in pay, which at first was hardly worthwhile. I was told the salary offered was the top of the range but in six months, if I proved successful, a substantial increase was guaranteed.

My departure from Medicare was quite an affair. The entire staff plus the Chairman and members of the Commission were present. There were the usual gratuitous speeches and I was presented with a very elaborate and expensive brief case. Following the ceremony the Executive Director wished me well and conceded that he was mistaken in not selecting me for the Assistant Director's job. I felt some comfort in his remarks.

At SaskPower it soon became apparent that the in house staff were so close to the forest they couldn't see the trees. In eighteen working days I solved a problem that had plagued them for years resulting in an immediate and substantial increase in their cash flow. I was the proverbial nine day hero, receiving accolades from all quarters including the Comptroller General. I was also assured once again that there was "a great future" for me with SaskPower.

I recall the chief accountant coming to my desk when, for the first time, his daily report indicated all billings were current.

"What has happened, apart from us hiring Frank Keeling," he said, "to bring about this extraordinary change?"

I told him the story of the very expensive plumber who justified his cost by knowing exactly where to wield the hammer. He was not amused and my popularity was short lived.

Shortly thereafter, unionised staff went on strike and management had to provide essential services. SaskPower provided service to everybody from the little shack with a few light bulbs to the inter-provincial exchange of power. Again, I was working all hours of the day.

I successfully completed my six-month probationary period but was not happy in Customer Accounts. There was a vacancy in Management Services that I wanted but the Comptroller refused to approve my transfer. I was somewhat disillusioned and decided I would not remain long in the employ of SaskPower. My remuneration and status were little improved over Medicare.

Around this time we received the first communication from the boys. They were in British Columbia and were full of praise for its climate and beauty. We were tired of the harsh winters and our family physician opined that a more moderate climate might be better for my back problem. After much discussion we decided to pack up and head west. We put the house up for sale but it would be another year before it sold. In the mean time, I was obviously being groomed for the Customer Accounts Management position; the incumbent was to retire in five years but I wasn't interested.

In June of 1967, Canada's centennial year, I told my superior that, either I am transferred to Management Services or I would quit, my request was refused. At the end of the month we received and offer on the house, not as much as we wanted but we accepted anyway and I handed in my notice.

The person buying the house liked the furnishings so much that he bought all but a few incidentals making our departure much easier. We bought a more modern station wagon and on Sunday July 23rd., our neighbours, Mary and Vic Makniak, threw a wonderful farewell party. The following morning we set off on yet another adventure.

This was our centennial project.

Thirty-three

A Fork In The Road

Most locals thought I was crazy but envied me none the less. I was leaving a secure nine to five job with all kinds of employee benefits including a pension at age sixty-five. I had no job to go to, I knew no one in lotus land and had no idea where we would live. Christopher Columbus had nothing on me.

We were excited about our adventure although at one point Joy shed a few tears at the loss of our beautiful home. I promised her even better in the future and she soon got over it. Our friends and neighbours openly admired our courage and many wished they could follow our example.

Jennifer was eleven and it wasn't easy for her to leave home and her many school friends, especially best friend Lori who lived next door. On the other hand, Michelle now almost five was a happy child and showed little emotion at the prospects of a new life on the West Coast.

Foremost in our thoughts were the two boys and a desire to help them start a new life. We had received letters from Dennis and reading between the lines it seemed they missed their family and were anxious to make something more of their lives. By the time we left Regina, Michael was taking a welding course; pipelines were being built all over the place so it seemed a worthy endeavour.

Our farewell was quite emotional with neighbours crowding around the car as we left. I had packed it with priceless personal effects and hoped for an early start. But it was almost ten in the morning before we closed the door of 3515 Wascana Street for the last time leaving the key inside.

We would take our time and enjoy western Canada in a leisurely manner but aimed for Calgary the first night; it wasn't to be. We were held up just outside Regina by the derailment of a freight train blocking the highway, forcing us to make a long detour. So we only made it to Brooks, Alberta.

Our first overnight stop was at a government rest area, one of many created on the recently constructed Trans-Canada highway. In those days they were spartan but cost nothing and we had to watch our pennies.

We had paid off our debts except for the car, leaving us with two thousand dollars from the sale of the house. Not much these days but a substantial amount then. I had no idea how long it would have to last so prudence was the watchword. Each night we stopped, unloaded the car and slept in it. Then up bright and early, cooked breakfast on our Coleman stove repacked the car and hit the road again.

I shall never forget that first night at Brooks. There were just three strands of barbed wire separating us from a herd of cows. They were not Joy's favourite animals, she had never forgotten her encounter in Colchester and was uneasy as we settled down for the night. As well, Michelle had a bout of car sickness and Joy had to take her to the bumby which was located at the very spot where the cows congregated for the night. I must confess I began to have some misgivings, but we survived.

The second night we spent in Revelstoke and were plagued with mosquitoes. But after that, the breathtaking beauty of British Columbia with its magnificent Rocky Mountains, the Fraser Canyon and the mighty river of the same name, all made our venture worthwhile.

We decided to take the scenic route into Vancouver and turned onto number seven highway at Rosetown making Golden Ears Provincial Park our last campsite. It was dense forest, damp, dark and foreboding. But we slept well, rose early from our makeshift beds and after a hearty breakfast, made our way to an emotional family reunion. As we drove out of the campsite a deer and her fawn strolled nonchalantly across the road. It was the first time Jennifer and Michelle had seen a real live "bambi" in its natural habitat.

After meeting with Dennis and Michael we registered at a nearby motel, determined to live out the rest of that week in a little more comfort. We were not happy campers but it was fun while it lasted.

We spent more time with the boys at the weekend discussing their future. Michael was content with his welding course; Dennis, anxious to rejoin the family, go back to school and embark on a meaningful career. He was twenty-one, Michael a year younger and they had a lot of catching up to do. But before any of that could take place, we had to get established, I had to find a home and a job.

On the Monday morning we checked out and headed toward Vancouver. In those days number seven was a narrow, two-lane highway and the traffic was heavy. Driving along I pondered the tasks that lie ahead. I had promised to help and support the boys in their efforts to start a new life. We would need a three-bedroom home. Dennis wanted to upgrade his education, so initially he would be dependent on me for room and board and money for incidentals. Michael would, presumably, find a job and be self-supporting but it still was an enormous task. To this day I don't think either of them realise what was involved.

Once again we were a family of six; I had no home, no job and limited finances. How would it all end? I wondered. I knew Joy was worried although she said little. The first thing though was to decide where we would live. I'd heard how expensive it was in Vancouver and would soon learn the cost of living anywhere on the West Coast was far higher than in Regina.

Anyway, I decided we should try the suburbs, but which one? A road sign told me we were approaching a fork in the road, straight ahead for Vancouver and to the left New Westminster. The junction was controlled by a traffic light and it took a couple of light changes to reach the stop line. As I waited for the light to change I recalled that Tommy Douglas, the former Premier of Saskatchewan and founder of Medicare was now the Federal member of parliament in these parts. And although he had left the Provincial government for Ottawa before I joined it, he had returned several times to review progress and was aware of some of my activities.

Maybe his office could help me get established, I thought, and activated my left turn signal. So when the light turned green our domicile was decided. We made our way through Port Coquitlam, Maillardville and into New Westminster looking for a motel, there were none. So over the Pattullo bridge onto King George highway where there were two, but no vacancies. We were directed to Green Timbers just off the Frazer highway in Surrey.

We rented a unit with a kitchenette and set about the task of getting re-established. The first day we met a couple from Ontario. He was a schoolteacher she a secretary, they had one little boy about two years old. Like us, they had come west in search of a better life. We remained good friends, Joy and Dianne spending their days together with the children while we two men went in search of employment. They all joined in the celebration of Michelle's fifth birthday while we were there.

Then we moved to a better motel on King George Highway and met another couple from Windsor, Ontario. They had come west because of the climate. A few days later they asked if we would like to take over an agreement they had signed with the manager of an apartment block in Maillardville. This was the predominantly French quarter of Coquitlam. They were going back to Windsor because he couldn't find satisfactory work and were anxious to extricate themselves from the deal.

It was interesting; the Manager's mother had occupied a fully furnished, two bedroom suite for years. She had passed away and the entire contents, all good quality, were sold to our friends for four hundred-fifty dollars. And they had agreed to rent the suite on the first of the month. After looking into the deal a little more we accepted, and so Maillardville was our first home in the west. Michelle Josephine felt quite at home.

I spent August and September searching for work. Many potential employers said they could use my services for a period of reorganisation or upgrading but nothing permanent. As I listened to their comments I was reminded of a quotation attributed to Lord Byron, the nineteenth century English philosopher. A Professor Raymond Byers, in a lecture I attended while at the University of Saskatchewan had used it.

"If you look long enough and hard enough at what you are doing, you can always find a better way of doing it."

I was suddenly inspired and at once became a Management Consultant; and used the quotation many times when selling my services to potential clients.

I had letterheads and business cards printed and, full of confidence and enthusiasm, launched the F.D. Keeling Company - Management Consultants. If people could use my services for short periods, so be it. And it was an instant success.

My first contract was with, Credit Union and Co-operatives Health Services Society (CU&C). British Columbia's largest, private, non-profit health care carrier. I spent three months on the project.

Word of my expertise quickly spread and my services were sought by a number of associated entities. So much so, that at one time I had to employ an assistant, another expatriate from Saskpower. I quickly expanded into the welfare and pension fields, sub-contracting the legal and actuarial work where necessary. I also worked out a deal with IBM on West Georgia Street for computer services.

Meanwhile, Jennifer and Michelle attended school in Maillardville. The transition was easy for Michelle, but not for Jennifer. Looking back, the move from Regina had a much greater effect on her than we realised. Leaving the security of a beautiful home, a good school and many dear friends, for what? Motels and apartments, in a strange environment surrounded by mostly French speaking children, plus the sense of uncertainty we all felt. It was a very traumatic experience for her. In January we moved to a three-bedroom apartment in Coquitlam to accommodate Dennis and Michael. This meant another change of school for the girls.

Before long and to our everlasting despair, Jennifer drifted into Anorexia Nervosa. It was then that I learned, for the first time, of an incident involving sexual abuse by a neighbour's children back in Regina. I believe it was this, together with the trauma of moving that triggered the onset of the disease.

For the next seven years we struggled to provide the love and support so necessary to combat the condition. I was working long hours and was away from it most of the time but for Joy it was a continuous struggle. It was only recently that she confided the extent of her frustration and despair at the dawn of each day.

Only Jennifer can know and understand what she went through; fortunately she was eventually able to control her condition so that by age eighteen, she could lead a near normal life. As events unfolded, however, life for Jennifer was never easy.

Dennis enrolled at the Vancouver College to upgrade his education but it didn't last long. He just couldn't hack it, he said. Things didn't improve and he left home again, Michael followed shortly thereafter. The next thing I heard from Dennis was in December 1968, a telegram saying he had married Carol in Regina. We wired them a hundred dollars as a wedding gift. They moved to Calgary and Dennis embarked on what became a very successful career in the Overhead Door Business.

In the spring of 1968, we took a quick trip back to Regina and apart from the occasional weekend trip, sometimes to Vancouver Island, that was the only relief we had from my busy schedule. Once again it was all work and very little play.

At eight o'clock on the night before Christmas Eve, I was still in the Boardroom of a client and not feeling well. I finally managed to get free, bought a few gifts on my way home and retired early to bed. Next morning I had my usual bowel movement and saw blood in the toilet bowl. A tiny droplet appeared at the opening of my urethra so I knew it was urinary in origin. Obviously something was wrong and now I knew why I'd been feeling so ill.

I saw a doctor in Vancouver close to where I was working. He referred me to a Urologist and an Xray of a perfect bladder was produced. He gave me some sulphur tablets, told me not to worry but to lay off any drink over the holidays and he would order a cystoscopy at Vancouver General, just to make sure.

On Monday afternoon, January 6, 1969 I was admitted for the cystoscopy at eight o'clock the following morning. It was a beautiful, clear, sunny morning as they wheeled my gurney down to the operating room. Not to worry, I'd be back in an hour. When I came to, I glanced out the window and it was pitch dark, there was an IV in my arm and a very uncomfortable catheter leading from my penis to a container at the side of the bed. Obviously this was more than a cystoscopy.

The Urologist eventually came and broke the news; he had removed a malignant papiloma the size of his thumb from my bladder. Through my exposure to the treatment of such conditions I was well aware that cancer of the bladder could be one of the most painful and mine lived up to its reputation and then some.

For the next six days I suffered the most excruciating pain and at times felt sure I was going to die. All this had a major impact on the way I looked at things, nothing traditional about life was as important anymore. Approaching fifty, I was more than half way through my expected life span and I felt much of it had been squandered; I'd spent all my time watching it go by. I realised the frailty of humankind and my own mortality and sank into a deep depression. But if I survived, I told myself, things were definitely going to change.

In the past it had been work, work, work. Being self employed on a contract basis was far more difficult than I had imagined. It entailed working for one client, often doing follow-up work for the previous one and always looking for the next. I had been under enormous stress, moving to the coast, getting established in a home and a job and dealing with a myriad of family problems. I realised I had absolutely no other interests in life. All this will change, I repeatedly told myself, but I could not have imagined how.

I was released from hospital after three weeks and went straight back to work; couldn't afford to do otherwise, here we go again. It wasn't long before I found myself drifting into another brief encounter. Some call it mid life crisis, numerologists will tell you that it's all to do with being fifty. One thing I do know, it wasn't hormonal overdrive, as some would have it.

Without making excuses, I do believe middle aged men experience physical and mental changes including mood swings. I am convinced that it was this state of mind coupled with the horrifying experience with cancer that led to my philandering.

Whatever it was, it caused irreparable harm to the family, especially to Joy, the one I would least want to hurt. As well, it was grossly unfair to the other person, a warm, loving and caring individual. She was also deeply hurt.

Certainly I was under a lot of stress and there were serious problems at home but, in retrospect, my behaviour was inexcusable. I had taken on the responsibilities of a family and I should have stuck with it. To my surprise, Joy told me to leave and get it out of my system. I don't think she really thought it through because doing so caused her a great deal of heartbreak.

Eventually I returned home assuring Joy that what had happened was no reflection on her. I was forgiven but it was never forgotten and I paid dearly for my transgression. From time to time, almost till the day she died, something would trigger a recollection of the event, in particular the writing of this book. She would have preferred I not mention it but I suggested that not doing so would destroy my credibility.

At the time my cancer was diagnosed, the Urologist also expressed concern over the state of my prostate. It was severely constricted and hardened and surgery was the only way to deal with it, he insisted. And so, as soon as I could afford the time, I went into St. Mary's hospital in New Westminster and had a trans-urethral resection. Another very painful operation and I was off work for several weeks.

In mid January 1973, I was awarded a three-month contract with the Health Security Programme Project in Victoria. A comprehensive review of health care in BC, commissioned by the Minister of Health. I was one of 126 individuals or groups specialising in a particular area of health care. I was to examine the management of the existing system for the delivery of services and make recommendations for change.

After less than two months the Director, Dr. Richard Foulkes asked me if I would consider giving up my clientele in Vancouver and move to Victoria on a permanent basis. There was, he said, enough work to last till I was sixty-five. Also the project itself was in need of improved management. To direct and co-ordinate such a large number of professionals was no easy task.

I would be appointed Deputy Director with a substantial increase in pay plus the usual public service benefits, and all expenses of moving the family would be paid. I accepted the offer and on March 1st., Joy and the girls joined me in Victoria. We stayed at the old Crest Hotel on Belleville Street at first, then rented a house on Victoria Avenue in Oak Bay and finally, in March of 1974, bought a house in Gordon Head.

Incidentally, contrary to the belief of many media pundits, I was never a member of any political party when hired by any government or agency in Canada or the US. In other words, mine was never a "political appointment."

The job lasted three years to the day. Then the newly elected Social Credit government terminated anyone hired by the previous administration. I decided against litigation, which was the more popular action under such circumstances and negotiated a reasonable severance package. One month's pay for each year of service plus holiday pay.

As usual, I had been working long hours and six, sometimes seven, days a week; Joy was getting tired of it. And so, when a vacancy arose with the Municipality of Saanich for a nine to five job I applied and was accepted. From the very beginning though, I had serious misgivings about my tenure. This was one of thirteen little fiefdoms in the Greater Victoria area, extremely parochial in its approach to doing things and not entirely receptive to major change; enough to make Lord Byron turn in his grave.

In April of 1976, I went public with some of my concerns, a cardinal sin, of course, and I was invited to resign. I did so, then sued for wrongful dismissal, settled out of court for six thousand dollars and took some time off.

During this time I had one cataract removed and an acromionectomy on my right shoulder, both legacies from world war two. I built a garden shed, topped off the concrete retaining walls in the front of the house with rich, red bricks and built two pillars at the end of the drive. Then a huge fireplace, using the same red bricks and finished off the rest of the basement. Like Winston Churchill, I found bricklaying very therapeutic.

It was during this year, 1977, that Joy went to our family physician and first presented a tiny pea sized lump well above the right breast. He examined it and assured her it was nothing to worry about. Returning home she told me about it.

"If John says there's nothing to worry about, there's nothing to worry about," I said he is an excellent physician, a friend and I trust his judgement.

By this time Joy had developed glaucoma and I was much more concerned about that.

Just before we moved to Victoria I had received a `phone call from Albert George, my son from the first marriage. There was a time when he was referred to as Al, but later it became AG. He had been searching for me for years, he said. It was a long conversation during which he advised that Rose had died in 1962 of cancer. I couldn't help thinking how strange it was that so many people with whom I'd had a close relationship had died in 1962. My mother, Frank Bunton and now Rose.

I ended the call with an open invitation for him and his family to visit us at any time. In June 1974, he and his wife Samantha spent three weeks with us. I asked why he had spent so much time and effort tracing me.

"Oh, just curiosity," he said with an air of nonchalance. I was disappointed. During his stay he also made reference to having read harsh letters from me to his mother. Because she was not there to defend herself I refrained from going into any detailed explanations; in retrospect, I should have.

Jennifer got along with them so well that the following year, at their invitation, she went to England and stayed with them. She got an excellent job chaperoning children all over the world and could have gone on to greater things but got home sick and returned.

She then got a job with the Workers Compensation Board in Victoria, did very well, was promoted and transferred to Cranbrook. A few months later, she had a nasty accident while cycling to work and we had to fly there and bring her back, ending her career. Then she moved to Nelson, met a CP Rail employee, married and had two children, Corey and Jessica. But all was not well.

On another sad note, Michael had become a Jehova Witness. In the beginning he was fanatical, trying desperately to convert every member of the family. He could not accept the fact that we simply were not interested in changing our beliefs. It caused a serious rift in the family that just about broke his mother's heart and to this day has left its mark. Although we enjoy a good relationship, there remains a kind of invisible barrier between us.

Thirty-four

North Of Fifty-four And Back

In those days removing a cataract was a delicate operation with a longer period of convalescence than now. In addition, there was the shoulder surgery. I had that extra money and we hadn't had a holiday since 1972, so we decided I should remain off work until completely recovered.

We took the time to explore, first the south and central part of Vancouver Island, then the north and west, something we had wanted to do for many years. But there came a time when I had to get back to work.

My attention was drawn to a national advertisement for a Director of Health Services for Northern Saskatchewan. The pay was excellent, accommodation was provided and all moving expenses paid. It seemed like a real challenge. After much discussion with Joy I applied and was selected.

Michelle was happy attending Lambrick Park Secondary School had lots of friends and was reluctant to move. The position carried the customary six months probationary period so we agreed I would go on my own. I left on June 28, 1978. From the beginning it was difficult for Joy. She had been plagued with double vision for almost three months and was then diagnosed with Glaucoma.

In retrospect, this is when her health began to deteriorate although she never complained. In any case, by August she could no longer cope with the separation. She joined me and arranged for Michelle to stay with a friend until we returned to Victoria for Christmas. Then we all made the long journey back to the frozen north. Michelle's fiancé Wayne joined us shortly afterwards following the tragic death of a friend in a motor vehicle accident in which Wayne was the driver.

Of all our adventures this was the most challenging. The government of Saskatchewan had decided that all health services north of the fifty-fourth parallel would be administered from La Ronge, about three hundred miles north of Regina. The permanent population of this area of 142 thousand square miles was about thirty-five thousand. But with several large uranium mines and lots of exploration underway, the population was increased fourfold at times and they all needed adequate health care. It was felt that the needs could best be met by a decentralised delivery system based in La Ronge.

And so it was that I became responsible for every aspect of health care for the region. There were large, fully equipped hospitals at La Ronge and Ile-a-la-Crosse with smaller ones at La Loche and Uranium City. All communities had a health centre staffed by a minimum of two, sometimes three specially trained Public Health Nurses. They provided primary diagnosis and emergency care as well as an excellent home care programme. There were seventeen resident physicians and five dentists. Specialists in every discipline visited key areas on an itinerant basis at least once a year and there was a Public Health physician with three inspectors to deal with environmental issues.

They had no emergency programme and all emergency supplies were stored in Prince Albert, 150 miles away. And so I appointed myself "Emergency Measures Co-ordinator" for Northern Saskatchewan and, with the help of the Airport Manager, organised and trained local personnel in search and rescue and related activities. I also had all the equipment shipped to La Ronge and stored in the basement of the local hospital.

We had at least one over flight of a Boeing747 every day and the local airport had more aircraft landing and taking off in a day than did Regina International Airport. We had several downed aircraft to deal with and many exploration people wandering away from their work sights and getting lost in the wilderness. The R.C.M.P. would 'phone me and I would provide the necessary personnel and equipment to meet the emergency. Also, being the co-ordinator I had to set up a command post in our living room to direct operations, and wouldn't you know it, most emergencies arose on weekends. But it was interesting and rewarding when, for instance, our search and rescue crews found someone who had been lost for days.

There was one horrific incident where a taxi carrying eleven people including a small baby, collided head on with a semi trailer on a gravel road many miles north of La Ronge. It was in the winter time so I dispatched a twin engine Otter equipped with skids to the scene carrying doctors, nurses and a rescue team. The pilot found the accident sight but because of the terrain couldn't land. The search master told me later that they all held their breath while he very gently landed the plane on the makeshift highway. My informant expressed amazement that the pilot managed to avoid the power lines alongside the road. There was a host of similar incidents but that gives some idea of our activities.

We lived in a three bedroom trailer at first having closed the house in Victoria. We paid a young guy across the street fifty bucks a month to tend the garden and check on things occasionally. And our good neighbour opposite parked his van in our driveway after work to give the appearance of it being occupied. Then a year later our Director of Air Services, yes we had our own airforce, decided to return to Victoria and needed somewhere to live. We took his new three-bedroom house and rented ours to him.

Soon after our arrival in La Ronge, Joy had a medical check-up and drew the doctor's attention to that tiny lump. The lady doctor promptly expressed the same opinion, "There is nothing to worry about," I felt vindicated. Joy was still not entirely convinced but didn't mention her concern again.

Meanwhile, Michelle was attending Churchill High School and I was able to get her a part time job as switchboard operator/stenographer. She graduated in 1980, worked there for the summer then returned to Victoria with Wayne. Joy and I were alone for the first time in thirty-four years. Needless to say we made the most of our newly won freedom.

There was only one paved highway in the entire region, number two from Regina to La Ronge, the rest were gravel trails. The majority of the communities, however, were accessible only by air or water thus the airforce. We had water bombers for fighting forest fires and a variety of other aircraft ranging from amphibious Cessna 185's to the most modern Lear jets. I was amazed at the sight of Joy climbing aboard a Cessna 185 floatplane. There was a time when she wouldn't even fly a kite.

I was fortunate in that, whenever I flew, if there were empty seats I could take Joy and or Michelle. In the course of the two years I was there they flew all over the north in every type of plane we had. Most memorable was a trip to Regina in a Lear jet.

At breakfast that morning I invited Michelle and Joy to join me on the flight. They spent the day with Mary a former neighbour across the street, meanwhile I went to work at the Legislative buildings. The plane arrived at eight that evening for the return journey. We took off in a typical prairie thunderstorm, climbed to thirty-five thousand feet and enjoyed an amazing show of the Aurora Borealis for the remainder of the journey. Mary had supplied us with lots of wine at supper so no one was scared.

An amusing incident occurred on a business trip to Meadow Lake. We had a Doctor of East Asian descent who had trained and worked in England for several years then joined us. He and I went to Meadow Lake to negotiate with disgruntled local physicians outside our juristriction but who were affected by some of our administrative policies. We landed at Meadow Lake airport and were picked up by the one and only taxi driver.

After spending the day successfully arguing our case with the locals, we had supper then took the same taxi back to the airport. To make conversation obviously, the taxi driver said, "Been doing a little work at the hospital doctor?" Without batting an eyelid the doctor calmly replied, "Yes, just a little brain surgery." There was dead silence for the remainder of the journey, the driver not knowing whether to believe him or not. We had a good laugh once in the airport.

One of my responsibilities was to monitor the uranium mining operations and although I had inspectors, management somehow knew ahead of time when they were due. So occasionally, I would drop in unannounced. On one such visit I was exposed to some yellow cake as it was called. Ten years later I was diagnosed with lung cancer. The surgeon advised me that lab tests revealed the tumour was not as a result of smoking. An Oncologist opined that the exposure could have been the cause.

The weather was a major problem. It would often start to snow on Joy's birthday in September and still be snowing for Jennifer's in April. The temperature frequently dipped to fifty below with snow and blowing snow; blizzards were commonplace. In summer, the reverse. Temperatures nearing the hundred degrees mark for days on end bringing out millions of black flies. Then there were the caterpillars, swarms of them; they covered our house from top to bottom. Joy spent one afternoon hosing them down with tide in the water, someone had told her that would get rid of them. But all it did was give us the cleanest caterpillars in La Ronge.

It had its bright side though, I recall with some degree of nostalgia fishing on Black Lake, near Uranium City at midnight in broad daylight. Then returning to the Health Clinic and enjoying a meal of freshly caught pickerel.

Joy kept herself busy with needlework and knitting, our home is bedecked with her works, including one particular objet d'art; a beautifully embroidered tablecloth that took her seven years to complete. On one occasion she was knitting on a circular needle and it broke. She phoned around but nobody had one so I said, "What the heck, let's go and buy one," and we drove the three hundred-mile round trip to Saskatoon and back all for a knitting needle. We've laughed many times over that.

We had a call from Dennis in November of 1979. He had the opportunity to buy a house in Surrey but was short two thousand dollars for the down payment. Much to his surprise we put a cheque in the mail the same day. Joy and I were pleased to help and furthermore, half of it was a belated wedding gift. Dennis was overwhelmed.

On November 16, 1979, Jennifer gave birth to Corey in Kamloops. She had written asking her mom to attend but at the time I was just recovering from the removal of my second cataract so, Joy, torn between loyalties, chose to remain with me. Jennifer 'phoned from the delivery room, we were staying at the Cavalier Hotel in Saskatoon at the time.

That Christmas was a memorable occasion. The doctors based at Ile-a-la-Crosse chartered a plane at their own expense and invited Joy and I to join them for the holidays. We flew in a single engine Otter loaded with gifts for the doctors and their families as well as some of the senior nursing staff, we had a great time.

Whenever we went back to Victoria on holiday we always drove the Yellowhead highway through Edmonton then south on number five to Kamloops. This is where Jennifer and Kevin were living. In April 1980, they bought a house atop the mountain at Pinantan Lake. We had to loan them a thousand dollars for their down payment; since we had bought them a washer and dryer as a wedding gift they repaid us.

Anyway, we arrived at their new home one Saturday in August, to find a new, 1979, fire engine red Firebird in the driveway as well as Kevin's truck. Turned out he had swung an incredible deal for this limited edition beauty but was having difficulty with the payments. I offered him four thousand dollars cash plus my car to take it off his hands; he accepted. It was a great car, heads turned everywhere we went. But whenever I stopped for gas the attendant would say, "So, you borrowed your son's car today huh?" or some such remark.

We then went on to spend the last few days of that holiday with Dennis and family in their new home. During our last meal before leaving, Dennis suggested I quit my job and join him as a partner in Overhead Doors of Victoria Ltd., he had been offered the Vancouver Island franchise. It was an interesting proposition and Joy and I talked about it on our way back to La Ronge.

By this time we had been up there for two years, the average length of stay before burnout often begins. I enjoyed the challenge but the daily grind was beginning to take its toll. We decided that as soon as Dennis made formal application we would join him. Another adventure; I was tiring of the health field anyway.

Soon after Michelle left, Dennis phoned saying the franchise was ours for the taking. I gave a month's notice and in mid September Dennis and Carol flew to Sankatoon, picked up a U Haul then drove to La Ronge. We spent the evening packing and left very early the next morning.

We stored our furniture in Dennis' basement and over the next few days pursued the formalities of establishing the franchise in Victoria. Overhead Doors is an International Company with Headquarters in Dallas, Texas. This was no two-bit outfit we were dealing with.

Reading the fine print, there were a couple of stipulations that didn't please me at all. One, they reserved the right to split the Island and two, they reserved the right to sell our products to competitors. At lunch with Dennis and his boss, I expressed my concern. Dennis visited the men's room and in his absence his boss confided that there was no way he would take on the franchise under those terms. That was good enough for me and I told Dennis we should forget it; he agreed but did press me to join him in a Vancouver venture in competition with his company. Joy would have nothing to do with that proposal, she was homesick for Victoria.

And so, in October we returned to Victoria, regained possession of our house and I wish I could say we lived happily ever after but it was not to be.

One of the first things we did was to re-establish relations with our family physician. For the next two years, Joy continued to express concern about the lump on her chest. He repeated his original diagnosis, "There is nothing to worry about." Years later she would tell me that on one occasion he actually laughed at her continuing concern.

I was sixty years old, I was tired of the health field so what should we do? After much discussion, we concluded that the four-bedroom house was too much for us so we'd sell it and invest the proceeds in a business where I could work at a less strenuous pace. And so the house was put on the market and the search for a suitable enterprise began.

We sold the house in December for $119,000.00, seventy thousand more than we paid for it in 1974, and moved into Harrington House on January 1, 1981. Meantime the search for the right business deal continued. Within two weeks I found exactly what I was looking for. At least, so I thought.

Thirty-five

Caveat Emptor

With the sale of the house we had paid off all our debts and traded the Firebird for a more modest, less costly vehicle. We substantially improved our R.R.S.P fund and had about fifty thousand left over which would be our investment. I was entitled to U.I.C benefits but had enough to live on for the first year anyway.

In the second week of January, having settled in our new condominium, an ad appeared in the Business Opportunities section of the local newspaper. It was for an investment of fifty thousand dollars in an International Communications Centre for Vancouver Island. A toll free number was available for further details.

I phoned the number and was eventually contacted by the President of the Company. The service involved the use of the Wide Area Telephone System. (WATS). The Head Office and operations centre was located in a prestigious suite of offices in West Vancouver, with branch offices in most major cities across Canada including Toronto. I believe there was a total of nineteen investors in the company.

Joy and I made several trips to the facility. We saw the operations room with an array of communications equipment manned by operators who appeared to be busy handling calls. We met other administrative staff and all in all, it appeared to be a hive of industry, especially one Sunday morning when the lines were literally ringing off the hook. There was a special deal in progress we were told.

We visited their bank, the manager was on long term sick leave suffering with cancer and I believe she later died. Our discussions with the Assistant manager led us to believe that this was a viable and successful business operation. We also talked to other franchise operators, including one in Toronto and the previous operator in Victoria. The latter had withdrawn due to ill health. We spoke to customers both large and small and except for minor complaints, everything checked out fine. But I was leery of the franchise business and wasn't inclined to risk my entire savings in such an enterprise. We returned to Victoria after making our decision known to the Company's Principal and started looking elsewhere.

A week later we were again approached by the same Company, this time the investment was to be forty thousand and another person was interested in a half share once the franchise was up and running. In the mean time, he would work as an employee on a commission basis. He couldn't invest immediately we were told, because his money was tied up with another franchise in Ladysmith but was to be released within days. We checked that out and it was confirmed.

So, with the risk reduced to twenty thousand and an experienced franchiser as a partner, the deal appeared a lot more attractive. Joy and I talked it over at length and finally, on February 10, 1981, decided to go for it. The following day we went to West Vancouver and handed over a cheque for forty thousand dollars. A contract was drawn up and we were in business. I was the President of International Communications Vancouver Island Ltd. Joy, the Secretary Treasurer.

On February 23, I invested another thousand dollars to set up a small one-room office in the Sayward Building on Douglas Street for one hundred dollars a month. My partner from Ladysmith joined me and we set about the task of re-establishing the franchise. There was one large customer still using the service in Victoria, a hotel on the Pat Bay Highway. They had assured me the service was an asset to their operation and that when controlled from West Vancouver was very good. But when local people took over the service went downhill. It sounded encouraging.

Trouble was everything continued to go downhill despite my best efforts. After only one week my partner and potential co-investor quit for personal reasons. So we were left holding the bag for the entire forty thousand dollars.

Not to be deterred I battled on alone, arousing considerable interest in the service but no sales. Then I received a 'phone call from the Toronto office saying that some of his clients, while in the US, were having difficulty getting access to toll free lines. Had I had any problems? I said, "No, but would monitor the situation." It wasn't long before we found the reason. 'Phone bills to Telephone companies were not being paid, lines were being disconnected and, in fact, the company was in a state of bankruptcy and had been for months.

It came as a terrible shock. How could this have happened after we were so careful to investigate? How could this state of affairs have been so cleverly disguised? We would soon learn we were dealing with skilled manipulators and that we were not the only victims. Caveat emptor, buyer beware, was the first thing that came to mind.

The day after this came to light I was admitted to hospital suffering with an acute case of kidney stones, a very uncomfortable condition. I contacted my landlord, terminated my lease, asked her to disconnect the phone, return the office furniture I'd rented and close the office. We were out of business.

I won't go into all the details. Suffice it to say that, on 21 May 1981, the two principals were charged with various counts of fraud. In June I hired a lawyer to pursue a civil action but it was not until August 1984 that a three weeks criminal trial took place. I was on the witness stand for a week. The perpetrators were found guilty; one was sentenced to a year in prison, the other to three months. The court issued an order for restitution but to date has proven of no more value than the paper on which it was written.

At the time it was all a sickening affair, the loss of our hard earned savings a severe blow. But in the course of time, the financial loss proved of little consequence. In the mean time, there were much more serious matters to be dealt with. Matters concerning the most important thing in life, our health.

I was sixty-five and had not worked since the ICC fiasco. We had lived, first on UIC then cashed our R.R.S.P's plus a ten thousand dollar tax refund resulting from an over payment in two consecutive years while working in Saskatchewan. It had come to light quite by accident. But before we get into that, other things had been happening.

Thirty-six

A Never Ending Battle

When Michelle returned to Victoria in 1980, she immediately got a full time job with the Victoria School Board. Her part time employment with the Department of Northern Saskatchewan and the reference she was given no doubt contributed to her success. But after five years her relationship with Wayne came to an end.

She took up skiing with Laurie her friend since grade school and they spent many hours at Mount Washington. On one such trip she met Rick, the manager of the Ski Shop and thus began another romance. Each weekend she would visit him in Campbell River despite the long and tedious drive. The highway wasn't improved until the nineties.

On Saturday 5 February 1983, at about ten o'clock in the morning the phone rang. Joy and I had showered and were in the bedroom dressing. A physician introduced himself by saying he was a classmate of our family physician, I wondered what he was leading up to. Finally, he broke the news that Michelle had been involved in a very serious automobile accident en route to Mount Washington and was in critical condition in St. Joseph's hospital in Comox.

"I think she will pull through, he said."

We were both in shock but left immediately.

On arrival we spoke with the surgeon who had operated. He described her injuries, in particular the dreadful state of her feet. He said that he had great difficulty finding all the tiny pieces of broken bones but was hopeful of a near normal recovery. She also sustained injuries to her head and shoulder.

Later, we visited the RCMP office in Courtney and were given a description of the accident. Apparently, Rick and Michelle along with Laurie and her Friend Tim, had stopped at a store to buy coffee and doughnuts. The girls returned to the car and Rick took off while they were handing out the goodies and before they had fastened their seat belts. Both girls were thrown out of the car, Michelle sixty feet. She landed on her feet then her shoulder and finally her head. Had it been the other way around she would have been killed instantly. The car had skidded on black ice.

We stayed in Comox until Michelle was discharged from hospital then took her home and the long, tedious rehabilitation began. Joy had to do almost everything for her so severe were her injuries. But there is a happy ending to the story. On her twenty-first birthday they became engaged, Rick gave her the ring in our living room at Harrington House. There followed a long and protracted court battle with ICBC but eventually, Michelle was awarded damages which they used for a down payment on their first home.

Meanwhile, living in an expensive, two-bedroom condo was becoming a financial burden for us and we thought about down sizing. On several occasions Dennis had suggested we live with them in their very attractive basement suite. Carol was finding it difficult to handle a full time job and at the same time cope with a family, including two teen-age girls. The proposal was that Joy handle the housework and cooking and me the maintenance, in return we would live rent-free. Joy had previously turned down the idea, she hated Vancouver. But now it seemed a move that would make life easier for everybody and so on 1 July 1983 we moved in with Dennis and family.

It worked out well for everybody. We all got along fine, the suite was comfortable and large enough for all our furniture and we had our own telephone. So apart from eating together we led our own lives.

We were invited to spend Christmas 1983, with Jennifer and family at Pinantan Lake. While there we met her in laws who had driven from Brandon, Manitoba.

At the time I was wearing, what I called my beer bottle glasses, designed to replace the natural lens of the eyes. By now I'd had both cataracts removed and without them everything was blurred, I was legally blind. One morning I was wearing them as, Joy was dressing and for the first time noticed the lump on her chest had grown bigger.

"When we get back to Dennis' we're going to have that lump checked out, I don't like the look of it." I said.

"Well, I've been complaining about it for years but everyone keeps saying it's nothing to worry about," she replied a little testily.

Back in Surrey, we made an appointment with a new doctor. Joy repeated the previous physician's opinion that there was nothing to worry about.

"Well I'm certainly worried about it," he replied.

An appointment was made for her to see a surgeon that afternoon, a biopsy was performed and it was malignant; Joy had cancer.

"I've been telling you all along that something was wrong," was all she said.

As for me, I was overwhelmed with guilt as I realised the implications. For seven years Joy had complained, early detection was the key to a cure and I had ignored it. I had stubbornly kept faith with our family physician when I should have demanded a second opinion. For the rest of my life that decision would haunt me.

On 8 March 1984, Joy had a lumpectomy followed by three weeks of radiation at the Vancouver Cancer Clinic. She had a very difficult time during the treatments, chronic nausea and vomiting. The most devastating news, however, was given to me in private by one of the doctors.

"Mrs. Keeling's condition is very serious," he said, "she could live as little as six months or as long as five years but the latter would be very optimistic."

I was stunned and we discussed whether, Joy should be told. I felt she shouldn't, I was sure it would be too much for her. The shock of having cancer and the difficulties she had with radiation were bad enough, I didn't think she could tolerate more. It was agreed she should not be told but I told the children.

The decision not to tell her was vindicated in later years when, in the belief that her disease was in remission, I told her about it. Her reply was that she was glad I hadn't told her.

At her first post-operative visit to the surgeon he asked our permission to report the family physician involved to the College of Physicians and Surgeons.

"Of course if you are thinking of litigation, I fully understand and will help you in any way I can," he continued.

This was, indeed, a surprise. Rarely does one hear such talk from a doctor. We said we would think about it. In retrospect, his comments may have been made in haste because when later interviewed by a lawyer he was evasive, although he did not deny his earlier remarks.

Joy was angry and bitter and insisted we proceed with litigation. Eventually, there was a preliminary hearing in Victoria but the case was dropped shortly thereafter. The surgeon was non co-operative and there was insufficient corroborative evidence. About a year later that same surgeon was killed in a bizarre automobile accident in the Frazer Canyon. A huge boulder crushed his car killing him instantly.

Joy was put on the wonder drug Tamoxifen for the next two years and the disease seemed to be under control. But there was no way she could continue looking after two families. Under her supervision, I did everything until on 1 April 1985, we returned to a one-bedroom condo at Harrington House in Victoria. But I'm getting ahead of myself.

Back on 8 June 1984 it was my turn. Michelle was visiting, busy preparing for her upcoming wedding. I had driven her and Joy all over the place looking at wedding dresses, catering arrangements and a host of other activities relating to the great day. We all gathered for supper and had a glass of wine. Soon I began to feel peculiar, chest pains and nausea. I excused myself and went down stairs and lay on the bed.

After a while, Joy and Michelle came to see what was wrong, I told them not to worry I just wasn't feeling too good.

"I don't like the look of Dad, I'm going to call the ambulance," Michelle said.

I didn't argue. Turned out to be an acute angina and I spent the next six days in the intensive care unit at Surrey Memorial Hospital. I also quit smoking cold turkey and it didn't bother me one bit.

It was a slow recovery but I made it for Michelle's wedding in Campbell River on 11 August, her birthday. It was a glorious sunny day and the ceremony was held in beautifully landscaped acreage of the best man. Michelle looked radiant in white, she reminded me very much of Princess Diana, I know that sounds pretentious but it's true. A fine reception at a shoreline hotel followed the exchange of vows.

In the fall of 1985, Joy's only brother, Francis paid us a visit on his way back to Australia from Germany. It was a happy occasion for all concerned, we had not seen him since 1954. Two years later his wife Eve visited us. She gave us a set of four small Japanese hand paintings she'd bought in Tokyo. We had them framed and they too adorn our living room wall. In October 1997, she died of breast cancer.

Joy was visiting the Cancer clinic every three months and, so far, so good. Financially, we were doing quite well. Since we had both served in World War Two we each qualified for a small war veteran's pension, which enabled us to live comfortably. In fact, we started saving for a long dreamed of trip back to our homeland. If we still had that forty thousand dollars or any income from it, we would not have qualified. So in the end its loss made little difference. One thing bothered me, however, rents in Victoria were skyrocketing. Ours remained reasonable but for how long I wondered? I put our names down for seniors housing just in case.

By this time, Jennifer's marriage had failed and she was granted a divorce. Her ex husband wrote to me admitting that the break up was entirely his fault.

There was another hasty marriage to one who proved to be an unsavory character. He was a pharmacist and was eventually jailed and lost his license to practice, for trying to peddle prescription drugs on a downtown street. Following the divorce, Jennifer settled down on her own and continued to upgrade her education.

Also in 1985, another traumatic event took place. For ten years I had been legally blind. I was only able to see properly by wearing those hideously thick glasses. Anyway, I had inter-ocular implants inserted. It was quite an experience to walk along Dallas Road and once again see things and people as they really are. And what a thrill to have twenty-twenty vision again.

In May of 1987 we found, to our dismay, that Joy was not a Canadian Citizen. Somehow there had been a bureaucratic screw-up in 1963, when I was granted mine. She applied, passed the necessary tests and was granted citizenship in September of that year. So now we were all set for our trip to England the following year.

On 24 July 1988, Dennis entered into his second marriage to Laureen, who had two children, Amber and Codie. We were unable to attend the wedding because I was in hospital having kidney stones removed again. Laureen was a lovely person and we were pleased to accept Amber and Codie as grandchildren.

A few months into their marriage, a sad case of child abuse involving Amber and her maternal grandfather came to light. Joy and I went to New Westminster where they were living and sat around their dining room table offering what comfort and advice we could. It was then that I disclosed the facts of my own abuse, everybody was shocked, of course, but benefited from my experience. Then, in fairness to the other children, I told them; without exception they were both sympathetic and supportive.

We flew to London, England for a memorable seven-week holiday on 27

July. It included a return visit to Broadstairs where we met in 1945 and visits to surviving members of our respective families that we had not seen since our departure in 1957.

We were guests of AG and Samantha at their comfortable, middle class home in London. On the day of our arrival we met Mary in the afternoon and in the evening with Angela and husband Dan. During the latter visit, conversation drifted toward the break-up of my marriage to their mother and her subsequent marriage to Sid. I reminded them that there had been others before Sid and offered to tell them my side of the entire story but suggested it might come as a bit of a shock to them. I felt comfortable in doing so because Joy was present and could bear witness to much of what I would have to say.

"No, I don't think mum would want us to know," AG said hastily.

Nothing more was ever said and they were all very kind to us throughout our stay. On Samantha's birthday, Mary hosted a reunion for the entire family the only exception being her daughter who was living abroad. It was particularly gratifying for me to finally meet all my children, grandchildren and great grandchildren on that side of the family.

During that holiday we also visited Cousin Arthur in Coventry. This was the son of Arthur senior who, it will be recalled, was the executor of my stepfather's estate. His wife, Agnes, was killed in the massive air raid on Coventry. Arthur junior was with his mother at the time and was seriously injured but survived.

We were invited to supper and spent most of the time reminiscing about the Ince side of the family. Toward the end of the evening Arthur produced a stack of legal documents relating to my stepfather's estate, now of little interest. But then he gave me what had eventually become my mother's diary; it had lain in a drawer since Fred's death in 1966, twenty-two years.

Just as old Annie Mason had intoned back in September 1939, the inscription on the cover read, "Emma Draper. Given to her by her mother on her 12th., Birthday, 1884." Later, I spent hours pouring over its contents, which I've already described. It is a beautiful little thing, has a religious connotation and, as I write, is 116 years old.

Back at home, we decided to change doctors. Ours was nearing retirement and we wanted someone younger, more up to date in his approach to health care. And so it was that, Michael Winston Vaughan B.A., B.Sc., B.Med., M.D., a native of Jamaica, became, and is to this day, not only our family physician but a much admired and trusted friend.

He promptly ordered a chest X-ray for me that uncovered a spot on the upper lobe of my right lung. A biopsy was performed and it was malignant. For the second time I had cancer. On 14 December I entered the Royal Jubilee hospital and had the offending tumor removed. The surgery was a success and I made a speedy recovery. But the surgery left me with a hiatus hernia for which I have to take daily doses of Famotadine and chew endless amounts of Gaviscon. What next, I wondered? As it turned out, I only had to have hearing aids during the rest of that year but it wouldn't be long before I was once again under the knife.

Joy had an appointment at the Victoria cancer clinic on 6 April 1989. It was now five years since her cancer was first detected. The Oncologist was pleased with her condition and didn't want to see her for another year. We were all thrilled and convinced that the disease was in remission. I got the impression that the experts were somewhat perplexed by Joy's favourable condition.

On 2 December 1990, I was again admitted to the emergency department at Royal Jubilee hospital for a cholesystectomy, the fancy medical term for the removal of one's gall bladder. There were stones in the duct so I couldn't have the latest laparoscopic procedure, instead, it was removed the old fashioned way. Much more uncomfortable and a much longer period of convalescence.

The most newsworthy events of 1991 were Michelle and family moving to Everett, Washington in the United States where Rick was offered the management of a new store. It made visiting them more difficult because now we had the ferry to contend with. But it was a wonderful opportunity for them and they made the most of it.

The other event was the invasion of Kuwait by Saddam Husain and the ensuing Gulf War. It affected us because we had planned to go to England again but cancelled because of the threat of terrorism. We'd go the following year, we said.

But 1992 got off to a bad start. On 16 February, Joy's sister Pearl died of lung cancer. It was all very sudden, one day we were told she was in hospital and before our get-well bouquet arrived she was dead, and only sixty-seven years of age.

I was reading the paper on the morning of Saturday 9 May when suddenly there was a piercing scream followed by a mournful, "Oh no." Joy was showering so I assumed something had gone wrong with the hot water. But the moaning continued so I rushed into the bathroom expecting to find she had fallen or something but no, she had discovered lumps under her right arm. We both knew this meant her cancer had returned and had spread to her lymph system. Tamoxifen was again prescribed but she had an adverse reaction and was put on Megase. This too was a failure and so in August they tried Tamoxifen again, this time it worked.

Shortly after this, Joy had a bone scan, which indicated the cancer had spread to the humerus, the large bone between the shoulder and the elbow. She was given five zaps of radiation at one time, this time feeling no side effects

It was at about this time that Joy came under the care of Doctor Sharon Allan a Medical Oncologist at the cancer clinic. She was thrilled to have a female doctor and over the next six years a very close and sincere relationship developed. Joy had nothing but the highest praise and admiration for the doctor who patiently guided her through her horrifying experience. I too became an admirer of her skill and demeanour, even when I became impatient because nothing could be done to help Joy's lymphedema, she showed the utmost professionalism and restraint.

"I don't know what I would do without Doctor Allan," Joy would say after almost every visit.

She was, indeed, a wonderful doctor and a very fine lady.

The cancerous nodes were surgically removed on 28 May, and for the second time we had to cancel our flight plans and claim a refund. Thank goodness we had taken out travel insurance. But we made up for it because by August, Joy was well enough to travel so we went to Pennsylvania to visit her sister, Thelma.

We had a great time including a trip to Atlantic City where we had a beautiful room on the thirty-fifth floor of Balley's. We visited the casinos but declined to get involved, I was not in a gambling mood. In fact, I spent most of the time in the hotel room not feeling well.

The year ended with me visiting a surgeon for tests relating to a continuing abdominal problem. On 13 April 1993, after more tests, it was discovered I had colon cancer and on the19th., I had an abdominal perineal resection. In other words, a chunk of my colon was removed, it was a long and painful recovery.

Jennifer married Ron on 21 May, the ceremony taking place at the Emily Carr house in Victoria. The reception, which Joy and I provided was held at the Empress hotel, how I got through it I will never know, I was in such discomfort.

On Wednesday 2 June I was admitted to emergency and at midnight, an attempt was made to stretch the colon because I had developed a constriction. In so doing the colon was perforated but that turned out to be the least of my worries.

At eight-twenty the following morning I suffered a massive heart attack. I spent the next six days in intensive care and although I was apparently quite lucid, I remember little of it. On Friday the 4th., I underwent angioplasty to remove the blockage in my arteries. Then on the 8th., I was given a temporary colostomy and for the next year had to use a bag. I was embarrassed at first but soon adjusted to it.

While in the hospital, I was visited by an Oncologist who glibly informed me I was scheduled for three weeks of radiation treatment followed by one year of chemotherapy. This would increase my chances of survival for a five-year period from forty per cent to eighty percent. I said I would take my chances with the forty per cent and refused the radiation and chemo. I'd had enough thank you very much. There followed predictions of doom and gloom but I stuck with my decision.

At the end of June our landlord sold the condo we were renting and we moved to Fern Street. This was quite a financial blow because our rent had been well below market value, now we would have to pay the going rate.

AG 'phoned from England on 26 September informing us that Angela's only child had been killed instantly in an automobile accident. His car went out of control on a wet road as he was driving home at night. Angela was never the same after that. What more could possibly happen? I asked myself. It wouldn't take long to find out.

By December tests had shown more cancer in Joy's left breast. She was admitted for a wedge resection but on entry the surgeon found the cancer was so widespread that a bilateral mastectomy was recommended. On 31 December,

Joy had both her breasts removed. In the meantime, I was admitted on 16 December to have corrective surgery. So I was in hospital for all of Christmas and Joy for all of New Year's. We almost passed in the hallway.

Then she was prescribed yet another cancer drug in an effort to control the disease. The question of reconstructive surgery arose. We visited a plastic surgeon and explored the options but in the end Joy decided on a prosthesis. She'd had enough surgery and I didn't blame her.

Losing her breasts was a terrible shock and she was very self-conscious. She said how glad she was that we slept in twin beds. I did my best to console her by assuring her that I was fully prepared for it. I was well aware of the repugnance felt by some spouses but it didn't bother me at all.

It was not until after her death, when we found a journal she had started that we realized just how much it did bother her.

"I still can't get over having my breasts off," she wrote, "it's such a shock, if it weren't for my wonderful husband, I don't know what I would do. It makes me love him more and more." She went on, "I love the times when he says, `come into my bed and let's have a cuddle,' and at the oddest times he hugs me."

It was very gratifying to learn her true feelings.

On 11 April 1994 Dennis' wife, Laureen died of a massive heart attack, she was but thirty-four years of age. It had been a happy marriage and for seven years Dennis had been a good father but the children, Amber and Codie, opted to return to their biological father. This was a shock to us all; we had become so attached to them.

In August 1994, Michelle and family moved to Spokane, Washington. Rick had been assigned to manage a much larger store. It was a promotion for him but such a long way away. At times like this we needed our children around us but, of course, life must go on; so we did a lot of driving.

For the rest of that year, Joy attended the cancer clinic every month and I was having periodical check-ups for my colon. It was, it seemed, a never-ending battle.

On 10 February 1995, we moved to a Senior's Complex. Into a pleasant little suite on the second floor, Joy loved it from the start. Located across from the playing fields of an elementary school, we enjoy the daily laughter of children at recess. From a large living room window we look out at a big Japanese cherry tree that in spring is awash with delicate pink blossom. To the right there are two graceful silver birch trees with a huge evergreen bush reaching up to their lower branches, an ideal home for hundreds of wild birds. As well, the lower rent enables us to enjoy the luxury of a new T.V., "Surround Sound"stereo and air conditioning.

My last surgery was 5 June1995, to repair a ventral (abdominal) hernia. Chicken feed compared to the big stuff and I quickly recovered. The following day, Joy had a CAT scan and there were no more abnormalities.

On the second day of June, we attended Jennifer's convocation ceremony at the University of Victoria. What a proud day it was; the first member of the Keeling clan to earn a degree, with honours too. We sat in the balcony and watched as Jennifer waddled, seven months pregnant, to the podium to receive her degree. Afterwards, I took everybody to lunch at the Oak Bay Marina. It was a day I shall never forget.

This event marked the end of an era, so to speak, in the raising of our children. They were all enjoying successful careers now; Dennis in a senior position with his Company and Michael doing very well as a Longshoreman. Michelle and Rick were having great success with their new store in Spokane and now Jennifer was well equipped for a professional career in Child and Youth Care.

Then, on 3 August 1995 the icing on the cake. Jennifer gave birth to a bouncing baby boy, 8lbs.13oz., Aaron Alexander. He lives close by and brings much joy, pardon the pun, to my lonely life.

We finally made it to England again in September of that year but it was not entirely successful. We intended to stay three weeks, the maximum Joy could be away, but returned after only two. The strain of travelling was too much for her and I too was having problems. So, after doing some research for this tome in Epping, Romford and Chelmsford we returned home.

The next two years saw the cancer spreading relentlessly throughout Joy's body. It started in late May, 1996 with an overnight stay at Dennis' in Maple Ridge. She complained of not feeling well but was determined to continue on to Michelle's in Spokane, Washington the following day.

We arrived at Michelle's at five in the evening, the excitement of seeing her made Joy feel a lot better. But as the weekend progressed her condition deteriorated. Late Sunday afternoon, Michelle asked her neighbour, a Registered Nurse, to take a look at her mom.

The nurse sounded her chest then turned to me.

"I think you'd better return to Canada immediately," she said, "your wife has a very serious lung condition."

We left the following morning.

Thirty-seven

Infiltrating Ductular Carcinoma

We left Michelle's at eight and I pushed my 1980 Chevy Citation to its limits on that four hundred-mile journey. I stopped only twice, once for gas and once for a short picnic lunch on the outskirts of Everett. All Joy would take was water and by the time we reached the ferry terminal at Tswassan she was feeling very ill.

I tried to console her by saying it was probably pneumonia, which these days was not considered as serious as in the past. I didn't really believe what I was saying and I know she too was sceptical. During the ferry ride she lost control of her bowels and spent most of the time in the toilet trying to repair the damage, she was terribly embarrassed.

We saw Doctor Vaughan on the Tuesday afternoon and he ordered an immediate X- ray. The next morning he phoned to say he was concerned with the results and had made an appointment for her to see Doctor Allan at the Cancer Clinic the next day.

Joy was always apprehensive about going to the Clinic and this time was no exception. I tried to ease her mind but she was so tormented by what might be wrong that nothing I said was of comfort. We spent a restless night and her appointment was not until late in the day. As the day wore on she could hardly contain herself, such is the fear this dreadful disease creates.

She entered the examining room full of misgiving, I could see the fear in her eyes. The nurse performed the routine preliminaries and told her to "Slip into a gown," it was heart-rending to watch as she fumbled to undress. I had to do almost everything for her.

It didn't take long for Doctor Allan to break the news. The X-ray was displayed on the screen and it clearly indicated the cancer had spread to her right lung.

"This is very serious," the doctor said.

I looked at Joy, her face was ashen.

"How long have I got," she meekly asked.

I was surprised, hitherto she hadn't wanted to know.

"People with your type of cancer sometimes live as little as six months . . . . ."

The words reverberated throughout my brain, they were the very same we had hidden from her for so many years and only recently divulged.

"In most instances," the doctor continued, " it's about two years but it is so unpredictable, it's hard to say."

Joy was silent for a moment.

"Two years . . . May 1998, that's not so bad," she quietly replied.

I was again overcome with that sense of guilt and had difficulty controlling my emotions. In a faltering voice I explained my feelings to Doctor Allan. She gently placed her hand on my arm.

"You know, Mr. Keeling, your wife's disease is so insidious it would probably have spread anyway. You should not condemn yourself."

I found some comfort in her words but the guilt persisted

Up to this point I had never been able to ascertain the clinical name for Joy's disease although I knew it was rare and something to do with the lymph system. And so when Doctor Allan left the room for a moment I took a peek at the chart. Under diagnosis it was written: "Infiltrating Ductular Carcinoma."

As we drove home I again tried to comfort Joy.

"This prognosis is based on statistics," I said, "and they were proven wrong before so there's no reason why they shouldn't be wrong again."

But Joy, as always, was pessimistic.

Then began the dreadful task of telling the children. In each case it was a tearful conversation, a mixture of shock and disbelief. By the time all four were informed we were utterly exhausted.

Joy was registered with the Hospice programme and over the next two years, almost to the day, there followed a series of bizarre incidents. A succession of cancer drugs was prescribed and one by one they failed to control the dreaded disease. Tamoxifen and Megase had already failed. She was then prescribed; Aminoglutethimide followed by Lenteron, a bi-weekly injection then Aremidex and Halotestin.

Later, at one of her clinic appointments the question of chemotherapy was raised. There were two types available, a mild one and a strong one. The chances of success were thirty and fifty percent respectively.

"How much longer would it give Joy," I asked.

"About six months," the doctor replied.

We said we would think about it.

Back at home we had long and sometimes emotional discussions about chemotherapy. Hair loss wasn't an issue because she could have a wig. The doctor had assured her that the associated nausea could be controlled with drugs but Joy found that difficult to believe. None of the prescribed drugs were curing the present nausea, how could they do so for chemo? She wondered aloud.

Also, we knew of two cases where patients wasted away in hospital, full of hope but in considerable discomfort for the remainder of their lives. We visited one of them regularly and afterwards spoke of the futility of it all. Then there were two deaths at the cancer clinic caused by improper administration of chemotherapy. They were widely publicised in the press. After a day or two, Joy solemnly announced her decision.

"Considering everything," she said, "it's not worth the discomfort and the risk for the sake of a thirty percent chance of living another six months. I would rather enjoy the best possible quality of life for whatever time I have left."

I could not in all conscience disagree and greatly admired her courage.

We advised Doctor Allan on the next visit, making no reference to the deaths. Joy said she liked her so much she didn't want to cause embarrassment. The doctor accepted the decision with little comment.

Meanwhile, other things were happening. Another bone scan revealed the cancer had spread to three areas of her spine. It wasn't long before she had to take morphine four times a day to control the pain. This played havoc with her bowels and required huge doses of Senakot, a laxative and Docusate, a softener. Joy began to despair at the number of drugs she was taking to control all her various conditions.

On 10 December 1996, there was a tragedy of another kind. I phoned Vic Bunton, it being his birthday. His son Michael answered only to inform me that Vic had died at three o'clock that morning. Of all the Bunton deaths, this one hit me the hardest. My earliest memories in life were centred on Vic; he had been my big brother for as long as I could remember. And he had died on his eightieth birthday!

Next, the cancerous fluid infiltrated Joy's heart, known as a pericardial effusion, this lead to rapid and irregular heartbeats. It was not serious enough to drain so she was put on Dygoxin to make the heart pump harder and Rythmol to control the rate. The combination of these two drugs caused the most severe nausea and it took much experimentation with dosages before life was anything like tolerable.

Finally, she broke out in a hideous rash covering her upper body. The doctor said it was the cancer cells permeating the skin. It didn't cause any pain or discomfort, just looked unsightly. Joy saw a Radiation Oncologist and there was some talk of experimental radiation in Vancouver but she quickly squashed that idea.

By now, everything was centred on making her life as comfortable as possible. To this end, we spent every moment of our lives together. Wherever, Joy was, there was I. Our closeness and devotion became the talk of the neighbourhood. Rightly or wrongly, we neglected or gave up all friendships, something that, in retrospect, I am beginning to question. At the time though, it seemed the right thing to do. To me nothing but Joy's well being mattered. She would often comment about how good I was to her and how many of her household duties I was performing. I simply pointed out that she had been doing it for me for over fifty years, it was pay back time.

In early February 1997, things began to improve. She was taking the cancer drug Aremidex, a new drug that had great potential. We began to venture further afield, even went to French Beach and she climbed the steep hill back to the parking lot with ease. At last we dared to think of a future, even to the point of discussing the possibility of spending New Year's Eve, 1999 together, my childhood dream. Alas, life can be so cruel, our enthusiasm was short lived.

Dennis had been courting Rena and on Valentine's day, 1997, they were married. She had a beautiful little girl, another, Jessica as well as a widowed mother, Hanni. All of whom were welcomed into the Keeling family circle. We made it to Maple Ridge for the ceremony, it was difficult for Joy but she was determined. As it turned out, it was a disaster from the moment of our arrival.

We were asked to pick up Amber and Codie and in doing so were somehow excluded from the wedding pictures. Joy was devastated, how could such a thing happen, she wailed. Then there was a long delay at the banquet. We had journeyed from Victoria, it was late in the evening and we'd had little to eat. Finally, Joy could stand it no longer and we left. Early next morning we returned to Victoria somewhat disillusioned. Dennis phoned from his honeymoon suite at Harrison Hot Springs full of apologies and was at a loss to know how it could have occurred.

In July Joy underwent a series of physiotherapy sessions in an attempt to reduce the fluid in her arm but like the pump treatment she had tried previously it proved useless. Nothing it seems, despite all the technology and research can solve what appears to the layman to be a relatively simple problem.

Nevertheless, we flew to Spokane, Washington, on 3 September 1997, for a ten-day visit with Michelle and family. The travelling was difficult for Joy but it was a most enjoyable holiday and one that we relived many times thanks to our video camera. But the insidious cancer was silently engulfing her body.

During the long period of pain and discomfort, she would become increasingly angry and embittered at her fate. So much so that I felt compelled to reason with her. She placed the entire blame on the original doctor and the extent of her bitterness was unhealthy, doing little to relieve the situation.

"Health care is a human activity," I said to her, "doctors are only human and occasionally mistakes are made."

I also pointed out that I too was at fault for not demanding a second opinion.

"I should have known better," I said.

But my reasoning did little to ease her feelings.

"That may be so," she replied, "but why me."

Of course, no one could answer that.

We spent Christmas day with Jennifer and family, it was a joyous occasion. For this historic day set-aside for rejoicing, we forgot everything and plunged into all the festivities. So much so that it seemed we were all subconsciously treating it as if it were the last. We both had oysters, something we had not enjoyed for a long time. On Boxing Day Joy became quite ill. We first blamed it on the oysters but it was something far more sinister.

In early January our niece, Janie and husband paid us a short visit. This is Joy's sister, Phyllis's youngest daughter. We were shocked to learn she had been diagnosed with ovarian cancer a year earlier. Initial treatment indicated all was well but it had returned and she was awaiting further treatment. They were full of hope that a cure would come eventually but it was not to be. She died within six months at age forty-three.

By mid January 1998 Joy's condition began to deteriorate even further. It started with a visit to the emergency room for breathing problems. It was the same old problem, infiltration. Aremidex, like all the other drugs had failed. She was then prescribed the last one in the arsenal, the male hormone Halotestin that has ghastly side effects. Apart from nausea and vomiting, there is growth of facial hair and lowering of the voice. Joy didn't suffer all the side effects but said she could feel subtle changes within her body.

"I'm turning into a man," she said, her voice full of pain and despair.

While on the drug she lay around listless, no appetite and suffered acute nausea.

"This is no life, sometimes I wonder if it's all worth while," she would often say. It was pitiful to watch as she struggled to get through each day.

Finally, on Wednesday, 11 April 1998, she said,

"I've had enough, throw that damn drug in the garbage."

We discussed the consequences of her action but she was adamant, again I had to admire her courage. I did, however, keep the drug just in case she changed her mind.

One of the drugs she had taken increased her appetite and she put on weight. I told her it suited her, made her look homely. But when she reached 138 pounds she began to worry, none of her clothes would fit. Then the next one did the opposite; she had no desire to eat, was completely turned off all her hitherto favourite foods and dropped to 120 pounds. There were times when she wouldn't eat enough to keep a sparrow alive. The mere sight of food made her feel sick.

Her right arm continued to swell to enormous proportions and she could do little with it. She was naturally right-handed but began to do more and more with the left. It was pitiful to stand by and watch her try to do her hair. The most difficult thing though was to sign her name. She would haul her right arm up onto a desk or table with the left hand as if it were a piece of dead meat then struggle to produce something resembling her signature.

Buying new clothes was a problem. She fell in love with one particularly attractive light green, two piece outfit, but couldn't begin to get her arm through it. She bought it anyway, then took material from the inside and inserted a long tapering piece the full length of the sleeve. It didn't show and everybody admired it, but I shall never forget the struggle and the torment she and I went through trying to manipulate the sewing machine.

Then, for a while she was incontinent and had to wear a pad whenever we left home. She was terribly embarrassed about that but after a while it disappeared as suddenly as it had started much to everyone's relief. There was a time when she could walk miles and at a pretty brisk pace, but gradually she was reduced to a crawl and just a few hundred yards. We frequently suggested a wheelchair but she was reluctant to give in.

By this time, she was taking a total of twenty-seven pills a day consisting of a dozen different drugs. I almost needed a degree in pharmacy to keep track of them all. One day, in a fit of frustration over taking so many, she threatened to,

"Throw the whole damn lot in the garbage."

I had a hard job reasoning with her but finally she agreed it would not be wise. Nevertheless, I checked the drug supply regularly just in case.

On Saturday 24 January, unbeknown to Joy, I phoned Michelle. I told her it was my feeling that if she wanted to see her mom alive again, she should come as soon as possible and I would pay for her flight. She arrived on the Wednesday and stayed for a week. It did wonders for Joy and Michelle left feeling things were looking up. Six weeks later, on 18 March, we were back in emergency, more lung problems, another pleural effusion.

Joy was attending the cancer clinic every two weeks and we were juggling the dosage of drugs in an attempt to relieve her nausea but nothing seemed to work. She lay on the couch all day, every day, with no appetite and feeling miserable. It was heartbreaking to watch.

At about this time, she received two visits from a male Hospice counsellor.

"He's very nice but I don't think it helps. You're my best counsellor and I love talking things over with you," she said following the second visit.

Ray came only once more after that and it was as an assistant to a Hospice nurse on an emergency visit. But his efforts were much appreciated.

Michelle paid another surprise visit for Easter, it was good to have her back to help me and again, it did wonders for Joy. The day before her arrival we had, after a lot of arm twisting, finally persuaded Joy to accept a wheelchair. Her first ride was on Dallas Road with Michelle pushing her. She enjoyed it so much that, weather permitting, we took her out every day. Twice, after Michelle left, I took her on the inner harbour it was her favourite. To mingle, even in a wheelchair, among the tourists and linger a while on the lower causeway was the highlight of her last days.

We were well known by many of the perennial vendors on the causeway having walked it hand in hand for years. Seeing her in a wheelchair brought out the compassion in all those who did know her. The Balloon Man gave her two small balloons to exercise her grip. And an elderly lady gave her a piece of driftwood with, "# 1 Grandma" burnt on it with a magnifying glass and the sun's rays.

On the last visit to the lower causeway, I placed the wheelchair right against the chain fence at the water's edge. After a few moments, a harbour seal popped up just a few feet away from where Joy sat. It was as if it was greeting her, then disappeared.

"This is wonderful, I shall remember this for the rest of my life," she said.

There was an abrupt change in the weather on Wednesday 6 May, it was cool, windy and wet so there was no more wheelchair outings. And I wept uncontrollably the day the wheelchair had to be returned.

But what is most amazing about this whole episode is, here I am almost seventy-nine, with a heart condition, less than full lung capacity and normally walking with the aid of a cane, pushing Joy all over the place in a wheelchair!

"I don't know where you get all your energy," she said repeatedly.

Neither did I, but from somewhere deep down I found an inner strength I didn't know I had. It's surprising what the human body can achieve in times of crisis.

At nine-thirty that evening, I was getting the beds ready when I heard a faint cry for help. Joy was gasping for breath and her pulse was erratic. I phoned Hospice and they were there in minutes. They made her comfortable for the night but on Thursday she could hardly walk. Her legs were swollen so badly that we could only shuffle her to and from the bathroom. Jennifer came and sat with her in the evening while I went grocery shopping. The next day I phoned each of the children and told them I feared the end was near.

Friday night, Jennifer visited again. She told her mom, among other things, how she and Ron were trying to figure out a way to carry her downstairs to the wheelchair, it was his day off and they wanted so badly to take Joy for a walk with Aaron. But Jennifer could sense that her mother was slipping away and gently asked her if Michelle should be summoned.

"No, tell her to wait a little while," she replied.

Jennifer 'phoned Michelle and told her mom's reaction.

Saturday morning, the ninth day of May, almost the full two years that had been projected, Joy could not get out of bed. Michelle was told to come at once but could get no further than Seattle that night so left Sunday morning.

The rest of the day saw Joy drift in and out of consciousness. I sat for hours holding her hand watching her gradually slip away. At one point she slowly opened her eyes and with just the hint of a smile whispered, "I love you."

"I love you too," I responded but she didn't hear, she had drifted off again.

At five o'clock, during a period when she was conscious I said,

"I think I'll make myself a bowl of soup."

"What about me?" she whispered."

"Would you like some soup?" I said.

Slowly and deliberately she whispered, "I would like a bowl of soup."

So I made soup for two but she took only three spoonfuls before drifting off again.

Jennifer, Ron and Aaron came about seven. It was hugs and kisses all round and little Aaron, not yet three years old, sang "You are my sunshine" for "Nanna," then they left. At seven-thirty, the Hospice team came and made Joy comfortable for the night. Her nighty was too hot so we dressed her in one of my cotton pyjama tops. They gave her an injection of Atropine and left three more syringes for me to inject at later intervals. This was supposed to make her breathing easier.

By nine o'clock it was worse, I gave her another injection and advised Hospice. I was told the team would be back as soon as they had finished with another patient.

At nine-forty I decided to make myself a cup of tea. I gently let go of Joy's hand and went to the kitchen. I made my tea and was returning to the bedroom when there was silence. Ah, I thought, the Atropine has kicked in but I was wrong. I turned on the light and Joy had lost her battle. In death she looked so beautiful, skin like marble, not a wrinkle to be seen.

I gently closed her eyes, her open mouth would not respond to my touch. I asked her why she left me when I went to make a cup of tea.

"I so badly wanted to be with you right to the end," I said.

I looked at my watch it was nine fifty-seven. I phoned Hospice, they apologised for the fact that I had been left alone but said the team would be there as soon as possible.

From that moment on, I moved about in a trance only vaguely aware of what was going on around me. At ten o'clock there was a knock at the door, barely conscious of my actions I opened the door, it was Jennifer and her daughter Jessica who had travelled all day by bus from Kamloops to be with Grandma only to miss her by three minutes.

With that, two Counsellors from Hospice arrived, one male, one female. I remember the man's name was Caelin. I asked if they called him Kato, referring to the notorious houseguest of O.J. Simpson.

"No, but it's a good idea," his colleague said.

Why would I jest at a time like this? I asked myself. It seemed so out of place and I felt guilty. I suppose it was because I was in a state of shock.

I explained how Joy's last breath came while I was making tea and how sad I was not to have been there at the end. They all insisted she chose that moment to let go. I wonder?

The Hospice team arranged for Joy to be taken away within the hour. Jennifer and Jessica lit a candle and performed a little private ritual. I spent some time alone with Joy, saying my personal farewell, all the time weeping on her shoulder. Then it was time for someone else to take over.

The sight of Joy's body, wrapped in the pink blanket from her bed being manipulated out of the bedroom door, into the hallway and out of sight will haunt me till the day I die. It was like watching a corpse being removed from the scene of a homicide on TV.

Jennifer offered to spend the night with me but I declined, preferring to be alone in my grief. Besides, she had Ron and Aaron to think about. I slept little and moved around the next day like an automaton. Michelle arrived and she and Jennifer took the clothing Joy would wear in the casket. The funeral was arranged for Thursday, 14 May 1998.

Thirty-eight

A Puddle By The Roadside

At Joy's request there was no funeral service; just a private family viewing at a downtown Funeral Chapel from ten till eleven in the morning, then a public viewing from twelve till three. Much to our disappointment, many people overlooked the Book of Remembrance. Some, including staff from Thrifty Foods in the Fairfield Plaza, insisted I take the book to them, so that they could record their personal thoughts. We had shopped there for many years and Joy was well known and liked. They even have an enlarged picture of the two of us in the centre of the illuminated directory above isle five.

Following the viewing, we all assembled in the lounge of Townley Lodge. Michelle provided the refreshments and Jennifer and Ron served. Then we sat around in a circle and with a little prompting from Jennifer, everyone related his or her favourite memory of Joy. The comments were so touching I had difficulty controlling my emotions. The gathering ended with each female member of the family being presented with an item of jewellery belonging to Joy. They were moved by her thoughtfulness.

Finally everybody left, including Michelle. She wanted to spend a few hours with her family. I would miss her company but realised she had to go, she had been away from Rick and the children for three days and they were leaving early on Saturday. She was staying till Wednesday so they would be separated again.

Back in the solitude of my suite I was overcome by reality. We had been together for fifty-three years, now Joy was gone and I was alone. But then I recalled the many kind words spoken at the gathering and realised that amidst the sorrow and the tears, she still lives in the hearts of all those she touched.

She was a wonderful person. From the beginning she accepted my faults and they were many. She pardoned my mistakes without forgetting but hoped I would learn from them. She accepted good fortune along with the bad and rarely complained. Deeply loved by all that knew her, she was a nurturing mother, a devoted wife and a woman of many talents. She was a superb cook, she could sew and knit and her embroidery was without equal. Her home was immaculate and all that entered were made to feel welcome.

She loved life and all it had to offer, she had a great sense of humour, was a good listener and loved to share life's stories. An avid reader, she became my most valued critic. And she was so determined this manuscript be completed and her story told as well as mine, that in the last days of life, when time together was so precious she insisted I, "Do a little on the book." As well, though her end was near, her greatest concern was for her niece, Janie. She repeatedly insisted I phone Don to enquire after her. "Poor, Janie," she would say, "only forty-three, too young to die." Then she would speak about the tragic coincidence of her sister Phyllis, Janie's mother, dying of cancer at age forty-five.

The following days were difficult for me, thank goodness I had Michelle for company. Without her I would not have survived. At my insistence, her and Jennifer disposed of all Joy's belongings, with most of her clothes being donated to "Women in Need." Unlike many people, I simply could not live with her things around me; too many memories and in my grief I couldn't handle it. No doubt some will think me callous, so be it, everybody deals with tragedy in a different way. One should also bear in mind that her passing was not sudden or unexpected, it had begun two years earlier.

On Tuesday, 19 May 1998, Joy's remains were interred at the Veterans cemetery in Esquimalt. It was a simple but moving ceremony. At the chapel door I was handed the solid oak urn containing her ashes. Then, with Jennifer at my side followed by Michelle, Ron carrying Aaron, and Laurie, Michelle's friend, we proceeded up the hill to Joy's final resting place. A few appropriate words were recited, a poppy placed on the urn followed by a flower from each of us including little Aaron. Then we all spread a handful of earth over the tiny container and it was all over.

Tears impaired my vision and my body wracked with uncontrollable sobbing as I drove away. I should have been driven home but nobody was thinking straight.

Michelle returned to Spokane the next day and I settled down to the ordeal of living alone. My loss was the end of a fourteen-year battle. I can handle it, I told myself, how naïve. Ron as Joy's Executor, dealt with all the legal and procedural matters for which I am most grateful. I must also pay tribute to Rick who went to work and looked after the children while Michelle stayed with me.

Contrary to my earlier position, I found myself in need of counselling and sought the help of Hospice. For several weeks I enjoyed a visit from a charming and skilful bereavement counsellor. As well, to ensure my mind is kept fully occupied in the years to come, I purchased the latest in computer technology just in case I decide to write another book. On second thoughts, maybe I'll just relax and enjoy myself on the Internet.

Our wedding anniversary was on Friday 3 July. Although we had actually been married only forty-four years, we have always counted from the time we started living together, so this was the fifty-third. It was a particularly hard day, so many memories of happy anniversaries. The last one celebrated at the Empress Hotel followed by a romantic stroll on Dallas Road.

I awoke on Sunday, 26 July1998, realising it was the fifth anniversary of the day I started writing this tome. It also meant a visit to the cemetery; I do so every Wednesday and Sunday. Afterwards, I stroll along the Gorge, one of Joy's favourite walks and only a few minutes drive from the cemetery.

I'd promised Joy the book would be finished by today and had yet to write an ending. I'd written several in the past; one had Joy and me sitting together on New Years Eve 1999 with a glass of wine waiting to welcome the new millennium. Another ended with a quote from Shakespeare's Richard II. "I count myself in nothing else so happy, as a soul remembering my good friends." I was going to substitute the word "family" for "good friends." And there were more, but none seemed appropriate now.

As I went about my daily chores, I hoped for some kind of inspiration but the morning past and nothing came. I yearned for Joy's presence, if she were here she'd think of something. She was my editor in chief, everything I wrote was read to her and she made many suggestions. I finally gave up, deciding to tell her I couldn't think of an appropriate ending.

I phoned Jennifer as usual just to let her know I was all right. Sometimes she offers to come with me but not today. After my walk on Sundays I go to hers for supper which makes a pleasant change. I get to spend time with little Aaron. It's sad Joy didn't live to see him grow up. She often expressed disappointment that she would be denied that privilege.

We missed so much of our grand children's growing up because of Joy's illness. We flew to Michelle's in September of '97, and although she didn't complain, I knew it was hard for her. When we returned she said, "No more travelling, I just can't stand it." So we had to rely on videotapes, which was better than nothing.

Now, as the days pass life is an even greater challenge. Jennifer and Ron are good to me but nothing, it seems, can ease the pain and despair that loneliness brings. I try to keep busy, sometimes to extremes. I nag myself far more than, Joy ever did especially when I do something foolish. There are times when I think I'm becoming senile. I dread the thought of being warehoused in an old folk's home. Like Joy I want to die at home, preferably in my favourite armchair, the one she bought me from her lottery winnings back in 1986, and despite my protests insisted it be re-covered a couple of years ago.

I also find myself thinking more than ever about my family in England and about my grand children here. Memories are all I have now. But to paraphrase Sir James Barrie, we were given memories so that in moments of darkness or despair we might relive and enjoy the beautiful things that happened in our lives.

I think of Amber and Codie leaving and another Jessica, Rena's little girl, being welcomed into the family; of Niki and Angela, Dennis' two daughters now mothers in their own right, and their children, my great grand children, Ashley, Taylor and Kaitlyn. Then there's David, a product of Michael's first marriage to Sue. He's grown into a fine young man, I'm very proud of him. Deidra and Mikey, I prefer to call him "Junior" from Michael's second marriage are two very interesting characters. Deidra wants to be a writer, I hope her dream comes true. Junior, I predict, will live to become a very wise person; he has a curious mind and reads a lot.

Corey, Jennifer's oldest, graduated from high school this year, I'm proud of him too. And her Jessica, a sweet person who I love dearly and wish she lived closer. Then there's Kyle and Cory, Michelle's two boys, full of life and lots of fun to be with. And last but not least, little Aaron. He lives close by so I get to see more of him.

"I count myself in nothing else so happy, as a soul remembering his family."

At the cemetery I parked the car in the shade across from the entrance to the old Maritime Chapel. To walk up the hill is difficult for me so I paused beside the grave of twenty-nine year old John Gill who died in 1891. How much he was missed from his place at home was inscribed upon his tombstone; that a shadow had been cast over the lives of those left to grieve. It spoke too, of the sunshine in his face, his willing hands and his fond and earnest care. "Our home is dark without you," it concluded, "we miss you everywhere."

Well-chosen words and a fitting epitaph for my loved one, I told myself.

I pushed on almost to the top then made my way across to Joy's grave. It is the last one in the row, right against the fence and under the shade of a giant fir; she always preferred the shade. The geraniums in their red, terra cotta planter looked strong and healthy now. They were doing poorly at first so I fed them a little nourishment and talked nicely to them.

It was very still. Not a sound, save for the lively chirping of an agitated robin perched restlessly on the fence. And the occasional smack of a nine iron striking the ball on a nearby Fairway followed by the muffled comments of a player.

It's so peaceful here. I enjoy these visits.

I fussed over the flowers, removing little bits of debris from last night's storm then chatted a while with Joy. I told her all the latest goings on, including my problem with the book ending. I found that helpful, it was as if she were there at my side. Then it was time for my usual farewell.

"Bye dear, loves ya, see you on Wednesday,"

And it was back to the car and reality.

I went for my usual stroll along the Gorge Waterway. A heavy thunder-shower had fallen earlier in the day and there was a puddle by the roadside. I stopped to look and in it saw a patch of cloud decked sky, and as I lingered I saw Joy's face reflected there.

The End

ISBN 1552124991
9 781552 124994